CLOUD TO EDGEWARE

Wireless Grid Applications, Architecture and Security for the *Internet of Things*

CLOUD TO EDGEWARE

Wireless Grid Applications, Architecture and Security for the *Internet of Things*

TYSON T BROOKS
Syracuse University, USA

World Scientific

NEW JERSEY • LONDON • SINGAPORE • BEIJING • SHANGHAI • HONG KONG • TAIPEI • CHENNAI • TOKYO

Published by

World Scientific Publishing Co. Pte. Ltd.
5 Toh Tuck Link, Singapore 596224
USA office: 27 Warren Street, Suite 401-402, Hackensack, NJ 07601
UK office: 57 Shelton Street, Covent Garden, London WC2H 9HE

Library of Congress Control Number: 2023048945

British Library Cataloguing-in-Publication Data
A catalogue record for this book is available from the British Library.

CLOUD TO EDGEWARE
Wireless Grid Applications, Architecture and Security for the *Internet of Things*

ISBN 978-981-4630-80-1 (hardcover)
ISBN 978-981-4630-81-8 (ebook for institutions)
ISBN 978-981-4630-82-5 (ebook for individuals)

For any available supplementary material, please visit
https://www.worldscientific.com/worldscibooks/10.1142/9354#t=suppl

Desk Editor: Logeshwaran Arumugam/Steven Patt

Typeset by Stallion Press
Email: enquiries@stallionpress.com

Preface

The world we live in today is increasingly interconnected. Technology has woven a complex web of interconnectivity from our homes to workplaces, from urban centers to remote areas, enabling various devices and systems to communicate and collaborate. At the heart of this digital revolution lies the "Internet of Things" (IoT), a network of interconnected devices, sensors, and actuators that collect, analyze, and exchange data to make our lives more efficient, convenient, and sustainable. The IoT has the potential to transform industries, revolutionize cities, and enhance the quality of life for individuals around the globe. However, this potential can only be fully realized if we overcome the challenges of connecting and managing a diverse and vast ecosystem of devices and applications. One of the key enablers in this journey is the evolution of wireless grid technologies, which provide the infrastructure and capabilities to extend the reach of the IoT from the cloud to the Edge of our networks.

In this book, *Cloud to Edgeware*: *Wireless Grid Applications, Architecture and Security for the Internet of Things*, we explore the various aspects of building and securing wireless grid applications for the IoT. We delve into the fundamental concepts, technologies, and architectures that underpin this paradigm shift while addressing the pressing concerns of security, scalability, and reliability. Throughout the chapters, we will examine the challenges and opportunities of the convergence of cloud computing, wireless grids, and Edge computing.

We will explore the different wireless grid technologies and discuss the crucial architectural considerations for designing efficient and resilient IoT systems, ranging from network topologies and protocols to Edge computing models and risk management frameworks. Moreover, security is a paramount concern in an increasingly connected world. Thus, we dedicate a substantial portion of this book to exploring the security challenges and solutions specific to wireless grid applications. We delve into authentication, encryption, access control, and privacy mechanisms that safeguard IoT deployments from malicious actors and potential vulnerabilities.

"Cloud to Edgeware" is intended for a diverse audience, including researchers, engineers, architects, and decision-makers who seek a comprehensive understanding of wireless grid technologies and their practical applications in the IoT landscape. Whether you are a novice exploring the vast possibilities of the IoT or a seasoned professional seeking to enhance your knowledge and expertise, this book provides a valuable resource to navigate the intricacies of wireless grid architectures, applications, and security considerations.

About the Author

Tyson Brooks is an adjunct professor in the School of Information Studies (iSchool) at Syracuse University. Dr. Brooks has over 25 years of professional experience in the engineering design, architecture, and information security of complex information systems in the US and overseas. Dr. Brooks's expertise includes work in the areas of information assurance, cyber-security, penetration testing, and network-based intrusion analysis and defense in both the public and private sectors. He also holds the Network+, Security+, CISSP, C|EH, CEA, GCIH, CAS-ISM, and PMP certifications. He was the past Editor-in-Chief of the *International Journal of Internet of Things and Cyber-Assurance* (*IJITCA*) and is an Associate Editor for IEEE Access. Dr. Brooks is also a Senior Member of IEEE and the Association of Computing Machinery (ACM).

Acknowledgment

I would first like to give honor to my Lord and Savior Jesus Christ whom all my blessing and strength come from in my life. To my parents, my dad [the late] F. Burrell Brooks and my mom, W. Michelle Brooks for all their love, encouragement, and guidance over my life. An extra special thanks to the loves of my life — my wife Lisa and children, Tyson Jr., and Taylor, for always supporting and loving me in whatever initiative "keeps me in the basement on the computer".

In addition, the author would like to thank the Syracuse University School of Information Studies (iSchool), a beacon of knowledge and innovation. The iSchool has consistently been a nurturing ground for forward thinkers and has played an instrumental role in the imagination and fruition of this book. Additionally, I would like to thank the following individuals who contributed to this book: Dr. Lee McKnight, Dr. Jerry Robinson, Dr. Michelle Kaarst-Brown, Dr. Carlos Caicedo, Dr. Joon Park, Dr. Shiu-Kai Chin and David Jones.

Contents

Introduction

The dawn of the 21st century presented an unprecedented surge in connectivity, ushering in a new era of technological advancements and possibilities. The Internet of Things (IoT) stands at the forefront of this revolution, transforming how we interact with our surroundings, how businesses operate, and how cities function. With each passing day, the IoT continues to grow, linking an ever-expanding array of devices, sensors, and systems, seamlessly interconnecting our physical and digital worlds. Wireless data systems have been available worldwide for several years. The wireless data communications market was the domain of vertical commercial enterprises with specialized needs. Many large organizations needed a way to stay in touch with their mobile sales force and remote field service representatives.

Organizations with inherently "mobile" components, such as delivery services, must keep track of vehicles and packages. The requirements of these organizations were met with wireless data networks. Wireless data networks were developed and deployed as specialized applications for individual companies. However, the technology used in these applications was soon commercialized and, in some instances, even expanded to national coverage. These early systems were dedicated mobile data networks (i.e., they handled data only and did not carry voice transmissions). When dedicated mobile data systems emerged, wireless voice transmission was serviced by the newly developed cellular telephony networks. This first generation of cellular networks focused on voice transmission at the expense of data transmission. These networks were analog and used circuit-switched technology, and by contrast, the dedicated mobile data systems used packet-switching technology.

At the core of this interconnected web lies the concept of wireless grid applications, where data flows effortlessly between the cloud and the edge of our networks. The transition from traditional centralized architectures to a distributed, decentralized paradigm reshapes the IoT landscape. It paves the way for unprecedented opportunities in diverse domains, including smart cities, industrial automation, healthcare, agriculture, and more. The central element of wireless computing networks, the Wi-Fi transmission standard IEEE 802.11, was introduced in 1997, with limited range and reliability and speeds of just a few megabytes per second (MBps).

Over the years, mobile computing capabilities have also progressed significantly with the introduction of Cloud Computing and IoT architectures. Wireless grids utilizing "Edgeware" technology are becoming increasingly popular. These wireless grid "Edgeware" systems give users greater mobility and flexibility. Although these characteristics of services provide several advantages, especially towards their integration into IoT architectures, they leave these wireless grids "Edgeware" devices vulnerable to attacks and other security-related problems. It is exactly the mobile nature of the devices that exposes them to a greater risk of data loss or theft. This contrasts with the wired service, which terminates in one location, such as the home or office, making it more safeguarded.

The trend of integrating these new complex systems with advanced computer and communication technologies has introduced serious cybersecurity concerns, especially in these new architectures, where the environment will no longer be regarded as reliable to support communications as before. For example, due to the critical role of the smart grid as the vital energy IoT infrastructure, the information infrastructure needed to route data by providing the dynamic *ad-hoc* sharing of heterogonous devices and the need to protect its information security is a critical task that can significantly contribute to security issues given the threat of cyber-attacks. Traditional security mechanisms, such as identification/authentication and access control (authorization), are complicated in these new environments, requiring new standards and the development of new security products.

However, only recently has the market begun to experience rapid growth in mobile service clouds and IoT functionality. This is due to several factors, which include the extensive spread of the Internet, high penetration of mobile phone usage, powerful new portable computing platforms, and smaller wireless devices. In addition, all of these are converging, which in turn is making the wireless telecommunications market increasingly data-centric. Due to their physical broadcast nature, these new communication networks are generally more vulnerable to malicious and accidental threats than their wired counterparts.

Cloud to Edgeware: Wireless Grid Applications, Architecture, and Security for the Internet of Things is a comprehensive exploration of the critical aspects of harnessing the power of wireless grid technologies to propel the IoT forward. In this book, we delve deep into the foundational principles, practical applications, and robust security measures necessary to unlock the full potential of the IoT ecosystem. The chapters are as follows:

Chapter 1: Exploring the Fusion of Artificial Intelligence and Wireless Grids Edgeware
Chapter 2: Authenticating Devices in Fog-Mobile Edge Computing Environments through a Wireless Grid Resource Sharing Protocol
Chapter 3: Conceptualizing a Secure Wireless Cloud
Chapter 4: Securing Wireless Grids: Architecture Designs for Secure Wiglet-to-Wiglet Interfaces
Chapter 5: A Failure to Communicate: Security Vulnerabilities in the GridStreamX Wireless Grid Edgeware Application
Chapter 6: Secure the Edge? Understanding the Risk Toward Wireless Grids Edgeware Technology
Chapter 7: Edge Computing and Cyber Warfare: Strategies for Future Operations in a Wireless Grid SDN-Enabled World
Chapter 8: Developing a CyberAssurance Multiple Adversary Risk Model for Wireless Grids Edgeware
Chapter 9: An Internet Control Device Embedded Sensor Agent (IcdESA) for Wireless Grids
Chapter 10: Zero Trust Security in 5G O-RAN Wireless Grid Networks: Designing a System-of-Systems Intrusion Detection Systems (SoSIDS)

Whether you are an aspiring wireless or IoT professional, a researcher, or a decision-maker seeking to navigate the complexities of wireless grid architectures and their application to the IoT, this book equips you with the knowledge and tools necessary to thrive in this ever-evolving landscape. "Cloud to Edgeware" is a comprehensive guide for anyone seeking to explore the boundless possibilities of wireless grid applications in the IoT. It is a testament to the transformative power of technology, inspiring readers to embrace innovation, overcome challenges, and contribute to the continuous growth of the IoT ecosystem.

Chapter 1

Exploring the Fusion of Artificial Intelligence and Wireless Grids Edgeware

ABSTRACT

This chapter explores the fusion of artificial intelligence (AI) and wireless grids Edgeware, examining the transformative potential of this integration in optimizing the performance, efficiency, and reliability of wireless grid systems. By providing an overview of the convergence of AI and wireless grids Edgeware, this section highlights the significance of this fusion in addressing the complex challenges modern grid infrastructure faces. The chapter delves into the architectural considerations, algorithms, and methodologies for integrating AI into wireless grids Edgeware. It further explores the implications and impacts of AI in enabling intelligent decision-making, proactive monitoring, predictive maintenance, and advanced analytics in wireless grid systems. By leveraging the power of AI and wireless grids Edgeware can unlock new possibilities for optimized resource allocation, increased energy efficiency, enhanced grid operations, and improved resilience. Finally, it highlights the importance of understanding and harnessing the fusion of AI and wireless grids Edgeware for unlocking the full potential of next-generation smart grid technologies.

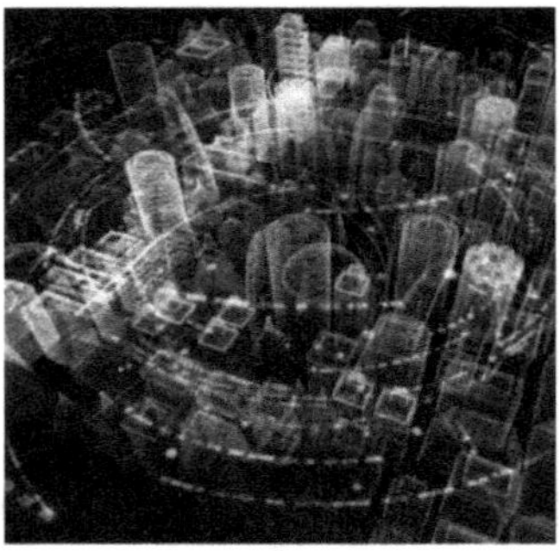

INTRODUCTION

Artificial intelligence (AI) and wireless grids Edgeware are two interconnected fields that have the potential to revolutionize various aspects of technology, communication, and infrastructure. In its broadest sense, AI refers to the development of intelligent machines capable of simulating human-like intelligence [13]. AI encompasses a wide range of subfields, including machine learning (ML), natural language processing, computer vision, robotics, and expert systems. ML, a subset of AI, enables computers to learn from data and improve performance without explicit programming [7]. This branch of AI has witnessed remarkable advancements in recent years, fueled by the availability of vast amounts of data and powerful computing resources. The applications of AI are diverse and extend across numerous sectors. For example, in healthcare, AI is being used for disease diagnosis, drug discovery, and personalized treatment recommendations. In finance, AI algorithms are employed for fraud detection, risk assessment, and algorithmic trading. AI-powered virtual assistants, such as Siri and Alexa, have become integral to our daily lives, facilitating voice-based interactions and automating routine tasks. Autonomous vehicles are another prominent application of AI, where complex algorithms enable cars to perceive their surroundings and make decisions without human intervention.

Wireless grids Edgeware, on the other hand, focuses on the integration of wireless communication technologies with Edge computing capabilities to enable efficient and intelligent data processing at the network edge [9]. The proliferation of Internet of Things (IoT) devices and the exponential growth of data have created the need for Edge computing solutions to handle the massive volume of data generated and provide real-time insights. Wireless grids Edgeware leverages the power of distributed computing, where data is processed closer to its source, reducing latency and optimizing network bandwidth. By combining AI and wireless grids Edgeware, we can unlock a plethora of innovative applications. For instance, in smart cities, AI algorithms can analyze sensor data collected from various IoT devices deployed throughout the city to optimize energy consumption, traffic flow, and waste management. Integrating AI and wireless grids Edgeware can also enhance the efficiency and reliability of wireless networks by dynamically allocating network resources based on real-time demands, improving network performance and user experience.

However, some challenges need to be addressed in both AI and wireless grids Edgeware. In AI, issues related to data privacy, transparency, and bias must be carefully considered. As AI algorithms make critical decisions that impact individuals and society, ensuring fairness and accountability becomes paramount. Furthermore, the integration of AI and wireless grids Edgeware requires addressing concerns related to security, privacy, and interoperability. The distributed nature of Edge computing introduces new vulnerabilities that need to be mitigated to safeguard sensitive data and maintain network integrity.

Looking ahead, the future of AI and wireless grids Edgeware appears promising. Advances in AI research, coupled with the rapid deployment of 5/6G networks and the proliferation of Edge computing infrastructure, will create new opportunities for innovation and growth. AI will continue to evolve, enabling machines to understand human intent, interpret emotions, and engage in natural conversations. Wireless grids Edgeware will play a crucial role in supporting AI applications by providing the necessary computational resources and low-latency connectivity.

OVERVIEW

Wireless grids Edgeware introduces a novel concept in wireless networking and will begin to leverage the capabilities of AI. The foundations of AI in wireless grid Edgeware encompass a deep understanding of AI principles and techniques, ML algorithms, and the role of data and data analytics in the integration of AI within wireless grid systems. This technology provides a platform for different types of devices on a network to communicate and share resources efficiently, effectively creating a kind of "shared intelligence" across the grid.

The fundamental AI-driven approach enables the network to learn from the behaviors, interactions, and preferences of the devices and users connected to it. It adapts to these patterns and can predictively allocate resources based on these learned patterns. In addition to improving efficiency and usability, this AI integration facilitates the implementation of advanced features like smart automation, predictive maintenance, and enhanced security protocols, making it a transformative technology in the field of wireless communication. The deployment of AI in wireless grids Edgeware has the potential to significantly alter the landscape of networking, bringing about unprecedented levels of connectivity and integration. To begin, let's delve into the fundamentals of AI/ML.

AI refers to the development of intelligent machines capable of mimicking human-like intelligence encompassing various subfields, including ML, natural language processing, computer vision, robotics, and expert systems [13]. AI is a subfield of computer science that aims to create systems capable of performing tasks that would normally require human intelligence [13]. These tasks can include things like understanding natural language, recognizing patterns, solving problems, making decisions, and even exhibiting creativity.

AI can be categorized into two types: (1) Narrow AI and (2) General AI. Narrow AI systems refer to AI systems that are designed to perform specific tasks or functions within a limited domain [10]. Unlike general AI which aims to replicate human-level intelligence and understanding across various domains, narrow AI focuses on specialized tasks and operates within predefined parameters [10]. Narrow AI systems are designed to excel in specific areas, such as speech recognition, image classification, natural language processing, or autonomous driving. These systems typically rely on ML algorithms and large datasets to learn and improve their performance in their specific tasks. While narrow AI demonstrates impressive capabilities within its specific domain, it cannot generalize knowledge or understand contexts beyond its specialized area. Narrow AI has found widespread applications in various industries, including healthcare, finance, manufacturing, and customer service, revolutionizing processes and augmenting human capabilities in these domains [10].

General AI possesses the capability to understand, learn, adapt, and implement knowledge in a wide variety of tasks, essentially mirroring human intelligence. This refers to the concept of creating intelligent machines or systems that possess the ability to understand, learn, and apply knowledge across diverse domains, similar to human intelligence [8]. Unlike narrow AI, which focuses on specific tasks, general AI aims to replicate human-level intelligence and cognitive abilities. General AI systems are not limited to pre-defined tasks or domains and can exhibit intelligence and problem-solving capabilities in a wide range of contexts. These systems can reason, understand natural language, learn from experiences, and adapt to new situations [8]. General AI is often associated with the concept of machine consciousness, wherein machines possess subjective experiences and self-awareness. While general AI remains a subject of ongoing research and development, achieving it poses significant challenges, including the need for advanced cognitive architectures, human-level understanding of natural language and context, and the ability to generalize knowledge across domains [8]. The development of general AI has the potential to revolutionize various fields, including healthcare, robotics, education, and scientific research, but also raises ethical and philosophical questions regarding its impact on society and the human condition.

ML is a subfield of AI that focuses on the development of algorithms and models that enable computers to learn and make predictions or decisions without explicit programming [7]. It is based on the idea that machines can analyze and interpret data, identify patterns, and learn from examples to improve their performance on a given task. ML algorithms are designed to automatically learn and iteratively adjust their models based on the available data, allowing them to make predictions or take actions without being explicitly programmed for every specific scenario. ML can be categorized into three main types of learning: (1) supervised, (2) unsupervised, and (3) reinforcement [4].

Supervised learning is where the model is given a dataset in which the "correct" answers (known as labels) are provided [4]. The algorithm analyzes the data and learns the relationship between the features (input data) and the labels. Once trained, the model can apply this learned relationship to new, unseen data to make predictions. In unsupervised learning, the model isn't given any labels, so it must find structure in the data on its own [4]. This is often used for clustering (grouping similar items) or anomaly detection. Unsupervised learning involves finding patterns or structures in unlabeled data without predefined output labels. Reinforcement learning (RL) is when an agent learns how to behave in an environment by performing actions and receiving rewards or penalties [4].

The agent's goal is to learn a policy, which is a strategy for choosing actions that maximize the sum of rewards over time. ML requires large amounts of high-quality data for training and evaluation. It involves tasks such as data preprocessing, feature engineering, model selection, and evaluation to ensure accurate and reliable results. Advances in computational power, data availability, and algorithmic improvements have contributed to the rapid growth and adoption of ML in various industries and domains, enabling intelligent systems to make accurate predictions and automated decisions based on patterns and insights derived from data.

WIRELESS GRID AI ALGORITHMS

In the context of wireless grid Edgeware, AI techniques, and algorithms play a crucial role in optimizing network performance, resource allocation, and decision-making processes. These techniques leverage the power of AI to analyze large volumes of data generated by wireless grid systems, identify patterns, and make intelligent predictions. By integrating AI into wireless grid Edgeware, we can enhance the efficiency, reliability, and scalability of wireless networks. One prominent AI technique for wireless grid Edgeware is RL. RL involves training agents to make decisions and take actions based on trial and error, to maximize a cumulative reward wireless grid Edgeware is RL [12]. In the context of wireless grids, RL algorithms can be employed to optimize resource allocation, such as dynamically adjusting transmission power, channel allocation, and routing decisions. RL enables wireless grid systems to adapt to changing network conditions, improve energy efficiency, and enhance overall system performance.

Another vital AI technique for wireless grid Edgeware is deep learning (DL). DL involves training deep neural networks with multiple layers to extract high-level representations from raw input data [12]. DL has revolutionized several domains, including computer vision and natural language processing. In the context of wireless grids, DL can be utilized for tasks such as signal processing, spectrum sensing, and interference mitigation. For example, DL models can learn to identify and classify different wireless signals, enabling more efficient utilization of the available spectrum.

Furthermore, data plays a central role in the integration of AI within wireless grid Edgeware. The availability of large-scale datasets is crucial for training AI models and enabling accurate predictions. In wireless grid systems, data can be collected from various sources, such as IoT devices, sensors, and network infrastructure. This data provides valuable insights into network performance, user behavior, and environmental conditions. By leveraging data analytics techniques, such as data preprocessing, feature extraction, and anomaly detection, we can extract meaningful information from raw data and make informed decisions.

Data analytics also enables predictive modeling in wireless grid Edgeware. By analyzing historical data, AI models can predict future network conditions, anticipate demand patterns, and optimize resource allocation accordingly [2]. This proactive approach helps in mitigating network congestion, optimizing energy consumption, and improving Quality of Service (QoS) for end-users. Additionally, data analytics techniques, including clustering and classification, can be employed for network management and fault detection, aiding in the identification and resolution of network issues. The integration of AI and data analytics in wireless grid Edgeware offers several benefits. Firstly, it enhances network performance by optimizing resource allocation, improving spectral efficiency, and reducing interference. Secondly, AI enables self-organizing and self-healing capabilities, allowing wireless grid systems to adapt to dynamic network conditions and mitigate disruptions. Thirdly, AI techniques facilitate intelligent decision-making processes, enabling efficient traffic management, load balancing, and routing in wireless grid networks.

However, there are several challenges and considerations in the application of AI in wireless grid Edgeware. One significant challenge is the need for sufficient training data. The success of AI models heavily relies on the quality and quantity of training data available. Collecting and labeling large-scale datasets for wireless grid systems can be a resource-intensive task. Additionally, ensuring data privacy and security is crucial, as wireless grid systems handle sensitive user data and network information. Moreover, the deployment of AI models in wireless grid systems requires careful optimization and scalability considerations. AI algorithms often involve computationally intensive operations, requiring efficient hardware infrastructure and distributed computing resources.

Real-time processing and latency constraints in wireless grids pose additional challenges in deploying AI models. Balancing the trade-off between accuracy and computational complexity is crucial to ensure practical implementation and some of these algorithms are identified as follows.

Channel Equalization using Recursive Least Squares (RLS)[1] is crucial to mitigate the effects of multipath fading in wireless communication. RLS is an adaptive filtering algorithm used for channel estimation and performing RLS in real-time for multiple users in a wireless grid demands efficient hardware infrastructure and distributed computing resources due to the iterative nature of the algorithm and matrix computations involved. The algorithm updates filter coefficients in real time using the following equation:

$$w(n+1) = w(n) + \frac{\mu}{R(n) - 1u(n)} e(n)$$

where

- $w(n)$ is the filter coefficient vector at time n,
- μ is the step size controlling the adaptation speed,
- $R(n)$ is the autocorrelation matrix of the input vector $u(n)$,
- $e(n)$ is the error between the received signal and the estimated signal.

Multiple-Input, Multiple-Output (MIMO) Detection using Sphere Decoder[2] systems provides increased data rates in wireless grids. Sphere decoding is an algorithm used to detect transmitted symbols in MIMO systems. MIMO detection using sphere decoding is computationally intensive, especially for large MIMO systems with many antennas and symbols. Real-time processing of sphere decoding in wireless grids may require distributed computing resources to achieve low latency. The algorithm aims to find the maximum likelihood solution among a set of candidate symbols using a sphere-bound equation:

$$||y - Hx||^2 \leq \text{bound}$$

[1] https://www.imeko.org/publications/wc-2015/IMEKO-WC-2015-TC4-124.pdf.

[2] https://www.researchgate.net/publication/224363254_Two-level-search_sphere_decoding_algorithm_for_MIMO_detection.

where
- y is the received signal vector,
- H is the MIMO channel matrix,
- x is the transmitted symbol vector,
- bound is a predetermined threshold.

Orthogonal Frequency Division Multiplexing (OFDM) Signal Generation[3] is a widely used modulation technique in wireless communication. It involves converting data symbols into time-domain samples through Inverse Fast Fourier Transform (IFFT) operations. In wireless grids, generating OFDM signals in real time demands efficient hardware infrastructure and distributed computing resources, especially when dealing with multiple users concurrently. The algorithm for OFDM signal generation is

$$x(t) = \text{IFFT}\,(\text{modulate}(\text{data}))$$

where
- $x(t)$ is the time-domain OFDM signal,
- modulate(data) maps data symbols to the frequency domain,
- IFFT is the Inverse Fast Fourier Transform.

Network Flow Optimization using Linear Programming[4] is essential for efficient resource allocation in wireless grids. Linear Programming (LP) is a mathematical technique used to optimize network flows. Solving large-scale LP problems for resource allocation in real-time wireless grids may require distributed computing resources and efficient hardware infrastructure due to the computational complexity involved. The objective function and constraints are represented as linear equations, and the optimization problem can be formulated as follows:

$$\text{Maximize } c^T x$$
$$\text{Subject to } Ax \leq b, \quad x \geq 0$$

[3] https://ieeexplore.ieee.org/abstract/document/4772401.

[4] https://optimization.cbe.cornell.edu/index.php?title=Network_flow_problem.

where

- c is the cost vector,
- x is the flow vector to be optimized,
- A and b are matrices and vectors representing constraints.

Nonlinear Beamforming[5] techniques can improve wireless communication performance. Genetic Algorithms (GAs) can be employed to optimize nonlinear beamforming weights to maximize the signal-to-interference-plus-noise ratio (SINR). Optimizing nonlinear beamforming weights using GAs in real-time requires efficient hardware and distributed computing resources to handle the complexity and achieve low latency. The optimization problem can be represented as follows:

$$\text{Maximize SINR} = \frac{\left|h^H w\right|2}{\sum_{i=1,\, i\neq k}^{n} |\, h^H w_i\, |^2 + \sigma^2}$$

where

- h is the channel vector between the transmitter and receiver,
- w and w_i are the beamforming weight vectors for the user of interest and interfering users, respectively,
- N is the total number of users,
- Σ^2 is the noise power.

Implementing these algorithms in real-time within wireless grids demands computational power beyond the capabilities of standard devices, necessitating the use of efficient hardware infrastructure and distributed computing resources. Through the integration of AI techniques, such as RL and DL, wireless grid systems can achieve optimized resource allocation, intelligent decision-making, and proactive network management. The utilization of data and data analytics enables predictive modeling, anomaly detection, and network optimization. While challenges exist, the application of AI in wireless grid Edgeware holds great promise in enhancing network performance, scalability, and adaptability. Continued research and innovation in this domain will drive future advancements and widespread adoption of AI in wireless grid systems.

---

[5] https://www.researchgate.net/publication/251828411_A_Nonlinear_Beamforming_algorithm_for_wireless_Communication_Systems.

AI-ENABLED GRID MONITORING AND MANAGEMENT

AI-enabled grid monitoring and management has emerged as a transformative approach in the field of energy infrastructure [6]. By leveraging the power of AI, grid operators can proactively monitor, analyze, and optimize the performance of their grids. Proactive monitoring and fault detection are crucial aspects of AI-enabled grid management. Traditional grid monitoring methods often rely on manual inspection and reactive responses to grid failures. AI changes this paradigm by enabling proactive monitoring, where real-time data from grid sensors and smart meters are continuously analyzed to detect potential faults and anomalies. ML algorithms, such as anomaly detection and pattern recognition, can identify abnormal grid behavior, equipment malfunctions, and potential failure points. By detecting faults in advance, grid operators can take preventive measures, minimize downtime, and optimize grid performance.

Predictive maintenance and asset management are integral components of AI-enabled grid monitoring [6]. With AI, grid operators can employ advanced analytics to predict the health and performance of grid assets, such as transformers, power lines, and substations. ML models can be trained using historical maintenance records, sensor data, and environmental factors to forecast the probability of equipment failures or performance degradation. By leveraging these predictions, grid operators can schedule maintenance activities more efficiently, reduce costs, and extend the lifespan of critical assets. Predictive maintenance also enables the use of condition-based monitoring, where sensors continuously monitor equipment parameters, allowing for timely maintenance interventions.

Real-time grid monitoring and anomaly detection are essential for ensuring the reliability and stability of the power grid [6]. AI techniques, such as real-time data analytics and intelligent algorithms, enable grid operators to monitor grid parameters, voltage levels, and load demands in real-time. ML models can analyze vast amounts of data to identify patterns, detect anomalies, and predict potential grid disturbances or instability. Real-time monitoring facilitates grid operators' decision-making processes, enabling them to take immediate actions to mitigate risks, prevent blackouts, and optimize grid operation.

To provide a clear example, let's assume we're monitoring a smart grid, an electricity supply network that uses digital communication technology for monitoring, control, and analysis.[6] An AI-enabled system might monitor various nodes (i.e., smart meters, power generators, substations, etc.) within this grid to ensure efficiency, security, and reliability. Let's represent each unit of network traffic as a "packet", which is a formatted unit of data carried by a packet-switched network. Each packet could include various pieces of information as follows:

Packet 1: Enumeration and Mapping
AI to Smart Meter: PING
Smart Meter to AI: ACK, Meter ID: 12345, Location: Substation A, IP: 192.168.1.2

Packet 2: Data Collection
AI to Smart Meter: REQUEST_DATA, Parameters: Energy Usage
Smart Meter to AI: DATA_RESPONSE, Energy Usage: 300 kWh

Packet 3: Anomaly Detection
AI to Central Server: LOG_METRIC, Meter ID: 12345, Energy Usage: 300 kWh, Status: NORMAL
Central Server to AI: ACKNOWLEDGED

Packet 4: Predictive Modeling
AI to AI: SIMULATE, Scenario: Energy Usage increases 20%, Meter ID: 12345
AI to AI: SIMULATION_RESULT, Scenario: Energy Usage increase 20%, Outcome: Sufficient Capacity

Packet 5: Automated Adjustments
AI to Smart Meter: ADJUST_PARAMETER, Parameter: Energy Draw, New Value: Reduced by 10%
Smart Meter to AI: ADJUSTMENT_CONFIRMED

---

[6]This example is highly simplified and represents a conversation between AI and the devices. In practice, this communication will be in specific protocols (like MODBUS or DNP3 for smart grids) and often secured and encrypted. Furthermore, real network traffic would be significantly more complex, involving a much larger number of packets, diverse communication types, and various error-checking and correction methods.

Packet 6: Alerts and Reporting
AI to Central Server: REPORT, Meter ID: 12345, Adjustment: Energy Draw reduced by 10%, Current Usage: 270 kWh
Central Server to AI: REPORT_RECEIVED

The integration of AI and grid monitoring systems generates significant benefits. Firstly, it improves grid reliability and resilience by enabling early fault detection and proactive maintenance. By identifying potential issues before they escalate, grid operators can minimize outages and optimize grid performance. Secondly, AI-enabled asset management enhances the utilization and longevity of grid assets. Predictive maintenance allows for targeted interventions and reduces the need for unnecessary maintenance activities. It optimizes resource allocation and reduces costs by replacing equipment only when necessary. Thirdly, real-time grid monitoring and anomaly detection enable quick responses to dynamic grid conditions. Grid operators can identify abnormal grid behavior, such as voltage fluctuations or grid imbalances, and take corrective actions promptly.

However, challenges exist in the implementation of AI-enabled grid monitoring and management. One significant challenge is the availability and quality of data. Grid operators need access to accurate and reliable data from sensors, smart meters, and other grid devices. Data integrity, consistency, and interoperability across different systems are critical factors for successful AI implementation. Additionally, ensuring data privacy and security is of utmost importance when dealing with sensitive grid data. Another challenge is the interpretability and transparency of AI models. While AI algorithms can make accurate predictions and detect anomalies, understanding the reasoning behind these decisions can be challenging. Interpretable AI models that provide transparent insights into their decision-making processes are crucial for building trust among grid operators and stakeholders. Furthermore, the scalability and computational requirements of AI algorithms need to be considered. Grid monitoring systems produce vast amounts of data, and AI algorithms must be capable of processing and analyzing this data in real time. Grid operators need to invest in robust computational infrastructure and cloud-based solutions to handle the computational demands of AI-enabled grid monitoring and management.

By leveraging AI techniques such as proactive monitoring and fault detection, predictive maintenance and asset management, and real-time grid monitoring and anomaly detection, grid operators can optimize grid performance, reduce downtime, and enhance reliability. Overcoming challenges related to data quality, interpretability, and scalability will be crucial for the successful implementation of AI in grid monitoring systems. Continued research, technological advancements, and collaborations between grid operators, AI researchers, and industry stakeholders will drive future advancements and widespread adoption of AI in grid monitoring and management systems.

AI-DRIVEN RESOURCE ALLOCATION AND OPTIMIZATION

Intelligent load balancing and demand response are critical aspects of AI-driven resource allocation [5]. Load balancing refers to the distribution of electrical load across different power sources and grids to ensure optimal utilization and efficiency. AI algorithms can analyze real-time data on power demand, generation capacity, and grid conditions to make intelligent decisions on load distribution. ML techniques, such as RL and optimization algorithms, can dynamically adjust load allocation, considering factors like cost, reliability, and environmental impact. By intelligently balancing the load, AI can help reduce grid congestion, enhance stability, and optimize resource usage [5].

Demand response is another key aspect of AI-driven resource allocation. It involves dynamically adjusting consumer electricity consumption in response to supply-demand imbalances or grid conditions [5]. AI algorithms can analyze historical consumption patterns, weather forecasts, and pricing information to predict and influence consumer behavior. By providing real-time insights and incentives, AI-driven demand response systems can incentivize consumers to shift their energy usage to non-peak hours, reducing strain on the grid during periods of high demand. This helps grid operators manage peak loads, minimize blackouts, and optimize overall grid efficiency.

The optimization of energy distribution and storage is another important application of AI in resource allocation [5]. AI algorithms can optimize the routing of electricity from various sources, including renewable energy generation, storage systems, and the traditional grid. These algorithms can consider factors such as energy availability, cost, carbon footprint, and grid stability to determine the most efficient distribution routes.

AI can also optimize energy storage systems, such as batteries, by predicting energy demand, generation patterns, and grid conditions. By intelligently managing energy distribution and storage, AI can facilitate the integration of renewable energy sources, improve grid resilience, and reduce reliance on fossil fuels.

In a wireless grid network, an AI-driven system might manage resource allocation for various connected devices, balancing loads and providing demand responses as needed. This could be seen in applications like wireless sensor networks, mobile computing, or IoT deployments. For simplicity, let's assume this system operates using a request/response protocol.[7]

Packet 1: Network Mapping
AI to Network Node: PING
Network Node to AI: ACK, Node ID: 56789, Location: Building B, IP: 192.168.2.3, Current Load: 45%

Packet 2: Load Reporting
AI to Network Node: REQUEST_LOAD
Network Node to AI: LOAD_STATUS, Current Load: 55%, Capacity: 100%

Packet 3: Load Balancing and Resource Allocation
AI to Network Node: REDISTRIBUTE_LOAD, Transfer Load: 10% to Node ID: 67890
Network Node to AI: LOAD_REDISTRIBUTION_COMPLETE, Current Load: 45%

Packet 4: Demand Response
AI to Network Node: INCREASE_CAPACITY, Parameters: +15%
Network Node to AI: CAPACITY_INCREASE_COMPLETE, New Capacity: 115%

---

[7]This represents a hypothetical and simple back-and-forth between the AI and a network node. In a real-world scenario, the AI would be managing many such conversations concurrently, constantly adjusting loads and capacities based on ongoing monitoring and predictive analysis. Actual protocols for communication would depend on the specific application and might use a variety of technologies for wireless communication, such as Wi-Fi, Zigbee, or cellular networks.

Packet 5: Monitoring
AI to Network Node: REQUEST_LOAD
Network Node to AI: LOAD_STATUS, Current Load: 45%, Capacity: 115%

Packet 6: Reporting
AI to Central Server: REPORT, Node ID: 56789, Adjustment: Capacity Increased by 15%, Load Redistribution: 10% to Node ID: 67890, Current Load: 45%, Capacity: 115%
Central Server to AI: REPORT_RECEIVED

AI-driven decision support systems play a crucial role in enabling grid operators to make informed decisions in real time. These systems utilize AI techniques, such as ML and data analytics, to process and analyze vast amounts of data from sensors, smart meters, and grid infrastructure. By integrating historical data, real-time measurements, and predictive models, AI decision support systems can provide grid operators with actionable insights and recommendations. These insights can include optimal maintenance schedules, grid optimization strategies, and emergency response plans. AI-driven decision support systems empower grid operators to manage grid operations efficiently, enhance grid resilience, and improve overall performance.

However, several challenges must be addressed for the successful implementation of AI-driven resource allocation and optimization. One major challenge is the availability and quality of data. AI algorithms rely on large-scale, high-quality datasets to make accurate predictions and decisions. Grid operators need access to comprehensive data on energy consumption, generation, weather conditions, and grid infrastructure. Data collection, management, and privacy considerations are crucial aspects that must be carefully addressed to ensure data quality and protect sensitive information. Another challenge is the interpretability and transparency of AI algorithms. AI-driven resource allocation and optimization often involve complex algorithms such as DL neural networks or RL models. Understanding the reasoning behind AI-driven decisions and ensuring transparency is critical for building trust among grid operators, regulators, and end-users. Explainable AI techniques that provide interpretable insights and explanations for AI-driven decisions are gaining attention to address this challenge.

Scalability and computational requirements are additional challenges in AI-driven resource allocation and optimization [5]. As power grids produce enormous amounts of data, AI algorithms need to scale efficiently to process and analyze this data in real time. Advanced computational infrastructure, cloud computing, and distributed computing technologies are crucial to handle the computational demands of AI-driven resource allocation and optimization. From intelligent load balancing and demand response to optimization of energy distribution and storage, AI empowers grid operators to make data-driven decisions and improve grid efficiency, stability, and sustainability. Addressing challenges related to data quality, interpretability, and scalability will be essential for the widespread adoption of AI in resource allocation and optimization. Continued research, collaboration between stakeholders, and policy frameworks are necessary to realize the full potential of AI-driven resource allocation and optimization in the power grid.

AI-SECURITY AND RESILIENCE OF WIRELESS GRIDS EDGEWARE

AI plays a vital role in enhancing the security and resilience of wireless grids Edgeware. Threat detection and prevention are critical aspects of securing wireless grids Edgeware against various cyber threats [3]. AI techniques, such as ML and DL, can be utilized to analyze vast amounts of network data, system logs, and user behavior to identify and mitigate potential threats. By training AI models on historical data, these models can learn to recognize patterns associated with cyber-attacks, anomalies, and malicious activities [1]. This enables the detection of emerging threats, including malware, distributed denial-of-service (DDoS) attacks, and unauthorized access attempts.

ML algorithms can be employed for anomaly detection, where deviations from normal network behavior are flagged as potential security threats. These algorithms learn the normal behavior patterns of wireless grids Edgeware and can identify anomalies that indicate a security breach or intrusion. By continuously monitoring network traffic, AI-powered systems can detect and respond to suspicious activities in real time, allowing for prompt mitigation measures to be taken [11]. Additionally, AI-driven cybersecurity measures help protect wireless grids Edgeware against evolving cyber threats. AI algorithms can analyze system vulnerabilities, identify potential attack vectors, and recommend security measures to strengthen the network infrastructure [11]. This includes measures such as implementing strong encryption protocols, access controls, and secure authentication mechanisms. AI can also assist in the automated patch management process, ensuring that system vulnerabilities are promptly addressed and protected against potential exploits.

Intrusion detection is another crucial aspect of securing wireless grids Edgeware [3]. AI algorithms can continuously monitor network traffic and detect unauthorized access attempts, intrusions, and data breaches. These algorithms can analyze patterns, identify abnormal activities, and trigger alerts or responses to mitigate the impact of the intrusion. Advanced AI techniques, such as behavior-based intrusion detection systems, can learn the normal behavior of wireless grids Edgeware and detect deviations indicative of an intrusion attempt. This proactive approach helps prevent potential security breaches and ensures the integrity and confidentiality of critical infrastructure. Resilience and self-healing mechanisms are integral components of AI-enabled security in wireless grids Edgeware. AI can enhance the resilience of wireless grids by analyzing real-time data, predicting potential failures or disruptions, and initiating appropriate measures to mitigate the impact [11]. AI algorithms can identify system vulnerabilities, anticipate grid failures, and dynamically allocate resources to ensure uninterrupted power supply. For instance, AI can optimize energy distribution, dynamically reroute power flows, and manage energy storage systems to maintain grid stability during adverse conditions or cyber-attacks.

One such intrusion detection utilizing AI is YARA[8] rules. YARA is a tool primarily used in malware research and detection which uses a rule-based approach to create descriptions of malware families based on textual or binary patterns. In the context of AI-driven wireless grid Edgeware networks, YARA could potentially be used to identify suspicious or malicious traffic patterns, although it's important to note that its use in network intrusion detection is less common than in malware detection.

As an example, let's assume we're dealing with an AI-driven system that has been trained to recognize certain patterns of network traffic that could indicate an intrusion. These patterns have been converted into

[8] https://yara.readthedocs.io/en/latest/.

```
rule AI_Driven_Intrusion_Detection
{
    meta:
        author = "SKYNET"
        description = "Detect potential intrusions in wireless grid Edgewar
        last_modified = "2023-07-23"

    strings:
        $network_packet_pattern_1 = { 23 45 67 89 ab cd ef 12 34 56 }
        $network_packet_pattern_2 = { fe dc ba 98 76 54 32 10 ef cd }
        $malicious_IP = "192.0.2.0"
        $malicious_payload = "BadPayload123"

    condition:
        any of ($network_packet_pattern_*) and
        ($malicious_IP in network_traffic) and
        ($malicious_payload in network_traffic)
}
```

Figure 1. Sample AI YARA Rule

YARA rules. Here's a hypothetical YARA rule that might be used in this context[9] (see Figure 1):

In this rule:

- network_packet_pattern_1 and network_packet_pattern_2 are byte sequences representing specific patterns in the network packets that the AI system has identified as potentially indicative of an intrusion.
- malicious_IP represents an IP address that has been flagged as associated with malicious activity.
- malicious_payload is a string that has been identified as part of a potential malicious payload.
- The condition for the rule specifies that any of the network_packet_pattern_* strings, when found along with the malicious_IP and malicious_payload in the network traffic, will trigger the rule.

[9]Note that YARA is traditionally used for file scanning, and its use in wireless network IDS's will require additional tools or approaches, such as deep packet inspection. The above sample is highly simplified, and IDS are significantly more complex, often utilizing a combination of signature-based, anomaly-based, and policy-based detection methods.

Furthermore, AI-driven self-healing mechanisms enable wireless grids Edgeware to autonomously detect and respond to system failures or attacks. AI algorithms can automatically identify compromised components, isolate affected areas, and initiate recovery processes; this includes tasks such as system reconfiguration, automatic patching, and rerouting of energy flows to ensure minimal disruption and rapid restoration of grid functionality. AI-enabled self-healing mechanisms reduce the reliance on manual interventions, enhancing the efficiency and effectiveness of grid resilience [13]. However, several challenges exist in the implementation of AI in the security and resilience of wireless grids Edgeware. One significant challenge is the dynamic and evolving nature of cyber threats. AI models need to be continually updated and trained with the latest threat intelligence to effectively detect and respond to emerging threats [11]. Moreover, the interpretability and explainability of AI algorithms are crucial for building trust and understanding the reasoning behind their decisions while explainable AI techniques are gaining importance to address this challenge.

Data privacy and security are also critical concerns in AI-enabled security [11]. Protecting sensitive data collected by wireless grids Edgeware is paramount. Security measures, such as encryption, access controls, and secure data transmission protocols, must be implemented to ensure data confidentiality and integrity. Additionally, collaboration between grid operators, cybersecurity experts, and AI researchers is crucial to establishing comprehensive cybersecurity frameworks and best practices. Scalability and computational requirements present additional challenges. Wireless grids Edgeware generate vast amounts of data that need to be processed and analyzed in real-time. AI algorithms must be scalable, efficient, and capable of handling the computational demands of large-scale grid systems. Advanced computational infrastructure, distributed computing technologies, and cloud computing play vital roles in addressing these challenges.

AI plays a pivotal role in ensuring the security and resilience of wireless grids Edgeware [3]. By enabling threat detection and prevention, implementing cybersecurity measures, facilitating intrusion detection, and implementing resilience and self-healing mechanisms, AI empowers grid operators to protect critical infrastructure from cyber threats and maintain grid functionality in the face of disruptions. Addressing challenges related to dynamic threat landscape, data privacy, interpretability, and scalability will be crucial for the successful integration of AI in securing wireless grids Edgeware. Continued research, collaboration, and industry-wide efforts are necessary to advance AI-driven security and resilience in wireless grids Edgeware.

AI CHALLENGES AND FUTURE DIRECTIONS

Data quality is a crucial challenge in AI for wireless grid Edgeware. The success of AI algorithms relies heavily on the availability of high-quality data. However, collecting and maintaining large-scale, diverse, and accurate data can be complex and resource-intensive. Challenges include data consistency, data cleaning, data privacy, and data labeling. Efforts must be made to ensure data integrity, standardization, and adherence to privacy regulations. Collaboration between grid operators, researchers, and data providers is vital to address data quality challenges and establish robust data collection and management frameworks.

As wireless grid systems generate vast amounts of data, AI algorithms must be scalable to handle the increasing data volume, velocity, and variety. Scalable ML algorithms, distributed computing technologies, and cloud computing solutions are necessary to process and analyze data in real time. Research in efficient parallel processing, distributed learning, and edge computing can help address scalability challenges and enable the deployment of AI at scale in wireless grid Edgeware. Interoperability changes pose challenges when integrating AI in wireless grid Edgeware. Wireless grid systems consist of diverse devices, sensors, and communication protocols from different vendors and generations. Achieving seamless interoperability between these components and AI systems requires standardized communication protocols, data formats, and interfaces. The development and adoption of open standards, such as IEEE 2030.5[10] and IEC 61850,[11] can facilitate interoperability and promote collaboration between different stakeholders.

Human–machine collaboration and trust are crucial aspects in the application of AI for wireless grid Edgeware. Trust in AI algorithms and decision-making is vital for effective adoption. AI systems should be transparent, explainable, and auditable, enabling human operators to understand and validate their outputs. Ensuring human oversight and

[10] https://standards.ieee.org/ieee/2030.5/5897/.

[11] https://ieeexplore.ieee.org/abstract/document/7543038.

control over AI-driven processes is essential to build trust and ensure accountability. Human-machine collaboration frameworks should be developed, where AI systems assist human operators in decision-making, optimization, and response to complex grid scenarios.

Advancements and emerging trends in AI for wireless grid Edgeware offer promising future directions. Explainable AI techniques, such as interpretable ML models and rule-based systems, are gaining importance to enhance transparency and trust. Federated learning, which allows AI models to be trained collaboratively on decentralized data sources, addresses data privacy concerns while promoting model performance and knowledge sharing. RL algorithms, such as multi-agent systems, enable decentralized control and coordination in wireless grid Edgeware. Emerging trends include the integration of AI with emerging technologies such as 5G, edge computing, and IoT. AI can optimize network resource allocation, facilitate dynamic spectrum access, and enable real-time analytics in 5G-enabled wireless grids. Edge computing enables AI algorithms to be deployed closer to the grid's edge, reducing latency and enhancing real-time decision-making. IoT devices provide additional data sources for AI algorithms, enabling fine-grained monitoring, control, and optimization of wireless grid Edgeware.

The future directions in AI for wireless grid Edgeware encompass several key aspects. Research and development efforts should focus on enhancing data quality through data cleaning, standardization, and privacy-preserving techniques. Scalability solutions, such as distributed learning and Edge computing, need to be advanced to handle the increasing data volume and computational demands. Standardization bodies should collaborate to establish interoperability frameworks and promote open standards. Human-machine collaboration frameworks must be developed to leverage the strengths of both humans and AI algorithms in grid management. Furthermore, continued research in explainable AI, federated learning, RL, and integration with emerging technologies will drive the advancements in AI for wireless grid Edgeware.

CONCLUSION

In conclusion, this chapter explores the integration of AI in wireless grids Edgeware, showcasing the transformative potential of AI technologies in optimizing grid operations, enhancing energy management, improving security, and fostering sustainable development. By embracing AI-powered solutions, wireless grids Edgeware can leverage advanced analytics, predictive capabilities, and intelligent decision-making to enable efficient resource allocation, proactive monitoring, and resilient grid systems. The chapter highlights real-world examples and case studies to demonstrate the successful integration of AI in wireless grid deployments. AI brings both challenges and future directions for wireless grid Edgeware. Overcoming data quality, scalability, interoperability, human-machine collaboration, and trust challenges will be essential for successful AI integration. Advancements and emerging trends, such as explainable AI, federated learning, RL, and integration with 5G, edge computing, and IoT, offer promising future directions. Continued research, collaboration, and industry-wide efforts are necessary to realize the full potential of AI in wireless grid Edgeware and transform the energy sector.

REFERENCES

[1] Ahmetoglu, H. & Das, R. (2022). A comprehensive review on detection of cyber-attacks: Data sets, methods, challenges, and future research directions. *Internet of Things*, 11, 100615.

[2] Bega, D., Gramaglia, M., Fiore, M., Banchs, A., & Costa-Perez, X. (2019). DeepCog: Optimizing resource provisioning in network slicing with AI-based capacity forecasting. *IEEE Journal on Selected Areas in Communications*, 38(2), 361–376.

[3] Brooks, T. T. (Ed.) (2017). *Cyber-Assurance for the Internet of Things*. John Wiley & Sons, Hoboken, New Jersey.

[4] Chinnamgari, S. K. (2019). *R Machine Learning Projects: Implement Supervised, Unsupervised, and Reinforcement Learning Techniques using R 3.5.* Packt Publishing Ltd., Birmingham, UK.

[5] Firouzi, F., Farahani, B., & Marinšek, A. (2022). The convergence and interplay of edge, fog, and cloud in the AI-driven Internet of Things (IoT). *Information Systems*, 107, 101840.

[6] Jiang, J., Lin, C., Han, G., Abu-Mahfouz, A. M., Shah, S. B. H., & Martínez-García, M. (2022). How AI-enabled SDN technologies improve the security and functionality of industrial IoT network: Architectures, enabling technologies, and opportunities. *Digital Communications and Networks*. https://doi.org/10.1016/j.dcan.2022.07.001.

[7] Kreuzberger, D., Kühl, N., & Hirschl, S. (2023). Machine learning operations (mlops): Overview, definition, and architecture. *IEEE Access*, 11, 31866–31879.

[8] Hassani, H., Silva, E. S., Unger, S., TajMazinani, M., & Mac Feely, S. (2020). Artificial intelligence (AI) or intelligence augmentation (IA): What is the future? *AI*, 1(2), 8.

[9] Ramnarine-Rieks, A. & McKnight, L. (2010). Exploring cyberlearning with wireless grids. In *ICERI2010 Proceedings* (pp. 5576–5585). IATED.

[10] Page, J., Bain, M., & Mukhlish, F. (2018, August). The risks of low level narrow artificial intelligence. In *2018 IEEE International Conference on Intelligence and Safety for Robotics* (*ISR*) (pp. 1–6). IEEE.

[11] Truong, T. C., Zelinka, I., Plucar, J., Čandík, M., & Šulc, V. (2020). Artificial intelligence and cybersecurity: Past, presence, and future. In *Artificial Intelligence and Evolutionary Computations in Engineering Systems* (pp. 351–363). Springer, Singapore.

[12] Ullah, Z., Al-Turjman, F., Mostarda, L., & Gagliardi, R. (2020). Applications of artificial intelligence and machine learning in smart cities. *Computer Communications*, 154, 313–323.

[13] Zhang, B., Zhu, J., & Su, H. (2023). Toward the third generation artificial intelligence. *Science China Information Sciences*, 66(2), 1–19.

Chapter 2

Authenticating Devices in Fog-Mobile Edge Computing Environments through a Wireless Grid Resource Sharing Protocol*

ABSTRACT

The rapid growth of the Internet of Things (IoT), cloud computing, Fog computing, mobile edge computing, and wireless grids has ushered in the extensive deployment of relatively nascent technology. These technologies, which are predominantly set to utilize 5G wireless communication networks, are gaining popularity due to their rapid deployability with minimal infrastructure requirements, making them conducive to environments with an abundance of internet-connected devices (ICDs). Nevertheless, there exist significant challenges for security designers, engineers, and implementers of these networks in ensuring that they deliver adequate security levels. Owing to the ever-present threat of exploitation, these networks necessitate the protection of a robust security architecture, given the persistent security issues that plague these technologies. The authentication of smart ICDs to IoT networks emerges as a pivotal mechanism in achieving security for these novel information

*Revised article. Originally published as Brooks, T. (2022). Authentication devices in fog-mobile edge computing environments through a wireless grid resource sharing protocol. *International Journal of Ubiquitous Computing* (*IJU*), 13(1/2).

system platforms. This chapter underscores the authentication process requisite for these ICDs, which will need to authenticate their identities to an IoT, fog-mobile edge computing (FMEC) cloud network through a wireless grid authentication process. The objective of this chapter is to propose a generic authentication methodology for the use of these FMEC clouds within an IoT architecture. The proposed methodology, dubbed wg-IoT, should incorporate the integration of Fog computing, wireless grids, and mobile edge computing clouds to forge this innovative IoT architecture. An authentication process, which is based on the resource sharing protocol (RSP) of a wireless grid, is initially developed and proposed for the authentication of ICDs. The core components of the wireless grid must be incorporated in IoT devices or sensors based on their ability to manage five primary functions: management of identification [ID] and presence, permissions management, data transferability, application-programming interface [API] utilization, and security.

INTRODUCTION

The IoT paradigm, which consists of a network of embedded sensors connected to the Internet, is rapidly gaining ground in wireless telecommunications [8, 60]. However, only recently has the IoT market begun to experience rapid growth. This is due to several factors, which include the extensive spread of the Internet, next-generation 5G networks, high penetrations of mobile device usage, new cloud computing platforms, fog-mobile edge computing (FMEC), and microbrowsers.[1,2] The Fog computing market is expected to reach $617.3 million by 2025[3] and over $5.6 billion of devices will utilize mobile edge computing, primarily in the manufacturing, energy, and transportation industries.[4] All of these market forces are converging, which in turn is making the IoT market increasingly data-centric.

Any cloud network is subject to becoming the target of exploitation by individuals or groups outside of the authorized group of intended users and/or devices [22]. In addition, the advances in wireless technology have

[1] https://www.transparencymarketresearch.com/mobile-edge-computing-market.html.

[2] https://www.ibm.com/developerworks/library/wa-browse/index.html.

[3] https://www.grandviewresearch.com/press-release/global-fog-computing-market.

[4] https://www.thorntech.com/2017/11/edge-computing-and-the-cloud-future-of-iot/.

given the common individual the ability to establish a communication connection with anyone at any time. This ability has created a general addiction to connectedness and has opened new opportunities for the exploitation of communications. The exploitation of a cloud network by adversaries is conducted for four main reasons: to gain access to data flowing over the network, to disrupt the flow of data on the network, to parasitically usurp the network resources (e.g., to use a network free of charge), and provide disinformation by injecting false data into the network in order to mislead and to cause confusion and doubt [2, 26]. However, this situation has now changed, as ICDs will be able to perform these exploitations with limited human interactions.

With these assumptions as background, authentication of [wireless] ICDs in these FMEC clouds must involve strong encryption to prevent eavesdropping and must involve mutual authentication to ensure that sensitive information is transmitted only over legitimate FMEC cloud networks [40]. Authentication will require that ICDs prove their identity through a hardware/software token, a challenge/response mechanism, or a combination of these and other methods of identification. Authentication should be two-way, the ICD must authenticate to the network, and the network should authenticate to the ICD. This lets the network know that it is communicating with a valid, non-malicious ICD. By having the network authenticate to the ICD, it is less likely that an unauthorized ICD will be able to pose as valid in the network. The purpose of this chapter is to hypothesize a generic authentication methodology for ICDs in FMEC clouds utilizing the IoT architecture.

WIRELESS GRIDS AND 5G ENABLING TECHNOLOGIES

Wireless Grids

As displayed in Figure 1, a wireless grid is an augmentation of a wired grid that facilitates the exchange of information and the interaction between heterogeneous wireless devices [1]. The IoT is an integrated part of the future Internet including existing and evolving Internet and network developments and could be conceptually defined as a dynamic global network infrastructure with self-configuring capabilities [53]. This is based on standard and interoperable communication protocols where physical and virtual smart “things/objects” [e.g., wireless sensors,

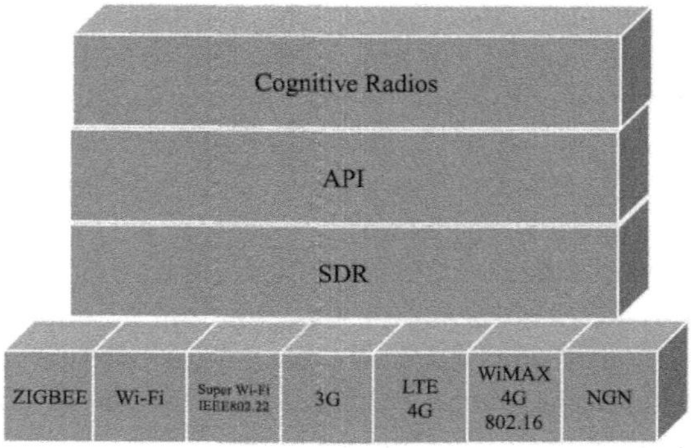

Figure 1. WIGIT Open Framework

actuators, radio frequency identification (RFID) tags, smart mobile devices, mobile robots, etc.] have identities, physical attributes, and virtual personalities, use intelligent interfaces, and are seamlessly integrated into the information network [53]. The application of wireless grids, FMEC, and IoT architectures is a key objective which facilitates information sharing and provides a means for the system to get information (whether wired or wirelessly) to individuals to satisfy their needs.

In the IoT, smart "things/objects" (i.e., internet-connected devices or ICDs) are expected to become active participants in business, information, and social processes where they are enabled to interact and communicate among themselves and with the environment by exchanging data and information sensed about the environment [12, 49, 53]. Services will be able to interact with these smart ICDs using standard interfaces that will provide the necessary link via the Internet, to query and change their state and retrieve any information associated with them, considering security and privacy issues [53]. "Things" can only become context-aware, sense, communicate, interact, and exchange data, information, and knowledge if they are suitably equipped with appropriate object-connected technologies unless of course, they are human "things" or other entities with these intrinsic capabilities [10]. In this vision, using intelligent decision-making algorithms in software applications, appropriate rapid responses can be given to physical phenomena, based on the very latest information collected about physical entities and consideration of patterns in the historical data, either for the same entity or for similar entities [53, 56].

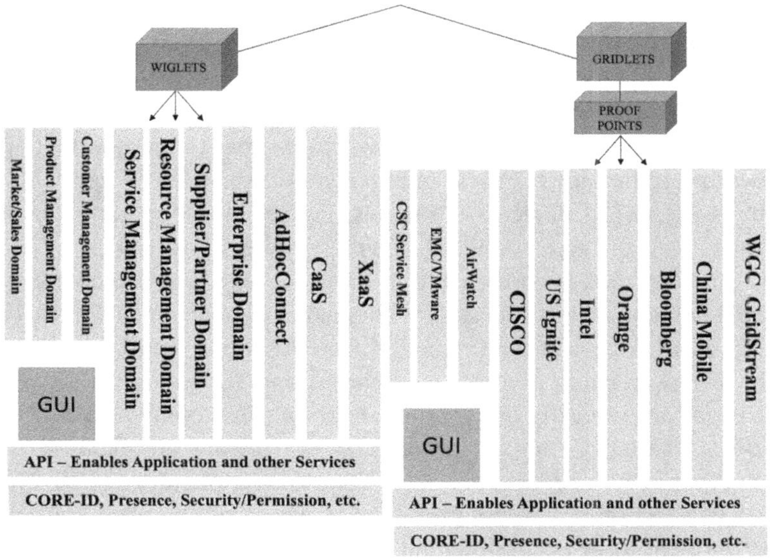

Figure 2. Edgeware Grid Core

However, the application of authentication of these ICDs within this environment brings about new and challenging problems from an information security perspective. Traditional security mechanisms, such as identification/authentication and access control (authorization) are complicated in these environments, requiring new standards and the development of new products. Counter-intuitively, the more wireless grids, FMECs, and IoT architectures that exist, the more vulnerable they will toward cyber-attacks. This is because, with wireless grids, FMECs, and IoT architectures, every user/device/thing/object may have the right to access the system causing errors and flaws. For this reason, individual users/devices/things/objects will continue to be the primary targets of malicious software (or malware) attacks.

Wireless Grid "Edgeware"

As displayed in Figure 2, Edgeware, a new class of software applications, enables the *ad hoc* connection of people, devices, software, and services in a personal cloud, supported by personal cyberinfrastructure [9, 39].

Edge devices are routers, switches, routing switches, integrated access devices (IAD), multiplexers, and a variety of metropolitan area network (MAN)/wide area network (WAN) access devices that provide entry points into enterprise or carrier/service provider core networks which translate between one type of network protocol and another [39]. Edgeware applications can dynamically make use of content and resources present in devices — phones, laptops, PCs, cameras, printers, screens, etc. — through connectivity via a wireless grid [39].

The vertical boxes on the right in Figure 2 represent Edgeware applications that sit on a user interface, which in turn sits on an API [39]. These may represent dozens or hundreds of different sorts of mini-programs that enable different kinds of resource sharing and functionality. Edgeware applications are typically delivered as a service; and come in two primary varieties: Gridlets, that is, proprietary Edgeware applications, and Wiglets, that is, non-proprietary open Edgeware applications [39]. Not all devices enabled on a wireless grid need to have an Edgeware application sitting on them to be accessible and active.

The only thing that must be deployed for a wireless grid to work is for the Grid Core to be on some intelligent machine, somewhere, with rights to control other "edge" resources such as sensors that may not have the capability to have the core components installed, which may be facilitated by one or more Gridlets and/or Wiglets [39]. Other network hardware, software, services, and content may be controlled and shared through the wireless grid "Edgeware" as these may not be or cannot become self-aware devices on the grid. However, if those "edge" resources are in a relationship with other hardware, software, and services, which are part of the wireless grid, they may function as if they were fully cognitive [39]. A further differentiation in the varieties of Edgeware applications may also be drawn between peer-to-peer implementations, and cloud-to-edge applications, which may appear at first glance to be a basic client-server implementation. In both cases, however, the Edgeware application may be able to interact dynamically with other types of Edgeware applications. The architecture and open specifications presented here allow for *ad hoc*, peer-to-peer applications and services to interact with cloud services [39].

The Grid Core components are represented by the green box and embedded in certain devices or sensors depending on their capability which makes every device a node on the wireless grid [39]. This core is extremely "light" and easy to embed on a wide range of different kinds of equipment. Reference [39] identified that users are allowed to share and manage the digital resources at their fingertips through applications of the architecture's eight core components:

- the authentication and authorization component [AAC],
- the billing, accounting, and charging component [BAC] which provides access to the things/objects financial information,
- the messaging and presence component [MPC] which provides scalable messaging, manages the availability of a thing/object and the method or language of communication with that thing/object,
- the metadata component [MC] which creates, edits, and generally manages the metadata for an ICD, (5) the resource management component [RMC] which is responsible for aggregating and searching metadata about things/objects within the context of authentication and works closely with the AAC and MPC,
- the economic and legal policy component [ELP] which supports economic and legal policies,
- the communication protocols component [CPC] which is a subsystem that manages the interaction with specific types of resources, such as printers, files, etc., and is needed to interact within a wireless grid, identifies and manages network and internetwork communications including IP and other protocols (e.g., Bluetooth), provides connections with other wireless grids and across the internet, and
- the security component.

The wireless grid architecture core components handle four primary functions, which make the grid-enabled ecosystem possible: management of identification (ID) and presence, permissions management, data transfer ability, and API/interfacing [39]. The layers above the core are comprised of the API which enables connections with other applications and services, the User Interface (which may or may not be necessary depending on the device upon which it sits), and finally the Edgeware applications are shown in the vertical boxes in Figure 2.

Once a grid is established then resources can be published or accessed across the grid, enabling the infinite functional possibilities of the Grid technology. There are three classes of wireless grid applications [39]:

- **Class 1:** Applications aggregating information from the range of input/output interfaces found in nomadic and mobile devices.
- **Class 2:** Applications utilizing the locational and contextual characteristics in which the devices will be found.

- **Class 3:** Applications leveraging the mesh network capabilities of groups of devices: Workplace-As-A-Service (WpaaS), Compute-Infrastructure-As-A-Service (CIaaS), and Virtual Private Cloud (VPC) are reference architectures that potentially can meet the unique requirements to satisfy enterprise-grade customers.

These wireless grid Edgeware systems give the user greater mobility and flexibility. Although these characteristics of services provide a number of advantages especially toward their integration into IoT architectures, they leave these wireless grids Edgeware devices vulnerable to attacks and other security-related problems [9]. It is exactly the mobile nature of the devices that exposes it to a greater risk of data loss or theft, and this contrasts with the wired service, which terminates in one location, such as in the home or office, making it more safeguarded [9].

The trend of integrating these new complex systems with advanced computer and communication technologies has introduced serious cyber-security concerns, especially in these new architectures; where the environment will no longer be regarded as reliable to support communications as before [9]. For example, due to the important role of the smart grid as the key energy IoT infrastructure, the information infrastructure needed to route data by providing the dynamic *ad hoc* sharing of heterogonous devices and the need to protect its information security is an extremely important task, which can significantly contribute to security issues given the threat of cyber-attacks [14, 34]. Traditional security mechanisms, such as identification/authentication and access control (authorization) are complicated in these new environments, requiring new standards and the development of new security products.

Due to their physical broadcast nature, these new communication networks are generally more vulnerable to malicious and accidental threats than their wired counterparts. As a result of this inherent vulnerability, security is a mandatory component. While it's more difficult and potentially more important to secure this communication, the issues, threats and the respective required services to adequately respond to these threats are mostly the same for wired and wireless technology. Alternatively, the task of providing security services for these networks is more complicated than in wired networks. Power and bandwidth limitations, often non-existent in wired networks, impose considerable constraints on the complexity and efficiency of security protocols.

Millimeter-Wave Communication

Millimeter-wave (mmWave) communication is a promising technology that enables high-speed wireless data transmission in the frequency range of 30–300 GHz [35]. With its ability to provide significantly increased bandwidth, mmWave communication holds immense potential for addressing the ever-growing demand for faster and more reliable wireless connectivity [35]. By utilizing a broader spectrum, mmWave technology can support data rates in the multi-gigabit range, facilitating applications such as high-definition video streaming, virtual reality, augmented reality, and real-time cloud-based services (see Figure 3).

One of the key advantages of mmWave communication is its ability to support massive data capacity [23]. The large bandwidth available in the mmWave spectrum allows for the simultaneous transmission of a vast amount of data, enabling seamless connectivity for a large number of devices in densely populated areas. Additionally, mmWave technology offers low latency, allowing for near-instantaneous communication and response times, critical for time-sensitive applications such as autonomous vehicles, telemedicine, and industrial automation [23]. However, mmWave communication also poses unique challenges. The high-frequency nature of mmWave signals results in shorter propagation distances and increased susceptibility to obstacles, such as buildings and foliage. The limited penetration capabilities of mmWave signals require the deployment of denser network infrastructure, including small cell

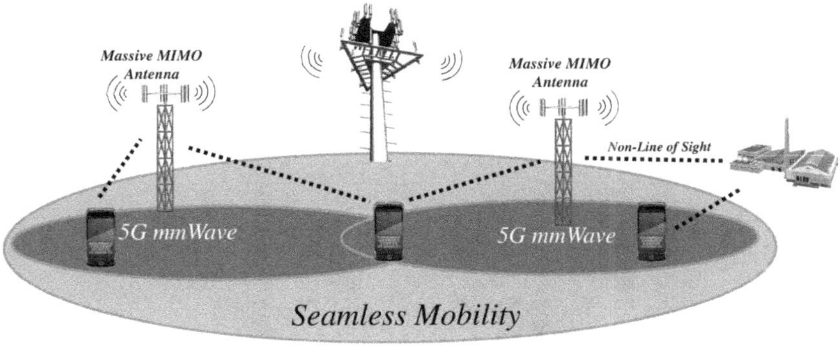

Figure 3. mmWave Communication

deployments and beamforming techniques to overcome signal attenuation and maintain reliable connectivity.

Overall, mmWave communication holds immense potential in enabling next-generation wireless connectivity with ultra-high data rates and low latency. Its deployment can revolutionize various industries, from entertainment and healthcare to transportation and manufacturing. However, addressing the technical challenges associated with mmWave propagation and infrastructure deployment is crucial for the widespread adoption and realization of its benefits in real-world applications.

Massive MIMO

Massive multiple-input multiple-output (MIMO) is an advanced antenna technology that revolutionizes wireless communication by utilizing a large number of antennas at the base station as displayed in Figure 4 [16]. Unlike traditional MIMO systems that employ a few antennas, Massive

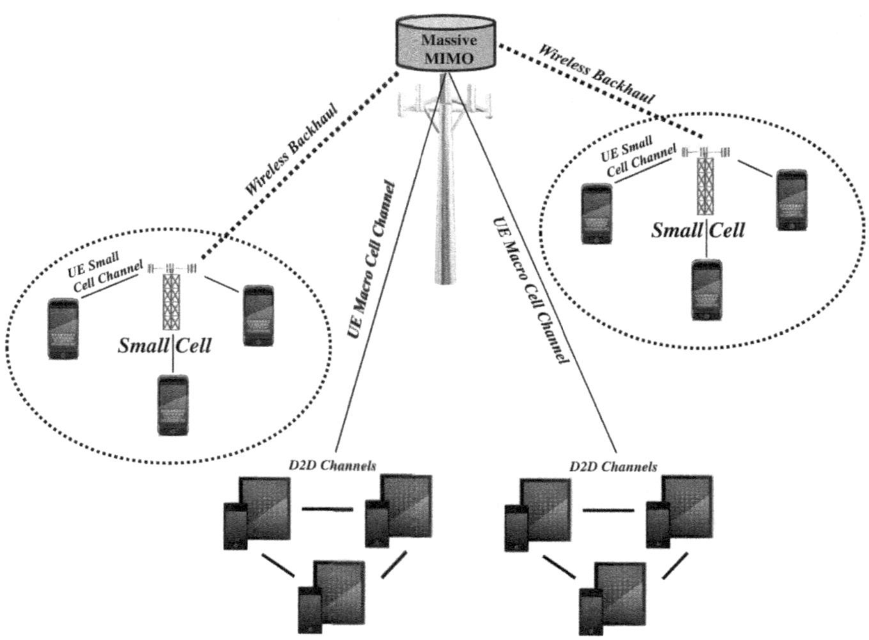

Figure 4. Massive MIMO

MIMO can simultaneously transmit and receive data using dozens or even hundreds of antennas [20]. This technology significantly enhances spectral efficiency, capacity, and overall network performance.

The key advantage of Massive MIMO lies in its ability to serve multiple users simultaneously, enabling concurrent data transmission to multiple devices at the same time-frequency resources. By exploiting spatial multiplexing, Massive MIMO can separate user signals in the spatial domain, mitigating interference and increasing network capacity [16]. The large number of antennas also improves the accuracy of channel estimation, enabling more precise beamforming and enhancing signal quality and coverage. Moreover, Massive MIMO offers significant gains in energy efficiency and reduced power consumption. By optimizing the transmit power and exploiting the spatial diversity of multiple antennas, the system can improve the signal-to-noise ratio and reduce interference, resulting in better signal quality and reduced power requirements.

Massive MIMO technology has the potential to revolutionize wireless communication systems, particularly in 5G networks [18]. Its ability to enhance capacity, coverage, and energy efficiency makes it well-suited for densely populated areas and high-traffic scenarios. However, implementing Massive MIMO also requires overcoming technical challenges, such as increased hardware complexity, efficient channel estimation, and the need for advanced signal processing algorithms. Despite these challenges, Massive MIMO is poised to play a critical role in meeting the ever-increasing demands for high-speed, reliable, and efficient wireless communication.

Ultra-Dense Small Cells

Ultra-dense small cells are a key component of next-generation wireless networks, designed to meet the growing demand for high-capacity and high-speed connectivity in densely populated areas [30]. Small cells are low-power, short-range base stations that enhance network capacity and coverage by offloading traffic from traditional macrocell towers, see Figure 5. Ultra-dense small cell deployments involve the deployment of a large number of these small cells in a concentrated area, typically in urban environments or venues with high user density. The main advantage of ultra-dense small cells is their ability to provide localized and targeted coverage. By deploying a higher density of small cells, network operators can improve network capacity and performance, ensuring seamless connectivity even in areas with high user demand [30]. These small cells operate on different frequency bands and can be strategically placed to address specific coverage and capacity requirements, such as indoor coverage in shopping malls, airports, or stadiums.

Furthermore, ultra-dense small cells enable more efficient spectrum utilization by utilizing smaller coverage areas. This approach allows for the reuse of frequency resources, increasing overall network capacity and reducing interference. Additionally, small cells support better signal quality and higher data rates due to their proximity to users, resulting in improved user experiences and faster download and upload speeds. However, deploying and managing ultra-dense small cell networks pose technical challenges. These include efficient network planning and optimization, backhaul connectivity, interference management, power management, and coordination between small cells and macrocells. Overcoming these challenges is essential to ensure the seamless integration of ultra-dense small cells into existing network infrastructure and to provide the promised

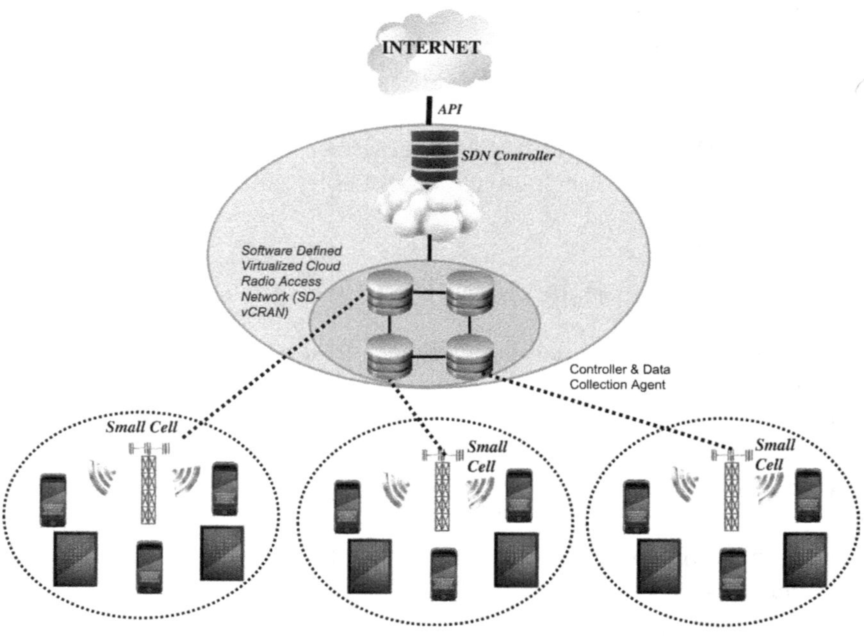

Figure 5. Ultra-Dense Small Cells

benefits of increased capacity and improved user experiences in densely populated areas.

Machine-to-Machine and Device-to-Device

Machine-to-machine (M2M) and device-to-device (D2D) communications are two important aspects of modern wireless networks that enable direct communication between devices without the need for human intervention (see Figure 6). M2M communication refers to the exchange of data between machines or devices, enabling them to communicate, interact, and share information autonomously [61]. This technology enables a wide range of applications, such as smart homes, industrial automation, healthcare monitoring, and smart transportation systems. M2M communication relies on wireless connectivity to establish seamless connections between devices, enabling them to share data, coordinate actions, and make decisions in real time.

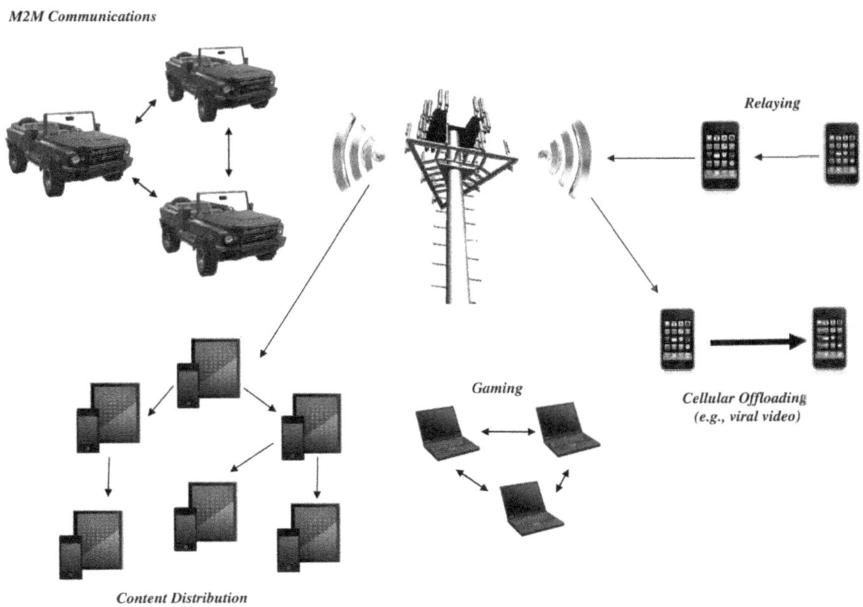

Figure 6. Machine-to-Machine and Device-to-Device

D2D communication, on the other hand, focuses on direct communication between user devices without the need for intermediate infrastructure or network resources [48]. With D2D communication, devices in proximity can establish direct wireless links, allowing for efficient data exchange and collaboration. D2D communication enables various applications, including local file sharing, multiplayer gaming, and proximity-based services. It enhances communication efficiency, reduces network congestion, and improves the overall user experience. Both M2M and D2D communications rely on underlying wireless technologies, such as Bluetooth, Wi-Fi, or cellular networks, to establish connections and exchange data. These technologies provide the necessary infrastructure and protocols to support reliable and secure M2M and D2D communication. As wireless networks evolve, M2M and D2D communications are becoming increasingly important in enabling efficient and intelligent device-to-device interactions. These communication paradigms open up new opportunities for automation, improved efficiency, and enhanced user experiences across various industries and domains.

Cloud-based Radio Access Network

Cloud-based radio access network (RAN) is an innovative approach to network architecture that leverages cloud computing principles to enhance the performance and scalability of wireless networks (see Figure 7). Traditionally, RAN consists of base stations and radio equipment deployed at specific locations. In a cloud-based RAN, the baseband processing functions are moved to a centralized cloud infrastructure, while the remote radio units (RRUs) are distributed across the network [47]. By centralizing the baseband processing in the cloud, cloud-based RAN brings several advantages including pooling of resources, allowing for efficient utilization of processing power, memory, and storage [47]. This centralized processing also enables advanced signal processing techniques, such as coordinated multipoint transmission and reception (CoMP), which can improve network capacity, coverage, and overall performance.

Another benefit of cloud-based RAN is its flexibility and scalability. The cloud infrastructure can dynamically allocate resources based on network demand, allowing for efficient scaling of capacity to handle fluctuations in user traffic. Additionally, cloud-based RAN enables network virtualization, where multiple virtual network functions (VNFs) can be

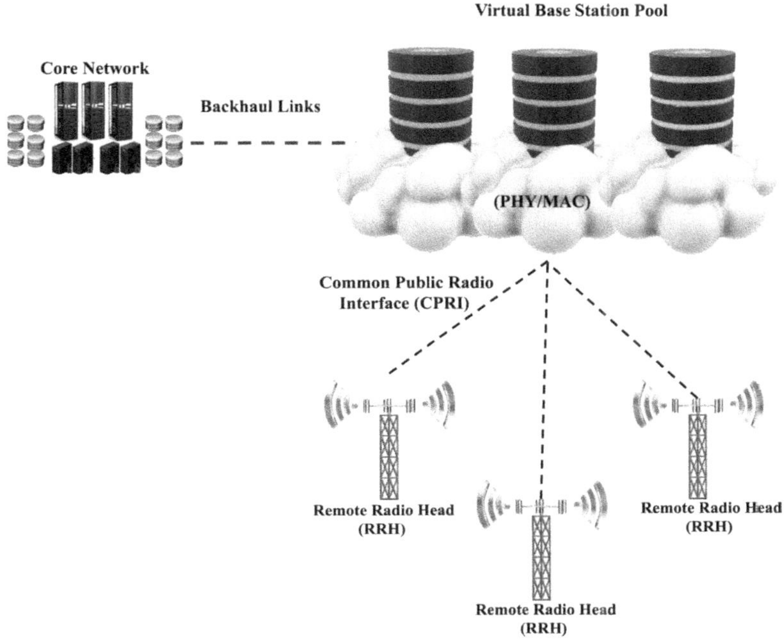

Figure 7. Cloud-based Radio Access Network

deployed on the same hardware infrastructure, reducing equipment and operational costs.

With centralized processing, it is essential to ensure the integrity and confidentiality of data transmitted between the cloud infrastructure and the remote radio units. Encryption, secure protocols, and authentication mechanisms are implemented to protect against unauthorized access and data breaches [25]. Overall, cloud-based RAN holds great promise in transforming the way wireless networks are designed and operated. It offers improved resource utilization, scalability, flexibility, and advanced signal processing capabilities, paving the way for more efficient and adaptive wireless communication systems.

Software-Defined Networking

Software-defined networking (SDN) is a revolutionary approach to network architecture that decouples the control plane from the data plane, enabling centralized management and programmability of network resources [5]. In traditional network architectures, network devices make autonomous decisions about forwarding traffic based on pre-configured rules. However, SDN introduces a centralized controller that dynamically controls and manages the behavior of network devices through an open and programmable interface. The key advantage of SDN is its ability to provide a centralized view and control of the network, allowing for greater agility, flexibility, and scalability. The controller can dynamically allocate network resources, define traffic paths, and enforce policies based on real-time network conditions and application requirements [5]. This enables organizations to rapidly adapt to changing network demands, optimize traffic flow, and implement new services or policies with ease (see Figure 8).

Moreover, SDN brings simplification and automation to network management. By abstracting the control plane from underlying network devices, administrators can manage the network through a centralized software-based controller. Furthermore, by separating the control plane from the data plane, SDN enables efficient resource allocation, dynamic network management, and rapid innovation in network services. This eliminates the need for manual configuration of individual devices and reduces the complexity associated with managing network infrastructure.

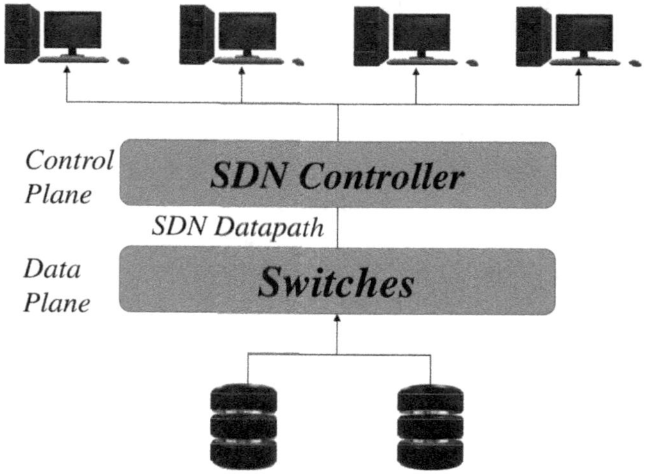

Figure 8. Software Defined Networking

Overall, SDN is revolutionizing the way networks are designed, operated, and managed. Its centralized control, programmability, and automation capabilities provide organizations with greater agility, scalability, and security.

Network Function Virtualization

Network function virtualization (NFV) is a transformative concept in network architecture that aims to virtualize traditional network functions, such as firewalls, routers, and load balancers. NFV decouples network functions from dedicated hardware appliances and abstracts them into software-based instances that can run on standard off-the-shelf servers, switches, or even cloud infrastructure (see Figure 9) [44]. By virtualizing network functions, NFV offers greater flexibility, scalability, and cost-efficiency.

One of the key advantages of NFV is the ability to deploy and scale network functions on-demand, without the need for physical hardware provisioning [44]. This allows for more agile network management,

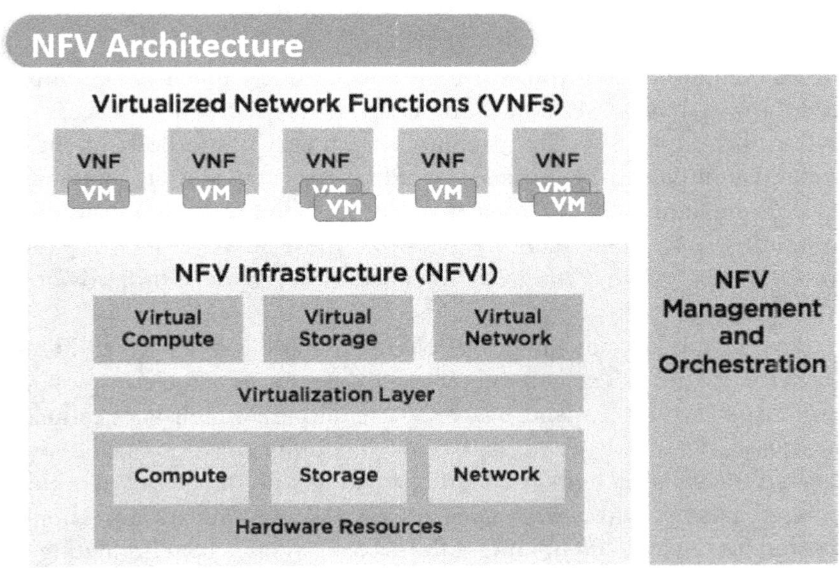

Figure 9. Network Function Virtualization

enabling organizations to quickly adapt to changing network requirements and traffic demands. With NFV, new network services and functions can be provisioned or decommissioned dynamically, reducing the time and cost associated with traditional hardware-based deployments. NFV also enables the consolidation and optimization of network resources. Multiple VNFs can be hosted on a single physical server, leading to better resource utilization and cost savings. Additionally, NFV facilitates network automation and orchestration, as VNFs can be easily instantiated, interconnected, and managed through SDN controllers or orchestration platforms.

Virtualized network functions can be encapsulated and isolated within their own virtual environments, providing enhanced security and isolation between different network services [42]. Additionally, NFV enables the deployment of security functions, such as virtualized firewalls and intrusion detection systems, in a more scalable and flexible manner. With NFV, organizations can achieve greater agility, resource optimization, and automation in network management, while also improving security capabilities. As the demand for dynamic and scalable network services continues to grow, NFV plays a crucial role in transforming the way networks are designed, deployed, and operated.

Cloud Computing

Cloud computing is a transformative technology that has revolutionized the way businesses and individuals store, access, and process data and applications [54]. Cloud computing involves the delivery of on-demand computing resources, including servers, storage, databases, networking, and software, over the Internet (see Figure 10). With cloud computing, users can access and utilize these resources on a pay-as-you-go basis, without the need for upfront investment in hardware or infrastructure.

One of the key advantages of cloud computing is its scalability and elasticity as providers can quickly allocate or de-allocate computing resources based on demand, allowing users to scale their applications or services up or down as needed. This flexibility enables businesses to respond to changing market conditions and handle fluctuating workloads more efficiently, without the need for excessive hardware provisioning. Furthermore, cloud computing offers cost savings by eliminating the

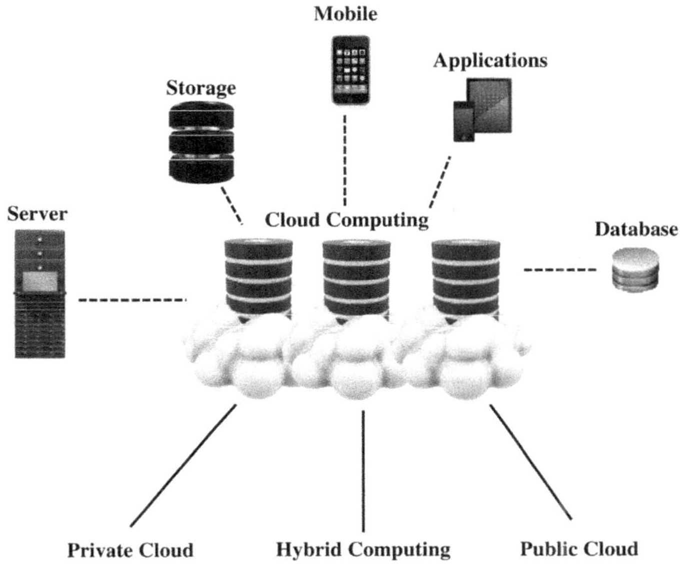

Figure 10. Cloud Computing

need for organizations to manage and maintain their own physical infrastructure.

With cloud services, users can leverage shared resources and economies of scale, reducing the operational and capital expenses associated with traditional on-premises data centers. Additionally, Cloud service providers employ various measures, such as encryption, access controls, and data isolation, to ensure the confidentiality and integrity of user data. However, users must also take responsibility for implementing proper security measures and managing access to their cloud resources.

Network Slicing

Network slicing is a cutting-edge concept in the field of telecommunications that enables the creation of multiple virtual networks within a single physical infrastructure as displayed in Figure 11. It allows network operators to partition their resources and allocate them to different virtual networks, each tailored to specific requirements and use cases. Network slicing is particularly prominent in the context of 5G networks, where it offers significant advantages in terms of flexibility, efficiency, and customization [55].

With network slicing, a single physical network can be divided into logically independent slices, each with its own dedicated set of resources, including compute, storage, and network capacity. Each slice can be customized to meet the unique needs of different applications or user groups, such as autonomous vehicles, industrial IoT, or virtual reality [55]. This level of customization enables optimized performance, security, and quality of service for each slice and also provides efficient resource utilization, as resources are dynamically allocated based on the demand of each slice. This ensures that resources are not wasted on underutilized services and can be efficiently shared among different slices. Additionally, network slicing allows for quick provisioning and deployment of new services, as each slice can be created and managed independently.

Moreover, network slicing enhances the overall network management and orchestration capabilities. By abstracting the underlying physical infrastructure, network operators can centrally manage and control the different slices through SDN and NFV technologies [55]. This centralized

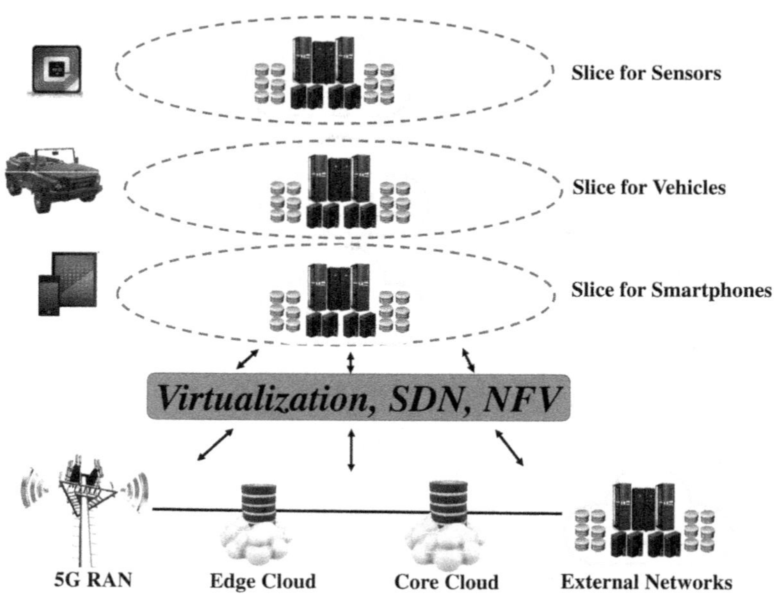

Figure 11. Network Slicing

management simplifies operations and enables dynamic optimization of resources.

Management and Orchestration

Management and orchestration (MANO) is a critical component of modern network architectures, enabling the efficient provisioning, configuration, and control of virtualized network resources as displayed in Figure 12 [11]. MANO encompasses the management and coordination of various network functions, including VNFs and infrastructure resources, to ensure optimal performance and service delivery. At its core, MANO provides the framework for automating and orchestrating the deployment and management of virtualized network services including functions such as service orchestration, lifecycle management, fault management,

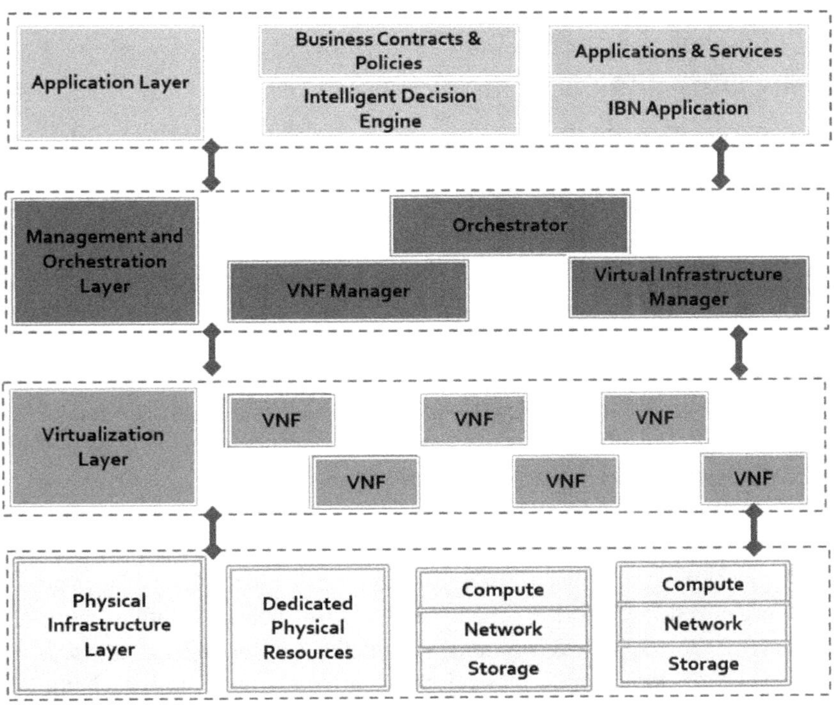

Figure 12. Management and Orchestration (MANO)

performance monitoring, and resource optimization [11]. By automating these processes, MANO simplifies network operations, reduces manual intervention, and accelerates service delivery.

MANO facilitates the dynamic allocation and scaling of virtualized resources based on demand, ensuring efficient utilization of network resources while enabling the seamless deployment and scaling of network services in response to changing network conditions, user demands, or service level agreements (SLAs) [50]. This agility and flexibility are crucial for enabling rapid service innovation and achieving cost-effective operations. MANO provides a centralized management and control framework, allowing network operators to have a holistic view of their network resources and services. Moreover, MANO facilitates policy-based management, allowing operators to define and enforce policies for service quality, security, and resource allocation. By automating and orchestrating network functions and resources, MANO enables operators to deliver scalable, agile, and cost-effective network services while ensuring optimal performance and customer satisfaction.

FOG COMPUTING

Cisco, Inc. defines the Fog as "an extension of the cloud to be closer to the things that produce and act on IoT data, processing IoT data closer to where it is produced and needed solves the challenges of exploding data volume, variety, and velocity and accelerating awareness and response to IoT events by eliminating a round trip to the cloud for analysis" [12, 13]. The National Institute of Standards and Technology (2018) recently defined Fog computing as [28]:

> A layered model for enabling ubiquitous access to a shared continuum of scalable computing resources. The model facilitates the deployment of distributed, latency-aware applications and services, and consists of fog nodes (physical or virtual), residing between smart end-devices and centralized (cloud) services. The fog nodes are context aware and support a common data management and communication system. They can be organized in clusters — either vertically (to support isolation), horizontally (to support federation), or relative to fog nodes' latency-distance to the smart end-devices. Fog computing minimizes the request-response time from/to supported applications, and provides, for

the end-devices, local computing resources and, when needed, network connectivity to centralized services.

The characteristics of the Fog (proximity and location awareness, geo-distribution, hierarchical organization) make it the suitable platform to support both energy-constrained wireless grids [7]. However, this implies a number of characteristics that make the Fog a non-trivial extension of the cloud including edge location, location awareness, and low latency [62]. The Fog, for instance, will play an active role in delivering high-quality streaming to moving vehicles, through proxies and access points positioned along highways and tracks. Localization of data processing is a fundamental and essential issue for operational wireless sensor networks (WSNs) [45].

A large number of Fog nodes, as a consequence of the wide geo-distribution, as evidenced in sensor networks in general and the Smart Grid in particular will provide support for mobility [19, 41]. It is essential for many Fog applications to communicate directly with mobile devices, and therefore support mobility techniques, such as the Locator ID Separation Protocol (LISP) 1, that decouple host identity from location identity and require a distributed directory system [62]. With support for online analytics and interplay with the Cloud, the Fog is positioned to play a significant role in the ingestion and processing of the data close to the source [62]. Figure 13 presents the idealized information and computing architecture supporting the future IoT applications, and illustrates the role of Fog computing through compute, storage, and networking resources building blocks of both the Cloud, the Fog and the mobile edge of the network.

FOG MOBILE EDGE COMPUTING

A mobile grid combines mobile computing and grid computing and develops rapidly [59]. Fog mobile edge computing (FMEC) can be mobile, portable or fixed. However, in general, the mobile user unit is a mobile, wireless device. These user devices provide one basic function — connectivity with an access point or a base station providing mobile services. Reference [43] define FMECs as clouds that support autonomic communication at the wireless edge of the Internet, defined as those nodes that are one, at most a few, wireless hops away from the wired infrastructure. FMEC enables dynamic instantiation, composition, configuration,

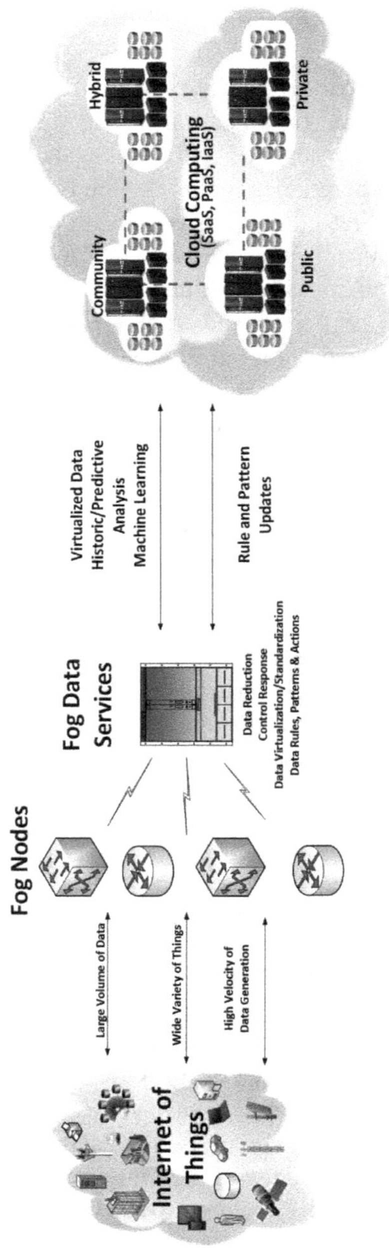

Figure 13. The Internet of Things and Fog Computing

and reconfiguration of services on an overlay network to support mobile computing [43]. FMEC provides a distributed infrastructure designed to facilitate rapid prototyping and deployment of services that enhance communication performance, robustness, and security and include a collection of low-level facilities that can be either invoked directly by applications or used to compose more complex services [37].

As displayed in Figure 14, the FMECs model supports dynamic composition and reconfiguration of services to support clients at the wireless edge and provide an infrastructure for composing autonomic communication services [43, 53]. FMECs (see Figure 3) allow information systems to mirror the integrated, evolving business processes of an enterprise to deliver specific capabilities and service levels. The ability of FMECs to change, evolve, and manage business processes throughout an enterprise is changing the way information technology development, integration and deployment work. Pervasive FMECs in an enterprise will identify and highlight cross-functional dependencies and encourage cooperation and communication between and among functional units and information technology.

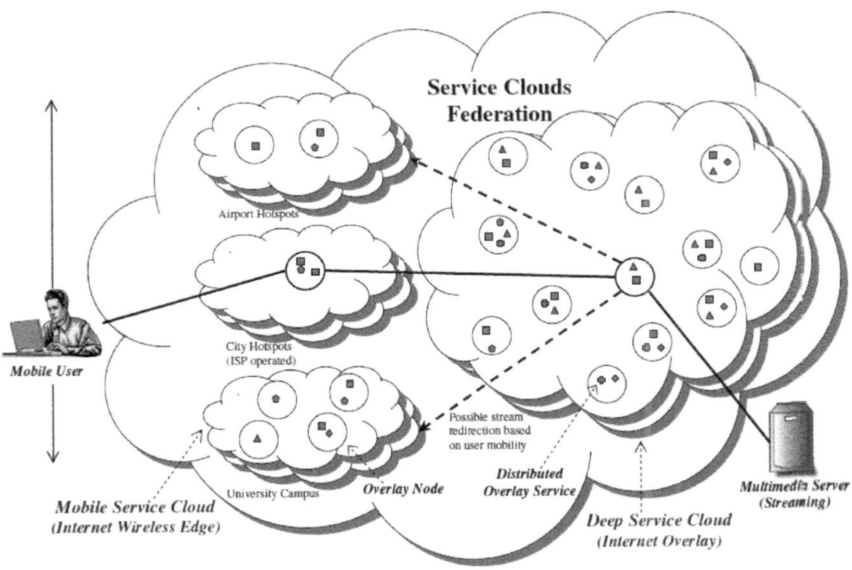

Figure 14. Fog Mobile Edge Computing

Wireless grids are infrastructure-less mobile *ad hoc* networks that can intelligently and dynamically interconnect users and stakeholders at multiple sites, transfer digital media, assume and respond to different equipment types, and adapt to low power conditions and diminished communications capabilities [38]. There are two modes of wireless grid creation, user mode and machine-based mode, as displayed in Figures 15 and 16, comparing a "human-user"-centric grid with a "node-based" grid [39]. In purely conceptual terms, it is evident that in both cases the outermost

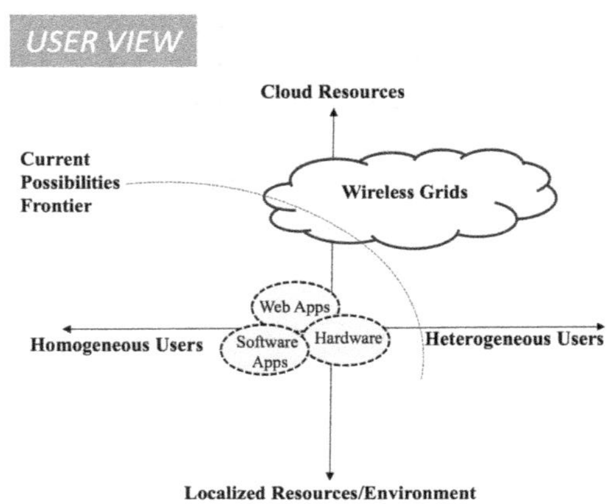

Figure 15. User View

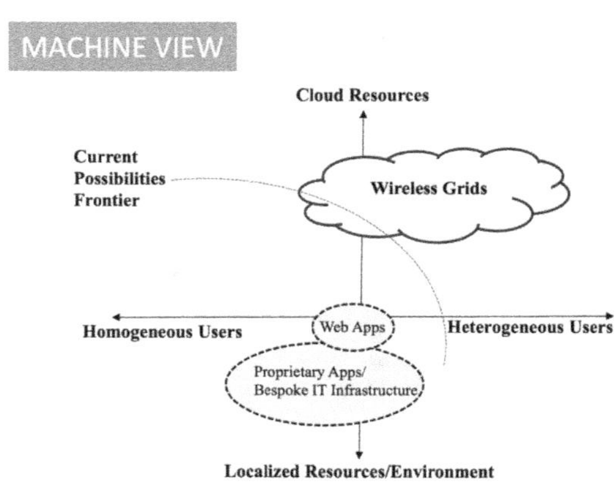

Figure 16. Machine View

frontier of what is currently possible (i.e., engaging the full range of user types) with device heterogeneity considered on an infinite axis only goes so far; the promise of the wireless grid technology is the capability of "M2M" communication via a virtual distributed operating system that enables the IoT [39].

The vision of the IoT will be driven by FMEC, wireless grids, Cloud computing and other various technologies, which also include improving information reliability and efficiency and enhancing customer participation. Given the obvious benefits of the IoT, its introduction has also posed severe security concerns. As a critical infrastructure, the IoT is expected to be a tempting target for hacking, service theft, sabotage, terrorism and other malicious attacks [34]. IoT security has been widely recognized as a major issue with potentially catastrophic implications. Due to its heavy reliance on the cyber-infrastructure for sensing and control, the IoT will be exposed to new risks from computer network vulnerabilities as well as inherit existing risks from physical vulnerabilities within existing systems [34]. Because of the significant role of the IoT as a key infrastructure, the cyber-attacks against it pose severe threats to the security of the architecture.

Both cascading failures and collapses are catastrophic events and will finally lead to large-scale shut-down of wireless grids, FMECs, and IoT architectures. Therefore, the authentication of ICDs will be key for wireless grids for the IoT architecture. An authentication model is needed to analyze the wireless grid ICDs for the wg-IoT architecture. In general, the framework provides a generic process for understanding the authentication and authorization component (AAC), the messaging and presence component (MPC), and the security component (SC) from the RSP [39]. In this chapter, the consideration is that the proposed framework can be easily extended to analyze a coordinated authentication cyber-attack launched by attackers trying to gain access to the overall IoT architecture.

EXTENSIBLE AUTHENTICATION PROTOCOL METHODS FOR WIRELESS GRID AUTHENTICATION

Authentication is the process of verifying a claimed identity. The simplest form of authentication is based on something that the authenticating parties know. For example, an individual (the user) being authenticated presents a password to the authority requiring authentication (the authenticator). If the user presents the correct password, authorization to gain access to something or to receive services is granted. For some purposes, simple password authentication like this can provide relatively strong security, but in order to do so, certain assumptions must hold true:

- The user must have some assurance that the authenticator is in fact the authority in question.
- The communication channel between the user and the authenticator must be secure so that the user and authenticator can be sure that no third party is listening.
- It must be highly unlikely that an attacker would be able to guess the password.
- In a nod to human frailty, the password must be easy to remember, but not so easy that it can be easily determined by a third party.

With these assumptions as a background, authentication for wireless networks must involve strong encryption to prevent eavesdropping and must involve mutual authentication to ensure that sensitive information is transmitted only over legitimate networks. The IETF's transport layer security (TLS) standard meets the challenges of strict encryption and authentication requirements.

Strict encryption and authentication requirements are met by IEEE 802.11-based wireless LANs through the implementation of the IEEE 802.1X standard [51]. This standard specifies the use of the extensible authentication protocol (EAP) directly over a link layer protocol. EAP is essentially a transport protocol that can be used by a variety of different authentication types, known as EAP methods. EAP was standardized by the IETF in March 1998. Among the EAP methods developed specifically for wireless networks are a family of methods based on public key certificates and the TLS protocol. These are EAP-TLS, EAP-TTLS, LEAP, and PEAP. Guidance is provided by the IETF on general EAP deployment considerations. IETF RFC 3748[5] [1, Section 7] enumerates the threat model under which EAP operates and the security claims that must be

---

[5] https://datatracker.ietf.org/doc/rfc3748/.

addressed by EAP methods. Specifically, the threat model identifies the following ten potential intruder actions[6]:

1. An attacker may try to discover user identities by snooping authentication traffic.
2. An attacker may try to modify or spoof EAP packets.
3. An attacker may launch denial of service attacks by spoofing lower layer indications or Success/Failure packets, by replaying EAP packets, or by generating packets with overlapping Identifiers.
4. An attacker may attempt to recover the pass phrase by mounting an offline dictionary attack.
5. An attacker may attempt to convince the peer to connect to an untrusted network by mounting a man-in-the-middle attack.
6. An attacker may attempt to disrupt the EAP negotiation in order to cause a weak authentication method to be selected.
7. An attacker may attempt to recover keys by taking advantage of weak key derivation techniques used within EAP methods.
8. An attacker may attempt to take advantage of weak cipher suites subsequently used after the EAP conversation is complete.
9. An attacker may attempt to perform downgrading attacks on lower-layer cipher suite negotiation in order to ensure that a weaker cipher suite is used subsequent to EAP authentication.
10. An attacker acting as an authenticator may provide incorrect information to the EAP peer and/or server via out-of-bound mechanisms. This includes impersonating another authenticator or providing inconsistent information to the peer and EAP server.

IEEE 802.11i Wi-Fi Protected Access 2

The 80211i, released in 2004, defines a new encryption method based on the advanced encryption standard (AES) in addition to temporal key integrity protocol (TKIP) encryption, AES based encryption can be used in a number of different modes or algorithms. The mode that has been chosen for 802.11 is the Counter Mode with CBC-MAC (CCM). Targeted at Wi-Fi equipment, it is hardware-accelerated for faster performance.

[6]RFC 3748: 3 of 3, p. 42 to 67. https://www.tech-invite.com/y35/tinv-ietf-rfc-3748-3.html.

WPA2 is the only Wi-Fi encryption protocol that fully implements the IEEE 802.11i standard [17].

The 802.11i specification applies across 802.11 versions a, b, and g. The full implementation of 802.11i is tentatively called Wi-Fi Protected Access 2 (WPA2). WPA2 (802.11i) upgraded the fundamental 802.11 WLAN encryption algorithm from TKIP/WEP to an AES-based approach [29]. 802.11i utilizes the same 802.1X authentication used with WPA and enabled a graceful transition from the earlier version through a mixed mode supporting 802.11i access points (AP) allowing both WPA and 802.11i clients.

A robust security network (RSN) as defined by 802.11i depends upon IEEE 802.1X to deliver its authentication and key management services [47]. IEEE 802.1X Ports (a new component) are present on all stations in an RSN. They reside above the IEEE 802.11 fragmentation and reassembly layer, and all data traffic that flows through the RSN MAC also passes through the IEEE 802.1X Port [46]. All stations and APs in an RSN contain an IEEE 802.1X entity that handles many of these services. The 801.11i standard defines how an RSN utilizes IEEE 802.1X to access these services. The 802.11i standard differentiates between an RSN and a TSN as a TSN is an RSN that also supports unmodified pre-RSN equipment [46]. A TSN is defined only to facilitate migration to an RSN and is insecure since the pre-RSN equipment can compromise the larger network.

An RSN provides a number of security features to the 802.11 architecture. These features include:

- Enhanced authentication mechanisms for both access points and stations,
- Key management algorithms,
- Dynamic cryptographic keys,
- Enhanced data encapsulation mechanism called CCMP and optionally temporal key integrity protocol (TKIP) and wireless robust authenticated protocol (WRAP) which consists of three parts: a key derivation procedure, an encapsulation procedure, and a decapsulation procedure.

A second component is the authentication server (AS). The AS is an entity that resides in the directory services (DS) that participates in the authentication of all stations (including APs) in the extended service set (ESS). It may authenticate the elements of the RSN itself (stations or APs) or it may provide material that the RSN elements can use to authenticate each other. The AS communicates with the authenticator address (AA) on each station, enabling the stations to be authenticated to the ESS and vice versa. Mutual authentication of both the ESS and the station is an important goal of the RSN. It is important to note that the AS is a logical entity only; in real implementations, it may be integrated into the same physical device as an AP, in order to accommodate low-end markets such as the home and small office/home office (SoHo).

802.1X was initially developed for the authentication of users on traditional wired LANs and therefore did not require strong encryption [40]. 802.11 data security additions include various encryption processes such as counter with cipher block chaining message authentication code protocol (CCMP), TKIP, and WRAP. CCMP is targeted at future WLAN equipment, while TKIP is targeted at legacy equipment. TKIP's main attraction is a frequent update of the encryption key as it generates new encryption keys for every 10 kilobytes of data transmitted [40]. TKIP can be added to an existing 802.11 interface by upgrading its software. A version of the TKIP mechanism called safe secure networks (SSNs), was already adopted by the Wi-Fi industry group prior to the approval of 802.11i [61]. CCMP is designed for wireless LANs as it needs more processing power than most adaptors and access points currently have to spare. It uses a version of the AES to encrypt data in transit.

The 80211i defines a new encryption method based on the AES in addition to TKIP encryption. AES-based encryption can be used in a number of different modes or algorithms. The mode that has been chosen for 802.11i is the Counter Mode with CBC-MAC (CCM). The 802.11i standard defines three data privacy protocols: TKIP, WRAP, and CCMP [17]. TKIP provides legacy hardware devices with a way to securely interoperate with 802.11i-capable devices. WRAP and CCMP are both protocols based on 128-bit AES, the first in offset codebook mode (OCB) mode, and the second in CCM mode. CCMP will be mandatory in all IEEE 802.11 equipment claiming RSN (802.11i) compliance. Implementation of TKIP and WRAP is optional for RSN compliance. Pre-RSN devices may be patched to implement TKIP, to interoperate -with RSN-compliant devices that also implement TKIP. The use of any of the privacy algorithms depends on local policies. Because of its weakness, IEEE 802.11 recommends not using TKIP except as a patch to pre-RSN equipment [32] RSN devices should implement TKIP only to allow interoperability with pre-RSN hardware implementing the TKIP patch.

IEEE 802.11i MAC Security Enhancements

IEEE 802.11i was initially intended to address both quality of service and security. This was then split with IEEE 802.11i for quality of service and IEEE 802.11i for security. Irrespective of the MAC protocol used — be it the original IEEE Std 802.11 providing up to 2 Mbps frequency-hopping spread spectrum (FHSS) or direct sequence spread spectrum (DSSS) in the 2.4GHz band or IEEE 802.11a's amendment for up to 54 Mbps orthogonal frequency division multiplexing (OFDM) in 5GHz band or IEEE 802.11b's amendment for up to 11 Mbps DSSS in 2.4 GHz band or IEEE 802.11g's mixture of DSSS and OFDM to give up to 54 Mbps in the 2.4GHz band or the future IEEE 802.11n's MIMO technologies promising over 100 Mbps effective — the IEEE 802.11i amendment provides MAC layer security to addresses all known vulnerabilities in the original 40-bit or 104-bit WEP encryption scheme.

Robust Security Network Association

IEEE 802.11i introduces the concept of the robust security network association (RSNA) that allows mutual authentication, and introduces key management protocols and new data encryption and integrity protocols [15, 32]. On top of the existing Open System authentication, where any station can be authenticated without credentials, a RSNA provides authentication based on IEEE 802.1X, or by using preshared keys (PSKs). The latter is not to be confused with the original "Shared Key" authentication, where a shared, secret, WEP encryption key is required. An RSNA specifically excludes the original "Shared Key" WEP authentication. IEEE 802.1X authentication utilizes an extensible authentication protocol (EAP) to authenticate STAs and the AS with one another. The EAP method is not specified but needs to allow mutual authentication. Also, IEEE 802.11i includes two new confidentiality protocols, the TKIP that is compatible with older hardware and the AES in Counter-Mode with Cipher-Block Chaining with Message Authentication Code (CTRICBC-MAC) Protocol (CCMP) [32].

The RSN architecture authenticates and secures an association to an access point, but does not provide ongoing access control functionality such as that provided by filtering routers or firewall devices. The only access control performed by IEEE 802.11i RSN access points is to prevent all communications over the IEEE 802.1X controlled port until the STA has successfully authenticated via the IEEE 802.1X uncontrolled port.

Once the STA has authenticated no filtering of traffic transmitted over the controlled port is performed. While the firmware in specific vendors' access points may implement some basic filtering, it is unlikely to support the range of filtering options and application intelligence found in more fully-featured firewall products. It is likely then, that an additional firewall component will need to be deployed to provide access control functions for a gateway system based on 802.11i RSN.

The IEEE 802.11i RSN relies on IEEE 802.1X port-based network access control and the EAP to provide a framework that supports higher layer authentication, to a RADIUS server for example. On successful completion of an EAP method, the station (STA) and AS will have mutually authenticated each other and established a pairwise master key (PMK). If the AS is not collocated with the authenticator (access point), the PMK must be securely transmitted to the AR The AP and STA now use the PMK as an input to the IEEE 802.11i 4-way handshake to derive the pairwise transient key (PTK) and establish the security association that will secure the link layer.

IEEE 802.1X Port-Based Authentication

This section will discuss the IEEE 802.1X Port-Based Authentication protocol and how it is used in WLANs to improve the MAC-layer security. IEEE 802.1X is not particular to WLANs but is a general purpose access control framework. In IEEE 802.1X parlance, the entity wanting to be authenticated is the Supplicant, which authenticates with the AS through the Authenticator. The authenticator is an entity the supplicant has to use to communicate with the AS. The authenticator allows the supplicant to communicate with the AS (so as to authenticate) but with no other part of the network until authentication is completed successfully. The authenticator does not do the authentication — it controls the traffic between the supplicant and the authentication server.

In IEEE 802.1X port-based authentication, the IEEE 802.1X Authenticator is an IEEE 802.1X "Port" device consisting of a "Controlled Port' and an "Uncontrolled Port". The Controlled Port provides access to all the network services but is initially blocked until the IEEE 802.1X Supplicant can successfully authenticate to the AS via the Uncontrolled Port. The Uncontrolled Port only allows communication with the AS. All other traffic must traverse the Controlled Port after successful authentication.

Where an RSNA uses IEEE 802.1X authentication, an AS mutually authenticates the STA, as the IEEE 802.1X Supplicant and the EAP peer, by communicating through the AP, as the IEEE 802.1X Authenticator (and thus controlling the ports between the wireless medium (WM) and the DS) and the EAP Authenticator. The AP does not actually perform the authentication but controls access to the infrastructure via the IEEE 802.1X Controlled Port on the basis of the authentication between the STA and the AS.

The AS communicates through the AP authenticator to authenticate each of the STA supplicants and vice versa. An RSNA depends upon the use of an EAP method that supports mutual authentication of the AS and the STA [15]. Between the supplicant and the authenticator, the protocol is IEEE 802.1X. The protocol between the authenticator and authentication server is not defined in IEEE 802.1X nor IEEE 802.11i but is typically remote authentication dial-in user service (RADIUS) (IETF RFC 2865) [15]. For an independent basic service set (IBSS), each STA also contains its own authenticator and AS, as well as being a supplicant.

Thus, to establish an IEEE 802.1li RSNA, the STA must first "authenticate" to the AP using "Open System" authentication (authentication is optional in IBSS mode but RSNA disallows the use of "Shared Key" authentication). Then the STA must associate with the AP — and that association will have a one-to-one mapping to an IEEE 802.1X Port on the AP, with the Controlled Port closed. Then the AP initiates the EAP exchanges for the AS to mutually authenticate the STA. Then the AP initiates a 4-Way Handshake of (HAP over LAN) EAPOL-Key frames to perform a key exchange and the Controlled Port is opened once the channel is secured.

Protocol Negotiation

As with 802.11i management frames, some EAP messages are unauthenticated and expose a DOS vulnerability. This section discusses the key exchanges and transient key establishment protocol negotiations in the following paragraphs. Note that the group cipher suite is the protocol used to encrypt broadcast traffic. The pairwise cipher suite list is a list of all confidentiality protocols allowed to be used for unicast traffic. The authentication and key management suite advertises if preshared key or IEEE 802.1X is being used [27].

IEEE 802.11i has its own EAPOL-key exchanges. The PMK comes from the authentication server or preshared password mapped into a

PMK. A pseudorandom function of the supplicant's MAC address, the authenticator's MAC address, a nonce from the supplicant, and a nonce from the authenticator, is run over the PMK to create the PTK.

The PTK is divided into three keys: the EAPOL-key confirmation key (KCK), the EAPOL-key encryption key (KEK), and the temporal key. The KCK is used by the EAPOL-key exchanges for authentication. The KEK is used by the EAPOL-key exchanges for confidentiality. The temporal key is used by the data-confidentiality protocols [27]. The group master key (GMK) is a random number chosen by the AP. A pseudorandom function of the authenticator's MAC address and a nonce from the authenticator is executed on the GMK to create the group temporal key (GTK).

IEEE 802.11i Specific Vulnerabilities

WLAN security has been under extensive scrutiny in the last few years and has received much attention from both academic and industrial sectors. However, despite the emergence of security standards like IEEE 802.11i [35] that improve the confidentiality and integrity protection of user data, WLANs still face a variety of serious threats and risks. These remaining threats are based on: a failure to adequately protect management frames used by the IEEE 802.11 state machine; a loose coupling between the state machines used by IEEE 802.11i and IEEE 802.1X; and vulnerabilities in supporting protocols, such as EAP and key management protocols [32].

IEEE 802.11i places emphasis on the protection of confidentiality and integrity of wireless data and ensures mutual authentication of the communicating parties. However little effort has been put toward ensuring the availability of the standard. This makes IEEE 802.11i particularly vulnerable to various DoS attacks. In addition, some potential implementation issues also present some practical problems.

Unauthenticated Management Frames

Management frames are medium access control (MAC) layer frames used in IEEE 802.11 WLANs to manage the association between a wireless station (STA) and an AP in infrastructure mode. The exchange of management frames moves an STA from the unassociated and unauthenticated state to the associated and authenticated state.

Once in the associated and authenticated state, the STA is able to transmit and receive data. Neither the original IEEE 802.11 standards nor the recent IEEE 802.11i standard specifies mechanisms for protecting the integrity of management frames, leaving IEEE 802.11-based WLANs vulnerable to management frame spoofing and the associated denial of service attacks that such spoofing permits [27].

Session Hijacking in IEEE 802.11 WLANs

Session hijacking is a common and serious threat to WLAN security that exploits deficiencies in the WLAN security state machine and can be launched using off-the-shelf hardware and software. Session hijacking combines denial of service and identity spoofing attacks. Typically an adversary forces a legitimate STA to terminate its connection to an AP by sending it a disassociation/de-authentication management frame with the source MAC address spoofed to be that of the AP. This results in the STA disconnecting from the network. The adversary can now associate with the AP, by masquerading the MAC address of the STA, and hence take over its session. The adversary can periodically spoof management frames to the legitimate STA to stop it from retrying to associate with its AP.

In an IEEE 802.11i session hijacking attack, a legitimate STA successfully authenticates itself to an AP via both IEEE 802.1X and Open Authentication steps. If the attacker now sends a disassociation management frame to the STA with the source MAC address spoofed to be that of the AP, the legitimate STA will terminate its connection to the AP. However, on the AP, only the RSN state machine transitions to an unassociated state, while the AP's IEEE 802.1X state machine still remains in an authenticated state. The attacker is then able to gain access to the network by spoofing the MAC address of the legitimate STA. As the TEFE 802.1X state machine of the AP still considers the STA to be in an authenticated state [49] the attacker is considered to be associated and authenticated.

Session hijacking attacks are possible in 802.11i wireless LANs due to the use of unauthenticated management frames and the loose coupling of the 802.11i and 802.1X state machines. Until the standards are updated to include techniques to adequately address session hijacking attacks, specialized wireless intrusion detection systems (WIDS) will be required to help manage these risks by detecting attacks in a reliable fashion [15].

Most of the threats mentioned above can be addressed using good administration and careful configuration parameter tuning of the APs and the STAs. However certain vulnerabilities can only be mitigated by introducing changes to the IEEE 802.11 standards such as the lack of protection for management and control frames. So the sensible choice is to monitor the airwaves for any abnormal or suspicious activity via a WIDS [15]. Even if the current vulnerabilities and threats are addressed in future releases of WLAN standards, deployment of WIDS in WLAN is still a fruitful activity as it enables logging and monitoring of WLAN activity for security policy compliance. Unapproved APs and STAs can only be reliably detected by constant monitoring of the airwaves for transmissions from such devices.

WIDS facilitates misuse detection and detection of any violation of the site's wireless security policy. WIDS can also help sanity-checking security measures implemented to protect wireless traffic. For example, rollback attacks and the use of appropriate EAP methods can be monitored using a WIDS, and any violations can be logged and reported. WIDS are passive devices which monitor and log all WLAN activity and detect any rogue APs or STAs. WIDS devices should also log all alerts and activity to facilitate the auditing process.

To provide maximum coverage and enhanced confidence in the intrusion detection process, multiple WIDS units should be deployed throughout the WLAN site. They should collectively cover the complete RF range of the WLAN over multiple channels used within the WLAN. Ideally, such a deployment of WIDS units will be centrally controlled and managed. The central management station can also implement correlation of alerts received from all WIDS units and hence provide a better understanding of security events occurring on the WLAN.

WLANs are a relatively new technology in comparison to wired LANs. Consequently, the wireless IDSs are also relatively immature (compared to wired IDSs). Currently, available WIDSs are still evolving and use techniques which are not very robust and reliable [27]. However, this is just a matter of time and building market demand rather than an indication of any critical shortcomings on the part of the WIDSs. Deployment of WIDS units should be used as part of a defense in-depth security management strategy. By no means do wireless 1DSs replace the functionality of wired IDSs. A WIDS only provides detection capabilities for attacks on the wireless medium. Higher layer traffic still needs to be filtered and checked for malicious content using conventional wired IDSs.

Even wired components of WLAN authentication, authorization, and access control architecture (e.g., RADIUS servers) need to be monitored for attacks by wired IDSs.

Some of the WIDS offerings have also started moving into the wireless intrusion prevention field. However, yet again the techniques used to implement wireless intrusion prevention are far from robust and accurate. Most exploit the lack of protection of management frames in the WLAN protocols to target an unauthorized AP or STA. In fact, one has to be very careful in carrying out these intrusion prevention techniques as they can easily affect other clients in the WLAN and/or not work appropriately. As wireless intrusion prevention techniques tend to be active, involving the injection of new traffic into the WLAN, they are also prone to passive fingerprinting. An adversary can passively monitor the WLAN for intrusion prevention traffic from the WIDS and fingerprint the kind of WIDS deployed [70]. Some of the prevention techniques used are also prone to evasion. For example, after detecting an unauthorized STA, a WIDS might try to force the STA to disassociate from the network by sending it a de-authentication management frame. If this frame is just sent to the STA and not to the AP, the AP might still consider the STA to have a valid association. The STA can (with a modified driver) choose to ignore the de-authentication frame from the WIDS and still continue with its association with the AP, hence rendering the prevention technique ineffective.

Therefore, it is necessary to carefully evaluate the wireless intrusion prevention techniques before use in an active WLAN deployment as they are evolving and still in the very early stages of development. Hence, presently it is advisable that WIDSs be used as purely passive monitoring and logging systems and not expose them to detection and other wireless-specific threats by making them actively participate in the WLAN to inject wireless traffic. WIDS should ideally be totally passive and undetectable. Wireless Intrusion Prevention Systems should be independent of the WIDS and use reliable techniques which should not have any adverse effect on other STAs or network performance.

Security Level Rollback

IEEE 802.11i specifies two broad categories to classify security algorithms used: RSNA and pre-RSNA. Pre-RSNA comprises WEP and classical 802.11 entity authentication. Whereas RSNA provides authentication using 802.1X, key management protocols, RSNA establishment procedure, and two data confidentiality protocols namely the temporal key integrity protocol (TKIP) and the countermode/CBC-MAC protocol (CCMP).

In a WLAN deployment, IEEE 802.11i allows both RSNA and pre-RSNA to co-exist in what is called a TSN. Although 802.11i does not allow the use of pre-RSNA algorithms when RSNA is being used, if not managed properly in a complex network, such a mixed setup can become the target of a security-level rollback attack. An STA might enable connection to both RSNA and pre-RSNA while roaming to boost its chances of uninterrupted network access. Similarly, the network access points might accept both RSNA and pre-RSNA clients to facilitate the transition from pre-RSNA to RSNA.

In a security-level rollback attack, an adversary would impersonate the authenticator by sending forged beacon and/or probe response management frames to the supplicant, hence misleading the supplicant to believe only pre-RSNA is available at the authenticator. Similarly, the adversary can trick the authenticator into using pre-RSNA by impersonating association frames from the supplicant.

Man-in-the-Middle Attack against Tunneled EAP Methods

To enable the migration of legacy remote client authentication protocols (such as plain EAP) to more secure protocols, IETF has proposed running them within secure tunnels. Examples of such tunneled protocols are pre-IKE credentials (PIC), protected EAP (PEAP), and EAP-tunneled TLS (EAP-TTLS). These protocols constitute a combination of two protocols: an outer protocol, and an inner protocol. The inner protocol is a legacy protocol which authenticates the client. The outer protocol protects the inner protocol messages and authenticates the network to the client. The outer protocol is solely responsible for generating the session key material. Therefore, the security association between the client and the network is based on the keys derived during the outer protocol run (where the network is authenticated to the client). The inner client authentication protocol is not aware of the outer protection protocol and any keying material generated (if any) during the inner protocol run is not used to establish the security association between the client and the network.

An attack was identified against tunneled EAP methods that permitted a man-in-the-middle to obtain legitimate supplicant credentials and derive the PMK used for securing subsequent network access. The following steps summarize how the attack is executed:

1. The attacker waits for a legitimate supplicant to use a legacy remote authentication protocol and captures the initial message sent by the supplicant.
2. The attacker initiates authentication with an authenticator using a tunneled protocol.
3. Now the attacker passes the legitimate supplicant's captured messages to the authenticator via its tunnel.
4. The reply authentication protocol messages from the authenticator are unwrapped and forwarded on to the legitimate supplicant.
5. After successful authentication of the legitimate supplicant, the attacker uses the tunnel keys to derive the session keys (PMK).

Hence, for the remote client authentication protocols that are already sufficiently secure, use of tunneling just exposes them to a new vulnerability. This attack can easily be mitigated by only using authentication methods that support mutual authentication (e.g., EAP-TLS).

Attacks Facilitated by Unprotected Frames

Unfortunately, IEEE 802.11i does not address the adequate protection of management and control frames. It is easy to spoof these frames and launch DoS attacks against WLANs using commodity hardware. The most common attack is to forge disassociation and de-authentication management frames and transmit them periodically to disconnect legitimate clients from the network. Control frames like request to send (RTS) and clear to send (CTS) can also be easily forged to launch a DoS attack against virtual carrier sensing in IEEE 802.11 networks. An adversary can also launch management/control frame flood attacks, e.g., association and authentication flood attacks where a large volume of forged requests are flooded at the authenticator with an aim to deplete resources and cause DoS.

Similarly, unprotected EAP frames can easily be forged to launch a DoS attack: an EAP-Start frame can be forged to prevent 802.1X authentication from succeeding, a spoofed EAP-Success frame can be used to activate an unauthenticated 802.1X data port; and forged EAP-Failure and EAP-Logoff frames can be used to disconnect legitimate supplicants. Association flood attacks can also lead to exhaustion of the EAP Identifier space (8 bits long) at the authenticator, where the authenticator stops accepting new connections, hence causing DoS.

Michael DoS attack

The TKIP in IEEE 802.11i uses the Michael algorithm to provide integrity protection (Message Integrity Code, i.e., MIC) for every frame. Michael is designed to provide 20 bits of security which means an adversary only needs to make 219 attempts at manufacturing a forgery. Considering current computing power, this is insufficient protection, hence a countermeasure has been adopted to limit the forgery rate. The countermeasure is to log the first MIC failure and if two failures are detected within one minute, then the transmission and reception is ceased for a minute. The authenticator can even disconnect the supplicant and rekey.

This countermeasure, however, can potentially be used to launch a DoS attack where the adversary might periodically send forged frames to the authenticator with the wrong MIC, causing all communication to stop for a minute every time. However in practice, to avoid this scenario, the protocol checks the frame check sequence (FCS), integrity check value (ICY), the TKIP sequence counter (TSC), and MIC sequentially. The MIC is only checked if a frame with the correct FCS, ICV, and TSC is received. However, a DoS attack is still possible if the adversary intercepts the frame before the receiver hears it. This way the adversary can use the TSC value of the frame unchanged. Then the adversary can update the frame and utilize weaknesses in the ICY algorithm to correct values of ICY and FCS. This frame would pass the FCS, ICV, and TSC checks and log a MIC failure on the authenticator. A large volume of these intercepted frames can be used to create a DoS.

RSN Information Element Poisoning

The RSN information element (IE) contains information such as authentication and pair-wise key cipher suite selectors, group key cipher suite selectors, an RSN capabilities field, pairwise master key identifier

(PMKID) count, and the PMKID list. The RSN IE is included in beacon and probe response frames to advertise the RSN capabilities and available cipher suites in the network. The supplicant also includes it in its association/reassociation requests advertising its RSN capabilities and supported cipher suites.

Both parties negotiate common cipher suites and use them for authentication, key management, and data encryption. In IEEE 802.11i, the supplicant and the authenticator are required to confirm the authenticity of each other's RSN IE. This is performed as part of the 4-way handshake where both send their RSN IEs to each other and compute a bitwise comparison against their own copies obtained from beacon/probe responses or association/reassociation requests. If the RSN IEs do not match then both parties will deauthenticate each other. This strict check prevents an adversary from deceiving either the supplicant or the authenticator into using a weaker security suite by forging the RSN IE.

Wi-Fi Protected Access

Wi-Fi Protected Access 3 (WPA3) represents a crucial step forward in wireless network security, delivering a suite of advancements over the earlier standard, WPA2, to provide robust, reliable, and resilient protection for Wi-Fi networks in an age of ever-increasing cyber threats [6]. Introduced by the Wi-Fi Alliance, WPA3 provides cutting-edge features to simplify Wi-Fi security and provides the capabilities necessary to support different network deployments ranging from corporate networks to home networks [33]. It also ensures cryptographic consistency using encryption algorithms such as AES and TKIP to defend against network attacks [33].

One of the key security implications of WPA3 lies in its safeguard against brute-force or dictionary attacks, which were a notable weak point in WPA2. In a dictionary attack, an attacker systematically tries all the possible passwords from a prearranged list of words or combinations, an approach that could crack weaker passwords in WPA2. WPA3 addresses this threat through the implementation of a cutting-edge protocol known as Simultaneous Authentication of Equals (SAE), also referred to as Dragonfly [52]. SAE demands direct interaction with the network for every single password guess attempt, making offline guessing attacks extremely difficult, if not impossible. An attacker can no longer make multiple password guesses offline after a single interaction with the network. This means that each attempt to crack the password necessitates a separate interaction, considerably slowing down any malicious effort and vastly enhancing the security of Wi-Fi networks against brute-force attacks.

Another crucial security feature introduced by WPA3 is its support for forward secrecy. In WPA2, if an attacker were able to capture an encrypted data stream and later managed to crack or otherwise obtain the network password, they could retroactively decrypt all of the previously intercepted data. However, with the forward secrecy feature, WPA3 ensures that even if a password is compromised in the future, past communication remains secure. This means that every session is independently encrypted, providing robust protection for historical data and significantly improving privacy for users.

WPA3 also includes a 192-bit security suite, which aligns with the Commercial National Security Algorithm (CNSA) Suite from the Committee on National Security Systems. This provides additional protection for networks with higher security needs, such as those in the financial sector, government, or other areas handling sensitive, confidential data. It's an enhanced level of security, beyond what was offered by WPA2, that ensures strong cryptographic key strength while delivering a consistent combination of cryptographic tools.

Additionally, WPA3 promises improved security for the rapidly growing world of IoT devices. These devices often come with limited or no display interface, making the secure addition of these devices to a Wi-Fi network a complex process under WPA2. WPA3 introduces a feature known as Wi-Fi Easy Connect to simplify this process. With this feature, users can add devices to a network by scanning a QR code, significantly simplifying the process while maintaining a high level of security. This innovative feature not only enhances user experience but also promotes better security practices in IoT devices, which are often seen as weak points in a network due to their limited security features.

Yet another improvement is WPA3's robust protection against key reinstallation attacks, commonly known as Key Reinstallation AttaCK (KRACK) attacks [36]. This was a significant vulnerability in WPA2 where an attacker could manipulate the handshakes used in the protocol to trick a victim into reinstalling an already-in-use key. In doing so, they could disrupt the inherent assumptions about key secrecy, potentially leading to data theft or network intrusion. WPA3 offers new handshaking procedures that are resistant to such attacks, thereby bolstering its overall security profile.

The transition to WPA3, however, is not without its challenges. As with any major technological upgrade, a full transition to WPA3 will take time, given it requires both hardware and software support. While newer devices will come equipped with WPA3 capabilities, older hardware might not be compatible with the updated security protocol, necessitating either hardware replacement or firmware updates, if they are available and feasible [15]. For large organizations, this can imply substantial logistical and financial implications. The Wi-Fi Alliance, understanding this issue, has ensured that WPA3 will coexist with WPA2, and the new devices will be compatible with older ones. This means networks can support a mix of WPA2 and WPA3 devices, facilitating a gradual transition rather than necessitating a sudden switch.

WPA3 marks a significant evolution in Wi-Fi security [31]. With enhanced protections against brute-force attacks, support for forward secrecy, a robust 192-bit security suite, simpler yet secure connectivity for IoT devices, and resilience against KRACK attacks, WPA3 provides a more secure and resilient framework for wireless connectivity. Despite the challenges in its adoption, its benefits underscore the importance of this security upgrade in addressing the increasingly complex threats in today's cyber landscape, making Wi-Fi networks safer and more secure for all users.

Extensible Authentication Protocol-Transport Layer Security

Extensible authentication protocol transport layer security (EAP-TLS) uses the TLS public key certificate authentication mechanism within EAP to provide mutual authentication of client to server and server to client [21]. With EAP-TLS, both the client and the server must be assigned a digital certificate signed by a Certificate Authority (CA) that they both trust. The EAP-TLS key system uses dynamic WEP or TKIP keys and uses a TLS handshake as the basis for mutual authentication. The server presents a certificate to the client, and, after validating the server's certificate, the client presents a client certificate. The certificate may be protected by the client by a passphrase, PIN, or stored on a smart card. One flaw in the EAP-TLS protocol noted by many observers is that the identity exchange proceeds in the clear before the exchange of certificates, so a passive attack can easily observe usernames.

Since the normal TLS keys are used in the handshake, and therefore should not be used in a different context, new encryption keys must be derived from the TLS master secret for use with PPP encryption.[7] For both peer and EAP servers, the derivation proceeds as follows:

To begin with, the values for master secret, pseudorandom function (PRF), and random value must be gathered. The master secret is negotiated by the TLS handshake. The pseudorandom function (PRF) is defined in the specification for the version of TLS being used. The random value is derived from the concatenation of the handshake message fields [client_hellosandom] and [server hello.random] (in that order). Next, two output strings are generated: one string for the value PRF (master secret, [client EAP encryption], random) is computed up to 128 bytes, and one string for the value PRF("Null", [client EAP encryption], random) is computed up to 64 bytes (where "Null" is an empty string).

The peer encryption key (the key used for encrypting data from peer to EAP server) is obtained by truncating to the correct length the first 32 bytes of the first PRF output string. The EAP server encryption key (the key used for encrypting data from the EAP server to peer) is obtained by truncating to the correct length the second 32 bytes of this same PRF output string. The client authentication key (the one used for computing MACs for messages from peer to EAP server), if used, is obtained by truncating to the correct length the third 32 bytes of this same PRF output string. The EAP server authentication key (the one used for computing MACs for messages from the EAP server to peer), if used, and if different from the peer authentication key, is obtained by truncating to the correct length the fourth 32 bytes of this same PRF output string.[8]

The peer initialization vector (IV), used for messages from peer to EAP server if a block cipher has been specified, is obtained by truncating to the cipher's block size the first 32 bytes of the second PRF output string. Finally, the server IV, used for messages from peer to EAP server, if a block cipher has been specified, is obtained by truncating to the cipher's block size the second 32 bytes of the second PRF output string. The use of these encryption and authentication keys is specific to the PPP encryption mechanism used. Additional keys or other non-secret values (such as IVs) can be obtained as needed for future PPP encryption methods by extending the outputs of the PRF beyond 128 bytes and 64 bytes, respectively.[9]

---

[7]RFC2716 — PPP EAP TLS Authentication Protocol.. http://rfc.eu/rfc/rfc2716.htm.

[8]RFC2716 — PPP EAP TLS Authentication Protocol.. http://rfc.eu/rfc/rfc2716.htm.

[9]RFC2716 — PPP EAP TLS Authentication Protocol.. http://rfc.eu/rfc/rfc2716.htm.

Extensible Authentication Protocol Tunneled Transport Layer Security

The extensible authentication protocol tunneled transport layer security (EAP-TTLS) is an Internet Engineering Task Force (IETF) standard and can be used to provide password-based authentication of a client [24]. EAP-TTLS has been implemented in some Remote Authentication Dial-In User Service (RADIUS) servers and supplicant software designed for use in 802.11 WLAN networks.

EAP-TTLS uses the TLS channel to exchange "attribute-value pairs" (AVPs), much like RADIUS. EAP-TTLS provides a sequence of attributes that are included in the message. The general encoding of information allows a TTLS server to validate AVPs against any type of authentication mechanism. EAP-TTLS implementations today support all methods defined by EAP, as well as several older methods (CHAP, PAP, MS-CHAP, and MS-CHAPv2). By including a RADIUS EAP message attribute in the message payload, EAP-TTLS can be made to provide the same functionality as PEAP. If, however, a RADIUS Password or CHAP-Password attribute is encapsulated, TTLS can protect the legacy authentication mechanisms of RADIUS. When the TTLS server forwards RADIUS messages to the home server, it decapsulates the attributes protected by EAP-TTLS and inserts them directly into the forwarded message. Because this method is so similar to PEAP, it is being used less frequently.

In EAP-TLS, a TLS handshake is used to mutually authenticate a client and server. EAP-TTLS extends this authentication negotiation by using the secure connection established by the TLS handshake to exchange additional information between client and server. In EAP-TTLS, the TLS handshake may be mutual; or it may be one-way, in which only the server is authenticated to the client. The secure connection established by the handshake may then be used to allow the server to authenticate the client using existing, widely-deployed authentication infrastructures such as RADIUS.[10]

Most password-based protocols in use today rely on a hash of the password with a random challenge. Thus, the server issues a challenge,

[10] Draft-funk-eap-ttls-v0-05 — Extensible Authentication Protocol Tunneled Transport Layer Security Authenticated Protocol Version 0 (EAP-TTLSv0). https://datatracker.ietf.org/doc/draft-funk-eap-ttls-v0/05/.

the client hashes that challenge with the password and forwards a response to the server, and the server validates that response against the user's password retrieved from its database. This general approach describes CHAP, MS-CHAP, MS-CHAP-V2, EAP/MD5 Challenge, and EAP/One-Time Password. An issue with such an approach is that an eavesdropper that observes both challenge and response may be able to mount a dictionary attack.[11]

EAP/TTLS Architecture

The EAP/TTLS network consists of logical entities. On the user side is the client. The client is a host or device that connects to a network through an Access Point. The Access Point is a network device that provides users with a point of entry into the network, and may enforce access control and policy based on information returned by a TTLS Authentication, Authorization, and Accounting (AAA) Server [24]. A TTLS AAA Server performs one or more AAA functions: authenticating a user prior to granting network service, providing authorization (policy) information governing the type of network service the user is to be granted, and accumulating accounting information about actual usage.[12] The AAA/11 Server is a AAA Server in the user's home domain, where authentication and authorization for that user are administered. Since these are logical entities, they may or may not be separate components of an actual physical network. For example, the TTLS AAA Server and the AAAJH Server might be a single component; the access point and TTLS AAA Server might be a single entity; or, the functions of the access point, TTLS AAA Server, and AAAJH Server might be combined into a single physical device [24].

The parts of the EAP/TTLS network communicate with each other using carrier protocols capable of encapsulating EAP. The client and access point communicate using a link layer carrier protocol such as PPP or EAPOL. The access point, TTLS AAA Server and AAAJH server communicate using an AAA carrier protocol such as RADIUS or Diameter. The client and access point initiate an EAP conversation to

[11]RFC 5281 (Aug 2008, Informational, 51 pages): 1 of 3, p. 1 to 19. https://www.tech-invite.com/y50/tinv-ietf-rfc-5281.html.

[12]*Ibid.*

negotiate the client's access to the network. Typically, the access point issues an EAP-Request/Identity to the client, which responds with an EAP-Response/Identity. Note that the client does not include the user's actual identity in this EAP-Response/Identity packet; the user's identity will not be transmitted until an encrypted channel has been established.[13]

The access point now acts as a passthrough device, allowing the TTLS server to negotiate EAP-TTLS with the client directly. An EAP-TTLS negotiation comprises two phases: the TLS handshake phase and the TLS tunnel phase. During the first phase of the negotiation, the TLS handshake protocol is used to authenticate the TTLS server to the client and, optionally, to authenticate the client to the TTLS server, based on public/private key certificates. As a result of the handshake, the client and TTLS server now have shared keying material and an agreed-upon TLS record layer cipher suite with which to secure subsequent EAP-TTLS communication. This allows phase 2 to proceed securely using the TLS record layer.

During phase 2 of negotiation, the client and TTLS AAA Server use the secure TLS record layer channel established by the TLS handshake as a tunnel to exchange information encapsulated in attribute-value pairs (AVPs). EAP-TTLS specifies how user authentication may be performed during phase 2. The user authentication may itself be EAP, or it may be a legacy protocol such as PAP, CHAP, MS-CHAP, or MS-CHAP-V2. When a client and TTLS server that have previously negotiated an EAP-TTLS session begin a new EAP-TTLS negotiation, the client and TTLS server may agree to resume the previous session. This significantly reduces the time required to establish the new session. This could occur when the client connects to a new access point, or when an access point requires reauthentication of a connected client. Session resumption is accomplished using the standard TLS mechanism. The client signals its desire to resume a session by including the session ID of the session it wishes to resume in the ClientHello message; the TTLS server signals its willingness to resume that session by echoing that session ID in its ServerHello message. If the TTLS server elects not to resume the session, it simply does not echo the session ID and a new session will be negotiated.[14]

---

[13] *Ibid.*

[14] Draft-funk-eap-ttls-v1-01. https://datatracker.ietf.org/doc/html/draft-funk-eap-ttls-v1-01.

Protected Extensible Authentication Protocol

Protected extensible authentication protocol (PEAP) is an Internet Engineering Task Force IETF standard authored by Cisco Systems, Microsoft, and RSA Security used to provide a secure password-based authentication mechanism [27]. The PEAP authentication type is designed to take advantage of server-side EAP-TLS and to support various authentication methods, including login passwords and OTPs.

PEAP uses a digital certificate for server authentication. For user authentication, PEAP supports various EAP-encapsulated methods within a protected TLS tunnel [27]. In a PEAP exchange, only the AS is required to have a certificate. After the initial communication with the AS, the public key from the AS certificate is sent to the client's computer. The client computer then generates a master encryption key and encrypts this key using the AS's public key and sends the encrypted key to the AS. Now that the master key is on both ends of the channel, this key can be used as source material to establish a secure tunnel between the AS and the client over which any subsequent authentication method can be used to authenticate the client computer to the AS. In many cases, it is expected that this will be some form of a password-based authentication protocol.

Where EAP is used for authentication in wireless networks, authentication latency is a concern. As a result, it is valuable to be able to do a quick re-authentication on roaming between access points. PEAP supports this capability by leveraging the TLS session resumption facility, and any EAP method running under PEAP can take advantage of TLS session resumption.[15]

The Microsoft version of PEAP supports client authentication by only MS-CHAP Version 2. This limits user databases to those that support MS-CHAP Version 2, such as Windows NT Domains and Active Directory. To use Microsoft PEAP, users must purchase individual certificates from a third-party CA to install on their authenticating server. The root CA certificate must be installed on each wireless client. Windows, however, includes the root certificates of many third-party CAs. If the authenticating server certificates correspond to an included root CA certificate, no additional wireless client configuration is required. If users purchase authenticating server certificates for which Windows does not include a

[15] Draft-josefsson-pppext-eap-tls-eap-06. https://datatracker.ietf.org/doc/html/draft-josefsson-pppext-eap-tls-eap-06.

corresponding root CA certificate, they must install the root CA certificate on each wireless client.

Lightweight Extensible Authentication Protocol

The lightweight extensible authentication protocol (LEAP) is a proprietary standard developed by Cisco Systems and was designed to be portable across a variety of wireless platforms [21]. It has gained popularity due to the fact that it was the first, and for a long time, the only password-based authentication scheme and it also provided this support across several different client operating system platforms. LEAP is based on a straightforward challenge-password hash exchange where the authentication server issues a challenge to the client and then the client returns the password to the authentication server after first hashing it with the challenge text sent by the authentication server. This mutual authentication protects against unauthorized (or "rogue") access points attempting to enter the network. The compatibility of Cisco LEAP running on Cisco Aironet wireless infrastructure and client devices from third-party companies is accomplished through the Cisco Compatible Extensions Program (CCX).

With LEAP, mutual authentication relies on a shared secret, the user's logon password, which is known by the client and the network. The authenticating server (i.e., RADIUS server) sends an authentication challenge to the client. The client uses a one-way hash of the user-supplied password to fashion a response to the challenge and sends that response to the RADIUS server. Using information from its user database, the RADIUS server creates its own response and compares that to the response from the client. When the RADIUS server authenticates the client, the process repeats in reverse, enabling the client to authenticate the RADIUS server. When this is complete, an EAP-Success message is sent to the client and both the client and the RADIUS server derive the dynamic WPA key.[16]

With Cisco's LEAP, security keys change dynamically with every communications session, thus preventing an attacker from collecting the packets required to decode data. The new keys generated through LEAP

[16]Burnette, J.R., *et al.* (2002). Tradeoff analysis for combat service support wireless communications alternatives. https://doi.org/10.2172/943415.

Table 1. Wireless Encryption Technology Comparison Table

	Cisco LEAP (with TKIP)	EAP-TLS (with TKIP)	EAP-PEAP (with TKIP)
Key Length (in bits)	128	128	128
Encryption Algorithm	RC4	RC4	RC4
Packet Integrity	CRC-32/MIC	CRC-32/MIC	CRC-32/MIC
Device Authentication	No	Certificate	No
User Authentication Type	Username/password	Certificate	Username/password or OTP
Certificate Requirements	None	RADIUS server/ WLAN client	RADIUS server
Single Sign-on Support	Yes	Yes	No
Additional Hardware	No	Certificate server	Certificate server
Per-user Keying	Yes	Yes	Yes
Protocol Support	Any	Any	Any
Client Operating System (OS) Support	Wide range	Wide range	Wide range

use a shared secret key method between the user and the access point. Because LEAP is proprietary to Cisco, it can be used only with a Cisco access point. LEAP also adds another level of security to the network by authenticating all connections to the network before allowing traffic to pass to a wireless device.

A quick comparison of the EAP encryption sub-types is provided in Table 1.

AUTHENTICATION IN A FOG-MOBILE EDGE COMPUTING ENVIRONMENT UTILIZING THE WIRELESS GRID RESOURCE SHARING PROTOCOL

Authentication is an important issue for the security of fog computing since services are offered to massive-scale end users by front fog nodes [57]. Reference [4] introduces a mutual authentication between Fog users at the Edge of the network and the Fog servers at the Fog layer proposing a fog user-fog server anonymous mutual authentication scheme; in which the fog user and fog server authenticate each other and establish a session key without disclosing user's real identity. This scheme is based on pseudonym-based cryptography (PBC), elliptic curve discrete logarithm problem (ECDLP), and bilinear pairing to establish the session key [4]. Reference [3] proposes a Fog computing-based security (FOCUS) system, which leverages a VPN to secure the access channel to IoT devices through a challenge-response authentication process to protect the VPN server against distributed denial of service (DDoS) attacks. Furthermore, with the emergence of biometric authentication, such as fingerprint authentication, face authentication, touch-based or keystroke-based authentication etc., in mobile computing and cloud computing, applying biometric-based authentication in fog computing will be beneficial [58].

Authentication requires that an ICD prove its identity. Authentication will require that the ICD authenticate to the IoT network, and the network should authenticate the ICD. The wireless grid core components must be embedded in IoT devices or sensors depending on their capability to handle five primary functions: (1) management of identification [ID] and presence, (2) permissions management, (3) data transfer ability, (4) application programming interface [API], and (5) security [39]. These are the elements that make the grid-enabled ecosystem possible and make every ICD a node on the wireless grid. The layers above the core are comprised of the wireless grid's API, which enables connections with other applications and services, the grid user interface (GUI), which may or may not be necessary depending on the thing/object upon which it resides, and finally the wireless grid "Edgeware" applications, which are typically delivered as services of resource sharing and functionality services and once a wireless grid is established, then resources and services can be published or accessed across the grid, enabling the infinite functional possibilities of wireless grid technology [39].

The wireless grid is made possible by the "Grid Core", which is software installed on any Grid-enabled, IoT device [39]. As identified in Figure 17, the resource sharing protocol (RSP) is the primary Grid Core function provided by the architecture's eight core components: AAC, BAC, MPC, MC, RMC, ELP, CPC and SC [39]. The RSP enables creating, joining and subscribing to a wireless grid through provision of the following services: resource identification, resource acquisition, resource advertisement/discovery, communication amongst wireless grids, communication with the internet, creating a wireless grid and joining and subscribing to a wireless grid [39].

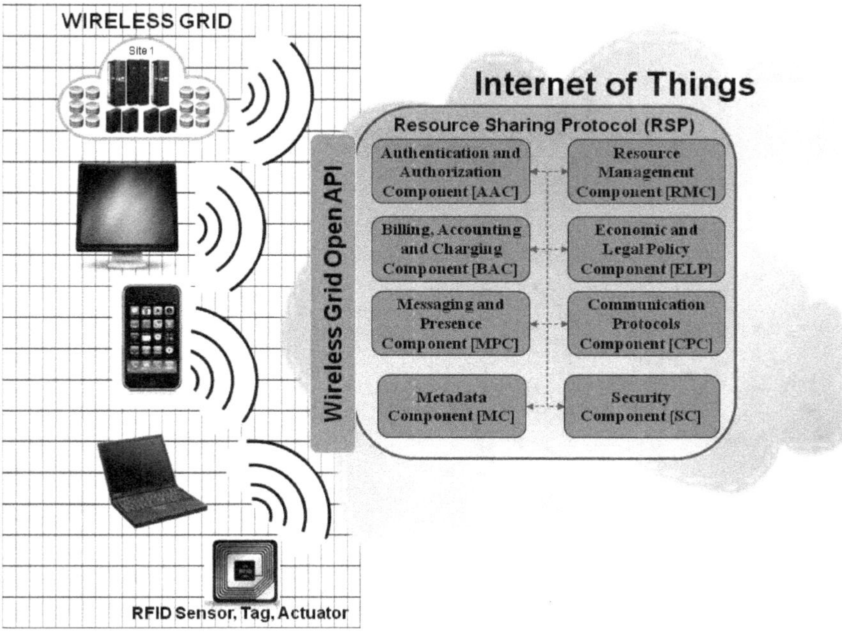

Figure 17. Open Wireless Grid API Map

WIRELESS GRID INFORMATION ELEMENT

Due to the processing nature of wireless grids for the IoT architecture (see Figure 18), a standard process for authentication needs to be defined that provides for a network-wide cryptographic challenge and response mechanism. This standard should provide for the ability to uniquely authenticate ICD's to legitimate mobile access points. In order to provide authentication for the ICD's in the IoT, the system must use standard cryptographic algorithms/ciphers for wireless and RFID systems (e.g., WPA2, Simon and Speck, AES, Skipjack, etc.) and the establishment of an information element known only to the service provider from the RSP. This information element is referred to as the "wireless grid information element (WGIE)", should be programmed into all mobile access points and known to the network infrastructure for the FMEC/IoT network.

The WGIE, as displayed in Figure 19, is a 256-bit cryptographic key variable stored in the semi-permanent memory of the mobile access point

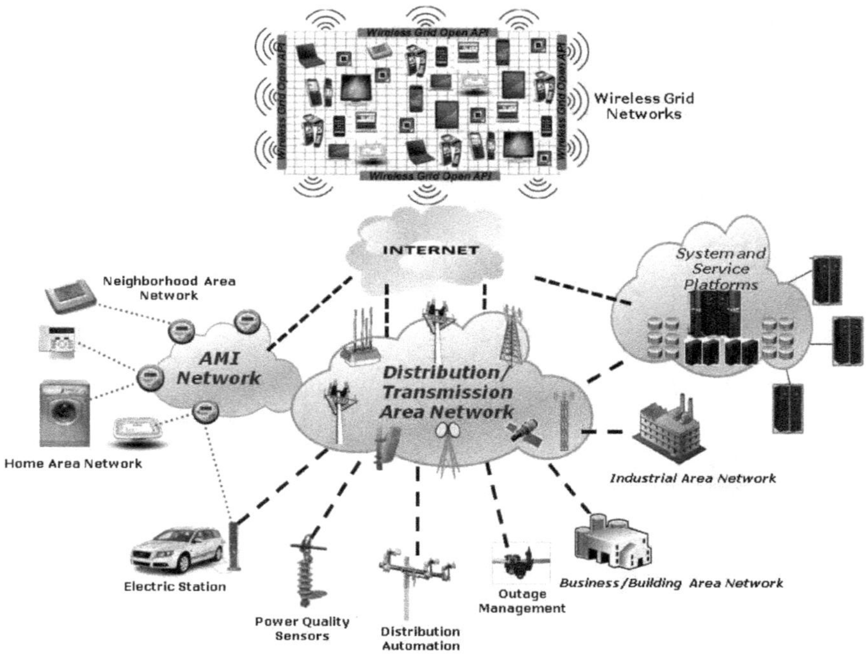

Figure 18. IoT Architecture

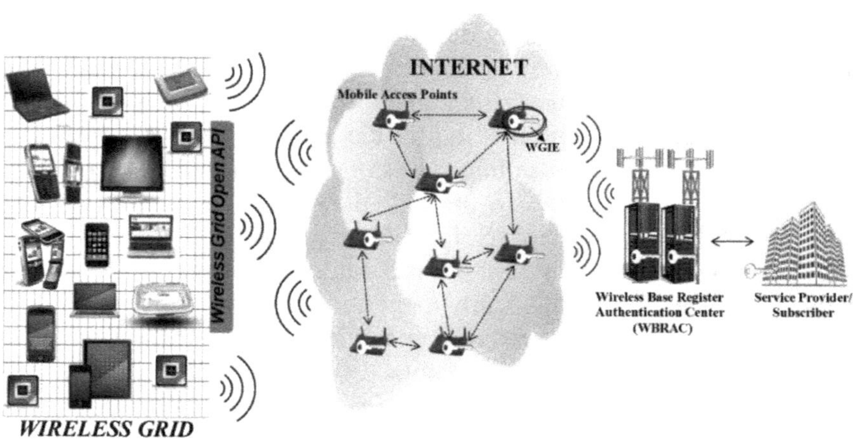

Figure 19. Wireless Grid Information Element

and is known to the wireless base register authentication center (WBRAC) of the IoT system.

The WBRAC provides identification, authentication and encryption for ICD's, provides a central location for supporting mobile access points and is the repository for all subscriber information. As a secured database that stores essential encrypted subscriber information, the WBRAC plays a key role in the operation of the wg-IoT network as it manages the services to which an ICD has subscribed. The WBRAC is constantly subjected to heavy load of traffic to identify service providers/subscribers, route, handle data, and provide security for the IoT system. The WBRAC is used to conduct the IoT network's primary security functions and it contains the wg-IoT network's set of algorithms necessary to authenticate an ICD.

THE "wg-IoT" AUTHENTICATION PROCESS

The wg-IoT authentication process (as displayed in Figure 20) is initiated when a mobile access point(s) attempts to confirm the identity of an ICD. This is based on the services identified from the Grid Core and generated in the wg-IoT system. Within the WGIE, the wg-IoT service data (IoT_SD) is a 128-bit pattern that resides in the ICD's semi-permanent memory. The IoT_SD is passed wirelessly across the air between the ICD and the mobile access point. The WGIE includes the 64-bit mobile access point's ESN and the ICD_IN which is also stored in the WBRAC. The IoT_SD is subdivided into two 64-bit potions called the IoT_SD_1 and the IoT_SD_2. The IoT_SD_1 supports the ICD's authentication procedure and the IoT_SD_2 supports privacy and message confidentiality. When the ICD sends a secure activation signal to the wg-IoT system, the ICD uses the WGIE (i.e., IoT_SD field, ESN, ICD_IN) to begin the generation procedure for the security component (SC) authentication key [SC_auth-K] (e.g., the SC_auth-K is a 128-bit long sequence that is stored in the ICD permanent security identification memory). This information is used to execute the authenticate-signature procedure from the Grid Core's RSP, which will yield a 128-bit numerical value for AAC.

The ACC component handles the authentication of the ICD and the authorization of resources; in effect, the AAC provides the protocols to identify the ICD and understands that ICD's relationship to a resource (i.e., what the ICD can or can't do with a resource). The AAC is used by all grid members and has an identity system that looks at all ICD's and allows policies to be made regarding the ICD's grid profile. The ICD then combines the AAC with two more numerical values from the Grid Core, the messaging and presence component [MPC] and the resource management component [RMC].

The MPC is a scalable messaging and presence protocol that manages the availability of an ICD and the method or language of communication with that resource. The RMC is responsible for aggregating and searching metadata about resources within the context of authentication and works closely with the AAC and MPC. The RMC has a scheduler to manage and coordinate resources, such as network access, and allows for ICD's to be identified as being available. The MPC and the RMC are filled in from values already residing in the ICD's memory. The MPC is a 128-bit long value that was received by the thing/object during its last access parameter message transmitted by the network over the wg-IoT communication channel. The MPC is periodically generated and issued by the wg-IoT system, and it is transmitted by the network to all mobile wireless base stations. The ICD stores and uses the most recent version of the MPC that

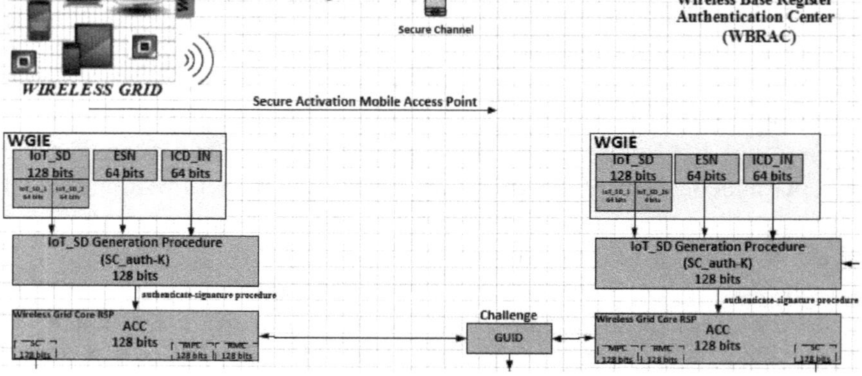

Figure 20. wg-IoT Authentication

it has in its authentication attempts. The RMC is a 128-count field stored in the ICD and updated whenever a parameter update order is received from the wg-IoT network on the wg-IoT secure traffic channel. After the ICD has assembled the AAC-MPC-RMC number, called the global unique identifier (GUID), it sends it to the mobile access point. The mobile access point compares the information it received from the ICD with its stored value for the AAC and MPC, along with its RMC derived from a stored service. If valid, the ICD is authenticated. If any of the comparison fails, the mobile access point initiates a unique challenged response process or starts an update value process.

In the update value process (see Figure 21, the wg-IoT system responds by calculating new authentication values and challenging the ICD. First, the WBRAC in the wg-IoT system sends an update message to the mobile access point telling it that the ICD is to be updated and it passes a value to the mobile access point. This random number that the WBRAC has used, together with the ICD to calculate the new value. Since the WGIE is stored in both the ICD and in the WBRAC, the mobile access point sends the value to the ICD in an update order over the wg-IoT secure traffic channel. When the update order arrives at the ICD, it causes the unit to execute an IoT_SD generation procedure. In this procedure, the ICD uses the AAC, ESN and the SC_auth-K to produce an IoT_SD_New value. Meanwhile, the WBRAC has also used the AAC and SC_auth-K to

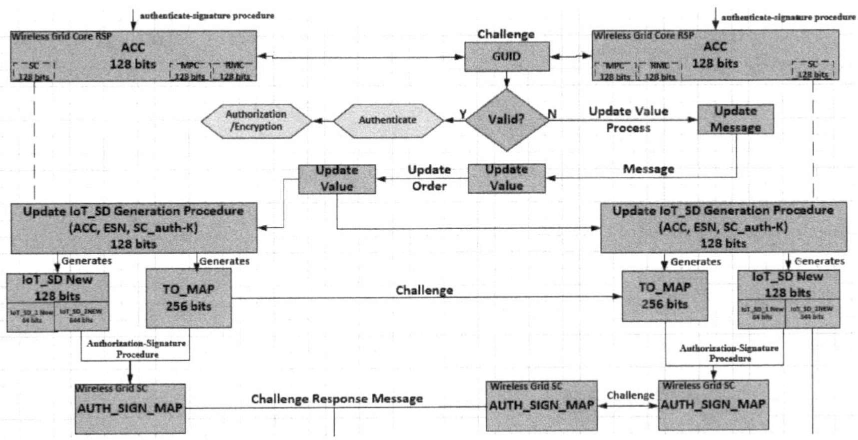

Figure 21. Update Value for AUTH_SIGN_MAP

generate its version of the IoT_SD_New value. Next, the ICD generates a random, 256-bit long number called the "thing-object mobile access point (TO_MAP)". The TO_MAP number is used to challenge the mobile access point. The mobile access point issues the challenge via a mobile access challenge order message that is transmitted via the wg-IoT secure traffic channel. The ICD continues on by running an authorization-signature procedure using its IOT_SD_New and the TO_MAP (coupled with the ESN and ICD_IN). The result is a new number called the AUTH_SIGN_MAP within the wireless grid security component.

At the same time that the ICD is calculating the AUTH_SIGN_MAP, the mobile access point received the TO_MAP from the ICD and has started its own authorization-signature procedure. The mobile access point forwards the challenge order to the WBRAC and sends an acknowledgement on receipt of the order to the ICD. The SC uses the TO_MAP (calculated by the ICD) and the IOT_SD_New (calculated by the WBRAC) to generate its own version of the AUTH_SIGN_MAP. The SC then sends its AUTH_SIGN_MAP to the mobile access point in a mobile access point challenge response message. The mobile access point sends this response to the ICD via a mobile access point challenge response order message via the wg-IoT secure traffic channel. The mobile access point challenge confirmation order must be received by the ICD within a timer period of 1s after it has received acknowledgement of reception of the challenge order. If it does not receive the confirmation order within the specific time, the ICD will discard the AUTH_SIGN_MAP and terminate the update value process.

Once the ICD has both copies of the AUTH_SIGN_MAP in its possession, it conducts a comparison of the two. If the comparison results in a successful match, the ICD resets the original IOT_SD_New, replacing them with the new values of the IOT_SD_1New and the IOT_SD_2New. If the comparison results in an unsuccessful match, the ICD discards the IOT_SD_1New and the IOT_SD_2New values and sends an update rejection message to the mobile access point; thus, denying the wg-IoT system access and causing the authentication procedure to begin again. With a successful match and reset, the ICD sends an update confirmation message to the mobile access point. After it has received this message, the mobile access point resets its IOT_SD_1 and the IOT_SD_New value using the IOT_SD_1 New and the IOT_SD_2 New values it received from the WBRAC. The ICD has now been authenticated and proceeds to the authorization and encryption process (see Figure 22).

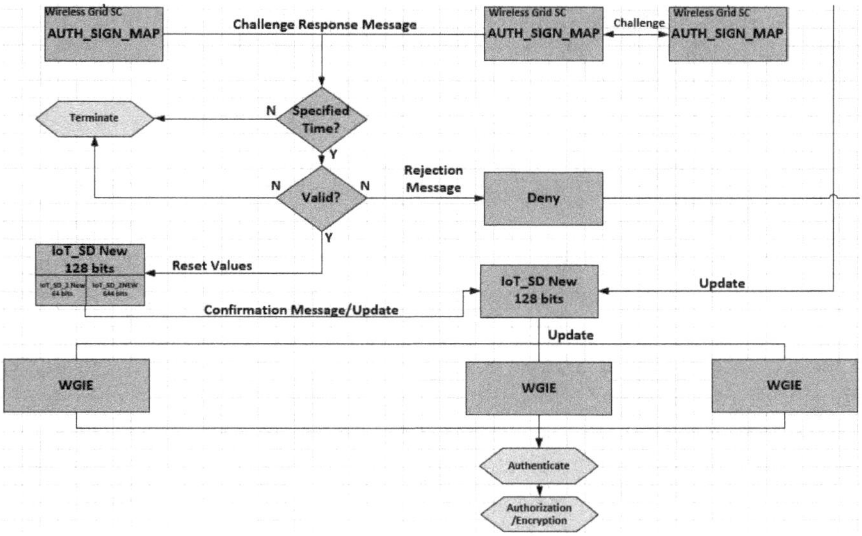

Figure 22. Validating the AUTH_SIGN_MAP

If any of the calculated values fails a comparison made by the mobile access point during an authentication procedure, then the mobile access point may deem the attempt unsuccessful. It can then terminate the current authentication procedure and initiate the unique challenge response process. This process can be carried out on the wg-IoT secure traffic channels since the mobile access point generates a 64-bit long value called the WMAP and send it to the ICD via the authentication challenge message. This message is sent on the wg-IoT secure traffic channel. When the ICD receives this message, it performs an authorization-signature calculation. Its takes the value and makes it the 64 most significant bits of the WMAP. It also takes the 16 least significant bits of the WBRAC and makes those the 16 least significant bits of the WMAP. The ICD then calculates the authorization-signature, which is used to fill the AUTH_SIGN_MAP field.

The AUTH_SIGN_MAP is then sent to the mobile access point. The mobile access point then compares the ICD AUTH_SIGN_MAP with its own version of the AUTH_SIGN_MAP. If the two do not match, the mobile access point will drop the attempt, deny any further attempt to access the wg-IoT network by the ICD or initiate an update process.

If authentication is successful, the mobile access point can move on to authorization and message encryption, which involves scrambling the data signal stream within the wg-IoT network as displayed in Figure 21.

CONCLUSION

Unlike wired networks, wireless grids and FMECs are not limited by physical space. This potentially opens up the network to attack from rogue ICDs and users who may spy on the wireless transmission or gain unauthorized access to the network from the inside or outside. Traditional thieves, hackers, high-tech criminals, government sponsored organizations, viruses, and other types of malicious code will continue to be causes for security concerns on these networks. The information passed on these networks is exposed to malicious attempts to obtain the information without proper authorization. These new systems must be designed to minimize the vulnerabilities of the networks and the information contained within them. However, as vulnerable as wired networks are for potential attacks, these networks are even more vulnerable.

The intent of this chapter is to hypothesize a generic authentication methodology for wireless grid/FMECs use for the IoT architecture. The proposed methodology, called wg-IoT, includes the integration of fog computing, wireless grids and FMECs to create this new IoT architecture and must be further researched. The authentication process developed from the wireless grid RSP still has to be developed and proposed for modeling the authentication of ICD's, which allows strategies and approaches for enhancing the information security architecture for further development. There are numerous complex considerations which must be considered when implementing this process and without adequate forethought these new ICDs and FMECs may be ill-advised.

REFERENCES

[1] Agarwal, A., Norman, D., & Gupta, A. (2004). *Wireless Grids: Approaches, Architectures and Technical Challenges* (Report No. 4459-04). Massachusetts Institute of Technology (MIT), Cambridge, MA.

[2] Ahmed, M. & Litchfield, A. T. (2018). Taxonomy for identification of security issues in cloud computing environments. *Journal of Computer Information Systems*, 58(1), 79–88.

[3] Alharbi, S., Rodriguez, P., Maharaja, R., Iyer, P., Subaschandrabose, N., & Ye, Z. (2017). Secure the internet of things with challenge response authentication in fog computing. In *2017 IEEE 36th International Performance Computing and Communications Conference (IPCCC)* (pp. 1–2). San Diego, CA, 2017. DOI: 10.1109/PCCC.2017.8280489.

[4] Amor, A. B., Abid, M., & Meddeb, A. (2017). A privacy-preserving authentication scheme in an edge-Fog environment. In *2017 IEEE/ACS 14th International Conference on Computer Systems and Applications (AICCSA)* (pp. 1225–1231). Hammamet, Tunisia, 2017. DOI: 10.1109/AICCSA.2017.57

[5] Aswini, C. & Valarmathi, M. L. (2023). Artificial intelligence based smart routing in software defined networks. *Computational Systems Science and Engineering*, 44(2), 1279–1293.

[6] Bednarczyk, M. & Piotrowski, Z. (2019, March). Will WPA3 really provide Wi-Fi security at a higher level? In *XII Conference on Reconnaissance and Electronic Warfare Systems* (Vol. 11055, pp. 369–376). SPIE.

[7] Bonomi, F., Milito, R., Zhu, J., & Addepalli, S. (2012, August). Fog computing and its role on the internet of things. In *Proceedings of the First Edition of the MCC Workshop on Mobile Cloud Computing* (pp. 13–16). ACM.

[8] Brooks, T. T. (Ed.) (2017). *Cyber-Assurance for the Internet of Things*. John Wiley & Sons, Hoboken, New Jersey.

[9] Brooks, T., Kaarst-Brown, M., Caicedo, C., Park, J., & McKnight, L. (2013, December). A failure to communicate: Security vulnerabilities in the gridstreamx edgeware application. In *2013 8th International Conference for Internet Technology and Secured Transactions (ICITST)* (pp. 516–523). IEEE.

[10] Brooks, T. & McKnight, L. (2017). A steady-state framework for assessing security mechanisms in a cloud-of-things architecture. In *Cyber-Assurance for the Internet of Things* (pp. 225–247).

[11] Chiang, Y., Zhang, Y., Luo, H., Chen, T. Y., Chen, G. H., Chen, H. T., … & Chou, C. T. (2023). Management and orchestration of edge computing for IoT: A comprehensive survey. *IEEE Internet of Things Journal.*

[12] Cisco Fog Computing Solutions (2015a). Unleash the power of the internet of things. Cisco Systems Inc. https://www.cisco.com/c/dam/en_us/solutions/trends/iot/docs/computing-solutions.pdf.

[13] Cisco Fog Computing (2015b). The Internet of Things: Extend the cloud to where the things are. http://www.cisco.com/c/dam/en_us/solutions/trends/iot/docs/computingoverview.pdf.

[14] Covington, M. J. & Carskadden, R. (2013). Threat implications of the Internet of Things. In *2013 5th International Conference on Cyber Conflict (CyCon)* (pp. 1, 12).

[15] Dalal, N., Akhtar, N., Gupta, A., Karamchandani, N., Kasbekar, G. S., & Parekh, J. (2022, January). A wireless intrusion detection system for 802.11

WPA3 networks. In *2022 14th International Conference on Communication Systems & Networks* (*COMSNETS*) (pp. 384–392). IEEE.

[16] Demir, Ö. T., Björnson, E., & Sanguinetti, L. (2021). Foundations of user-centric cell-free massive MIMO. *Foundations and Trends in Signal Processing*, 14(3–4), 162–472.

[17] Easttom, C. (2022). Virtual private networks, authentication, and wireless security. In *Modern Cryptography: Applied Mathematics for Encryption and Information Security* (pp. 309–327). Springer International Publishing, Cham.

[18] Eichhorn, J. (2010, November). GREENER, SAFER, SMARTER considerations in building a smart grid communications network, TROPOS network. http://slideplayer.com/slide/5850758/ (Accessed March 23, 2018).

[19] Ekanayake, B. N., Halgamuge, M. N., & Syed, A. (2018). Security and privacy issues of Fog computing for the internet of things (IoT). In *Cognitive Computing for Big Data Systems over IoT* (pp. 139–174). Springer, Cham.

[20] Elhoushy, S., Ibrahim, M., & Hamouda, W. (2021). Cell-free massive MIMO: A survey. *IEEE Communications Surveys & Tutorials*, 24(1), 492–523.

[21] El-Nagar, A. M., Abd El-Hafez, A. A., & Elhnawy, A. (2011, December). A novel EAP-moderate weight extensible authentication protocol. In *2011 Seventh International Computer Engineering Conference* (*ICENCO'2011*) (pp. 1–6). IEEE.

[22] Firdous, S., Baig, Z., Valli, C., & Ibrahim, A. (2017). Modelling and evaluation of malicious attacks against the IoT MQTT protocol. In *2017 IEEE International Conference on Internet of Things (iThings) and IEEE Green Computing and Communications (GreenCom) and IEEE Cyber, Physical and Social Computing (CPSCom) and IEEE Smart Data (SmartData)* (pp. 748–755). Exeter.

[23] Flamini, R., De Donno, D., Gambini, J., Giuppi, F., Mazzucco, C., Milani, A., & Resteghini, L. (2022). Toward a heterogeneous smart electromagnetic environment for millimeter-wave communications: An industrial viewpoint. *IEEE Transactions on Antennas and Propagation*, 70(10), 8898–8910.

[24] Funk, P., & Blake-Wilson, S. (2008). Extensible authentication protocol tunneled transport layer security authenticated protocol version 0 (EAP-TTLSv0) (No. rfc5281).

[25] Guo, F., Peng, M., Li, N., Sun, Q., & Li, X. (2023). Communication-computing built-in-design in next-generation radio access networks: Architecture and key technologies. *IEEE Network*. 10.1109/MNET.005.2300092.

[26] Gupta, S. & Gupta, B. B. (2018). XSS-secure as a service for the platforms of online social network-based multimedia web applications in cloud. *Multimedia Tools and Applications*, 77(4), 4829–4861.

[27] Hidayat, T. N. & Riadi, I. (2021). Optimation wireless security IEEE 802.1 X using the extensible authentication protocol-protected extensible authentication protocol (EAP-PEAP). *International Journal of Computer Applications*, 174(11), 25–30.

[28] Iorga, M., Feldman, L., Barton, R., Martin, M. J., Goren, N. S., & Mahmoudi, C. (2018). Fog computing conceptual model (NIST Special Publication 500-325). National Institute of Standards and Technology. Retrieved March 22, 2018, from https://doi.org/10.6028/NIST.SP 500-325.

[29] Kadhim, A. N. & Sadkhan, S. B. (2021, July). Security threats in wireless network communication-status, challenges, and future trends. In *2021 International Conference on Advanced Computer Applications (ACA)* (pp. 176–181). IEEE.

[30] Kim, E., Jung, B. C., Park, C. Y., & Lee, H. (2022). Joint optimization of energy efficiency and user outage using multi-agent reinforcement learning in ultra-dense small cell networks. *Electronics*, 11(4), 599.

[31] Kohlios, C. P. & Hayajneh, T. (2018). A comprehensive attack flow model and security analysis for Wi-Fi and WPA3. *Electronics*, 7(11), 284.

[32] Kutsak, S. V. (2021). Analysis of attacks in IEEE 802.11 networks at different levels of OSI model. *Scientific Bulletin of National Mining University*, (2), 163–169.

[33] Le, D. T., Tran, T. T., Dang, K. Q., Alkanhel, R., & Muthanna, A. (2022) Malware spreading model for routers in Wi-Fi networks. *IEEE Access*, 10, 61873–61891.

[34] Li, X., Liang, X., Lu, R., Shen, X., Lin, X., & Zhu, H. (2012). Securing smart grid: Cyber-attacks, countermeasures, and challenges. *Communications Magazine, IEEE*, 50(8), 38–45.

[35] Li, J., Niu, Y., Wu, H., Ai, B., Chen, S., Feng, Z., … & Wang, N. (2022). Mobility support for millimeter wave communications: Opportunities and challenges. *IEEE Communications Surveys & Tutorials.*

[36] Lounis, K. & Zulkernine, M. (2020). WPA3 connection deprivation attacks. In *Risks and Security of Internet and Systems: 14th International Conference, CRiSIS 2019, Hammamet, Tunisia, October 29–31, 2019, Proceedings 14* (pp. 164–176). Springer International Publishing.

[37] McKinley, P. K., Samimi, F. A., Shapiro, J. K., & Tang, C. (2006). Service Clouds: A distributed infrastructure for constructing autonomic communication services. In *Proceedings of the 2nd IEEE International Symposium on Dependable, Autonomic and Secure Computing* (pp. 341–348). IEEE.

[38] McKnight, L. W., Howison, J., & Bradner, S. (2004). Guest editors' introduction: Wireless grids–distributed resource sharing by mobile, nomadic, and fixed devices. *IEEE Internet Computing*, 8(4), 24–31.

[39] McKnight, L., Marsden, J., Treglia, J., Nanno, E., Hameed, A., & Lu, Y. (2015). Open specifications for wireless grids technical requirements, version 0.3 (pp. 1–45). Syracuse University.

[40] Moissinac, K., Ramos, D., Rendon, G., & Elleithy, A. (2021, January). Wireless encryption and WPA2 weaknesses. In *2021 IEEE 11th Annual Computing and Communication Workshop and Conference (CCWC)* (pp. 1007–1015). IEEE.

[41] Mukherjee, M., Matam, R., Shu, L., Maglaras, L., Ferrag, M. A., Choudhury, N., & Kumar, V. (2017). Security and privacy in fog computing: Challenges. *IEEE Access*, 5, 19293–19304.

[42] Nahi, H. A., Hasan, M. A., Lazem, A. H., & Alkhafaji, M. A. (2023). Securing virtual architecture of smartphones based on network function virtualization. *Metaverse Basic and Applied Research*, 2, 37–37.

[43] Samimi, F. A., McKinley, P. K., & Sadjadi, S. M. (2006). Mobile service clouds: A self-managing infrastructure for autonomic mobile computing services. In *Self-Managed Networks, Systems, and Services* (pp. 130–141). Springer, Berlin, Heidelberg.

[44] Sharma, S. & Nag, A. (2023). Cognitive software defined networking and network function virtualization and applications. *Future Internet*, 15(2), 78.

[45] Sheu, J. P., Chen, P. C., & Hsu, C. S. (2008). A distributed localization scheme for wireless sensor networks with improved grid-scan and vector-based refinement. *IEEE Transactions on Mobile Computing*, 7(9), 1110–1123.

[46] Singh, R. & Sharma, T. P. (2015). On the IEEE 802.11 i security: A denial-of-service perspective. *Security and Communication Networks*, 8(7), 1378–1407.

[47] Swain, S. R., Saxena, D., Kumar, J., Singh, A. K., & Lee, C. N. (2023). An AI-driven intelligent traffic management model for 6G cloud radio access networks. *IEEE Wireless Communications Letters*. 10.1109/LWC.2023.3259942.

[48] Turaga, H., Bommisetty, S. H., Vanukuru, C., Nandakumar, S., Preetha, K. S., & Velmurugan, T. (2023). Distinctive analysis of power and frequency allocation for device to device (D2D) communication. *Computers and Electrical Engineering*, 106, 108572.

[49] Uckelmann, D., Harrison, M., & Michahelles, F. (2011). An architectural approach towards the future internet of things. In *Architecting the Internet of Things* (pp. 1–24). Springer, Berlin, Heidelberg.

[50] Umrao, B. K. & Yadav, D. K. (2023). Placement of virtual network functions for network services. *International Journal of Network Management*, e2232.

[51] Xiao, Y., Chen, H., Yang, S., Lin, Y. B., & Du, D. Z. (2009). Wireless network security. *EURASIP Journal on Wireless Communications and Networking*, *2009*(1), 1–3.
[52] Vanhoef, M. & Ronen, E. (2019). Dragonblood: A *Security Analysis of WPA3's SAE Handshake*. IACR Cryptology ePrint Archive, 383.
[53] Vermesan, O., Friess, P., Guillemin, P., Gusmeroli, S., Sundmaeker, H., Bassi, A., & Doody, P. (2011). Internet of things strategic research roadmap. In *Internet of Things—Global Technological and Societal Trends*, 1, (pp. 9–52).
[54] Williamson, B. (2023). Governing through infrastructural control: Artificial intelligence and cloud computing in the data-intensive state. *The SAGE handbook of digital society*. SAGE, Thousand Oaks, CA.
[55] Wu, L., Gan, C., Xu, Z., & Hui, J. (2023). (Network value)-based adaptive dynamic bandwidth allocation algorithm for 5G network slicing. *Transactions on Emerging Telecommunications Technologies*, 34(3), e4722.
[56] Yan, X., Şekercioğlu, Y. A., & Narayanan, S. (2010). A survey of vertical handover decision algorithms in fourth generation heterogeneous wireless networks. *Computer Networks*, 54(11), 1848–1863.
[57] Yi, S., Qin, Z., & Li, Q. (2015, August). Security and privacy issues of fog computing: A survey. In *International Conference on Wireless Algorithms, Systems, and Applications* (pp. 685–695). Springer, Cham.
[58] Yi, S., Li, C., & Li, Q. (2015, June). A survey of fog computing: Concepts, applications and issues. In *Proceedings of the 2015 Workshop on Mobile Big Data* (pp. 37–42). ACM.
[59] Zeng, W. Y., Zhao, Y. L., Zeng, J. W., & Song, W. (2008, October). Mobile grid architecture design and application. In *4th International Conference on Wireless Communications, Networking and Mobile Computing, 2008*. WiCOM'08 (pp. 1–4). IEEE.
[60] Zhang, Y., Yu, R., Nekovee, M., Liu, Y., Xie, S., & Gjessing, S. (2012). Cognitive machine-to-machine communications: Visions and potentials for the smart grid. *Network, IEEE*, 26(3), 6–13.
[61] Zheng, K., Yang, H., Xiong, X., Mei, J., Hou, L., & Zhang, K. (2023). Dynamic beam-based random access scheme for M2M communications in massive MIMO systems. *IEEE Transactions on Vehicular Technology*. 10.1109/TVT.2023.3286660.
[62] Zhu, J., Chan, D. S., Prabhu, M. S., Natarajan, P., Hu, H., & Bonomi, F. (2013, March). Improving web sites performance using edge servers in fog computing architecture. In *2013 IEEE 7th International Symposium on Service Oriented System Engineering* (*SOSE*) (pp. 320–323). IEEE.

Chapter 3

Conceptualizing a Secure Wireless Cloud*

ABSTRACT

The rising interest in cloud computing among organizations has incited a primary aspiration to enhance the effectiveness and efficiency of their information technology (IT) operations. Cloud computing empowers organizations to instantaneously provision scalable IT resources on a pay-per-use basis. Concurrently, the wireless grid presents a novel model for heterogeneous devices to share both physical and virtual resources within an *ad hoc* environment, eliminating the need for a dedicated server to manage the network. These technologies herald new opportunities for innovative architectures but also engender a host of security-related issues that concern many prospective users. Despite the prospective benefits, the integration of cloud computing and wireless grid architectures amplifies information security concerns beyond those associated with each architecture in isolation. As new paradigms for strategic organizational initiatives, these issues hinder the widespread adoption of cloud computing and wireless grid solutions as the prevalent integrations for operational systems. This chapter aims to delineate a wireless cloud architecture and identify potential vulnerabilities and threats intrinsic to a wireless cloud solution. We also broach the emergence of a

*Originally published as Brooks, T., Robinson, J., & McKnight, L. (2012). Conceptualizing a secure wireless cloud. *International Journal of Cloud Computing and Services Science (IJ-CLOSER)*, 1(3), 89–114.

promising wireless grid security architecture, centered around wireless cloud authentication, authorization, and access control processes.

INTRODUCTION

Computer networks and telecommunications backbones have made distributing computing power essential in the majority of industries and homes worldwide. The financial industry conducts trillions of dollars in transactions each day using current networking and distributed computing technology; and governments around the world maintain information on networks and in distributed databases. Each of these examples represents ways that telecommunications and network technologies are used to efficiently conduct daily operations. However, there is a downside. The information that is stored in and passed along global networks is exposed to malicious attempts to intercept it without proper authorization [10]. Information technology (IT) systems should be designed to minimize network vulnerabilities and protect the information contained within them [26].

Cloud computing represents the long-held dream of computing as a utility. It has the potential to transform a large part of the IT industry, making software even more attractive as a service by leveraging a data center's shared resources and shaping the way IT hardware is designed and purchased [3, 4]. Cloud computing is being touted as a new paradigm in computing, which will obviate an organization's need to build, manage, and fund internal data centers and complex IT infrastructures. Cloud computing infrastructures enable companies to cut costs by outsourcing computations, on-demand [64]. Many people in the IT industry are interested in advancing cloud computing and it is envisioned by many as the next-generation architecture of IT enterprises [33, 36].

Many organizations are beginning to see the potential in cloud computing solutions but may not be aware of the wireless grid and its potential integration with cloud computing for critical systems. However, organizations considering this integrated solution must carefully consider their specific needs, the security risks, and whether or not cloud computing will deliver value. Wireless grids provide the dynamic sharing of physical and virtual resources among heterogeneous devices [44]. A new wireless cloud option should be examined from a security perspective for potential business and technical benefits as it relates specifically to organizational IT assets.

This chapter discusses the implications of developing a wireless cloud and the potential security risks. We will identify a wireless cloud architecture, potential vulnerabilities, and threats to a wireless cloud solution, and propose the beginnings of a wireless grid security architecture, which focuses on an authentication, authorization, and access control process.

CLOUD COMPUTING

"Cloud" computing is a relatively recent term and builds on decades of research in virtualization, distributed computing, utility computing, and more recently networking, web, and software services [4, 32]. A definition of cloud computing is:

> "...a model for enabling convenient, on-demand network access to a shared pool of configurable computing resources (e.g., networks, servers, storage, applications, and services) that can be rapidly provisioned and released with minimal management effort or service provider interaction."[1]

As displayed in Figure 1, cloud computing has emerged as a new computing paradigm that arrays massive numbers of computers in centralized data centers to deliver web-based applications, application platforms, and services via a utility model [25, 59]. Reference [46] describes the four deployment models identified by the National Institute of Standards and Technology (NIST) for cloud services as the following: (1) private cloud — the cloud infrastructure is operated solely for an organization. It may be managed by the organization or a third party and may exist on-premise or off-premise; (2) community cloud — the cloud infrastructure is shared by several organizations and supports a specific community that has shared concerns (e.g., mission, security requirements, policy, and compliance considerations). It may be managed by the organizations or a third party and may exist on-premise or off-premise; (3) public cloud — the cloud infrastructure is made available to the general public or a large industry group and is owned by an organization selling cloud services and (4) hybrid cloud — the cloud infrastructure is a composition of two or more clouds (private, community, or public) that remain unique entities

[1] http://www.nist.gov/itl/cloud/upload/cloud-def-v15.pdf.

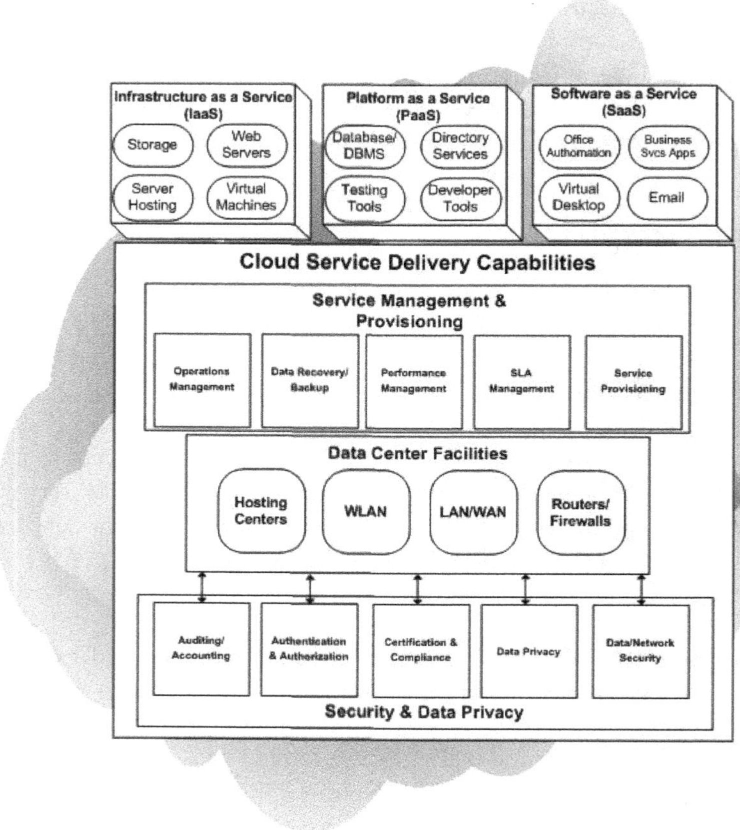

Figure 1. The Cloud Computing Framework

but are bound together by standardized or proprietary technology that enables data and application portability (e.g., cloud bursting for load-balancing between clouds).

There are a number of service offerings and implementation models within the cloud computing umbrella. These models, as displayed in Table 1, can be grouped into the following three categories: Infrastructure-as-a-Service (IaaS), which offers the ability to lease services such as storage or computing resources (e.g., Amazon Simple Storage Service[2] and

[2]Amazon Simple Storage Service: http://aws.amazon.com/s3/.

Table 1. Cloud Delivery Models

Delivery Model	Definition
Infrastructure-as-a-Service (IaaS)	Includes the foundational elements, such as storage, operating system instances, network, and identity management upon which development platforms and applications can be layered; the capability provided to the consumer is to rent processing, storage, networks, and other fundamental computing resources where the consumer is able to deploy and run arbitrary software, which can include operating systems and applications [14, 69].
Platform-as-a-Service (PaaS)	Cloud systems can offer an additional abstraction level: instead of supplying a virtualized infrastructure, they can provide the software platform which systems run. The sizing of the hardware resources demanded by the execution of the services is made in a transparent manner [14, 69].
Software-as-a-Service (SaaS)	Builds upon PaaS to offer complete applications customizable by the user to a limited degree and utilizing a security model developed by the provider; services of potential interest to a wide variety of users hosted in Cloud systems, which is an alternative to locally run applications. An example of this is the online alternatives of typical office applications, such as word processors, Google Docs, etc. [14, 69].

Elastic Compute Cloud[3]) [14], Platform-as-a-Service (PaaS), which provides the ability to lease an application development environment (e.g., Microsoft Azure Services Platform[4]) and Software-as-a-Service (SaaS), which offers network-accessible applications (e.g., Google docs.[5] These models provide distinct resources to the user/customer ranging from general infrastructure services provided by IaaS vendors to targeted customizable applications provided by SaaS vendors [69].

Instead of buying and maintaining costly servers, the IAAS cloud computing model, for example, allows one to control processing, memory,

[3]Amazon Elastic Compute Cloud: http://aws.amazon.com/ec2/.

[4]Microsoft Windows Azure: www.microsoft.com/windowsazure.

[5]Google Docs: https://www.google.com/docs/about/.

data storage, and network bandwidth dynamically and remotely from pools of these resources, providing the ability to specify and deploy computing capacity on demand [34, 37, 39]. If there is a need to scale up to accommodate sudden demand the necessary resources can be provisioned by the customer using a web browser. These same services are provided to multiple external customers (multi-tenancy), leveraging the shared resources of large data centers to achieve economies of scale and reduce the cost of the service [60]. Multi-tenancy enables the sharing of resources (and costs) among a large pool of users and provides reliability by way of multiple redundant sites, which makes it suitable for business continuity and disaster recovery. Clouds are advertised as a cheap alternative to supercomputers and specialized clusters. The cloud platform is much more reliable than grid platforms and it is more scalable [52]. The IAAS in cloud computing relies on large collections of commoditized computing resources provisioned via hypervisors.

Although cloud computing is in its early stages and its definitions vary greatly, the technologies used for the cloud include grid computing, utility computing, virtualization technologies, microservices, and containers. Grid computing is a form of distributed, parallel computing whereby processes are split up to leverage the available computing power of multiple central processing units (CPU) acting in concert [23]. Utility computing allows users to purchase computing capacity, such as CPU, storage, and bandwidth, from an IT service provider and to be billed based on actual consumption [3]. Virtualization technologies are virtual servers and virtual private networks, and they provide the ability to quickly reconfigure available resources on demand and provide the necessary security assurance, such as increased security protocols to protect against threats from the cloud environment and the data transported within the cloud [7].

Among the substantial challenges that hinder the widespread adoption of cloud computing are the security and privacy concerns of data in the cloud. Security has emerged as arguably the most significant barrier to faster and more widespread adoption of cloud computing [11]. Although cloud computing offers the benefits of moving computing resources to a cloud computing environment to take advantage of flexibility and cost savings, data confidentiality and integrity controls for the cloud need to be applied to limit exposure to unauthorized users [28]. Moving information assets to a cloud computing environment can reduce the costs of information management and storage but cloud-based systems are open to security threats and loss of control of data [64]. The cloud computing service deployment and architecture (e.g., private, community, public, or hybrid) chosen must fit the security and privacy needs of the organization adopting this type of environment [15, 39, 46]. Two key components

Microservices[6] are becoming increasingly popular in cloud computing as it enable organizations to achieve high scalability, performance, and availability. Microservices represent an architectural style that structures an application as a collection of services that are highly maintainable, testable, loosely coupled, independently deployable, and precisely focused. These services can be independently scaled and deployed, which helps developers take advantage of the distributed development across teams and locations.

The cloud's capabilities align perfectly with the dynamic, distributed, and modular nature of microservices as it offers functionalities like automated provisioning and scaling that allow services to quickly adapt to changes in demand. Further, the distributed nature of the cloud improves the resilience of microservices, as failure in one part of the system does not necessarily mean a complete system breakdown. However, with these advantages come unique security challenges. Unlike monolithic architectures where data flow happens within a single, secure domain, microservices require data to flow across various network points, potentially exposing it to vulnerabilities. Therefore, securing microservices in a cloud computing architecture requires special attention to network security, data encryption, secure APIs, identity and access management, and robust monitoring and logging mechanisms.

Containers and Kubernetes,[7] also known as K8s, play a pivotal role in today's cloud computing architectures, offering a highly scalable, robust, and flexible method to develop, deploy, and manage applications. When it comes to container technology, it's a lightweight, stand-alone, executable software package that includes everything needed to run an application, including the code, a runtime, libraries, environment variables, and config files. Containers provide a consistent and reproducible environment, ensuring that applications run the same way regardless of the deployment environment. Kubernetes, on the other hand, is an open-source platform designed to automate deploying, scaling, and managing containerized applications. It groups containers that make up an application into logical units for easy management and discovery. Kubernetes has

[6] https://microservices.io.

[7] https://kubernetes.io.

become the *de-facto* standard for orchestrating containerized applications, due to its robustness, scalability, and extensive community support.

In the context of security, containers, and Kubernetes have their own set of considerations. While containers are isolated from each other, they share the same host operation system (OS) kernel, which presents a unique set of security challenges. If a malicious entity were to gain access to one container, it could potentially exploit kernel vulnerabilities to affect other containers or the host system itself. To secure containers, it's crucial to adopt best practices such as using minimal base images, regularly scanning for vulnerabilities, not running containers with root privileges, and following the principle of least privilege. Additionally, it's essential to secure container images by signing them and using only trusted registries. On the Kubernetes side, security can be complex due to its inherent flexibility and broad feature set and must include application programming interface (API) security, role-based access control, network policies, Secrets management, and Pod security policies.

WIRELESS GRID

Reference [68] defines wireless grids as *ad hoc* dynamic sharing of physical and virtual resources among heterogeneous devices, content, and users. As the future of distributed computing, wireless grids (see Figure 2) will enable resource sharing among dynamic groups or social networks with individual profiles that are assigned a specific status relative to similar objects and resources with no dedicated server needed to manage the network [45]. Grid computing involves the aggregation of network-connected computers to form a distributed system for coordinated problem-solving and resource sharing [16, 17, 57]. McKnight *et al.* [44] can be credited with describing wireless grid infrastructures along three dimensions: the physical layer, the networking infrastructure, and the middleware. Literature from [42] and [2] identify wireless grids as three distinct architectures: (1) wireless sensor grid, (2) mobile wireless, and (3) fixed wireless. McKnight *et al.* [44] provide a classification of the wireless grid which differs from a typical wired network such as the:

- applications aggregating information from the range of input/output interfaces found in nomadic devices,

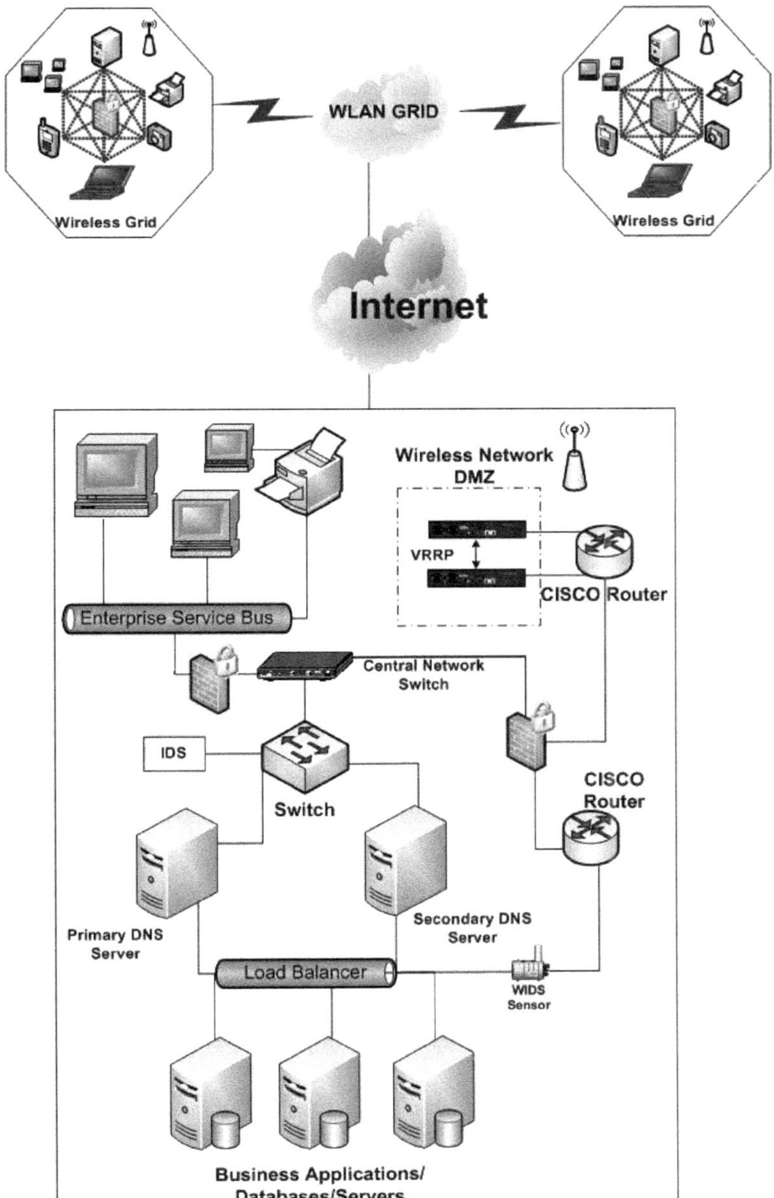

Figure 2. Wireless Grid

- applications leveraging the locations and contexts in which the devices exist, and
- applications leveraging the mesh network capabilities of groups of nomadic devices.

The wireless grid extends grid resources to wireless devices of varying sizes and capabilities such as sensors, mobile phones, laptops, special instruments, and edge devices [1]. These devices might be statically located, mobile, or nomadic, shifting across institutional boundaries and connected to the grid via nearby devices such as desktops [45]. Resources can be searched, found, viewed, and manipulated remotely from any other grid-enabled device or service, and devices on the wireless grid network can serve as both servers and clients. Reference [1] identifies these grids as an augmentation of a wired grid that facilitates the exchange of information and the interaction between heterogeneous wireless devices. These grids will enable shared resources among dynamic groups or social networks of computing and communication devices and are composed of objects and resources with individual profiles that are assigned a specific status relative to similar objects and resources [45]. Wireless grids can take ubiquitous computing to the next level by providing seamless wireless extensions to the wired grid. The architecture for these types of grids are of importance because they can be deployed to provide autonomous nodes that communicate with each other in a decentralized manner and how each node of the network connects others with wireless links and acts as both a host and a router in sending and receiving data.

Grid computing and grid topologies have been extended into wireless implementations and have been used to facilitate the exchange of information between heterogeneous wireless devices [1, 42]. Wireless grids can take distributed computing to the next level by providing seamless wireless extensions to the wired grid. Wireless grid computing consists of autonomous nodes that communicate with each other in a decentralized manner. Each individual node of the network connects with other nodes via wireless links and acts as both a host and a router.

One major issue with wireless grids is information security [1]. Integrating wireless grids with an existing information system (e.g., cloud computing) or traditional wired network raises new challenges in terms of routing, aggregating, and querying data from multiple sources on wirelessly connected heterogeneous devices. As with all wireless information, the communication devices in the grid communicate and pass information over standard radio frequencies which can be easily tapped [42]. Even if the wireless grid utilizes a firewall and proxy system that filters out any potentially malicious network packets or web content, data can still leak outside of the grid. The wireless grid will generally be more vulnerable to malicious and accidental threats than its wired counterparts. A defined security architecture must be a mandatory component of the wireless grid if this inherent vulnerability is to be properly addressed.

Security architecture and security analysis of communication protocols for mobile wireless networks must also be taken into consideration [48, 61]. Security is always an issue with mobile wireless devices since wireless transmission is susceptible to a wide range of attacks [57]. Because of the inherent nature of the wireless connection, protecting information is difficult. The diversity of the link quality, the potential unreliability of the end devices, the power constraints of the mobile device, and the enforcement of security and privacy policies all present major challenges in the wireless grid environment [1]. The Wireless Grid Innovation Testbed (WiGiT) at Syracuse University is one organization researching a deeper understanding of wireless grid security, application, device, network, user, and market behavior through academic, trade, and popular publications [68].

Most existing wireless security typically includes some form of security mechanisms [e.g., wired equivalent privacy (WEP)] that provide security on an access point-by-access point basis [22]. As wireless grid technology continues to grow, the grid will become increasingly heterogeneous, requiring data to transit across various trusted wireless networks. For this reason, users will come to demand more robust end-to-end security services. In order to make integrations more feasible, such as wireless grid and cloud computing services, grid services will have to be complemented by the addition of security services. This could potentially lead to the development of a new wireless cloud architecture.

THE WIRELESS CLOUD

Under emerging wireless grid architectures, however, such network-based security models are far from adequate. These new systems will be about net-centric information sharing and collaborating business functionality which will become service-enabled and exposed to external wireless clients via standard web services type protocols. These wireless clients, which themselves may be applications, will dynamically discover services and make real-time use of their code and data. Their services will be inherently location-independent, not necessarily bound to a physical location, which can change over time as services are relocated or for fail-over reasons. Since wireless grid clients and service providers may belong to different physical networks or even different service providers, these networks and/or organizations may be governed by entirely different security policies.

Therefore, in a wireless cloud environment, organizations will need to shift their focus from perimeter-based security models to a service-level view of security. Emphasis should be placed on network identities, trust, and authorization of both users and applications rather than on ownership and control. The architectural model of a wireless cloud computing environment is identified in Figure 3. Reference [39] identified the wireless cloud as a natural extension of the wireless grid. It provides seamless access to the internet, networked devices, and computing capabilities. The wireless cloud is a kind of next-generation wireless grid and as an emerging technology, there is very little in the literature about it [38].

Combining cloud computing and the wireless grid will create a new form of distributed computing. Through loosely coupled computers acting

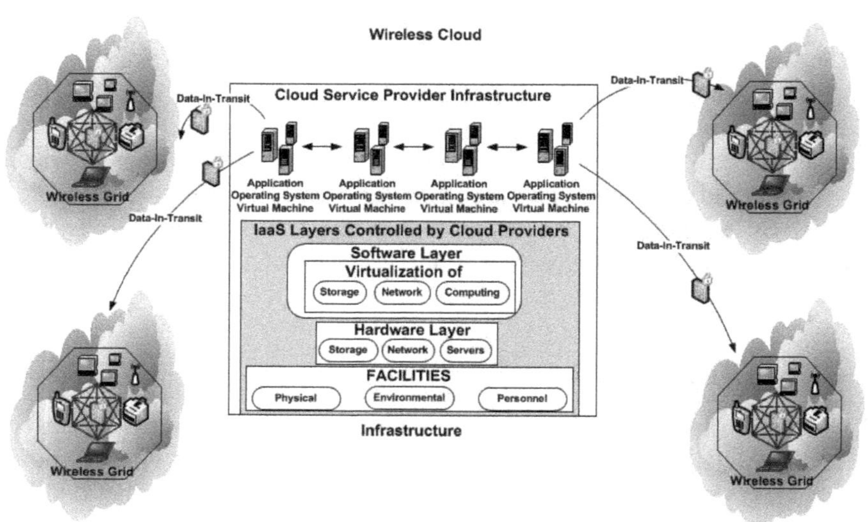

Figure 3. The Wireless Cloud

in concert to perform large tasks wirelessly, the packaging of computing resources, such as computation and storage, will provide a future architecture capable of a grid-utility-like model. The wireless cloud's device and location independence enables the wireless grid to access the cloud systems regardless of device location or what device they are using. System performance could be monitored and managed for consistency but may be affected by insufficient bandwidth or high network load. Since scalability changes system configuration to meet changing user demands, the wireless cloud could operate without having to engineer for peak loads which may result in lower operational costs.

This conceptual model also emphasizes the importance of architecting for the cloud versus simply deploying system components to the cloud to ensure that business requirements are met. Typical software and systems that are not designed to take advantage of the scalability and parallelism of the cloud will likely not achieve the full benefit that is provided by a cloud computing environment. Wireless cloud security may improve due to added security-focused resources but currently, there are some concerns about possible loss of control over sensitive data. The data residing in the wireless cloud has to be managed on all security devices. The enforcement of security policies must take place to ensure the network has the latest protection against threats. The solution must also provide end-to-end visibility to validate and audit security effectiveness and monitor security events.

As cloud and wireless technology advances, the wireless cloud architecture could progress from a distributed, decentralized architecture with a lot of data in "thin" access points (APs) to a centralized architecture using "thick" APs with data located in wireless switches. When considering the risks associated with a wireless cloud architecture, the most fundamental element that must be considered is how the wireless cloud environment affects the trust model. In thinking about this question, first consider a traditional computing model where applications reside on client machines, servers, or mainframes that are owned and controlled by the enterprise. In this environment, it is possible to levy a host of countermeasures to mitigate the security risks that exist in the IT world. Those countermeasures include firewalls, data encryption, antivirus solutions, tight access permissions, virtual or physical separation of networks, and more. Coupled with those technical countermeasures are the use of trusted network administrators, application developers, and internal processes. Now consider what happens when the applications move to a wireless cloud in which the business model is typically driven by the provision of common service to a wide variety of customers. At this point, the security of those applications and their data is largely a function of the skill, willingness, diligence, and ability of the wireless provider to protect the data and provide reliable service.

Due to this issue of the movement of the trust model from customer to provider, the wireless cloud represents a significant challenge from an information security perspective. While the specific concerns will vary somewhat depending upon the implementation of a wireless cloud solution, the question remains as to just how far the trust model extend. Certainly, vulnerabilities and threats must be identified in dealing with this type of solution, where security may be a shared responsibility and where the final installation of a blend of network elements, operation systems, and tools will have to provide an operational solution.

VULNERABILITIES AND THREATS TO THE WIRELESS CLOUD

As data flows in the wireless cloud, data confidentiality and integrity controls need to be applied to limit exposure to unauthorized users. The knowledge of information security threats is quite useful to system administrators, testers, and information assurance professionals, who need to understand how an information system might be attacked. The intention of a threat is to exploit a vulnerability or a weakness in an information system. In any risk assessment, threats must first be identified. Reference [13] defines a threat as "any circumstance or event with the potential to adversely impact organizational operations (including mission, functions, image or reputation), organizational assets, individuals, other organizations, or the Nation through an information system via unauthorized access, destruction, disclosure, modification of information and/or denial-of-service (DoS) attack".

Unlike a wired network, the wireless cloud is not limited by physical space. This potentially opens up the network to attack from rogue users who spy on wireless transmissions or gain unauthorized access to the network from the inside or outside [26]. Traditional thieves, hackers, high-tech criminals, government-sponsored organizations, viruses, and other types of malicious code are the typical causes of security concerns on wireless networks [73]. The targets for attacks are the files stored on hard drives and other media, data, and voice communications transferred between the remote clients and the internal networks, or the remote system since it is used to gain access to the main network.

Vulnerabilities exist in wireless networks that are interconnected with any other system. The entire network becomes more vulnerable because when one part of the system is compromised, the rest of the network can be affected as well. Unprotected wireless communications equipment is also vulnerable to vandalism and terrorism that may cause large-scale communications outages [73]. The scale of any attack against any wireless network depends on the type of network, the security precautions of the network, the location of the network, and the ability of the adversary that desires that information.

All the vulnerabilities that exist in a conventional wired network will apply to the wireless cloud. Malicious entities may gain unauthorized access to a given computer network through wireless connections, bypassing any firewall protections, and may steal the identity of legitimate users and masquerade them on internal networks [72]. These entities may be able to violate the privacy of legitimate users by tracking their movements or using third party, untrusted wireless network services to gain access to network resources. Malicious code or viruses may corrupt data on a wireless device and subsequently be introduced to a wired network connection. While it is more difficult and potentially more important to secure wireless communications, the issues, threats, and the respective required services to adequately respond to these threats are mostly the same for wired and wireless technologies.

Managing security threats and vulnerabilities in information system assets are two fundamental challenges for organizations [51]. Security engineers can reduce the risks associated with systems by identifying threats and making design or procedural changes in a system to reduce its vulnerability to those threats. This chapter identifies potential threats to a wireless cloud environment that can be used as a starting point to secure a wireless cloud architecture. While this list is not all-inclusive, it will likely be expanded as industry experience with wireless clouds grows, technologies evolve, and the ingenuity of attackers seeks new ways to achieve their ends.

The knowledge of threats is quite useful to system administrators, testers, and information assurance professionals, who need to understand how an information system might be attacked. The intention of a threat is to exploit a vulnerability or a weakness in an information system. In any risk assessment, threats must first be identified. For example, researchers such as [70, 71] have identified some of the following threats against the IEEE 802.11 WEP, the standard for wireless networking, as follows:

- **Traffic analysis:** A simple technique whereby the attacker determines the load on the communication medium by the number and size of packets being transmitted, the source and destination of the packets, and the type of packets.
- **Passive eavesdropping:** The attacker passively monitors the wireless session and the payload. If the payload is encrypted, this includes breaking the encryption to read the plaintext.
- **Active eavesdropping:** Involves the attacker injecting data into the communication to help decipher the payload and then the attacker not only listens to the wireless connection but also actively injects messages into the communication medium in order to assist them in determining the contents of messages.
- **Unauthorized access:** Not directed at any individual user or set of users on the wireless local area network (WLAN). Once an attacker has access to the network, additional attacks can then be launched, or free network use is provided.
- **Man-in-the-middle:** Used to read private data from a session or to modify the packets thus violating the integrity of a session.
- **Session high-jacking:** An attack against the integrity of a session; the attacker takes an authorized and authenticated session away from its proper owner.
- **Replay:** Used to gain access to the network with the authorizations of the target, but the actual session or sessions that are attacked are not altered or interfered with in any way.

While many of the attacks referenced above are common across wireless environments, the highly distributed and collaborative nature of the wireless cloud will have to take on increased security protocols to protect against threats from the wireless grid environment, the cloud environment and the data transported from the cloud to the grid (see Figure 4, Wireless Cloud Threat Model). While threats focus on specific attacks on computing environments, the model below takes into consideration that threats should consider the skill of the attacker, their propensity to actually launch an attack, their concern for risk of detection or attribution, and the likelihood of success. The assumption is that the most highly skilled, motivated

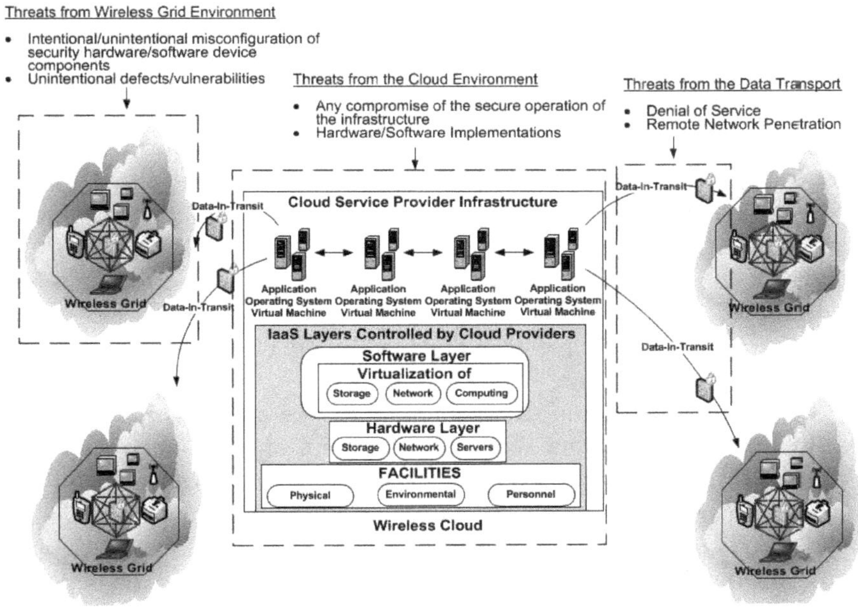

Figure 4. Wireless Cloud Threat Model

hackers would attack organizations that implement a wireless cloud within their environment.

Threats from the wireless grid environment cover those conditions involved in the actual use of operational wireless grid devices. Since each wireless grid location being connected to a cloud environment may be different, the worst-case environment would have to be considered from a risk assessment viewpoint. These conditions of use introduce the threat of people who have authorized access that may intentionally or unintentionally misuse, misconfigure, or bypass the security functions within the wireless grid. Threats related to people getting unauthorized, direct physical or logical access to the wireless grid devices security functions and any tampering or misconfiguration might occur as a result of a threat to this environment. This also includes those threats related to someone stealing or substituting hardware or software devices that provide security functions within the wireless grid.

Threats that arise from a vendor's supply chain of wireless grid devices for an organization may cause security concerns to the wireless cloud architecture. The supply chain security challenges posed by the threat of attacks have significant implications for enterprises and their suppliers [9]. The whole process of implementing, maintaining, upgrading, and patching hardware and software for wireless grid devices could introduce threats. Threats from the wireless grid hardware/software device supply chain include any related to having an adversary intentionally modify, bypass, or weaken the security functions during the development, production, distribution, maintenance, shipping, and warehousing/storage of these entities. Since such functions are not perfect in their implementation, there is also the threat of unintentional defects in the device hardware or software or in the overall wireless grid security architecture in which they exist.

Threats to a cloud computing environment are also of concern. There are multiple attack vectors within the software architecture of a cloud including virtualization software, web browsers, security software, and client/server operating systems [40]. Attacks could also be launched against major cloud services, such as Amazon Web Services (AWS) and Google Apps, potentially affecting thousands of cloud consumers. Web services could be targeted through the exploitation of vulnerabilities inherent in extensible markup language (XML), simple object access protocol (SOAP), and web services description language (WSDL). The provider and consumer security services, such as anti-virus and personal firewall applications, could be compromised. Attacks against web browsers can compromise communications between the consumer and the cloud provider and could allow attackers to intercept data (e.g., passwords, encryption keys, files); redirect web browsers to compromised sites; and prevent the web browser from functioning properly, thus inhibiting Internet communications.

One of the most critical and yet difficult challenges is ensuring continuous availability of wireless cloud resources. Protection of critical infrastructure components, such as routers, gateways, domain name system (DNS) servers, and the communications pathways between cloud provider and consumer, are key to maintaining resource availability and the integrity and confidentiality of data transmitted across these channels. Threats that impact communications can be either malicious, such as DoS attacks, aimed at wireless connections or devices, provider, consumer, or network resources; authentication and encryption infrastructure components; or inadvertent outages to include technical failures, power outages, Internet congestion, and natural disasters. Blacklisting of internet protocol (IP) addresses used by cloud consumers or cloud providers could also be a serious problem. Perceived inappropriate behavior by cloud consumers, which originate from within a cloud provider data center, may cause the IP set utilized by the provider to be blacklisted by internet service providers (ISP) and other cloud vendors. Whether the actions were inadvertent or malicious, the blacklisting of providers IP's would impact not only consumers from accessing cloud services but could be financially devastating to a cloud provider.

Physical security deals with access to computing facilities, infrastructure, and personnel that support the cloud provider, consumer, and communication pathways in between. While physical security is not unique to cloud computing, the shared resource environment of a wireless cloud architecture increases the potential to access data and computing resources of other organizations. A physical security breach within the cloud provider data center allows intruders potentially unauthorized access to the data of hundreds or thousands of users spanning various organizations [3]. Likewise, unauthorized access to computing assets at a consumer's facility may provide access to the cloud provider environment, allowing the attacker to inject malware into the infrastructure of the provider. Cloud provider administrators and maintenance personnel have physical access to the shared resources within the cloud (i.e., hardware, power, network, storage, firewalls).

Threats from the data transport from the cloud to a wireless grid environment must also be taken into consideration. Confidentiality and integrity of data must be protected at all times [58], whether that data is "at-rest" or "in-transit". The wireless cloud must provide protection against unauthorized alteration of messages and documents during data transit. This is especially important in a wireless cloud environment as cloud consumers will be accessing data, applications, and services across the great expanse of the Internet, increasing the exposure of sensitive data to interception, modification, and injection attacks. Protection of data within the boundaries of a wireless cloud environment is equally important as public clouds are environments where computing resources are shared among potentially thousands of different users and must be protected from the prying eyes of other cloud users. It's also important to protect the underlying communication (transport) as well as messages and documents that are carried over the transport so they cannot be made available to unauthorized parties.

Typical threats to data-at-rest within the wireless cloud could include the inadvertent or malicious alteration or deletion of data and files, data theft, and DoS attacks that prevent access to data, applications, and services. Inadvertent alteration or deletion of data and files is often due to improperly configured access controls versus malicious attacks perpetrated by hackers. Data-in-transit is susceptible to interception (e.g., man-in-the-middle attacks), injection, and modification, all of which pose serious risks to the confidentiality and integrity of the data. Data may be extracted without detection from improperly configured devices. Improperly protected end-user machines (i.e., at work or home) could spread malware to a virtual machine (VM), and in turn, spread to other users as they connect to the VM. As wireless cloud users connect to resources distributed across multiple VM's, malware may also spread. To reduce the potential spread of malware from unauthorized or personal devices, organizational security policies must address whether security services, such as anti-virus and personal firewall applications, will be extended to protect home personal computers (PC), Internet-enabled phones, or only allow users to connect to cloud resources with company-provided computing resources.

Much like an outside hacker, an insider with authorized access to a wireless cloud system could execute various attacks to gain unauthorized access to other systems or deny service to users of these other systems, and even manipulate files that facilitate the provision of services on virtual/remote machines. Insider abuse, when both malicious and accidental insider misuse of internal systems occurs, poses the most serious threat to wireless clouds. While organizations have to deal with insider threats today, the concentration of information and processing into wireless clouds will magnify the potential impact of insider abuse. Wireless clouds will be particularly threatened by malware for two reasons: (1) the homogeneous structure, rich interconnections, and large scale of a cloud raise the possibility of initial malware injection and can offer malware easy avenues for propagation, and (2) the concentration of value in a cloud offers potential attackers, both insiders and external adversaries, a high-value target for tailored, specialized malware.

Wireless cloud data owners will have to worry about two potential threats: accidental leakage of information outside the security enclave, and negative impacts to the integrity or availability of their information from the introduction of malicious code or DoS attacks. Wireless clouds will store and process information from various sources (e.g., clouds, devices, etc.), offer access to many different users, and connect to a wide variety of external systems. This increases the threat of cross-domain leakage of information. Therefore, wireless clouds will not have the luxury of keeping "customers" completely segregated but will have to provide controlled sharing. These sharing mechanisms will pose the greatest threat to leakage. As such, there must be securing mechanisms for addressing threats for securing wireless cloud environments.

SECURING THE WIRELESS CLOUD

Any communications network is subject to becoming the target of exploitation by individuals or groups outside of the authorized group of intended users. Traditionally, only the communications of governments and large corporations were regularly subject to such targeting. The military and diplomatic communications of governments were targeted for national secrets, while corporate communications were targeted for technology and trade secrets. Exploiting government and corporate communications networks required a large expenditure of resources. The exploitation of communications is conducted to gain access to data flowing over a network, disrupting the flow of data on the network and parasitically seizing the network's resources (i.e., to use a network free of charge). There is an additional reason for exploiting a communications network; however, it is used to a much lesser extent — disinformation. Disinformation can be injected into a communications network in order to mislead and cause confusion and doubt and can give a political, military, or economic advantage to the exploiter [66].

The first and foremost goal of the new wireless cloud security architecture is to ensure services can be invoked and managed in a secure fashion. As with just about every critical distributed system, there is a set of key security requirements that will need to be met which include authentication and authorization, confidentiality, data integrity, availability, non-repudiation, security policy exchange, intrusion detection, protection, and secure logging, manageability and accountability [6, 16, 18, 41]. For the wireless cloud, additional security measures will have to be implemented to ensure the cryptography (e.g., confidentiality, data integrity, entity authentication, and data origin authentication and availability) of all information that is acquired, processed, and transmitted due to the nature of its architecture [43]. The integration must ensure that security boundaries and security tools are designed and positioned to complement each other and interoperate as appropriate.

These include:

- **Interoperability:** The cornerstone of the wireless cloud architecture and must be preserved to the maximum extent by the security architecture. Major security integration points in the architecture — such as those between cloud computing service providers and wireless grid clients, between service providers and the security infrastructure, and between security infrastructures in different trust domains — must have stable, consistent interfaces based on widely adopted industry and government standards, which enables each domain or organization to implement its own market-driven solution while maintaining effective interoperability.
- **Tailored security policy constraints:** In a traditional security domain, resources and services are often protected by a uniform set of security rules that are not granular enough to meet specific application needs. Because customers who may access a resource may or may not be from the organization's local domain, different "strengths" of authentication and access control may be required. Consequently, security policies need to be expressive and flexible enough to be tailored according to both service providers' and wireless grid policy attributes.
- **"At-Rest" data security:** Focusing primarily on securing "in-transit" data, such as XML messages and resource access, security measures also need to be in place to protect data "at rest", which include but not limited to the protection of storage of credentials (private keys, etc.), protection of security infrastructure components, such as policy stores, and security logs.

Organizations must ensure the quality of data being processed and distributed with respect to the defense of the network at a level that is useful to the end user. The wireless cloud will have to provide the nature of each transaction, including the data standard, the content of the data, and the performance attributes of the data. Appropriate components must ensure that each of these parameters remains constant for data being relayed to wireless cloud activities, as well as meeting the performance standards defined within the wireless cloud. Data transported through the wireless cloud network must have a constant and reliable level of integrity, must not be undermined while passing through the network, and must maintain the quality of the data if latency occurs. For information that is processed or created for an external user, it must be guaranteed that the quality and timeliness of the data remain useful in the analysis and combat of threats to the network.

Because of the threat of exploitation, the wireless cloud will have to be protected by a well-defined security architecture. A security architecture encompasses IT security and data privacy requirements as well as solutions within the context of an over-arching enterprise architecture [5]. The wireless cloud model is one in which organizations will have less control over their security architecture than in traditional networks and at the same time are required to share IT infrastructure with other entities. This dynamic causes certain key challenges to rise in prominence in which the security architecture components for the wireless cloud must have an extensive security architecture in place. One such framework that could potentially address the wireless cloud security approach to creating secure, integrated, and interoperable grid services based on a set of security abstractions that unify formerly dissimilar technologies is the Grid Security Model [18, 49] as depicted in Figure 5.

A security framework ensures that basic security practices are implemented across an organization by integrating industry security best practices at multiple levels of the enterprise: information infrastructure design; software, hardware, and service procurement; application development; and training. This emerging Grid Security Model appears to offer an inherently practical framework in which to build and manage wireless cloud systems to meet security requirements [19]. For the purposes of this

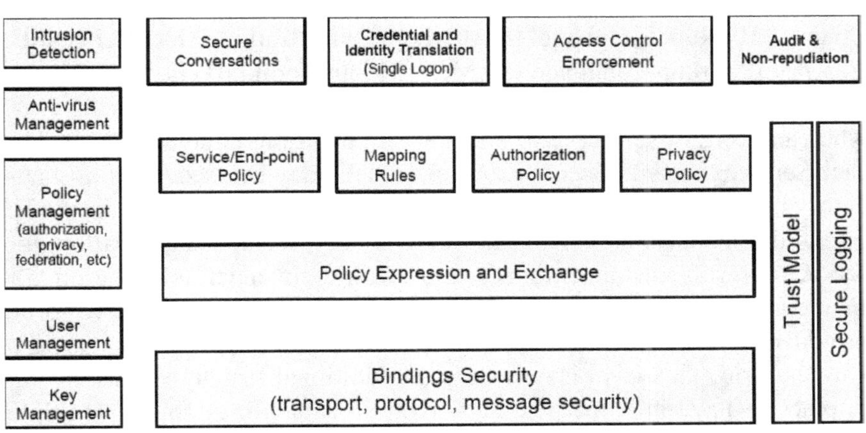

Figure 5. Grid Security Model

chapter, the authors are only addressing the authorization (including authentication) processes of this particular model.

AUTHENTICATION

One of the most important security controls of any IT system is the authorization, authentication, and access of the system [31]. Policies are one aspect of information which influences the behavior of objects within systems. To achieve both sharing of information and protection of information in a wireless cloud environment, it is necessary that common authorization and authentication policies and mechanisms be used. Whereas authorization is the process of giving user's access rights to computer resources based on their permissions and privileges [5], authentication is the verification of the identity or other attributes claimed by or assumed of an entity (user, process, or device) or verifying the source and integrity of data. The wireless cloud's authorization policy has to address the processes of ascertaining authorizations prior to allowing the performance of an action such as viewing or accessing information through authentication. Ideally, the authorization policy mechanism will have to provide interoperable authorization capabilities among cloud providers.

Cloud service providers will require that wireless grid organizations have authorization/authentication policies and contracts in place before granting them access to specified data. Different authentication mechanism standards should be leveraged, supported, configurable, and pluggable depending on service-specific requirements (e.g., eXtensible Access Control Markup Language [XACML] Authorization Model, Security Assertion Markup Language [SAML], Globus Toolkit [GT] 5.03 [35, 50, 67]. Control access to cloud services based on authorization policies (i.e., who can access a service, and under what conditions) may be attached to each service. Different access control models may be used, such as mandatory access control [53], discretionary [63], or role-based models [62]. The authorization implementation should also be extensible to allow for service-specific customizations (i.e., specific financial information for financial institutions). Ideally, the authorization policies will have to be provided by the cloud computing provider and the organizations using a wireless grid. This level is necessary, as additional structures must be put in place to have interoperable authorization capabilities among multiple enterprises (i.e., shared community space). Without procedures and methods in place to ensure that sharing takes place without ignoring appropriate protection of the information, collaboration is not possible.

A fully realized secure wireless cloud systems architecture will be highly dependent on a decentralized identity management and authentication architecture able to offload authentication. Authentication systems not only need to manage user identity certificates but also device-to-device certificates. Users utilize these certificates to authenticate to the policy enforcement point, while the devices utilize these certificates to authenticate each other and negotiate encrypted tunnels. Because of the lack of maturity of endpoint policy enforcement systems that can self-scan and automatically assure compliance as part of the authentication process, assurances of a secured endpoint remain the arena of hardened configurations and aggressive compliance scanning and remediation. For this reason, the initial implementation of this wireless cloud solution should focus on systems where internet connectivity and the use of highly efficient equipment can reasonably be restricted.

Authentication/authorization collectively generates, assigns, and manages identities and places those identities into credentials (i.e., X.509 certificates) [54]. Thus, authentication mechanisms are required so that the identity of individuals and services can be established, and service providers must implement authorization mechanisms to enforce policy over how each service can be used [49]. Authentication uses identities in the system and manages security-related attributes such as roles in the system. Figure 6 provides a generic Wireless Cloud Authentication, Authorization, and Access Control Process.

Authentication requires that the user (e.g., a cloud computing system) prove its identity. As data is received from the cloud to the wireless grid, a challenge/response mechanism is used as a method of identification. Authentication should be two-way, so once wireless grid credentials have been accepted and validated; policy enforcement must be enforced in order to render an authentication decision. This lets the system know that it is communicating with a valid user. By having the system authenticate to the user, it is less likely that an unauthorized third party will be able to pose as a system by inserting itself into the link between the user and the valid system (i.e., man-in-the-middle).

Wireless grid authentication should be based on wireless network authentication mechanisms [21]. Authentication for wireless grids must involve strong encryption to prevent eavesdropping and must involve mutual authentication to ensure that sensitive information is transmitted

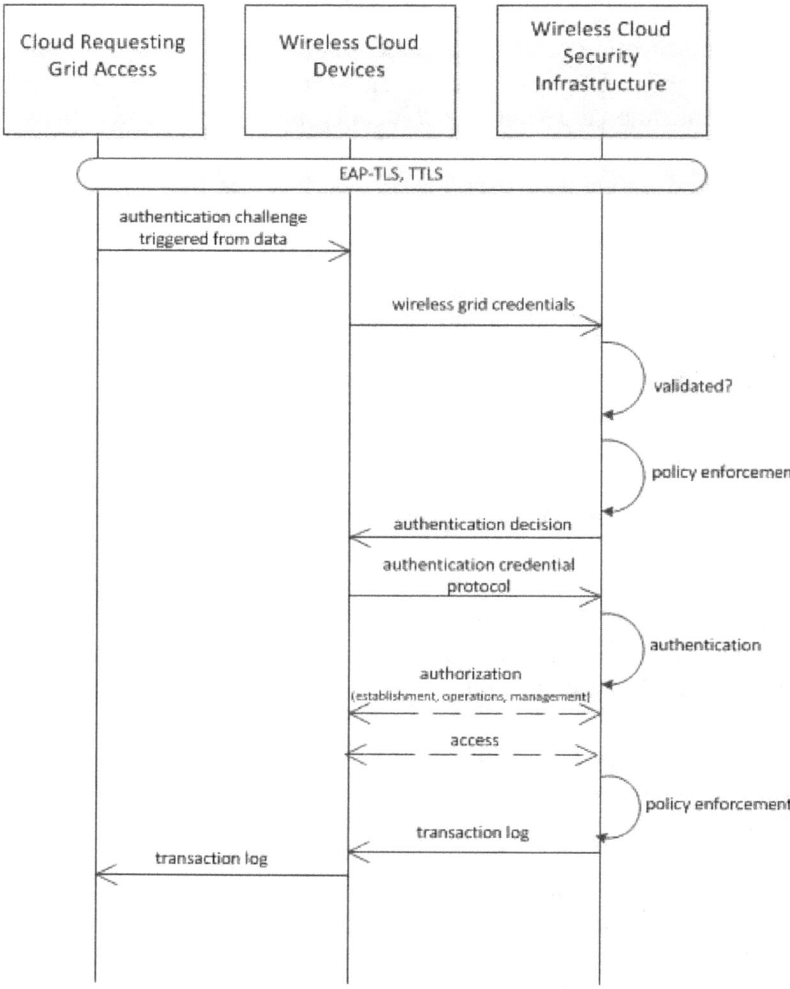

Figure 6. Wireless Cloud Authentication, Authorization and Access Control Process

only over legitimate networks. The wireless grid must also have strong authentication standards to meet the challenges of strict encryption and authentication requirements. Strict encryption and authentication requirements are met by IEEE 802.11-based wireless local area networks (LAN) through the implementation of the IEEE 802.1x standard. This standard specifies the use of the extensible authentication protocol (EAP) directly over a link layer protocol [24].

EAP is essentially a transport protocol that can be used by a variety of different authentication types, known as EAP methods. EAP was standardized by the Internet Engineering Task Force (IETF) in March 1999 [8]. Among the EAP methods developed specifically for wireless networks are a family of methods based on public key certificates and the transport layer security (TLS) protocol. These are extensible authentication protocol transport layer security (EAP-TLS) and the extensible authentication protocol tunneled transport layer security (EAP-TTLS).

EAP-TLS uses the TLS public key certificate authentication mechanism within EAP to provide mutual authentication of client-to-server and server-to-client [20]. With EAP-TLS, both the client and the server must be assigned a digital certificate signed by a certificate authority (CA) that they both trust. The EAP-TLS key system uses dynamic wired equivalent privacy (WEP) or temporal key integrity protocol (TKIP) keys. EAP-TLS uses a TLS handshake as the basis for mutual authentication [20]. EAP-TTLS has been implemented in some remote authentication dial-in user service (RADIUS) servers and supplicant software designed for use in 802.11 WLAN networks. In EAP-TLS, a TLS handshake is used to mutually authenticate a client and server [12]. EAP-TTLS extends this authentication negotiation by using the secure connection established by the TLS handshake to exchange additional information between client and server. In EAP-TTLS, the TLS handshake may be mutual, or it may be one-way, in which only the server is authenticated to the client. The secure connection established by the handshake may then be used to allow the server to authenticate the client using existing, widely deployed authentication infrastructures such as RADIUS [12].

AUTHORIZATION

After the user has proven who they present themselves to be, the next step is to provide authorization. Authorization is the granting of access to network resources and services, and entails restricting internal resources from users; it also determines access control [12]. In order to provide a complete authentication function in the wireless cloud system, three categories of an authorization sub-function have to be implemented: establishment, operations, and management. The first process is the establishment function; that is, those related to successfully initiating the function and getting it running correctly. The second is the operations functions, which are the ones that the authorization function performs to carry out its business purpose. The third category is the maintenance function, which deals with keeping the authorization operating properly.

Establishment Functions

The authorization process for the wireless cloud has to be pre-provisioned with the necessary values and information so that it can execute and deliver results. Figure 7 provides the Establishment Functions for the Wireless Cloud Authorization process.

The first step in the authorization process is to establish the pattern of the data being received. Once received, the provision identity (ID)

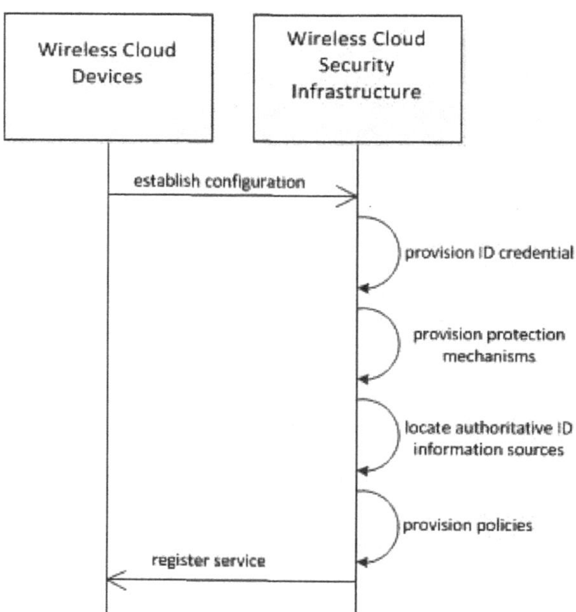

Figure 7. Establishment Process

credential process identifies the identity credential (e.g., PKI certificate) for its own use, so that it can be identified and authenticated in the system. This may come from a wireless identity management and/or credential management function. The protection mechanism has to protect the information it handles, both in transit and at rest. This might include cryptographic key material with which to encrypt and decrypt data. Trust anchors, with which to validate messages and signatures, have algorithms and signature key material to provide integrity.

Next, the locate authoritative ID information sources discovers the location within the system of enterprise services with which the function has to interact. In addition, this sub-function discovers the location of all authoritative sources with which the authentication function has to interact including the identification of specific types of content for each source and the materials necessary to validate that the source of transactions with each of these authoritative sources can be validated. The provision policies sub-function downloads any digital policy updates and installs and updates those policy updates. Finally, the register service makes the authorization function discoverable across the system. This should be the last establishment sub-function to be executed.

Operations Functions

Once the authorization function is established in a wireless cloud system, it can carry out its processing purpose. Figure 8 provides the Operations Functions for the Wireless Cloud Authentication process.

Once data is received, processing input messages come into the authorization function requesting a particular service (e.g., authorization of an entity, authorization of the source of the message, etc.). The first step is always for arriving messages to be processed to ensure that the message integrity is validated; that the message can be correctly decrypted if it is encrypted; that the message source can be authorized, if required, and that the message source is authorized to send such a message. If all tests pass, the message is passed to the main authorization function. A request to authorize an entity in the system will contain a claimed identity, and an authorization value showing that the entity is claimed identity. Depending on the system used, the authorization value will be a string signed or encrypted with the private key, to prove possession of the private key.

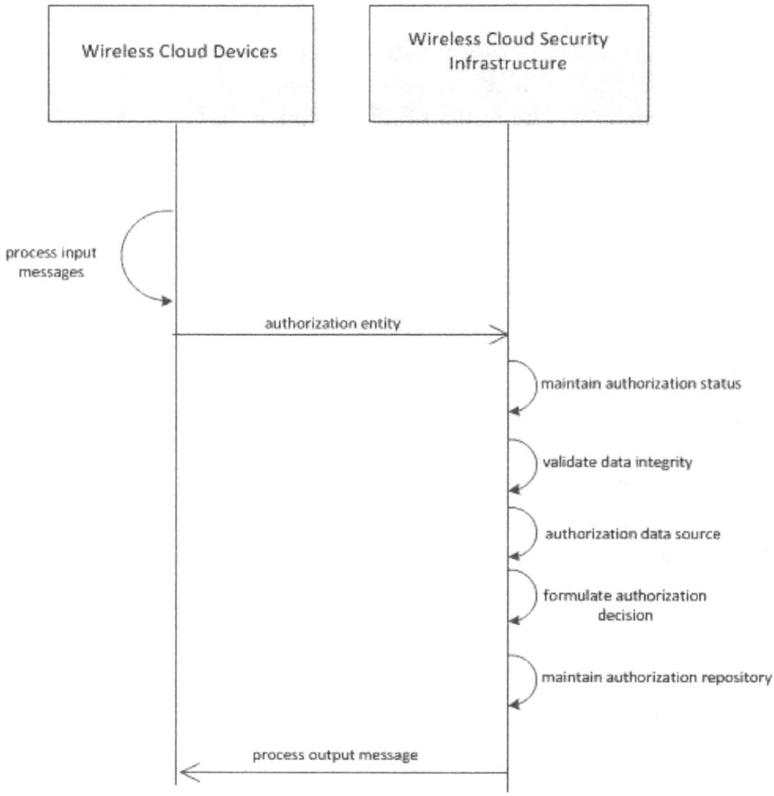

Figure 8. Operations Process

Next, maintaining the authorization status will track whether entities are currently authorized in the system. When an entity is authorized, this sub-function enters a record in the authorization repository. Policies dictate the parameters of the authorization (e.g., it is valid for 24 hours before re-authorization is required; it automatically expires after 10 minutes, etc.). This sub-function keeps a registry of all current and recently expired authorizations and can tell other functions when a new authorization is required. Validating data integrity determines whether any of the data contained in the message has been changed. Possible mechanisms that can be used include cyclic redundancy checks, hashed message authentication checks, and digital signatures.

Authorization of data source will require two steps to perform a source of authorization: (1) validating the integrity of the data to ensure it has not changed and (2) authorizing the entity that is the purported source of data. Calculating the assurance level calculates an assurance value for an entity authorization and passes it back to the requestor. Authorization decisions can be stronger or weaker based on a number of factors, including the type of authorization (e.g., two-factor authorization should be stronger than single-factor authorization), protection provided to the authorization channel (e.g., whether it is possible that an attacker copied a reusable authorization value, or injected a false value into the channel) and protection provided to the authorization database (e.g., whether it is possible that an attacker removed the true authorization value from the database and replaced it with a false one).

Finally, formulating the authorization decision takes the responses from the other sub-function and creates a response message that can be sent to the requestor. Maintaining the authorization repository needs a local repository for its own use, to store its policies, authorization decisions, and current authorization values. The process output message is responsible for determining the destination of a message and protecting it according to policy (e.g., encryption, integrity protection, digital signature).

Management Functions

Management functions are performed concurrently with operations functions. Management functions are those concerned with the health and functioning of the authorization function, rather than performing the purpose of the authorization function. Figure 9 provides the Maintenance Functions for the Wireless Cloud Authorization process.

As with procedures messages, all management messages must be processed to decrypt them if necessary and to determine their integrity source and the source's authorization. When a condition is detected that is not considered a normal condition, an exception is deemed to have occurred. In this case, the authorization function's maintenance must report the exception condition (e.g., system administer); determine the appropriate options (e.g., rebooting the system, restarting a process); and take action to restore the authorization function to normal operations.

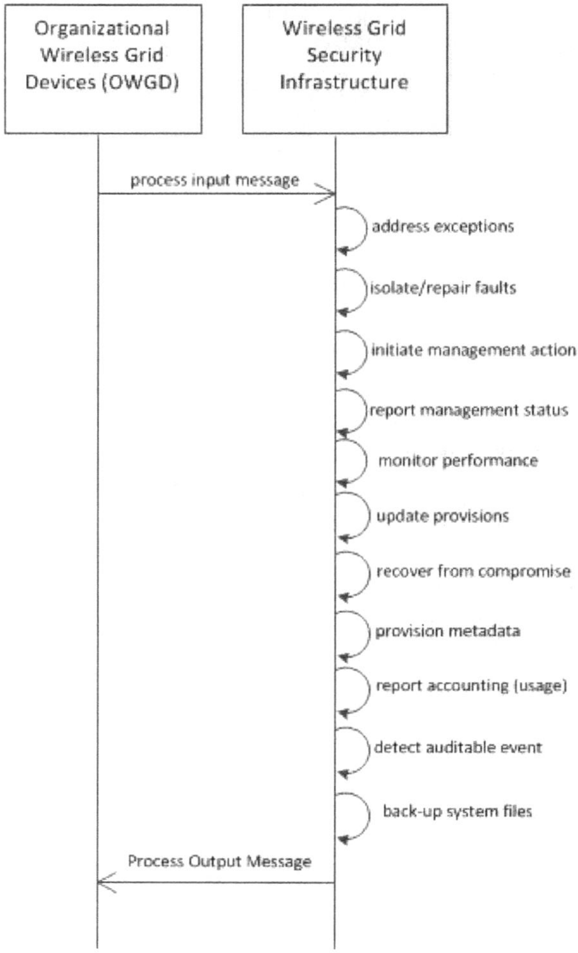

Figure 9. Management Functions

Authorization's fault process must include provisions to identify malfunctions or failures of the function mechanisms and resources (e.g., transport) upon which the function relies and initiate an appropriate means of remedying the situation while ensuring ongoing operations during the failure. The remedy may be initiating a repair action, activation of, or cutover to some space or stand-by capability, or some combination. When a fault has occurred, or performance has degraded below some acceptable level, a management action, whether automated or human-in-the-loop, must be started to address the issue.

In response to requests, the report management status can report on usage, detected faults, performance anomalies, management action status, provision status, incident status, response status, and other values. Monitoring performance monitors key performance indicators as specified in policies and reports or takes other action when performance degradation occurs, regardless of the cause. Updating provisions is responsible for reporting the status of and updating when necessary, any of a number of key values, including policies, configuration items, key materials, etc.

The recovery from compromise sub-function responds to the determination that a compromise to the system has occurred or suspicion that one has occurred. It includes capabilities to determine the impact of the compromise, identification of options for mitigating the effect of the compromise, and selection and execution of the mitigation response option. The provision metadata function initiates the discovery of metadata schemas required to assign valid discovery and metadata values from messages generated by the authorization function.

The report accounting (usage) sub-function maintains usage logs indicating when the authorization function is online and available as well as parameters and statistics about transactions. Examples of these parameters include the number of request transactions, specific requester and transaction requests, time of transaction occurrence, and the amount of time required before a response is initiated. The detect auditable event sub-function identifies the occurrence of events that specified by an audit policy. Upon detection, this function will generate an audit log event record, which it will protect and archive internally. Based on another input of digital policy, it will report the audit records. Finally, the backup systems files create and archive all information necessary to reconstitute or re-initialize the operation status of the authorization function. Just as for operational messages, processing output messages is responsible for determining the destination of a message and protecting it according to policy (e.g., encryption, integrity protection, digitally signing it).

ACCESS CONTROL

Wireless cloud access control deals with the processes and procedures to verify that an authenticated and authorized cloud computing/wireless grid system entity is assigned to a role (e.g., retrieve data, process data, store data, etc.). The system entity must have the authorizations needed to use or access a system resource and decide whether to permit access to information or execution of an operation based on wireless cloud security policy and the operational context of the entity. The system should only permit pre-selected entities which have access based on a wireless cloud access control list (WCACL). A WCACL[8] is operated and maintained by applications or data repositories to provide security management capabilities for wireless cloud access control activities.

A critical feature of any access control mechanism is the recording of transactions (processes accomplished) and events (unexpected occurrences) for subsequent audit or other analysis by a system or security management activities [29, 48, 56]. Systems implementing access control decision points must incorporate logging of transactions and events [62]. Systems implementing access control decision points must ensure the integrity of their transaction and event logs both in storage and in transmission [27]. Depending upon the log content, confidentially protection may also be required for storage and transmission. Figure 10 displays the Wireless Grid Access Control process:

Once an authenticated and authorized system entity invokes a session,[9] the system entity selects a wireless cloud point-of-service (e.g., sensor network) to contact based on what task they wish to accomplish. The entity's identifier (e.g., PKI certificate, etc.) is securely passed to the point-of-service. The identifier enables where the entity is physically located, the associated risk to information, and any security policy constraints or mandates associated with the location. To obtain system entity roles (and the authorizations associated with those roles) the wireless cloud point-of-service forwards via a secure path the entity's identity to the wireless cloud security infrastructure.

[8]The WCACL list would possibly include a list of authorized entities like system usernames and passwords, provide integrity protection for this information and may provide confidentiality protection for this information depending upon the function of the system.

[9]A session refers to the series of interactions between the entity and the point-of-service, plus all actions within the enterprise resulting from the entity's invocation of the particular point-of-service. The session ends when the entity receives their requested products or services and then terminates interaction with the particular point-of-service.

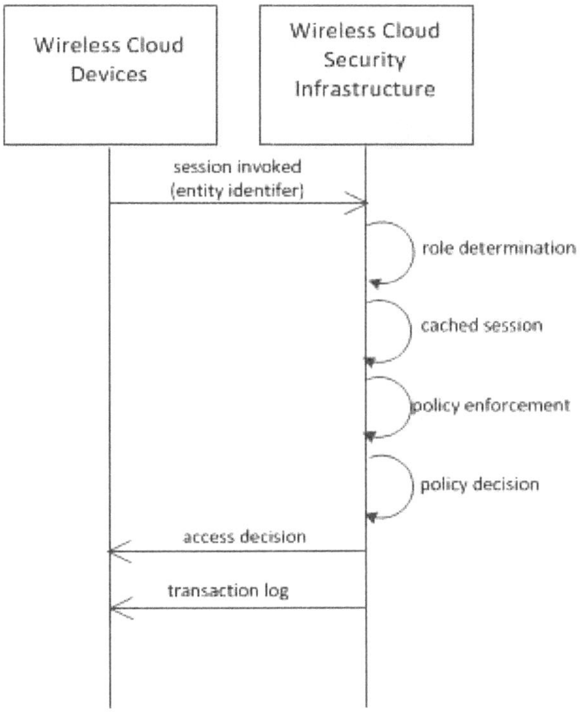

Figure 10. Access Control

Using the past entity identity, the wireless cloud security infrastructure looks up the roles (and associated authorizations) the entity has been assigned to for this particular process and returns, by secure means, the entity's roles (and associated authorizations) to the point-of-service. The wireless cloud security infrastructure caches the session parameters (entity identity, roles involved, etc.) for the duration of the functional session.

Simultaneously, the wireless cloud policy enforcement cross-checks this entity identity against the cache of other active sessions the same entity has underway to ensure the entity is not invoking mutually exclusive roles or triggering other policy concerns. If the additional role would cause a violation of security policy, a notification is sent to the wireless cloud point-of-service handling the offending role. In turn, the functional portal caches the entity's role (and authorizations) for the duration of the session and securely forwards the system entity's role-based authorizations when initiating interaction with any additional organizational capabilities (e.g., applications, query services, data brokers, etc.). All requests forwarded to these capabilities are within the entity's role-based authorizations and restrict all information flowing back to the system entity within the entity's role-based authorizations. The system then notifies the wireless cloud security infrastructure upon completion or termination of the entity's session with the wireless cloud point-of-service and logs all of the transactions for subsequent policy compliance audit or other analysis.

In some cases, authentication, authorization, and access control could be accomplished solely by a wireless point-of-service at the interface, allowing a system entity access only to those capabilities specifically authorized by the entity's role. In other cases, a combination of authentication, authorization, and access control points might be needed with multiple information brokers tailoring repository queries to ensure only role-allowable responses. An information broker interface, followed by an application review of the aggregated information and an operational system check by the wireless cloud, will initiate the information retrievals and forward the results through the wireless point-of-service to the entity.

To summarize, creating a wireless cloud must ensure adequate protection for information, systems, and sources. There must be flexibility in both the location and nature of the wireless cloud authentication, authorization, and access control decisions. To these ends, the wireless cloud may have to accommodate these decisions at many locations as well as at the interfaces between the receiving organization and external parties or other enterprises.

RECOMMENDATIONS

The wireless cloud system, applications, or services must include a defined set of authentication, authorization, and access control options appropriate for all possible use cases and sufficiently robust enough to ensure security policy compliance in a combined cloud computing/wireless grid environment. Alternative approaches must be considered and evaluated during system design rather than pre- or post-deployment. In some cases, the best option will be for the wireless cloud system itself to make all authentication, authorization, and access control decisions.

In other cases, the wireless cloud will need to rely on other systems or the information enterprise infrastructure for some or all of the required authentication, authorization, and access control processes.

Regarding the security issues addressed in this chapter, the following section provides some key wireless cloud architecture recommendations that will help to make the wireless cloud a more trusted computing platform.

Identity and Access Management Policies

Identity and access management (IAM) policies, contracts, and mechanisms must guide the process of determining which devices (and their respective users) in the wireless grid have the ability to access applications and/or data residing in the wireless cloud. Identity provisioning enables cloud service providers to securely on-board and off-board cloud users in a timely manner [65]. Setting up a robust identity provisioning platform will facilitate access management and control while enabling quick responses to requests for service access and termination. The authentication schema chosen must work across all cloud services, mesh with the customer's IAM schema for non-cloud services, and work on all devices connected to the wireless cloud.

Cloud customers will have the responsibility for creating, following, and maintaining IAM practices, policies, and procedures. The action or inaction of any one user of the wireless cloud in this key area has implications for all users. Extending IAM to the cloud takes careful planning and consideration of the user's current and future internal IAM platform. Cloud providers and wireless cloud architects must form partnerships to establish IAM policies, procedures, and contracts that will support the interoperable use of cloud services across organizations within the wireless grid. Such support is needed at the SaaS, PaaS, and IaaS service model levels. Assisting customers with IAM planning is likely to send a message to potential customers and current skeptics that providers are focused on security and privacy and are willing to play a part in protecting the services they provide against unauthorized access. Wireless cloud architects and cloud provider collaborations could potentially lead to the establishment of authoritative guidance on issues, such as IAM, as it relates to both the wireless cloud and cloud computing in general which would also lead to greater trust in this computing paradigm.

Encryption, Key Management and Cryptographic Inclusion

Some of the biggest fears that potential customers have related to cloud computing are data malicious alteration or deletion of data and files, data theft, and data loss and interception by unintended parties. In multi-tenant virtualized cloud environments, where data is managed by a third party, there is always a need to protect confidential data. In a wireless environment, the information that is communicated and passed between network nodes travels across standard radio frequencies that are vulnerable to being tapped by unintended third parties. Authentication and encryption have to work together to prevent eavesdropping as data moves across wireless networks and to make sure that sensitive information is transmitted across a legitimate network. In addition to protecting data already in the wireless cloud, customers need assurance that their credit card numbers, passwords, individual user identity, and cloud service identity information will remain secure while traveling over the Internet and between the grid and the cloud or sitting at rest on devices connected to the grid. Encryption and key management will be implemented by wireless cloud architects using the technologies and standards described earlier.

Cryptography uses mathematics to code and decode digital information, transactions, and digital computations [30]. By implementing cryptography in the cloud, providers can protect grid wireless organizations from malicious co-tenants and exploitable processes in the cloud by scrambling data so that it cannot be understood by unintended parties. Providers should offer encryption tools to IaaS customers that allow them to both encrypt data before sending it to the cloud for storage and decrypt data once it is retrieved from storage and back on the customer's premises. PaaS offerings should include standard tools to protect data at rest and/or in memory. SaaS customers should be told upfront that the provider alone has the ability to encrypt data at rest in the cloud [65].

Encryption service and support should be offered at the SaaS level to wireless cloud users without having to ask for it. In addition, cloud providers should do everything possible to support robust key management schemes where key stores are secure and keys in storage, in transit, and in the backup cannot be intercepted or stolen by unintended parties. Key stores inside the cloud should be managed in such a way that access to individual keys is limited to the entities that legitimately need them. Also, the roles of entities that use keys should be kept separate from the roles of entities that store them. Along with key storage policies, cloud service providers should have strong key generation and destruction policies as well as secure key backup and recovery capabilities.

It is undeniable that data security vulnerabilities are magnified when wireless grids are layered on top of cloud services and a robust solution to deal with these vulnerabilities is needed. However, making sure that data is of no use to unintended parties goes a long way in mollifying the impact of a data breach in the wireless cloud if it does occur. Until the cloud industry is able to come up with standards and end-to-end technology solutions that protect data at rest, in use, and in transit, wireless cloud architects and cloud providers should work together to build and maintain robust key management and encryption policies and practices.

Provenance

Increased data and service transparency in the cloud is another impediment to widespread cloud adoption. Many potential customers are reluctant to utilize the cloud because of the downside of rapid service provisioning: the inability of cloud providers to provide detailed information about data (e.g., movement, geographical storage location, multi-tenant/co-location information, etc.), which wireless cloud administrators will need in order to meet certain audit requirements. Provenance is a first step in that direction. Provenance is metadata that describes the origins of a digital object [47]. Service providers can use provenance to detect access patterns and unusual behavior as well as to improve offerings. Wireless cloud administrators and users can utilize provenance to keep track of data, comply with audit standards/requirements, and search through data even when it is encrypted. Commercial cloud providers, such as Amazon, Microsoft, and Nirvanix, provide some ability for customers to create, store, and retrieve provenance metadata from their own host devices. However, these providers are unable to automatically generate and store provenance data [47]. The responsibility for doing so belongs to the user of the cloud services. In order to make use of the provenance, wireless cloud organizations must subscribe to the cloud provider's database service so that provenance information generated by devices connected to the cloud can be stored. The organization can then use either client software or a software application built on top of the provider's database service to search through provenance data.

Provenance in the cloud is still under research and currently has some limitations. Unresolved questions related to the use of provenance include how to prevent users from providing false provenance, how to protect provenance from forgery or destruction, how to ensure data provenance consistency with the object it describes, and how to properly retain provenance (e.g., when the data object it describes no longer exists or is connected to unrelated objects [47]. As researchers, cloud providers, and consumers of cloud services work together to answer these questions the true potential of provenance is still unknown. The wireless cloud stands as a new use case for cloud computing and may introduce new issues related to the use of provenance in a distributed wireless environment. Wireless cloud architects should join the discussions around provenance and the potential benefits and challenges of using it in the wireless cloud.

Addressing Privacy during the Development/Selection of Wireless Cloud Services

As it stands, many see privacy as more of an afterthought than a forethought in the minds of cloud providers and software developers that design cloud services. For some major commercial providers, such as Google, cloud computing started out as a way to leverage and monetize excess capacity in data centers. In doing so these providers paid less attention to privacy and security and more attention to producing a marketable service offering when the cloud computing paradigm first developed. Currently, researchers such as Pearson [55], are pointing out the fallacy in that approach by saying that privacy should be considered during the development stage of new offerings.

According to Pearson [55], cloud service developers have a responsibility to follow design and development practices that avoid basic design and implementation flaws that can later lead to privacy violations. These practices include the following: (1) designing services that keep the amount of personal information sent to and stored in the cloud to a minimum; (2) giving users maximum control over who and under what circumstances personal data in the cloud can be accessed, managed, and changed; (3) providing a means for providers to make certain that personal data is being handled according to user specifications; and (4) providing feedback to customers and users on how personal data is being used and protected. Wireless cloud architects must serve as liaisons between cloud service providers and wireless grid organizations when it comes to privacy, particularly when the wireless cloud is being developed.

The privacy measures embedded in the wireless cloud should be seamless, complementary, and comprehensive. Wireless cloud architects must be sure to design interfaces between the provider and the grid environments that monitor the movement of data from and to the cloud as well as make use of any information the provider can or will one day be able to give concerning the use and protection of personal/confidential data in the cloud. Also, when choosing services from a cloud service provider wireless grid organizations should discuss privacy expectations with service providers. Rather than assume that data privacy is guaranteed by the service provider the organization must be diligent about understanding what the provider is and is not responsible for and what can be done by the adopting organization to ensure the privacy of wireless cloud user data.

CONCLUSION

This chapter discussed the implications of developing a wireless cloud and potential security threats from this architectural construct. It identified some of the academic literature around cloud computing and wireless grids, reviewed a conceptual model of a wireless cloud architecture, identified potential vulnerabilities in the wireless cloud, identified a proposed security solution for the wireless cloud and briefly discussed authorization policy issues, and developed a generic authentication/authorization process pertaining to its security architecture. The use of cloud computing and wireless grid integration for creating the wireless cloud should only exist in the context of clear business values and technical fit, including adherence to defined security and privacy standards.

The move to a wireless cloud architecture could potentially meet the business needs and service expectations of business users. This new platform could one day become a cost-effective solution, leading to a positive return on investment (ROI) for organizations. As part of an organization's transition to a wireless cloud environment, it will be important that organizations evaluate the potential cost-effectiveness to ensure that their IT funds are used wisely and to comply with management requirements. The positive ROI will likely be derived from reduced operational costs resulting from shared infrastructure and resources (e.g., hardware and software costs, staff resource costs, etc.). This aspect of the wireless cloud solution will require further research.

Critical to the success of transitioning to a wireless cloud is the requirement for cloud providers to ensure the continuum of data protection for their customers. Cloud providers must investigate new data-protection mechanisms to secure data privacy, resource security, and content copyrights [14]. Wireless cloud customers will face unique challenges not only in satisfying security imperatives but also privacy imperatives. Privacy in the wireless cloud considers the individual's contractual and statutory rights to control his or her own information, including decisions about submitting, using, disclosing, and protecting the data.

Wireless cloud customers must realize that using a wireless cloud will change how they define their system security boundaries. For example, how can they know that the integrity and confidentiality of their data are sufficiently protected? Data protection mechanisms need to be re-evaluated in the customer's own security strategy and the wireless cloud provider's architecture, to ensure that adequate self-protection of data (i.e., building protection into the data itself using cryptographic techniques), event and violation auditing and logging, disclosure/non-disclosure policies, and reporting, etc., are all included. Cloud customers must understand that their data protection needs will need to be addressed at the information security level to ensure their cloud-based data processing, storage, and transmission systems and applications operate as effectively and efficiently as their counterparts in traditional computing environments. This is especially true for ensuring the continuity of critical processes and operations.

Despite the challenges a wireless cloud introduces, none of the security requirements identified within this chapter are entirely new. Further research on wireless cloud security will help reduce risks, but it must be combined with security architecture, policy, governance, risk management, and risk mitigation. Successful, secure migration to a wireless cloud will require understanding cloud and wireless grid technologies and evolving government policies to adopt a comprehensive transition methodology and more collaboration between the cloud providers, wireless grid experts, community partners, and wireless networking security experts.

Critical to the success of a wireless cloud will be the ability to explore the possibility of cloud computing and wireless grid integration.

Future research areas around leveraging this type of architecture include addressing the following:

- How does threat exposure change when using a wireless cloud?
- How are the security responsibilities divided between cloud providers and wireless grid developers?
- What properties of a wireless cloud cause major security challenges?
- What properties of a wireless cloud result in major security advantages?
- What are the security controls I should expect to see in a wireless cloud?

For confidence in a wireless cloud implementation, the need to have sufficient visibility to see who was doing what and how across the infrastructure is paramount. This means the use of governance, or the ability to monitor, manage, and control, all aspects of the architecture, including the ability to trace issues with security down to the sources of the problems. Understanding that a wireless cloud architecture creates risks and requires a rethinking — but not reinvention — of security controls and architecture. However, with some forethought and planning, a wireless cloud computing-based system can be just as secure, if not more secure, as a traditional wired system.

REFERENCES

[1] Agarwal, A., Norman, D., & Gupta, A. (2004). Wireless *Grids: Approaches, Architectures and Technical Challenges.* Working Paper 4459-04, MIT Sloan School of Management.

[2] Ahuja, S. & Myers, J. (2006). A survey on wireless grid computing. *Journal of Supercomputing*, 37(1), 3–21.

[3] Armbrust, M., Fox, A., Griffith, R., Joseph, A.D., Katz, R., Konwinski, A., Lee, G., Rabkin, A., Stoica, I., & Zaharia, M. (2009). Above the *Clouds: A Berkeley View of Cloud Computing*. Technical Report No. UCB/EECS-2009-28. Electrical Engineering and Computer Sciences, University of California at Berkeley. http://www.eecs.berkeley.edu/Pubs/TechRpts/2009/EECS-2009-28.pdf.

[4] Aymerich, F., Fenu, G., & Surcis, S. (2008). An approach to a cloud computing network. In *Proceedings of the First International Conference on the Applications of Digital Information and Web Technologies* (pp. 113–118).

[5] Bernard, S. & Ho, S. (2008). Enterprise architecture as context and method for designing and implementing information security and data privacy controls in government agencies. In Saha, P. (Ed.), *Advances in Government Enterprise Architecture* (pp. 340–370), IGI Global, Hershey, Pennsylvania.

[6] Bishop, M. (2003). *Computer Security. Art and Science*. Addison-Wesley, Boston, MA, USA.

[7] Buyya, R., Yeo, C., Venugopal, S., Broberg, J., & Brandic, I. (2009). Cloud computing and emerging IT platforms: Vision, hype, and reality for delivering computing as the 5th utility. *Future Generation Computer Systems*, 25(6), 599–616.

[8] Bradner, S. (1999). The internet engineering task force. In Chris DiBona, Sam Ockman, & Mark Stone (Eds.), *Open Sources: Voices from the Open Source Revolution* (pp. 47–52). O'Reilly, Sebastopol, Calif.

[9] Closs, D. & McGarrell, E. (2004). *Enhancing Security throughout the Supply Chain* (pp. 1–52). IBM Center for Business of Government, Michigan, Michigan State University.

[10] Chan, H. & Perrig, A. (2003). Security and privacy in sensor networks. *IEEE Computer*, 36(10), 103–105.

[11] Chen, Y., Paxson, V., & Katz, R. (2010). *What's New about Cloud Computing Security?* Technical Report UCB/EECS-2010-5, EECS Department, University of California, Berkeley.

[12] Chen, J. & Wang, Y. (2005). Extensible authentication protocol (EAP) and IEEE 802.1x: Tutorial and empirical experience. *IEEE Communications Magazine*, 43(12), 26–32.

[13] CNSS Instruction 4009. (2010). National information assurance glossary. Committee on National Security Systems. http://www.cnss.gov/Assets/pdf/cnssi_4009.pdf.

[14] Dikaiakos, M., Katsaros, D., Mehra, P., Pallis, G., & Vakali. A. (2009). Cloud computing: Distributed internet computing for IT and scientific research. *IEEE Internet Computing*, 13(5), 10–13.

[15] Ekanayake, J., Qiu, X., Gunarathne, T., Beason, S., & Fox, G. (2010). High performance parallel computing with clouds and cloud technologies. In *Cloud Computing and Software Services: Theory and Techniques*. CRC Press (Taylor and Francis), CRC Press (Taylor and Francis), Boca Raton, Florida.

[16] Foster, I. (2002). What is the grid? A three point checklist. *GRIDToday*, 1(6).

[17] Foster, I., Kesselman, C., & Tuecke, S. (2001). The anatomy of the grid: Enabling scalable virtual organizations. *International Journal of Supercomputer Applications*, 15(3), 200–222.

[18] Foster, I., Kishimoto, H., Savva, A., Berry, D., Grimshaw, A., Horn, B., Maciel, F., Siebenlist, F., Subramaniam, R., Treadwell, J., & Von Reich, J. (2006). The open grid services architecture, version 1.5. http://www.ggf.org/documents/GFD.80.pdf.

[19] Foster, I., Kesselman, C., Nick, J., & Tuecke, S. (2003). The physiology of the grid. In Berman, F., Hey, A., & Fox, G. (Eds.), *Grid Computing — Making the Global Infrastructure a Reality* (pp. 217–249). John Wiley and Sons, Ltd., Hoboken, New Jersey.

[20] Funk, P. & Blake-Wilson, S. (2008). Extensible authentication protocol tunneled transport layer security authenticated protocol version 0 (EAP-TTLSv0). RFC 5281, Internet Engineering Task Force. http://www.ietf.org/.

[21] Gaynor, M., Moulton, S., Welsh, M., LaCombe, E., Rowan, A., & Wynne, J. (2004). Integrating wireless sensor networks with the grid. *IEEE Internet Computing*, 8(4), 32–39.

[22] Hendrickson, L. & Piotrowski, V. (2004). Wireless security: From WEP to 802.11i. http://www.micsymposium.org/mics_2004/Hendrick.pdf.

[23] Hoffa, C., Mehta, G., Freeman, T., Deelman, E., Keahey, K., Berriman, B., & Good, J. (2008). On the use of cloud computing for scientific workflows. In *ESCIENCE '08: Proceedings of the 2008 Fourth IEEE International Conference on eScience* (pp. 640–645). IEEE Computer Society.

[24] Institute of Electrical and Electronics Engineers, Inc. (IEEE) Std 802.11 — Wireless LAN Medium Access Control (MAC) and Physical Layer (PHY) Specifications (1999). IEEE, Inc. http://www.ieee.org/index.html.

[25] Jaeger, P., Lin, J., & Grimes, J. (2008). Cloud computing and information policy: Computing in a policy cloud? *Journal of Information Technology & Politics*, 5(3), 269–283. http://www.jitp.net/m_archive.php?p=7.

[26] Jajodia, S., Noel, S., & O'Berry, B. (2003). Topological analysis of network attack vulnerability. In V. Kumar, J. Srivastava, A. Lazarevic (Eds.), *Managing Cyber Threats: Issues, Approaches and Challenges* (Chapter 5). Kluwer Academic Publisher, Dordrecht, Netherlands.

[27] Jajodia, S., Samarati, P., Subrahmanian, V., & Bertino, E. (1997). A unified framework for enforcing multiple access control policies. *SIGMOD Record* (*ACM Special Interest Group on Management of Data*), 26(2), pp. 474–485.

[28] Jensen, M., Schwenk, J. O., Gruschka, N., & Iacono, L. (2009). On technical security issues in cloud computing. In *IEEE International Conference on Cloud Computing* (CLOUD-II 2009) (pp. 109–116). Bangalore, India.

[29] Johnson, H., Nilsson, A., Fu, J., Wu, S., Chen, A., & Huang, H. (2002). SOLA: A one-bit identity authentication protocol for access control in IEEE 802.11, In *Proceedings of IEEE Global Telecommunications Conference, 2002* (*GLOBECOM'02*) (Vol. 1, pp. 768–772).

[30] Katz, J. & Lindell, Y. (2008). *Introduction to modern cryptography*. Chapman & Hall/CRC; *Cryptography and Network Security*. Chapman & Hall/CRC, Boca Raton, FL.

[31] Kotz, D. & Baek, K. (2004). *A Survey of WPA and 802.11i RSN Authentication Protocols*. Technical Report TR2004-524, Dartmouth College, Computer Science, Hanover, NH, November 2004.

[32] Keahey, K., Figueiredo, R., Fortes, J., Freeman, T., & Tsugawa, M. (2008). Science clouds: Early experiences in cloud computing for scientific applications. In *Proceedings of the 1st Workshop on Cloud Computing and its Applications* (CCA), Chicago, USA.

[33] Khajeh-Hosseini, A., Sommerville, I., & Sriram, I. (2010). Research Challenges for Enterprise Cloud Computing, (unpublished). Submitted to *1st ACM Symposium on Cloud Computing*. Indianapolis, Indiana, USA, under paper id 54.

[34] Klems, M., Nimis, J., & Tai, S. (2009). Do clouds compute? Framework for estimating the value of cloud computing. In Weinhardt, C., Luckner, S., & Stößer, J. (Eds.), *Lecture Notes in Business Information Processing* (Vol. 22, pp. 110–123). Springer, Berlin, Heidelberg.

[35] Lang, B., Foster, I., Siebenlist, F., Ananthakrishnan, R., & Freeman, T. (2006). A multipolicy authorization framework for grid security. In *Proceedings of the Fifth IEEE Symposium on Network Computing and Application*. Cambridge, MA, USA.

[36] Leavitt, N. (2009). Is cloud computing really ready for prime time? *Computer*, 42(1), 15–20.

[37] Lenk, A., Klems, M., Nimis, J., Tai, S., Karlsruhe, F., & Sandholm, T. (2009). What's inside the cloud? An architectural map of the cloud landscape. In *Proceedings of the 2009 ICSE Workshop on Software Engineering Challenges of Cloud Computing* (pp. 23–31). IEEE Computer Society.

[38] Li, G., Sun, H., Gao, H., Yu, H., & Cai, Y. (2009). A survey on wireless grids and clouds. In *Proceedings of the 8th IEEE International Conference on Grid and Cooperative Computing* (pp. 261–267).

[39] Lim, H., Babu, S., Chase, J., & Parekh, S. (2009). Automated control in cloud computing: Challenges and opportunities. In *Proceedings of the 1st Workshop on Automated Control for Datacenters and Clouds* (*ACDC'09*) (pp. 13–18). ACM, New York, NY, USA.

[40] Lohr, H., Ramasamy, H., Sadeghi, A., Schulz, S., Schunter, M., & Stuble, C. (2007). Enhancing grid security using trusted virtualization. In *Autonomic and Trusted Computing, Lecture Notes in Computer Science* (pp. 372–384). Springer, Berlin, Heidelberg.

[41] Ma, Q. & Pearson, J. (2005). ISO 17799: Best practices in information security management? *Communications of the Association for Information Systems*, 15, Chapter 32.

[42] Manvi, S. & Birje, M. (2010). A review on wireless grid computing. *International Journal of Computer and Electrical Engineering*, 2(3), 469–474.

[43] Menesez, A., van Oorschot, P., & Vanstone, S. (1997). *Handbook of Applied Cryptography*. CRC Press, Boca Raton, Florida.

[44] McKnight, L., Howison, J., & Bradner, S. (2004). Wireless grids: Distributed resource sharing by mobile, nomadic, and fixed devices. *IEEE Internet Computing*, 8(4), 24–31.

[45] McKnight, L., Sharif, R., & van de Wijngaert, L. (2005). Wireless grids: Assessing a new technology for a user perspective. In *Designing Ubiquitous Information Environments: Socio-technical Issues and Challenges* (pp. 169–181). Springer.

[46] Mell, P. & Grance, T. (2009). The NIST definition of cloud computing, verison 15. National Institute of Standards and Technology. http://csrc.nist.gov/groups/SNS/cloud-computing/cloud-def-v15.doc.

[47] Muniswamy-Reddy, K.-K. & Seltzer, M. (2010). Provenance as first class cloud data. *ACM SIGOPS Operating Systems Review*, 43(4), 11–16.

[48] Nanz, S. & Hankin, C. (2006). A framework for security analysis of mobile wireless networks. *Theoretical Computer Science*, 367(1–2), 203–227.

[49] Nagaratnam, N., Janson, P., Dayka, J., Nadalin, A., Siebenlist, F., Welch, V., Foster, I., & Tuecke, S. (2002). The security architecture for open grid services. Open Grid Service Architecture Security Working Group (OGSA-SEC-WG). http://citeseerx.ist.psu.edu/viewdoc/download?doi=10.1.1.98.5693&rep=rep1&type=pdf.

[50] Naedele, M. (2003). Standards for XML and web services security. *Computer*, 36(4), 96–98.

[51] Onwubiko, C. & Lenaghan, A. (2007). Managing security threats and vulnerabilities for small to medium enterprises. In *Proceedings of the 2007 IEEE International Conference on Intelligence and Security Informatics* (s.244). New Brunswick, NJ.

[52] Ostermann, S., Iosup, A., Yigitbasi, N., Prodan, R., Fahringer, T., & Epema, D. (2008). *An Early Performance Analysis of Cloud Computing Services for Scientific Computing*. TU Delft, Technical Report. http://pds.twi.tudelft.nl/reports/2008/PDS-2008-006.pdf.

[53] Park, J. & Sandhu, R. (2002). Towards usage control models: Beyond traditional access control. In *Proceedings of the Seventh ACM Symposium on Access Control Models and Technologies* (*SACMAT'02*) (pp. 57–64).

[54] Park, J. & Sandhu, R. (1999). Smart Certificates: Extending X.509 for Secure Attribute Services. In *Proceedings of the 22nd National Information Systems Security Conference* (*NISSC*). Crystal City, Virginia, USA.

[55] Pearson, S. (2009). Taking account of privacy when designing cloud computing services. In *Proceedings of the 2009 ICSE Workshop on Software Engineering Challenges of Cloud Computing* (pp. 44–52).

[56] Perrig, A., Stankovic, J., & Wagner, D. (2004). Security in wireless sensor networks. *Communication of the ACM*, 47(6), 53–57.

[57] Phan, T., Huang, L., & Dulan, C. (2002). Integrating wireless devices into the computational grid. In *Proceedings of the 8th Annual International*

Conference on Mobile Computing and Networking (*MOBICOM 2002*) (pp. 271–278).

[58] Raghunathan, A., Potlapally, N., & Ravi, S. (2002). Securing wireless data: System architecture challenges. In *Proceedings of the ISSS 2002* (pp. 195–200).

[59] Rimal, B., Choi, E., & Lumb, I. (2009). A taxonomy and survey of cloud computing systems. In *Proceedings of the Fifth International Joint Conference on INC, IMS and IDC* (pp. 44–51). IEEE.

[60] Rochwerger, B., Breitgand, D., Levy, E., Galis, A., & Nagin, K. (2009). The reservoir model and architecture for open federated cloud computing. *IBM Systems Journal*, 53, 4.

[61] Rosado, D., Fernández-Medina, E., López, J., & M. Piattini (2010). Analysis of secure mobile grid systems: A systematic approach. *Information and Software Technology*, 52, 517–536.

[62] Sandhu, R., Coyne, E., Feinstein, H., & Youman, C. (1996). Role-based access control models. *IEEE Computer*, 29(2), 38–47.

[63] Sandhu, R. & Munawer, Q. (1998). How to do discretionary access control using roles. In *Proceedings of the Third ACM Workshop on Role-based Access Control* (*RBAC'98*), Fairfax, VA, October 22–23), C. Youman and T. Jaeger, Chairs. ACM Press, New York, NY, pp. 47–54.

[64] Santos, N., Gummadi, K., & Rodrigues, R. (2009). Towards trusted cloud computing. In *Proceedings of the 1st USENIX workshop on hot topics in cloud computing*. Berkeley, CA, USA.

[65] Security Guidance for Critical Areas of Focus in Cloud Computing version 2.1. (2009). *Paper Presented at the 2009 RSA Conference*. http://www.cloudsecurityalliance.org/guidance/csaguide.v2.1.pdf.

[66] Snyder, A. (1995). *Warriors of Disinformation: American Propaganda, Soviet Lies, and the Winning of the Cold War, An Insider's Account*. Arcade Publishing, New York.

[67] The Global Alliance (2011). Globus ToolkitVersion 5.0.3. http://www.globus.org/toolkit/.

[68] Treglia, J., Ramnarine-Rieks, A., & McKnight, L. (2010). *Collaboration in a Wireless Grid Innovation Testbed by Virtual Consortium. Networks for Grid Applications*. Lecture Notes of the Institute for Computer Sciences, Social Informatics and Telecommunications Engineering (Vol. 25, p. 139). Springer, Berlin, Heidelberg.

[69] Vaquero, L., Merino, L., Caceres, J., & Lindner, M. (2008). A break in the clouds: Towards a cloud definition. *SIGCOMM Computer Communications Review*, 39(1), 50–55.

[70] Welch, D. & Lathrop, S. (2003). Wireless security threat taxonomy. In *Proceedings of the IEEE Systems, Man and Cybernetics Society Information Assurance Workshop* (pp. 76–83).

[71] Yang, H., Luo, H., Ye, F., Lu, S., & Zhang, L. (2004). Security in mobile ad hoc networks: Challenge and solutions. *IEEE Wireless Communications*, (11)1, 38–47.

[72] Yau, P. W. & Mitchell, C. J. (2003). Security vulnerabilities in *ad hoc* networks. In *Proceedings of the 7th International Symposium on Comms Theory and Applications* (*ISCTA'03*) (pp. 99–104). HW Communications Ltd.

[73] Yi, S., Naldurg, P., & Kravets, R. (2001). *Security-Aware Ad-Hoc Routing for Wireless Networks*, UIUCDCS-R- 2001- 2241v Technical Report. http://www-faculty.cs.uiuc.edu/~rhk/pubs/UIUCDCS-R-2001-2241.pdf.

Chapter 4

Securing Wireless Grids: Architecture Designs for Secure WiGLET-to-WiGLET Interfaces*

ABSTRACT

Wireless grids facilitate the *ad hoc*, dynamic sharing of physical and virtual resources among heterogeneous devices. For wireless grids to ensure security, the primary communication device, termed a WiGLET, must exercise precise control over the distribution of information exchanges among devices, while also accommodating new devices and resources that span various trust levels. The absence of trust in the WiGLET-to-WiGLET interface impairs its capacity to safeguard information and to cooperate with unanticipated devices during unforeseen events when such collaboration is crucial. It's not merely that the WiGLETs need to concur on the sensitivity level of the data; they also need to ascertain if they all interpret that sensitivity uniformly. This chapter identifies three distinct types of wireless grid architectures and delineates specific security considerations for each type concerning the WiGLET.

---

*Originally published as Brooks, T. & McKnight, L. (2012). Securing wireless grids: Architecture designs for secure WiGLET-to-WiGLET interfaces. *International Journal of Information and Network Security* (*IJINS*), 2(1), 336–351.

INTRODUCTION

There are two significant events occurring at this point in time that are affecting communications throughout the world. First, there has been increased activity to improve the security of network and computer systems on a global scale, both to ensure reliability as the internet becomes more open due to social networking sites and to ensure the confidentiality of these data exchanges [1]. Second, there is a movement to adopt wireless technologies, especially wireless grids, due to their agility in using existing devices and infrastructure [47]. Wireless grids are starting to emerge as a new type of resource-sharing network which will eventually connect sensors, mobile phones, and other edge devices with each other and with wired grids [31].

The wireless grid extends grid resources to wireless devices of varying sizes and capabilities such as sensors, mobile phones, laptops, special instruments, and edge devices [25, 32]. These devices might be statically located, mobile, or nomadic, shifting across institutional boundaries and connected to the grid via nearby devices such as desktops [3, 33]. Reference [3] identifies these grids as an augmentation of a wired grid that facilitates the exchange of information and the interaction between heterogeneous wireless devices. These grids will enable shared resources among dynamic groups or social networks of computing and communication devices and are composed of objects and resources with individual profiles that are assigned a specific status relative to similar objects and resources [30, 31]. Wireless grids can take ubiquitous computing to the next level by providing seamless wireless extensions to the wired grid. The security architecture for these types of grids is of importance because they can be deployed to provide autonomous nodes that communicate with each other in a decentralized manner and how each node of the network connects others with wireless links and acts as both a host and a router in sending and receiving data.

Under emerging wireless grid architecture, however, such network-based security models are far from adequate. These new systems will be about net-centric information sharing and collaborating business functionality which will become service-enabled and exposed to external wireless clients via standard web services type protocols. These wireless clients, which themselves may be applications, will dynamically discover services and make real-time use of their code and data. Their services will be inherently location-independent, not necessarily bound to a physical location which can change over time as services are relocated or for fail-over reasons. Since wireless grid clients and service providers may belong to different physical networks or even different service providers, these networks and/or organizations may be governed by entirely different security policies. This chapter identifies three different types of wireless grid architectures and specific security considerations for each type around the WiGLET.

SECURING THE WiGLET-TO-WiGLET ARCHITECTURE

The paradigm shift towards wireless collaboration and composition also brings fundamental changes to security architecture. A security architecture encompasses IT security and data privacy requirements as well as solutions within the context of an over-arching enterprise architecture [5]. Most existing security solutions today assume that both clients and servers are located on the same physical [e.g., local area network (LAN)] or logical [e.g., virtual private network (VPN)] network. They generally rely heavily on perimeter-based security such as demilitarized zone (DMZ), firewalls, and intrusion detection to thwart security threats [44]. Similarly, security policies behind those solutions are also to a large extent perimeter-based. For example, obtaining access to an application usually requires the creation of a new user account on the machine or network where the application is installed, plus granting the user physical access to the facility where the machine or network is located. By contrast, application/system level security is usually regarded as not quite as critical as network security and oftentimes enforced simply by a username/password. However, for a WiGLET within a wireless grid, this may not be the case.

A WiGLET (see Figure 1) is a wireless semantics-aware unit of workload division, computation off-load, and data related to the processing task which interacts directly with the wireless grid user interface (UI), the application program interface (API), the connection, messaging, permissions and metadata (CORE operations) employing resource management and accounting of devices directly through the interface layers of a wireless grid architecture [46, 47].

The vertical boxes in Figure 1 represent "Edgeware" applications that reside on a user interface, which in turn reside on an API, and may represent dozens or hundreds of different sorts of mini-programs that enable

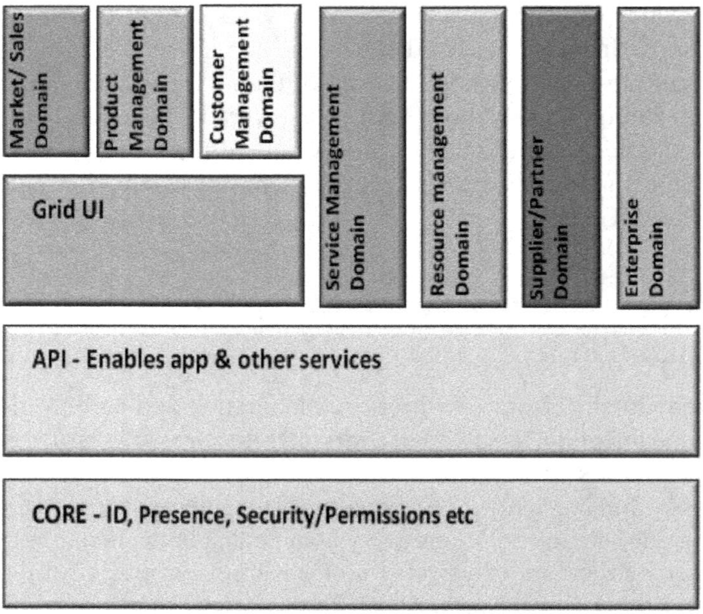

Figure 1. **WiGLET**

different kinds of resource sharing and functionality [34]. Wireless grids "Edgeware" technology sits at the outermost limits of existing networks, allowing all facets of a user's environment: printers, mp3, documents, photos, cell phones, PC and new plasma TV, etc. to be interoperated and shared easily [29, 47]. Other network hardware, software, services, and content may be controlled and shared through the wireless grid "Edgeware"; however, if those "edge" resources are in a relationship with other hardware, software, and services which are part of the wireless grid, they may function as if they were fully cognitive [34]. The Core components are embedded in certain devices or sensors depending on their capability, making every device a node on the wireless grid, extremely "light", easy to embed on a wide range of different kinds of equipment, and users are allowed to share and manage the digital resources at their fingertips through applications of the architecture's eight core components [34].

Reference [34] discusses that the wireless grid architecture core components handle four primary functions: management of identification (ID) and presence, permissions management, data transfer ability, and

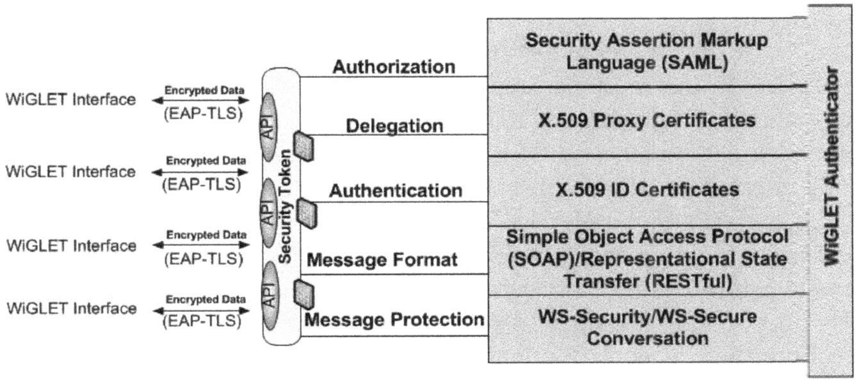

Figure 2. WiGLET Security Layer

API/interfacing. These are the elements that make the grid-enabled eco-system possible and the layers above the core are comprised of the API which enables connections with other applications and services, the User Interface (which may or may not be necessary depending on the device upon which it sits), and finally the Edgeware applications. Once a grid is established then resources can be published or accessed across the grid, enabling the infinite functional possibilities of the Grid technology.

Securing a WiGLET to WiGLET interface will rest on the principles of both protecting data and communication devices in the Wireless Grid. Such interoperability amongst WiGLET's is envisioned as shared devices with controlled and changing environments spanning trust levels within the grid. WiGLET's need to share not only data but also interactive exchanges of secure devices. A major issue with this problem space is the issue of revocable sharing, addressing the need to revoke access to data and/or resources formerly available to grid users who have either voluntarily withdrawn from the wireless grid or whose access has been involuntarily severed. WiGLET's will also need to work across multiple trust levels. The first step in securing this interface is to identify the functionality of the security token and the security standards/policies (authorization, delegation, authentication, message protection, and message format [21, 51] as displayed in Figure 2, which will need to be enforced.

Identified, authenticated and authorized WiGLET's should be able to access and process any service and data required to meet its specified purpose. Identification consists of the process that an information system uses to recognize an entity. Access control is accomplished by the resource owner (the provider) authenticating the entity seeking access (the requestor) to the resource, and then determining whether that entity is authorized and authenticated to access a WIGLET. As WiGLET's transmit encrypted data to other WiGLET's through defined application programming interfaces (API), it must first pass through a security token.

Authentication for WiGLET's must involve strong encryption to prevent eavesdropping and must involve mutual authentication to ensure that sensitive information is transmitted only over legitimate wireless grid networks. WiGLET's must also have strong authentication standards to meet the challenges of strict encryption and authentication requirements. Strict encryption and authentication requirements are met by the use of the extensible authentication protocol (EAP) directly over a link layer protocol [24]. EAP is essentially a transport protocol that can be used by a variety of different authentication types, known as EAP methods. EAP was standardized by the Internet Engineering Task Force (IETF) in March 1999 [6]. Among the EAP methods developed specifically for wireless networks are a family of methods based on public key certificates and the transport layer security (TLS) protocol for message protection. These are EAP transport layer security (EAP-TLS) and the extensible authentication protocol tunneled transport layer security (EAP-TTLS).

EAP-TLS uses the TLS public key certificate authentication mechanism within EAP to provide mutual authentication of client-to-server and server-to-client [20]. With EAP-TLS, both the client and the server must be assigned a digital certificate signed by a certificate authority (CA) that they both trust. The EAP-TLS key system uses dynamic WEP or temporal key integrity protocol (TKIP) keys. WEP is the security standard for all 802.11 standards with a goal to secure wireless local area networks (WLAN) at the same level as wired networks [41]. EAP-TLS uses a TLS handshake as the basis for mutual authentication [20]. EAP-TTLS has been implemented in some Remote Authentication Dial-In User Service (RADIUS) servers and supplicant software designed for use in 802.11 WLAN networks. In EAP-TLS, a TLS handshake is used to mutually authenticate a client and server [2005]. EAP-TTLS extends this authentication negotiation by using the secure connection established by the TLS handshake to exchange additional information between client and server. In EAP-TTLS, the TLS handshake may be mutual, or it may be one-way, in which only the server is authenticated to the client. The secure connection established by the handshake may then be used to allow the server to authenticate the client using existing, widely deployed authentication infrastructures such as RADIUS [2005].

The security token [or policy enforcement point (PEP)] is installed on the hardware device that the WiGLET carriers to authorize access to a wireless grid. The security token is embedded inside the WiGLET software and provides the first level of security assurance before authentication and authorization. A WiGLET will make a request to another WiGLET's security token and will form a request based on the WiGLET's attributes, the resource in question, the action, and other information pertaining to the request. The security token will then send this request to a policy decision point (PDP), which will look at the request and some policy that applies to the request and come up with an answer about whether data access should be authorized. That answer is returned to the PDP, which can then allow or deny access to the requesting WiGLET. The sending WiGLET has an identification number (ID#), which authorizes the WiGLET as the owner of that particular device. The device then displays a number which uniquely identifies the WiGLET to its specified service, allowing the WiGLET access to exchange encrypted data.

Before the WiGLET authenticator, which enforces authentication before access to services, allows access to the WiGLET, certain security parameters and standards should be met. For authorization, Security Assertion Markup Language (SAML) is a standard from the Organization for the Advancement of Structured Information Standards [OASIS] [38]. SAML defines a framework for exchanging security information in extensible markup language (XML) format, with the main design goal of supporting Single Sign-On (SSO). The authentication facts are represented in XML constructs called "assertions", which are managed by SAML Authorities [38, 8]. Interested WiGLET's could ask a SAML Authority whether an entity possesses a certain assertion, thus eliminating the need to authenticate the entity each and every time. SAML also maps seamlessly to the Simple Object Access Protocol (SOAP) and in many areas complements the Web Services Security [WS-Security] specification [27, 38].

In supporting delegation and authentication, X.509 proxy and identification (ID) certifications are the fundamental public key infrastructure-based technology critical for establishing identities and secure, trusted communications between the components [52]. In many cases, X.509 certificates may be used in place of SAML assertions to provide initiator identity (Lock and Sommerville, 2002). For the actual message format,

Simple Object Access Protocol (SOAP), which performs low-level XML communications for transmitting web service calls across the wire may provide a secure solution [50, 51]. Also, representational state transfer (RESTful) based web services often describe any simple interface which transmits domain-specific data over hypertext transfer protocol (HTTP) without an additional messaging layer such as SOAP [19, 13, 49]. Both SOAP/RESTful potentially provide a means of XML-based messaging between a WiGLET provider and a WiGLET consumer.

Other forms of message protection are needed to protect data from unauthorized (accidental or intentional) modification, disclosure, or destruction in protected messaging is needed. WS-Security is a standard jointly proposed by IBM, Microsoft, and Verisign and ratified by OASIS [35]. It serves as the foundation to address SOAP-level security issues, with three major propositions: (1) use of security tokens in SOAP headers for user identity and authentication, (2) use of XML-Signature standard for message integrity, and (3) use of XML-Encryption for message confidentiality [35, 36, 53]. There are of course many other security requirements that are not addressed by WS-Security, such as trust relationships and secure transactions. WS-Secure Conversation [WSSC], jointly proposed by IBM, Microsoft, and Verisign, also specifies the syntax and rules with which security tokens can be exchanged in SOAP [27, 36, 55]. These protocols and in particular their messaging constructs may potentially become another vehicle to carry the returned SAML authentication assertion for the WiGLET.

It is critical that only identified, authenticated, and authorized WiGLET's have access to other WiGLET's within the wireless grid. Identifying data from an incoming WiGLET to a receiving WiGLET may rely also upon a wireless identification and sensing platform (WISP) using a wireless access point (WAP) type of architecture. A WISP is a class of battery-free wireless sensors that scavenge power from ambient radio-frequency-identification readers to communicate sensed data using a usage model to enable a variety of distributed sensing applications [42]. This type of platform uses Radio Frequency Identification (RFID) technology for sensing and computing power to wireless devices [43]. A WAP point facilitates wireless connection between devices (e.g., sensors) and other wireless modules (e.g., routers, etc.) [10, 16]. The WISP also provides the interface for the WiGLET system resources for timing, power management, memory, central processing unit (CPU), and program and debug services.

Using WISP/WAP construct, identification and authentication data would be provided remotely, and authorization information would have to be embedded in a WiGLET security certificate. The WiGLET security certificate requires a service that presents the certificate as a proxy for the WiGLET to other WiGLET's as needed, as well as data that verifies the validity of the security token and manages WiGLET authorizations. Securing these WISPs and WAPs are obtainable through various wireless traffic encryption methods such as IEEE 802.1x/Remote Authentication Dial-In User Service (RADIUS) [14] and wired equivalent privacy (WEP) [45]. Additionally, the WiGLET embedded security kernel (as displayed in Figure 3) plays a vital role in the WiGLET to WiGLET security architecture.

A kernel can be defined as the code executing in the hardware's privileged mode in an embedded system [23]. The WiGLET embedded security kernel is used to protect the WiGLET from corrupt API interfaces, decrease the size of the core trusted code base, and put a clear, inviolable interface between the trusted code base and less trusted code within the WiGLET. The WiGLET embedded security kernel is responsible for enforcing the security mechanisms of the entire WiGLET system. The WiGLET embedded security kernel represents a small trusted system, and can be implemented by hardware, software, or a combination of the two with a direct interaction with the processor. It also protects the WiGLET's hardware initialization, device control, application scheduling, and application partitioning.

Even with this limited set of services and security features, the security kernel can run the services of a WiGLET while maintaining a high level of security. By enforcing a process (or application) separation policy, the secure kernel should guarantee that two independently running processes within the WiGLET will not be able to affect each other. This isolation process ensures that malicious code inserted into one isolation segment of the WiGLET kernel cannot access or steal resources, corrupt or read files, or otherwise harm the processes and data in another

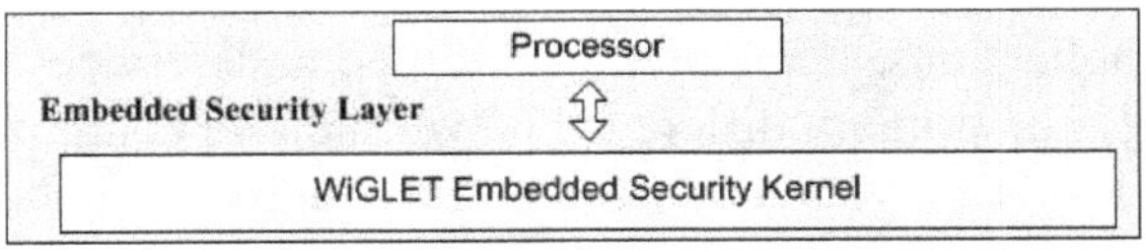

Figure 3. WiGLET Embedded Security Kernel

isolation segment. The WiGLET embedded security kernel must work directly with the other WiGLET's components to directly support the processing of secure data.

Access control mechanisms for the WiGLET must ensure that data is accessed and processed only by other authorized WiGLET's, including precise control over distribution (how many and when). A significant gap in access control that may affect this architecture is the lack of research, policies, standards, and mechanisms for this type of environment. For interoperability to exist, the WiGLET will need to be engaged in collaboration with multiple security domains at the same time. In order for such collaboration to be secure, WiGLET's in one domain must be secure and not able to access unauthorized information that resides in other domains. The shared data must be secured and protected during the identification and access control (authorization/authentication) process and internally using an embedded security kernel against threats, attacks, disclosure, corruption, and loss of availability (e.g., denial of service).

SECURING A WiGLET-TO-CLOUD COMPUTING ARCHITECTURE

Since the emergence of Web Services technologies, there has been a major paradigm shift in distributed computing: from distributed object architectures to service-oriented architecture (SOA) to cloud computing environments [4, 17]. There has been a growing need for increased integration and collaboration across organizational boundaries. A wireless grid WiGLET to cloud integration (Wireless Cloud) is well positioned to become the key technology enabler for such business drivers due to its decentralized, loosely coupled, and highly interoperable architecture. Securing the wireless cloud, however, faces new challenges that may not be fully addressed by existing information technology (IT) or wireless security solutions.

Cloud computing has emerged as a new computing paradigm that arrays massive numbers of computers in centralized data centers to deliver web-based applications, application platforms, and services via a utility model [4, 48]. The primary difference between cloud computing and previous software-as-a-service models (e.g., outsourcing or data center consolidation) is scalability. The premise is that as the scale of the cloud infrastructure increases, the incremental time and cost of application delivery trends toward zero. The term cloud computing refers to the practice of leveraging third-party computing resources such as network grids and server farms to extend IT capabilities and reduce the cost of ownership [15]. Most of the cloud providers today are data centers that have quickly adopted the technology to offer cloud computing services. Figure 4 illustrates the distinction in a cloud computing architecture.

Therefore, in a secure wireless cloud environment, organizations will need to shift their focus from perimeter-based security models to a service-level view of security, with emphasis not so much on ownership and control, but on network identities, trust, and authorization of both users and applications. The architectural construct of a secure wireless cloud computing environment is identified in Figure 5. Reference [26] identifies the wireless cloud as a natural extension of the wireless grid, which provides seamless access to the internet, networked devices, and computing capabilities. The wireless cloud is a kind of next-generation wireless grid, an emerging technology and the publication on it is limited [26].

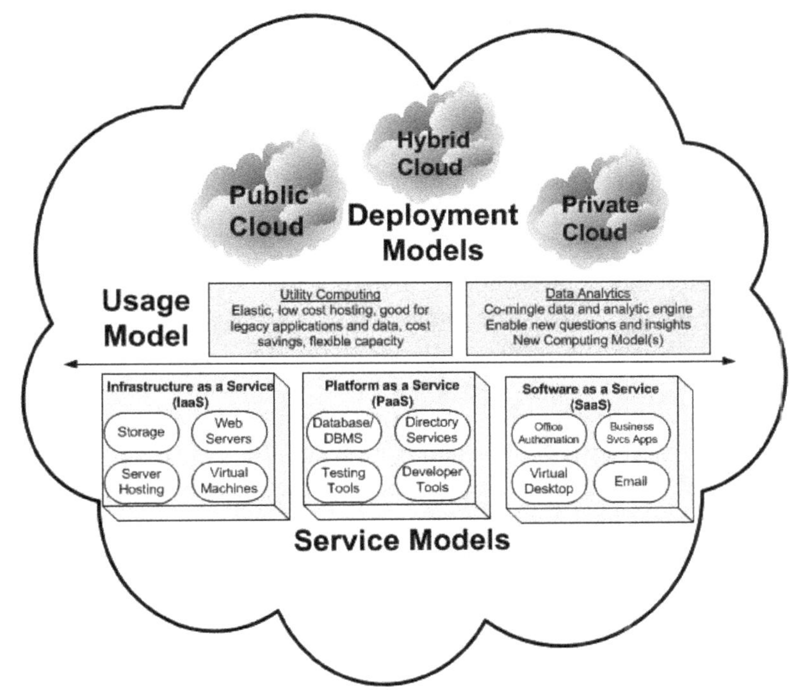

Figure 4. Cloud Computing

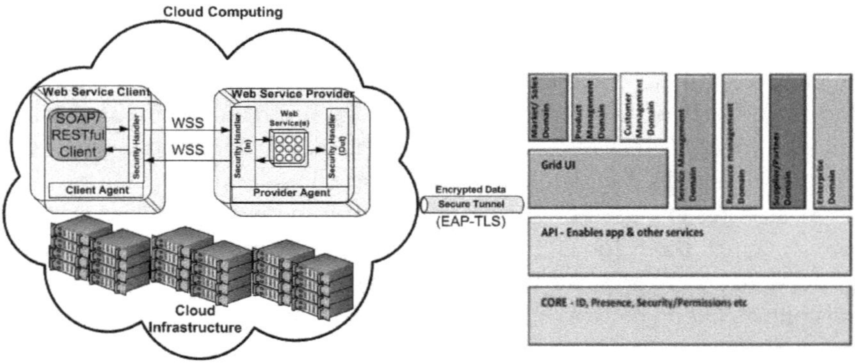

Figure 5. A Future Wireless Cloud Security Architecture

The wireless cloud security architecture is purposely kept technology-agnostic: there is no mention of any specific wire protocols, interfaces, or data models, except that everything will be web services based since the WiGLET interfaces directly with the cloud. Over time, the security standards will evolve, and new standards will continue to emerge and the conceptual architecture will not be inherently stable and may not remain the same. For this architecture, data exchanges will be transmitted through the use of encrypted data via a secure tunnel EAP-TLS/TTLS [9, 20]. This secure tunnel provides a secure interaction between the WiGLET and the Cloud software. A security token-based authentication (e.g., x.509 certificates) model could be used before invoking any secure web services. A cloud client needs to explicitly authenticate itself to a security token service which is one of the services offered by the WiGLET. After successful authentication, the client will be given a one-time security token, which is then passed in the regular web service request message to invoke a target service. The token essentially establishes a session whose duration is the lifespan of the token. During the session, the client can use the same token to invoke any services (subjecting to the local access control policy of course) and doesn't have to be authenticated again, thereby achieving service-level Single Sign-On (SSO). Compared with the direct authentication model specified in the WS-Security [WSS] standard [40], this approach improves performance by eliminating per-message authentication overhead, which is quite significant when asymmetric key exchange is involved.

In this hypothetical environment, the cloud client application issues a web service request in the form of a regular SOAP/RESTful message to the security handler. The security handler in the cloud client agent intercepts the SOAP/RESTful message. In the absence of a valid security token, the client agent presents WiGLET credentials to the security token service and obtains a security token upon successful authentication. The cloud client agent adds the security token in the SOAP/RESTful message header and sends the request to the target service provider. The cloud provider agent for the target service intercepts the SOAP/RESTful request and extracts the security token. It then checks with the policy decision service (PDS), which fetches needed resource attributes for the target web service from a service registry which acts as the resource attribute authority [54], in the WiGLET on whether this request can be authorized. The latter validates the token and checks the identity against the WiGLET access control policies and responds with a SAML authorization assertion which either permits or denies access. If access is granted, the provider agent forwards the SOAP/RESTful request to the target web service for processing. The invocation results are returned back to the client in a SOAP/RESTful response.

The WiGLET embedded security kernel provides transparent security enforcement using client/provider agent's software components installed in the client/provider application hosting environments in the cloud. At runtime, these agents reside in the same process space as the processor, analogous to linked code libraries, with the difference being these agents secure any exposed API interfaces. Using SOAP/RESTful message interception mechanisms (such as Java API for XML-Based RPC [JAX-RPC] [11] or Java API for XML Web Services [JAX-WS] [12] for message handler chains, these agents (among other things) transparently handle message-level security aspects such as authentication, token passing, and policy enforcement — all without the knowledge of the client or service applications. Moreover, third-party web services already developed without being security-aware can easily become so by plugging into the WIGLET security architecture with little or no modification.

The underlying security functionality such as security token management and policy management are themselves wrapped as web services in securing data to the WiGLET. When a web service invokes another service hosted by a different service provider on the client's behalf, the provider agent can transparently pass on the client's security token, thereby enabling the second provider to authenticate and authorize the client in the same manner. This is especially necessary to support dynamic service composition and orchestration, one of the most appealing features promised by the cloud. To ensure interoperability and API stability, fully standard compliant interfaces between architecture components may need to use SAML for authentication assertion/security token exchange between client agent and WiGLET, and for exchanging authorization decision assertions between provider agent and WiGLET. Also, WS-Security for attaching security tokens to SOAP/RESTful requests to target service providers, extensible access control markup language (XACML) for exchanging access control policies [39], and XML key management specification (XKMS) for key management [22] and PKI integration [2] may also have to be considered.

In a future wireless cloud environment with potentially millions of users and millions or more resources, having a central authorization authority simply won't scale. With this model, multi-level trust domains, policy management on the resources may have to be delegated down to the level where the resource is located and owned, from communities to organizations or even to individuals, effectively limiting the management span at each level. Information exchanged from the Cloud to the WiGLET needs to be secured because the overall security is only as strong as the weakest link in the system. There may be a need for new mechanisms to secure this type of architecture. These mechanisms not only ensure data integrity and confidentiality but also facilitate mutual authentication and non-repudiation.

SECURING A SERVICE-ORIENTED WiGLET ARCHITECTURE

SOA is a way of reorganizing a portfolio of previously siloed software applications and support infrastructure into an interconnected set of services, each accessible through standard interfaces and messaging protocols [18]. Under SOA, a set of network-accessible operations and associated resources are abstracted as a "service", which is described in a standard fashion, made available by publishing the service description to service registries and found by the service consumers via querying the registry (Figure 6). Four basic standards, SOAP, RESTful, Web Service Definition Language (WSDL), and Universal Discovery, Description, and Integration (UDDI), serve as the foundation of the web services protocol "stack" [7]:

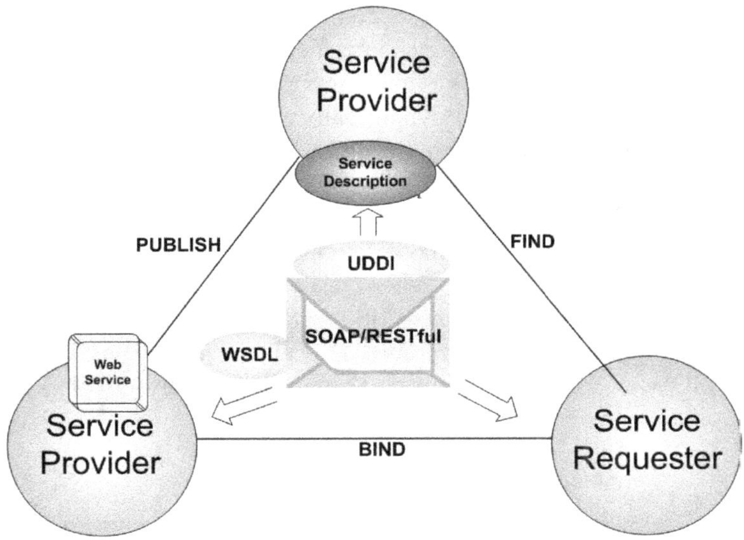

Figure 6. Service-Oriented Architecture

SOAP performs the low-level XML communications for transmitting web service calls across the wire [18]. It provides a means of XML-based messaging between a service provider and a service consumer. RESTful-based web services often describe any simple interface which transmits domain-specific data over HTTP without an additional messaging layer such as SOAP [13]. RESTful style is an abstraction of the architectural elements within a distributed hypermedia system and ignores the details of component implementation and protocol syntax in order to focus on the roles of components, the constraints upon their interaction with other components, and their interpretation of significant data elements [19]. WSDL is the language that defines the functional interfaces for a web service [18]. In other words, a WSDL document, which is itself in XML, represents the official "contract" between the service consumers and providers. These interfaces are described first in abstract message structures, and then bound to a concrete transport protocol and a communication "endpoint". UDDI is the emerging standard for organizing and accessing the service registry [18]. A service registry serves as the "yellow" page of a collection of web services, providing mechanisms for a service provider to publish its capabilities and for a service user to find matching services.

These protocols provide loose coupling of web services standards focused on defining the functional interfaces that represent the minimal understanding between service requestor and provider. Knowledge of the service provider is discovered dynamically from a service registry rather than statically coded in the client program. Simply put, web service calls are essentially XML messages over HTTP (or potentially other standard Internet protocols), which represents the "least common denominator" of network protocol stacks and makes it easier to overcome firewall and infrastructure constraints [7]. When it comes to information sharing among different autonomous networks, web services are likely to be the only viable option. The foundation of a service-oriented WiGLET architecture (SOWA) architecture is one that must be fully developed on a Trust Domain and Trust Model (as displayed in Figure 7), which has been

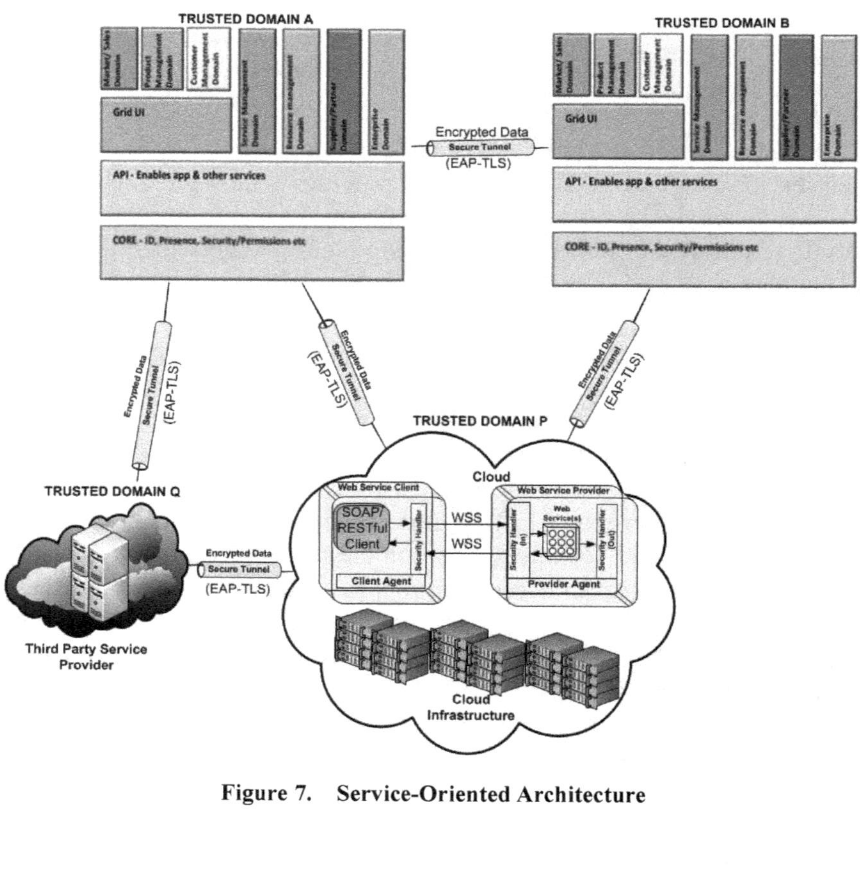

Figure 7. Service-Oriented Architecture

one of importance in distributed computing environments [37]. It may receive more attention (compared with other models such as virtual organizations) in the web services architectures, largely due to the growing acceptance of SAML and RESTful architecture.

In the context of SOWA, trust occurs at two levels: First, at the provider level (i.e. the trust domain level). Before information exchange or resource sharing can happen between two trust domains, a certain level of trust agreement must be established. The agreement can take many forms and is often domain-specific. For example, in exchanging data amongst WiGLET's, the cloud, and third-party service providers, there may be quite a number of legal constraints (e.g., in the form of US laws and government regulations) that dictate what information may or may not be shared among different parties. Other agreements may be more technical in nature, such as common attribute definitions and required certifications. Secondly, at the identity level: after the trust relationship has been put in place, interoperability can happen between WiGLET's or other system entities between the two trust domains.

First, we define what WiGLET trust domain means in technical terms. For example, when WiGLET domain A is said to be trusted with WiGLET domain B, the two domains are able to identify each other, able to locate and communicate with each other, and trust the transport on which secure data information is exchanged between each other. WiGLET domain B trusts A's process and mechanisms for authenticating its own identities. In other words, B is willing to acknowledge and accept a valid security token issued by A's as proof of identity. Domain B understands and trusts the attribute assertions issued by A for its identities. This also implies that the two domains share a common set of attribute definitions for identities. Given a valid security token and associated attribute assertions, domain B is willing to grant access to its resources based on its local security policy. The last point is especially worth noting because it stresses that trust domain is a necessary but not sufficient condition for a WiGLET in one domain to access resources in the other; the WiGLET will still be fully subject to the local access control policy in the target WiGLET domain.

Next, we formally define the trust model as the circle of trust consisting of multiple trust domains at multiple levels. A WiGLET domain may explicitly enter into a trust relationship with another by mutual agreement as defined in the terms above. The two domains are then called "integrated". A WiGELT domain may also join a "parent" trust domain through the same process. All peer domains within the same parent domain are implicitly considered integrated. Alternatively, the parent WiGLET domain may also instruct the child WiGLET domain to integrate with only some but not all of the other child WiGLET domains, based on its policies. Based on its discretion, a parent WiGLET domain can selectively pass its integration relationships down to its child WiGLET domains. For example, if WiGLET domain A is not integrated with another WiGLET domain Q while its parent WiGLET domain P does, and P decides to pass this relationship to A, then A is considered integrated with Q. Again, the integrated by no means grant unrestricted access; it is only a prerequisite.

Within a WiGLET trust domain, the local security policy governs access to local resources for both local identities and remote identities from other integrated domains. Trust is not permanent; it may be terminated by the parent WiGLET domain or either party of the peer WiGLET domains. Trust can be bilateral or unilateral, depending on the policies of the participating domains. In the unilateral case, for instance, WiGLET domain A's users can access resources in WiGLET domain B, but WiGLET domain B's users cannot access resources in A. The trust model should support both scenarios. Inter-domain trust relationships can be established in two ways, either explicitly between two domains or implicitly via joining a parent domain.

A WiGLET trust domain integrates with another peer WiGLET domain when the two domains have established mutual agreement on the trust relationship through a secure connection. Each domain simply needs to obtain the other party's identifier (which in this architecture is the domain name (DN) suffix of the domain) out-of-band and put in an internal "WiGLET Peer Domains" table. The DN needs to resolve to an actual uniform resource locator (URL) of the other domain's WiGLET; this is achieved through the security token process as is illustrated in Figure 8. To ensure authenticity, both domains may need to acquire and validate the other domain's digital certificate (e.g., the server), facilitated by the underlying security infrastructure.

Furthermore, WiGLET's may need to integrate with additional WiGLET's within the trust domain. Integrating with a "parent" domain is similar in the sense that the parent and child domains also need to exchange domain DNs and certificates. Additionally, the new child domain may retrieve the list of other child domains from the parent; these domains will implicitly become peer domains of the new child. The other child domains will also learn from the parent that a new child has joined, enabling them to integrate with the new WiGLET.

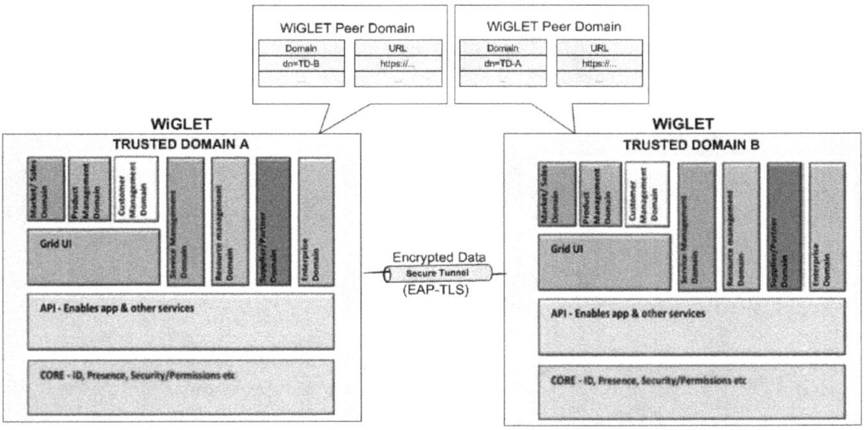

Figure 8. Explicit Integration of WiGLET Peer Domains

Invoking a web service through another trusted domain (e.g., cloud) assumes that the communication path to the remote domain, most likely SOAP/RESTful/HTTP based, can be established and the target web service has been discovered. The client agent authenticates with the local WiGLET domain's security token service and then passes the token in the outbound SOAP/RESTful request to the target service. This is the more typical scenario in which trust domain A would like to invoke a service in the cloud while connected to trust domain B and even though trust domain B doesn't have identity in that domain. Presumably, the security token in domain B has already learned about this intent beforehand and has assigned the appropriate permissions in the local security policy. The invocation process is shown in Figure 9.

When the WiGLET for the target service receives the request from the cloud or another WiGLET, it extracts the security token and queries the local PDS for a SAML authorization decision assertion, making no distinction where this request comes from. When the PDS receives the SAML query and recognizes by the DN suffix of the identity that the token is not issued by the local domain, it attempts to look up the WiGLET's domains list. The local PDS may also need to ask the remote domain to verify the security token is valid if the token is not signed. When an entry can be found, it sends a SAML attribute query to the remote domain's attribute management service (AMS), which requests a list of attributes it needs to make access control decisions. Example attributes may include "What is the WiGLET's request?", "How was the

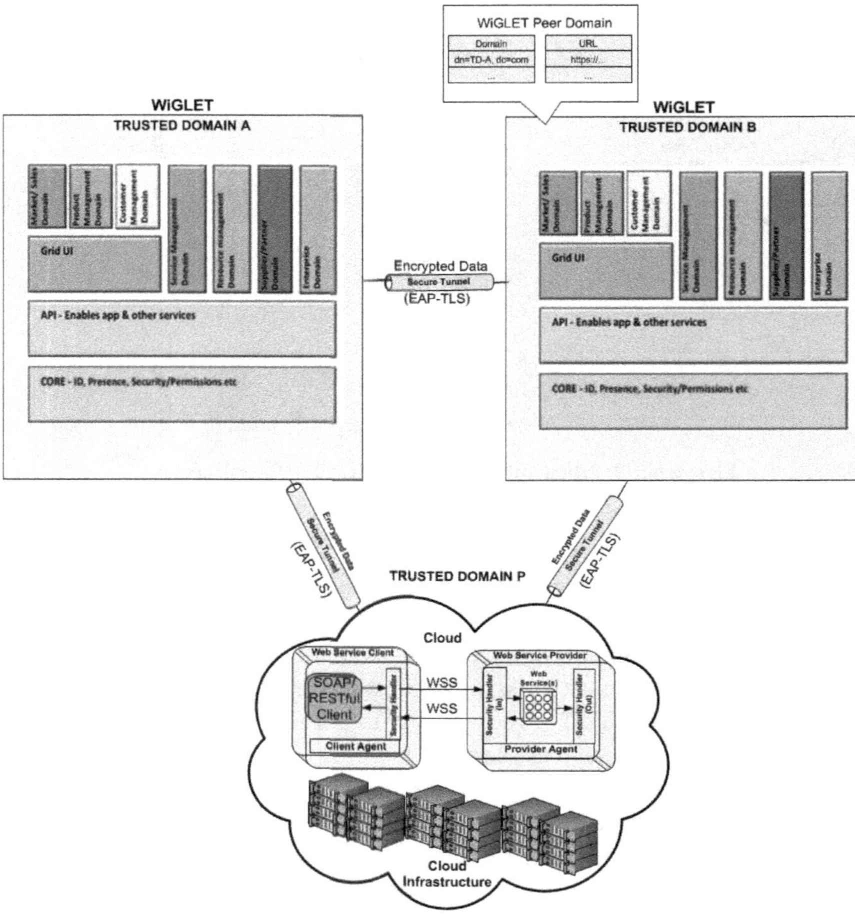

Figure 9. Invoking a Service in a Peer Domain

WiGLET authenticated?", "What data cloud is the cloud requesting?" and so on. If the query is successful, it feeds those attributes to the evaluation process against the local policy sets and either grants or denies the request.

When processing data from third-party service provider, the provider agent protecting a web service can pass the client's identity and security token on to another service, supporting service level "workflow" and composition. This feature is naturally extended to the inter-domain architecture, where security token forwarding across domain boundaries is governed by the trust as displayed in Figure 10.

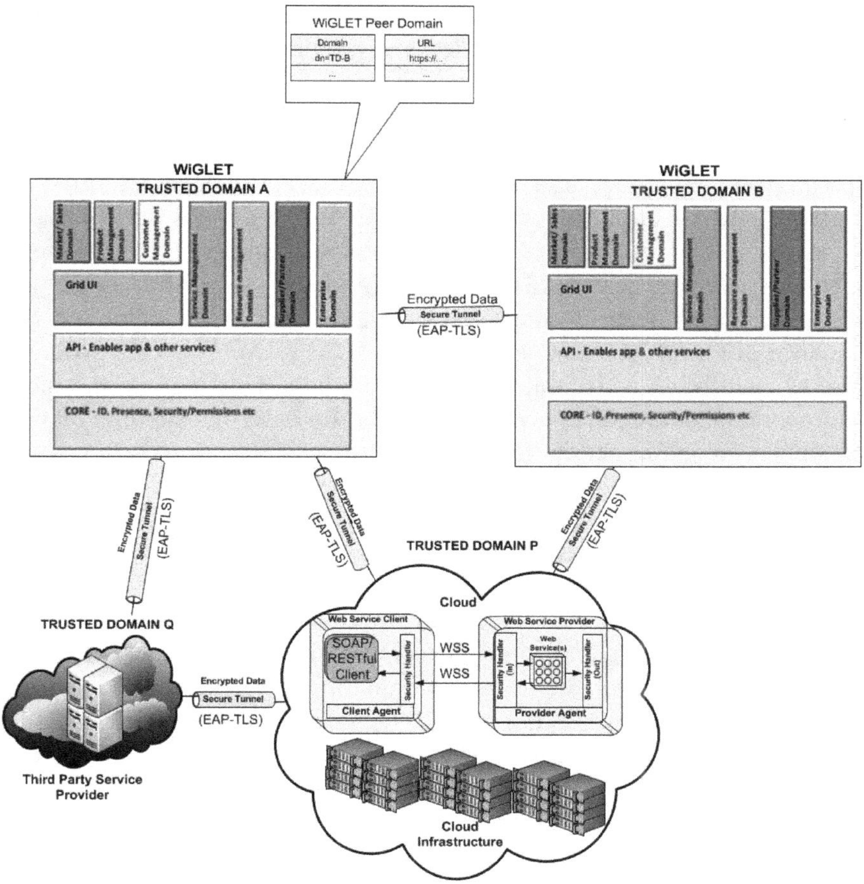

Figure 10. Inter-Domain Services

In this architecture, we assume a WiGLET trust domain A is integrated with WiGLET domain B. WiGLET domain B requests information from a third-party service provider through a cloud interface however, B is not directly integrated with the third-party service provider. Now a client from domain A successfully invokes a service in domain B and the cloud, which in turn needs to access another service located in domain Q from the third-party provider. The provider agent for the service transparently passes the security token from domain A to the target service in domain b. When B's PDS examines the foreign token, it should be able to find a secure domain from which attribute assertions can be retrieved, forcing it to accept the security token and provide its access to the target service.

In securing these types of new WiGLET SOWAs, it is almost certain that a core set of security services has to be developed in order to define service-level interfaces and domain-specific security services. First, it must include a security token service (STS) which defines the interfaces to access security tokens based on common authentication mechanisms, such as X.509 certificates [28]. Major operations could potentially include obtaining a new security token (based on the user credentials) and the issuance of a new one-time security token. The token may take different forms, such as a SAML authentication assertion. This may be the most interoperable, but requires good PKI support for assertion signing, renewing, and revoking a security token. As to protocols, because the service is only accessed within the trust domain, it can be implemented in a way that is more suitable to the existing tooling and user preferences. Options may include a regular web service interface, a SAML query interface, or a WS-Secure Conversation-based interface.

Another key component of securing this WiGLET SOWA is the inclusion of a PDS. The PDS serves as the PDP of the trust domain. It offers a SAML-compliant interface, accepting authorization queries and returns authorization decision assertions [54]. The heart of the service is basically a policy evaluation engine. The relevant policy rules are then evaluated against the attributes and a permit/deny decision is returned. Although hypothetical, this type of service-oriented architecture could potentially provide new business models for organizations using wireless grids.

CONCLUSION

All told, security is based on trust and the design of a solution of trust for the WiGLET is no simple task. A secure WiGLET transaction (i.e. communication) will rely on trust and WiGLET's engaged in a secure transaction must mutually trust each other's identities. This chapter identified three different types of wireless grid architectures and specific security considerations for each type around the WiGLET. Due to the inherent nature of the wireless grid connection, the potential unreliability of the end devices and the power constraints of the mobile device, securing this initial architecture represents the first major challenge in securing the wireless grid environment.

REFERENCES

[1] Abdulrahman, R., *et al.* (2011). Multi agent system for historical information retrieval from online social networks. In O'Shea, J., Nguyen, N., Crockett, K., Howlett, R., & Jain, L. (Eds.), *Agent and Multi-Agent Systems: Technologies and Applications* (pp. 54–63), Springer, Berlin Heidelberg.

[2] Adams, C. & Lloyd, S. (2003). *Understanding Public-Key Infrastructure* (2nd edition). Addison Wesley Professional, Addison Wesley Professional, Boston, Massachusetts.

[3] Agarwal, A., *et al.* (2004). *Wireless Grids: Approaches, Architectures and Technical Challenges.* MIT Sloan Working Paper No. 4459-04 (pp. 1–10). http://ssrn.com/abstract=489782 (Accessed February 5, 2012).

[4] Armbrust, M., *et al.* (2009). *Above the Clouds: A Berkeley View of Cloud Computing.* University of California at Berkeley Technical Report No. UCB/EECS-2009-28 (pp. 1–25). http://www.eecs.berkeley.edu/Pubs/TechRpts/2009/EECS-2009-28.pdf (Accessed February 5, 2012).

[5] Bernard, S. & Ho, S. (2008). Enterprise architecture as context and method for designing and implementing information security and data privacy controls in government agencies. In Saha, P. (Ed.), *Advances in Government Enterprise Architecture* (pp. 340–370), IGI Global, Hershey, Pennsylvania.

[6] Bradner, S. (1999). The internet engineering task force. In DiBona, C., Ockman, S. & Stone, M. (Eds.), *Open Sources: Voices from the Open Source Revolution* (pp. 47–52), O'Reilly Media, Sebastopol, California.

[7] Brooks, T. (2009). Service-oriented enterprise architecture (SOEA) conceptual design through data architecture. *Journal of Enterprise Architecture*, 5(4), 16–26.

[8] Cantor, S., *et al.* (2005). *Metadata for the OASIS Security Assertion Markup Language (SAML) V2.0. OASIS SSTC Document ID sstc-saml-metadata-2.0* (pp. 1–43). http://www.oasis-open.org/committees/security/ (Accessed June 5, 2012).

[9] Chen, J. & Wang, Y. (2005). Extensible authentication protocol (EAP) and IEEE 802.1x: Tutorial and empirical experience. *IEEE Communications Magazine*, 43(12), 26–32.

[10] Chen, Y., *et al.* (2009). Integrated wireless access point architecture for wireless sensor networks. In *Proceedings of the 11th International Conference on Advanced Communication Technology* (*ICACT 2009*) (Vol. 1, pp. 713–718).

[11] Chinnici, R. (2003). *Java API for XML-Based RPC (JAX-RPC) Specification 1.1.* Sun Microsystems, Inc. http://java.sun.com/webservices/jaxrpc/ (Accessed May 1, 2012).

[12] Chinnici, R., *et al.* (2005). *The Java API for XML Web Services (JAX-WS) 2.0 Java Specification Request 224*. Sun Microsystems Inc. http://java.net/projects/jax-ws (Accessed May 1, 2012).

[13] Costello, R. (2011). *Building Web Services the REST Way*. http://www.xfront.com/REST-Web-Services.html (Accessed June 5, 2012).

[14] Congdon, P., *et al.* (2003). *IEEE 802.1X Remote Authentication Dial in User Service (RADIUS) Usage Guidelines, RFC 3580*. https://tools.ietf.org/html/rfc3580 (Accessed May 1, 2012).

[15] Dikaiakos, M., *et al.* (2009). Cloud computing: Distributed internet computing for IT and scientific research. *IEEE Internet Computing*, 13(5), 10–13.

[16] Dong, S., *et al.* (2003). Improving the aggregate throughput of access points in IEEE 802.11 wireless LANs. In *Proceedings of the 28th Annual IEEE International Conference on Local Computer Networks* (*LCN'03*) (pp. 682–690).

[17] Erl, T. (2004). *Service-Oriented Architecture: A Field Guide to Integrating XML and Web Services*. Prentice-Hall, Upper Saddle River, New Jersey.

[18] Erl, T. (2005). *Service-Oriented Architecture (SOA): Concepts, Technology, and Design*. Prentice-Hall, Upper Saddle River, New Jersey.

[19] Fielding, R. (2000). *Architectural Styles and the Design of Network-Based Software Architectures*. Ph.D. Dissertation, University of California, Irvine.

[20] Funk, P. & Blake-Wilson, S. (2008). *Extensible Authentication Protocol Tunneled Transport Layer Security Authenticated Protocol Version 0* (*EAP-TTLSv0*) RFC 5281. Internet Engineering Task Force. http://www.ietf.org/ (Accessed February 5, 2012).

[21] Foster, I., *et al.* (1998). *A security architecture for computational grids. In Proceedings of the 5th ACM Conference on Computer and Communications Security*, 1998, pp. 83–92.

[22] Hallam-Baker, P. & Mysore, S. (2005). *XML Key Management Specification* (*XKMS 2.0*). W3C. http://www.w3.org/TR/xkms2/ (Accessed June 15, 2012).

[23] Heiser, G. (2007). *Virtualization for Embedded Systems* (pp. 1–30). Open Kernel Labs, Inc. http://www.scribd.com/doc/27250904/Technology-White-Paper (Accessed May 31, 2012).

[24] Institute of Electrical and Electronics Engineers, Inc. (IEEE) (2007). *Std 802.11 – Wireless LAN Medium Access Control (MAC) and Physical Layer (PHY) Specifications* (pp. 1–1232). IEEE. http://www.ieee.org/index.html.

[25] Kurdi, H., *et al.* (2008). A classification of emerging and traditional grid systems. *IEEE Distributed Systems Online*, 9(3), 1–13.

[26] Li, G., *et al.* (2009). A survey on wireless grids and clouds. In *Proceedings of the 8th International Conference on Grid and Cooperative Computing* (pp. 261–267).

[27] Liu, H., *et al.* (2005). Performance of web services security. In *Proceedings of the 13th Annual Mardi Gras Conference* (pp. 1–8).

[28] Lock, R. & Sommerville, I. (2002). *Grid Security and Its Use of X.509 Certificates* (pp. 1–14). Lancaster University http://www.comp.lancs.ac.uk/computing/research/cseg/projects/dirc/papers/gridpaper.pdf (Accessed June 2, 2011).

[29] Marsden, J. (2011). Determining the role of geospatial technologies for stigmergic coordination in situation management: Implications of the wireless grid. In *Proceedings of the 1st IEEE International Multi-Disciplinary Conference on Cognitive Methods in Situation Awareness and Decision Support* (*CogSIMA 2011*) (pp. 131–135).

[30] McKnight, L., *et al.* (2004). Wireless grids, distributed resource sharing by mobile, nomadic and fixed devices. *IEEE Internet Computing*, 8(4), 24–31.

[31] McKnight, L., *et al.* (2005). Wireless grids: Assessing a new technology for a user perspective. *Designing Ubiquitous Information Environments: Socio-Technical Issues and Challenges* (pp. 169–181). Springer.

[32] McKnight, L. (2007). The future of the internet is not the internet: Open communications policy and the future wireless grid(s). In *NSF/OECD Workshop on Social & Economic Factors Shaping the Future of the Internet* (pp. 1–4). http://www.oecd.org/dataoecd/18/42/38057172.pdf (Accessed June 1, 2011).

[33] McKnight, L., *et al.* (2010). Wireless grids or personal infrastructure: Policy implications of an emergent open standard. In *Proceedings of the TPRC 38th Research Conference on Communication, Information and Internet Policy* (pp. 1–23).

[34] McKnight, L., *et al.* (2012). Open specifications for wireless grids technical requirements, version 0.1. *WiGiT* (pp. 1–22). Syracuse University.

[35] Nadalin, A., *et al.* (2004). OASIS web services security: SOAP message security 1.0 (WS-Security 2004). OASIS Standard 200401 (pp. 1–56). http://docs.oasis-open.org/wss/2004/01/oasis-200401-wss-soap-message-security-1.0.pdf (Accessed June 1, 2011).

[36] Naedele, M. (2003). Standards for XML and web services security. *Computer*, 36(4), 96–98.

[37] Nagaratnam, N., *et al.* (2002). The security architecture for open grid services. Open Grid Service Architecture Security Working Group (OGSA-SEC-WG) (pp. 1–31). ftp://ftp.cigs.unimo.it/pub/OGSA-SecArch-v1-07192002.pdf (Accessed June 1, 2011).

[38] OASIS Open Standards. (2005). Security assertion markup language (SAML) v2.0. OASIS. http://www.oasis-open.org/standards#samlv2.0 (Accessed June 15, 2011).
[39] OASIS Open Standards (2005). eXtensible access control markup language v2.0(XACML). OASIS. http://www.oasis-open.org/standards#xacmlv2.0 (Accessed June 15, 2011).
[40] OASIS Open Standards (2005). Web services security (WSS) 1.1. OASIS. http://www.oasis-open.org/standards#samlv2.0 (Accessed June 15, 2011).
[41] Park, J. & Dicoi, D. (2003). WLAN security: Current and future. *IEEE Internet Computing*, 7(5), 60–65.
[42] Philipose, M., *et al.* (2005). Battery-free wireless identification and sensing. *IEEE Pervasive Computing*, 4(1), 37–45.
[43] Sample, A. & Smith, J. (2009). Experimental results with two wireless power transfer systems. In *Proceedings of the IEEE Radio and Wireless Symposium (RWS'09)* (pp. 16–18).
[44] Sherwood, J. (2005). *Enterprise Security Architecture: A Business Driven Approach.* CRC Press, Boca Raton, Florida.
[45] Stallings, W. (1999). *Cryptography and Network Security.* Prentice Hall, Upper Saddle River, New Jersey.
[46] Treglia, J., *et al.* (2010). Collaboration in a wireless grid innovation testbed by virtual consortium. *Networks for Grid Applications*, Lecture Notes of the Institute for Computer Sciences, Social Informatics and Telecommunications Engineering (Vol. 25, No. 6, pp. 139–146).
[47] Treglia, J., *et al.* (2011). Interoperability by 'Edgeware': Wireless grids for emergency response. In *Proceedings of the 44th Hawaii International Conference on System Sciences (HICSS'11)* (pp. 1–10).
[48] Vaquero, L., *et al.* (2008). A break in the clouds: Towards a cloud definition. *SIGCOMM Computer Communications Review*, 39(1), 50–55.
[49] Vinoski, S. (2008). RESTful web services development checklist. *IEEE Internet Computing*, 12(6), 95–96.
[50] W3C (2007). Simple Object Access Protocol (SOAP) 1.2, W3C, 2007. http://www.w3.org/TR/soap/ (Accessed June 3, 2011).
[51] Welch, V., *et al.* (2003). Security for grid services. In *Proceedings of the 12th International Symposium on High Performance Distributed Computing (HPDC-12)* (pp. 48–57).
[52] Welch, V., *et al.* (2004). X.509 proxy certificates for dynamic delegation. In *Proceedings of the 3rd Annual PKI RandD Workshop* (pp. 1–17).
[53] Weerawarana, S., *et al.* (2005). *Web Services Platform Architecture: SOAP, WSDL, WS-Policy, WS-Addressing, WS-PEL, WS-Reliable Messaging and More.* Prentice Hall.

[54] Yuan, E. & Tong, J. (2005). Attribute based access control (ABAC) for web services. In *Proceedings of the 3rd International Conference on Web Services (ICWS 2005)* (pp. 561–569).

[55] Zhuang, H. (2011). A secure framework for web service interaction. In *Proceedings of the 2011 International Conference on Electric Information and Control Engineering (ICEICE)* (pp. 95–98).

Chapter 5

A Failure to Communicate: Security Vulnerabilities in the GridStreamX Wireless Grid Edgeware Application*

ABSTRACT

Any communications network is subject to becoming the target of exploitation by criminal hackers looking to gain unauthorized access to an information system. As a computer information infrastructure, the wireless grid Edgeware technology model aims at aggregating ensembles of shared, heterogeneous, and distributed wireless resources to provide transparent services for various applications, systems, and devices. Currently, there is no research exploring the exploitation of technical vulnerabilities from a hacker's attack against a wireless grid Edgeware application. Using a quantitative research method from the theoretical perspective of an anatomy of a network attack, the central premise of this chapter is to compromise the confidentiality, integrity, and availability of a wireless grid called the GridStreamX Edgeware application for vulnerability exploitation through a laboratory experiment within the Syracuse University Wireless Grid Innovation Testbed (WiGiT).

---

*Originally published as Brooks, T., Kaarst-Brown, M., Caicedo, C., Park, J., & McKnight, L. (2013). A failure to communicate: Security vulnerabilities in the GridStreamX Edgeware application. In *Proceedings of the IEEE/Infonomics Society 8th International Conference for Internet Technology and Secured Transactions (ICITST-2013)*, December 9–12, 2013, London, UK.

The GridStreamX Edgeware application is a cloud to "worst-case scenario" emergency response wireless Grid resource, which can be utilized as a data communication vehicle during an enterprise network catastrophe and/or failure. This research makes a meaningful theoretical and managerial contribution because it represents the first empirical examination of researching the technical requirements of the open specifications for wireless grid Edgeware technology.

INTRODUCTION

As deceitful or malicious as it may appear, the ability to exploit a computer network (or system) is a valuable tool to those who possess it. This chapter focuses on performing an anatomy of an attack sequence to exploit (e.g., some degree of degradation or loss of service) vulnerabilities (e.g., a weakness in an information system; the absence of a safeguard on a system) in a wireless grid Edgeware technology product called the GridStreamX Edgeware application. The GridStreamX Edgeware application is a cloud to "worst-case scenario" emergency response wireless Grid resource, which can be utilized as a data communication vehicle during an enterprise network catastrophe and/or failure [1]. The GridStreamX Edgeware application is accessible on a virtualized cloud-based, wireless grid platform or a mobile computing environment to offer users ubiquitous computational and communications services through the combination of social networking (e.g., Facebook) type communications integrated with file sharing, video conferencing, calendar functions, and mobile device connectivity, without regards to location, and frequently and/or regards to environment or conditions [1].

This research used a laboratory experiment within the Wireless Grid Innovation Testbed (WiGiT) to exploit the GridStreamX Edgeware application in order to strengthen the understanding of the appropriate security mechanisms, protocols, and standards needed for securing this application. Due to the innovativeness of wireless grids and Edgeware technology, no previous research on how to protect against vulnerability exploitation by those who have the knowledge to do so (e.g., hackers) has been performed. Attacks and exploitations increase the vulnerability of these architectures due to the lack of research around the defined security standards, protocols, and policies of an integrated security architecture. While the average user of the GridStreamX Edgeware application may be unaware of the complexity and security infrastructure needed for interoperability, hackers who wish to gain access to the application may become experts in identifying weaknesses and vulnerabilities in an attempt to exploit them for their own purposes.

RELATED WORK

Although there has been research pertaining to Edge computing [2–5], there is not a significant body of related work toward computer network attacks against Edge computing (or Edgeware in general). Reference [6] performed research ensuring data security in an Edge computing platform through three schemes that enable users to check the correctness of query results produced by the edge servers. Reference [6] research is important because it shows that each scheme offers different security features (e.g., verifiability, unforgeability, identifiability, undeniability, and prevention of misuse) and imposes different demands on the edge servers, user machines, and interconnecting networks. Reference [7] research on network edge security developed a distributed firewall architecture designed to counter the insider threat, which is undeterred by existing firewall implementations. Reference [7] research addresses the security challenges of emerging technology trends like mobile computing, business-to-business computing, virtual private networks (VPNs), and wireless sensor networks by combining topology-independent policy management with strong security and scalability [7]. Although both of these studies are relevant, they don't specifically address the impact or harm from cyber-attacks toward edge devices themselves nor the mitigations an organization should take if such technology is compromised.

The most significant threat to the GridStreamX Edgeware application comes from vulnerability exploitation and cyber-attacks via CNA attacks [e.g., passive (sniffing) or active (Denial-of-Service, DoS)] performed by (external) criminal hackers, especially if the application is deployed in a cloud, virtualized or wireless environment. Reference [8] publication on cloud and grid computing security solutions identified CNA attacks consisting of cross-site scripting, structured query language (SQL) injections, DoS, IP spoofing, address resolution protocol (ARP) poisoning, and physical access of hardware components. Reference [9] identified the threat of criminal hackers performing cloud malware injection attacks, direct DoS attacks, and flood attacks as a significant concern to cloud environments. Reference [10] research on virtualization environments identified how the threat of hackers can originate security parameters from five different components using virtualization: (i) hardware, (ii) other virtual machines (VMs), (iii) the virtual machine monitor (VMM), (iv) the virtual machine monitors' management (VMMMs), and (v) network.

Therefore, research on the GridStreamX Edgeware application is essential. Without an understanding of the types of attacks or vulnerabilities to this type of wireless grid Edgeware application, the platform is run on could violate the semantics of protocol operation, or violate intended configuration, making vulnerabilities harder to detect. Hence, the GridStreamX Edgeware application could keep running but behave incorrectly by having the wrong set of access controls in the network propagating incorrect information in routing updates, or triggering forwarding anomalies that disrupt the operation of the entire organizational network. In addition, the GridStreamX Edgeware application could become increasingly "acceptable to an attack", with the use of highly flexible configuration languages, and the increasing use and deployment of WPaaS utilizing a cloud-based IaaS/VDI or mobile computing environment.

THE GRIDSTREAMX EDGEWARE APPLICATION

Reference [11] defines wireless grids as *ad hoc* dynamic sharing of physical and virtual resources among heterogeneous devices (see Figure 1). The wireless grid or "Grid" is software-driven, serverless, and infrastructureless (in the sense of dedicated infrastructure) and is made possible by the "Grid Core" which is a piece of software that is installed on any Grid-enabled device consisting of a common core library with binding for the local environment [12]. Wireless grids can intelligently and dynamically interconnect users and stakeholders at multiple sites (via cognitive radios), transfer digital media, assume and respond to different equipment types, and adapt to low power conditions and diminished communications capabilities [11,13]. Wireless grids "Edgeware" technology sits at the outermost limits of existing networks, allowing all facets of a user's environment: printers, mp3, documents, photos, cell phones, personal computers (PCs), new plasma TV, etc. to be interoperated and shared easily [14]. Other network hardware, software, services, and content may be controlled and shared through the wireless grid "Edgeware"; however, if those "edge" resources are in a relationship with other hardware, software,

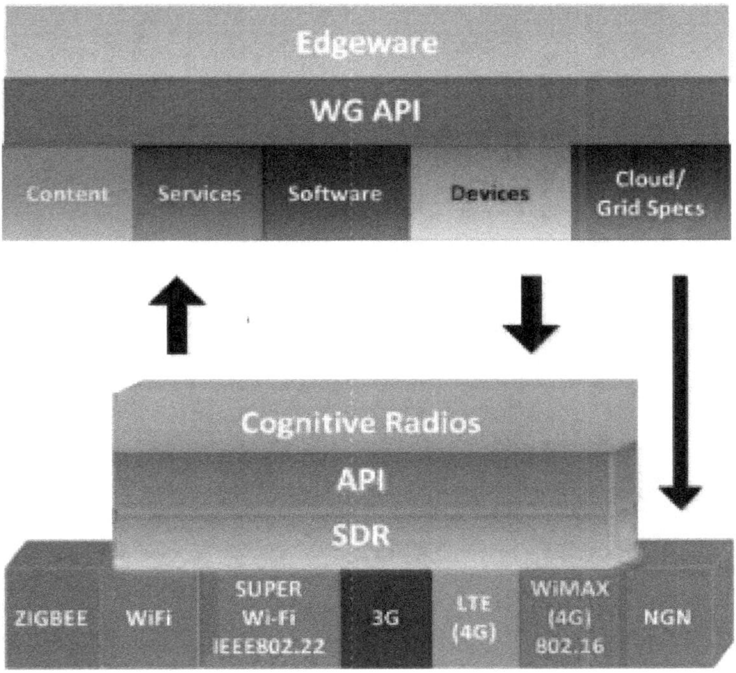

Figure 1. WIGIT Open Framework

and services which are part of the wireless grid, they may function as if they were fully cognitive [14].

Edgeware applications are typically delivered as a service on wireless grid platforms and come in two primary varieties: GriDLET (proprietary Edgeware applications) and WiGLET (non-proprietary open Edgeware applications). A GriDLET is a customized or targeted Grid application which resides in the application layer [14]. A WiGLET is a wireless semantics-aware unit of workload division, computation off-load, and data related to the processing task which interacts directly with the wireless grid user interface (UI), the application program interface (API), the connection, messaging, permissions, and metadata (CORE operations) employing resource management, and accounting of devices directly through the interface layers of a wireless grid architecture [15]. The vertical boxes in Figure 2 represent "Edgeware" applications that reside on a UI, which in turn reside on an API, and may represent dozens or hundreds of different sorts of mini-programs that enable different kinds of resource

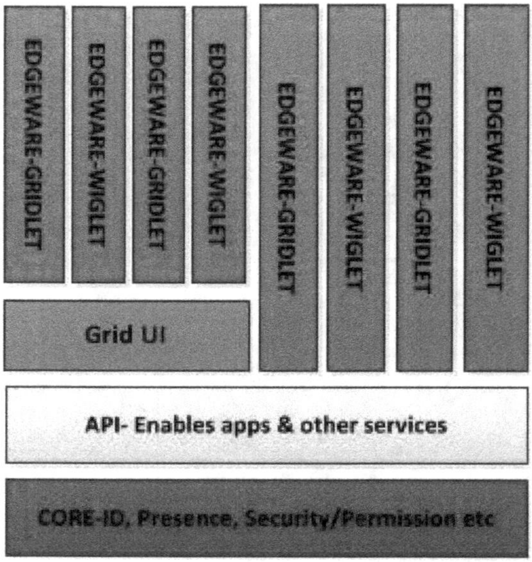

Figure 2. Edgeware Grid Core

sharing and functionality [16]. Edgeware, a new class of software applications, enables the *ad hoc* connection of people, devices, software, and services in a personal cloud, supported by personal cyberinfrastructure. Edge devices are routers, switches, routing switches, integrated access devices (IADs), multiplexers, and a variety of metropolitan area network (MAN)/wide area network (WAN) access devices that provide entry points into enterprise or carrier/service provider core networks which translate between one type of network protocol and another [14]. Edgeware applications can dynamically make use of content and resources present in devices — phones, laptops, PCs, cameras, printers, screens, etc. — through connectivity via a wireless grid [14]. A new Edgeware application which runs one of these of mini-programs is the GridStreamX Edgeware application.

Experimental Approach

To better understand the vulnerabilities in the GridStreamX Edgeware application (and for wireless grid Edgeware in general) and to assess the likelihood of compromising the application's security due to these vulnerabilities, a laboratory experiment was conducted using open-source technology. Through an anatomy of a network attack, specific vulnerabilities in the GridStreamX Edgeware application were identified. A laboratory experiment for studying vulnerabilities was produced at Syracuse University's WIGIT laboratory on a research network of two devices running the GridStreamX Edgeware application including one Dell Optiplex 380 desktop and an Asus X550 CA laptop. Both the desktop PC and laptop were cross-platform virtualized systems using Oracle's VM VirtualBox.[1] Oracle's VM VirtualBox is open-source software which extends the capabilities of computer systems to create a virtual environment to allow multiple operating systems to run concurrently. The attack laptop utilized an HP G71 laptop running the Kali Linux[2] attack tool in a virtualized Linux environment. As part of this research, the Kali Linux attack tool was chosen because it's an open-sourced product, well respected in the ethical hacking community, performs both passive and active attacks, and includes 60 built-in tools, which could address every aspect of an anatomy of a network attack. Since the application runs in a virtualized environment, the desktop and laptop utilized a peer-to-peer architecture through a hotspot on an Android phone (called "Woof-Woof") created specifically for the GridStreamX Edgeware application due to the lack of access to an actual cloud computing server during the time of the experiment.

Data Analysis and Results

The first step was to ensure that the GridStreamX Edgeware application was able to connect to each device in its virtualized operating environment. This was successfully achieved through the application having the ability to ping (e.g., the establishment of a range of IP addresses which map to live hosts) the other device through the network. When the Nessus external network scanner was run on the "Woof-Woof" network, 25 total vulnerabilities were found on the network [two identified as "medium risk" and 23 identified as "informational" (e.g., very low) risk]. Nessus will not attempt to exploit certain vulnerabilities because it could lead to a DoS of

[1]VirtualBox is a general-purpose full virtualizer for x86 hardware, targeted at server, desktop and embedded use https://www.virtualbox.org/.

[2]Previously called "BackTrack".

the system. The scan simply identifies, and reports noted vulnerabilities and security weaknesses in the target system/network. Given the open ports on the network and the number of medium risks identified, the risk of running the GridStreamX Edgeware application in this type of environment would be considered "low"; however, this laboratory environment does not mimic a real-world production environment of various clouds, VMs or smart devices.

Vulnerability Exploitations

Vulnerabilities (or failure of any component) within the GridStreamX Edgeware application can potentially reduce the security of one or more other components, and thus the security of the application and the systems it's on overall. For this reason, GridStreamX Edgeware application not only suffers from the vulnerabilities caused by its implementation in a virtualized network environment but also inherits the vulnerabilities associated with the programming language it uses (e.g., Ruby on Rails), the underlying virtual operating systems environment (e.g., Windows 7), the network and transport layers protocols used (e.g., router, TCP, Wi-Fi, etc.) as well as other supporting infrastructure used (e.g., desktop and laptop). Generally, vulnerability exploitations will result in loss of confidentially, integrity, and/or availability (known as the C-I-A triad) of an application, system, network, or the data it maintains. To further identify exploits to the GridStreamX Edgeware application, the Websploit automatic exploiter component was applied. The Websploit automatic exploiter module is an automatic exploit vulnerability component which utilizes an exploit module (called service autopwn) from the Metasploit module within BackTrack5 r3 tool. The module scans and exploits a target's application code on a device. Since the only targeted application service running in the laboratory environment was the GridStreamX Edgeware application, the targeted IP addresses were identified, and the attack engine was executed.

The purpose of this thesis research was not to identify all possible cyber-attacks leading to an exploit against the GridStreamX Edgeware application but to determine the vulnerabilities in its operating environment. The Metasploit application identifies the specific cyber-attacks and vulnerabilities to the GridStreamX Edgeware application. In order to begin building the exploit, the next step is just to tell Metasploit which module to use. This is performed by simply typing the "use" command followed by the name of the exploit. Once the desired exploit is identified, Metasploit provides instructions to craft its malicious payload. The consideration for categorization for this research was based on the following characteristics of the exploits: the Websploit/Metasploit service autopwn exploit contains metadata related to the vulnerability, there was a working Backtrack5 r3 exploit module for further exploitation for the vulnerability, a vulnerability was identified from the Nessus scan and the details of the vulnerability and exploit were rendered humanly readable (not just specific application code errors). Therefore, the following attacks were identified as "significant" for incorporation into this research and are displayed with their corresponding Metasploit exploit command option. Table 1 lists the cyber-attacks and vulnerabilities identified by this technology.

Table 1. GridStreamX Vulnerabilities

Cyber-Attack Implications	Vulnerabilities
Dictionary Attack	Overcomes weak passwords in XML, XHTML code, URLs, or URIs.
External Entity Attack	Injection of malicious data by pointing to the (unauthenticated) URI/datastore of malicious XML content.
Privilege Escalation Attack	Hacker changes the privilege level of a process and take control of it to bypass security controls.
Authenticated Check: Operating System Name and Installed Package Enumeration Attack	Gathers information about the remote host via an authenticated session and logs into the remote host using SSH, RSH, RLOGIN, Telnet, or local commands and extracts the list of installed packages.
Authentication of Administrators Attack	An unencrypted administrator password may be intercepted.
Checksum Spoofing Attack	An intercepted message with a hash attached is altered with a recomputed hash which will be the checksum for the hacker's replacement message; errors with messages with hash integrity mechanisms.

(Continued)

Table 1. (*Continued*)

Cyber-Attack Implications	Vulnerabilities
Sniffing Attack	Captures sensitive plaintext/poorly encrypted data.
RF Jamming Attack	All specific wireless signal transmissions and receptions are paralyzed simultaneously; causes causing data transmissions to be interrupted and terminated.
Flooding Attack	Repetitive XML messages are issued, overloading the application.
Impersonation Attack	A rogue version of the legitimate application program can be established.
Principal Spoofing Attack	Hacker may be able to impersonate the application on the virtual network.
Internet Explorer (IE) Unparsed XML Cross-Site Scripting (XSS) Attack	Failure to properly parse the XML files (such as due to a malformed XML document) will cause the query string data in the URL to be rendered by the browser; could be exploited to cause XSS attacks as the query string data may contain malicious scripts.
Registry Disclosure Attack	Hacker may gain access to a registry and obtain access to authentication information and audit logs.
Forceful Browsing Attack	Facilitates discovery of application services which are not explicitly publicized; can be used to gather information for future attacks via common gateway interface (CGI) programs.
Internal, Information Application Error Messages Returned to Users Attack	Reconnaissance information may be intercepted by hackers through administrator interfaces.
Routing Detours Attack	Hacker may compromise an application service access point and use it as part of a man-in-the-middle attack by inserting illicit routing instructions to send confidential data to a host of the hacker's choosing.
Symlink Attack	Hacker creates a symbolic link to a file to which the hacker does not have access, but which the application can access and then tricks the application using the symbolic link to grant de facto access rights to the hacker; usually found in Unix and Linux host operating systems.

Table 1. (*Continued*)

Cyber-Attack Implications	Vulnerabilities
Environmental Attack	Deny or disrupt wireless signals and damage its associated equipment, long-term power failure, pollution, chemicals or liquid leakage.
Remote OS Probing Attack	It is possible to guess the remote operating system using a combination of remote probes (TCP/IP, SMB, HTTP, NTP, SNMP, etc.).
Domain Name Attack	Possible to resolve the name of the remote host through the host's fully qualified domain name (FQDN) resolution.
Common Platform Enumeration (CPE) Attack	Possible to enumerate Common Platform Enumeration (CPE) names that matched on the remote system.
Device Type Software Integrity Attack	Possible to guess the remote device type based on the remote operating system.
Port Scanning (SSH) Attack	Remote open ports are enumerated via SSH; based on the remote operating system, it is possible to determine what the remote system type is (e.g., a printer, router, general-purpose computer, etc.).
DCE Services Enumeration Attack	By sending a Lookup request to the portmapper (TCP 135 or epmapper PIPE), it is possible to enumerate the Distributed Computing Environment (DCE) services running on the remote port; using this information, it is possible to connect and bind to each service by sending an RPC request to the remote port/pipe.
Microsoft Windows SMB Service Detection Attack	The remote service understands the Common Internet File System (CIFS) or Server Message Block (SMB) protocol, used to provide shared access to files, printers, etc. between nodes on a network.
Microsoft Windows SMB Log-In Possible Attack	The remote host is running Microsoft Windows operating system or Samba, a CIFS/SMB server for Unix. It is possible to log into it using one of the following accounts: NULL session, Guest account, Given Credentials.

(*Continued*)

Table 1. (*Continued*)

Cyber-Attack Implications	Vulnerabilities
Microsoft Windows SMB LanMan Pipe Server Listing Disclosure Attack	It is possible to obtain network information. It is possible to obtain the browse list of the remote Windows system by sending a request to the LANMAN pipe. The browse list is the list of the nearest Windows systems of the remote host.
Microsoft Windows SMB NativeLanManager Remote System Information Disclosure Attack	It is possible to obtain information about the remote operating system. It is possible to get the remote operating system name and version (Windows and/or Samba) by sending an authentication request to port 139 or 445.
Microsoft Windows NTLMSSP Authentication Request Remote Network Name Disclosure Attack	The remote service understands the Common Internet File System (CIFS) or Server Message Block (SMB) protocol, used to provide shared access to files, printers, etc. between nodes on a network.
SMB Signing Disabled Attack	It is possible to obtain the network name of the remote host. The remote host listens on TCP port 445 and replies to SMB requests. By sending an NTLMSSP authentication request, it is possible to obtain the name of the remote system and the name of its domain.
Service Detection Attack	Signing is disabled on the remote SMB server; this can allow man-in-the-middle attacks against the SMB server.
SSL Certificate Information Attack	It is possible to identify the remote service by its banner or by looking at the error message it sends when it receives an HTTP request.
SSL/TLS Versions Supported Attack	The remote service could be identified. It is possible to identify the remote service by its banner or by looking at the error message it sends when it receives an HTTP request. This connects to every SSL-related port and attempts to extract and dump the X.509 certificate.
SSL Compression Methods Supported Attack	The remote service encrypts communications. This script detects which SSL and TLS versions are supported by the remote service for encrypting communications.

Table 1. (*Continued*)

Cyber-Attack Implications	Vulnerabilities
SSL Trusted Certificate Attack	The remote service supports one or more compression methods for SSL connections. This script detects which compression methods are supported by the remote service for SSL connections.
Service Detection (HELP Request) Attack	The SSL certificate for this service cannot be trusted. The server's X.509 certificate does not have a signature from a known public certificate authority.
Vulnerable ActiveX Object in Internet Explorer Attack	It is possible to identify the remote service by its banner or by looking at the error message it sends when it receives a "HELP" request.
Internet Explorer XML Page Object Type Validation Attack	The Microsoft RDS.Dataspace ActiveX control, provided as part of the ActiveX Data Objects (ADO), may allow hackers to execute malicious code on a vulnerable system, with a potential result of the hacker taking complete control of the exploited system.
Improper Access Control Security Attack	Some versions of Microsoft IE could allow a remote hacker to execute malicious code in the application or on the host system; a hacker could create a malicious XML web page containing malicious objects embedded in the object data tags, which could be executed by the client's browser; the result of improper validation of object data types in some versions of IE when processing XML-based websites.
Improperly Configured SSL Security Level Attack	Hacker with less-than-administrator privileges may be able to access and exploit the administrative interface.
Race Condition Attack	Possible lack of separation between administrator sessions/ tunnels from user sessions/tunnels through administrative interface access.
PHP XML-RPC Library Attack	Caused by a hacker spawning multiple processes which attempt to access the same resources; if two threads of execution use a resource simultaneously, there exists the possibility that resources may be used while invalid, in turn making the state of execution undefined.

(*Continued*)

Table 1. (*Continued*)

Cyber-Attack Implications	Vulnerabilities
PAJAX Remote Code Injection Attack	Susceptible to arbitrary code execution due to unchecked user's input values being passed directly to the eval() call in the parseRequest() function on a server or host system; the hacker could create an XML file that uses a single quote to escape the eval() call to execute PHP code on the target server or host system.
Microsoft DCOM RPC Interface Buffer Overrun Attack	Parameter $methods and $args contain unchecked HTTP POST variables, which may contain malicious PHP code, and could eventually result in a directory traversals attack.
Format String Attack	A server or host system providing DCOM RPC services listens on TCP/UDP port 135, thus exposing itself to the execution of malicious codes with local system privileges on the server or host system.
Directory Traversal Attack	Hacker can exploit format string vulnerabilities introduced by programming errors to inject arbitrary data into the stack to gain control of the application.
Parameter Tampering Attack	Hacker can gain access to files on the host file system.
Schema Poisoning Attack	Insufficiently verified application method parameters allow for possible attacks on application service methods.
Canonicalization Attack	A stored schema may be replaced with a similar but modified one which may reject valid XML documents or allow malicious XML documents to be accepted.
Coercive Parsing Attack	Security decisions based on resource names (e.g., URIs, pathnames, usernames, etc.) can allow hackers to substitute malicious resources for the expected ones.
Intelligent Tampering and Impersonation Attack	Legitimate but large XML files cause the XML parser to treat them as valid but creates a DoS which processes a file big enough to consume all system resources.
Buffer Overflow Attack	A rogue version of the legitimate application service can be established, whilst appearing to be normal; hacker achieves this through deliberate tampering with or impersonating the application in an attempt to subvert its internal state.

Table 1. (*Continued*)

Cyber-Attack Implications	Vulnerabilities
XML Injection Attack	A DoS is created as a result of an oversized payload (e.g., transmitted data) input to the application causing the application to crash when part of the payload is executed; potentially malicious instructions may be loaded from the payload subverting the application service.
URL String Attack	Hacker may gain unauthorized access to XML content, or alter, insert, or delete data in a database accessed with XQuery, XPath, XACML, or gain unauthorized access to restricted portions of the application (or host), or make illicit modifications to the applications security policy; hacker may also be able to perform the equivalent of a cross-site scripting attack, effectively hijacking interaction with a legitimate application service.
Malformed Content Attack	Hacker may gain access to more information than the client's user is privileged to view. Hacker may hide malicious code in malformed XML payload data which is accepted and executed by the application.

SUMMARY OF RESULTS

Given the number of Nessus vulnerabilities identified (25) for the GridStreamX Edgeware application operating environment and the extreme amount of potential Metasploit exploits (927) against the application, there is a considerable risk to implementing this application within an organization's environment just from the "55" vulnerabilities/exploits identified from the research experiment. For this laboratory experiment, these vulnerabilities and exploits provide the foundation that covers all network protocols and types of interaction of the GridStreamX Edgeware application through an existing process model for vulnerability exploitation to build upon.

The research shows that wireless grid Edgeware technology will be vulnerable to cyber-attacks. For example, DoS attacks can be mounted at the RF physical layer or by abusing management frames in the TCP/MAC protocols. While these cannot be prevented, the presence of such attacks can be detected by a monitoring system, and when detected personnel should be sent to investigate the source of the offending transmissions. It may, however, not always be possible to locate and disable the source of these transmissions; therefore, wireless grid Edgeware communications should not be used in environments where availability is critical. Encryption will only protect user data, not TCP or MAC addresses, or information contained in wireless network management frames. Information regarding the name of the wireless grid Edgeware network and security configurations will be broadcast to anyone with an antenna sensitive enough to receive RF transmissions from the network access points. This means the wireless grid Edgeware network will remain vulnerable to wireless network information leakage and traffic analysis.

RECOMMENDATIONS

The results of this research demonstrate the need to further assess the security of GridStreamX Edgeware application modules, components, and the whole program in greater detail. The main objective will be to ensure that the application and its infrastructure environment have sufficient safeguards for the threat environment and aren't vulnerable to numerous cyber-attacks. Further research can also help verify that the GridStreamX Edgeware application exhibits its required security properties and behaviors.

Network Hardening for the GridStreamX Edgeware Application

Network hardening can be technical in nature when monitoring hacker activities or seeking out vulnerabilities in the GridStreamX Edgeware application network. By identifying attack paths, such that all the GridStreamX Edgeware application exploits in the path are necessary for achieving the attack goal, the attack paths can help network administrators determine the best way to harden their networks [17]. The GridStreamX Edgeware application network hardening should be technical in nature when hackers implement hardening tactics that more tightly monitor and control attack-related communications. For example, when a hacker compromises the communication channels in the GridStreamX Edgeware application, the network must increase its focus on operational security in order to protect itself from further malicious exposure.

Periodic GridStreamX Edgeware Application Code Security Review

The GridStreamX Edgeware application code security review should be repeated whenever the source code base changes, in order to identify any defects that may have been introduced into the new version of the code. Some portion of the security code review should be devoted to "black hat" analysis, which is similar in approach to a penetration test of black box software. A black hat code reviewer examines the source code the way an attacker would, specifically to locate defects that can be exploited to compromise the software's correct operation, its resources, or the data it "touches". In a black hat code review, only those parts of the code that are likely to contain exploitable defects are examined. Such a review should then be repeated after all the exploitable defects found through the first round of code reviews are thought to have been fixed, in order to assure that no residual vulnerabilities remain.

Review for Lack of Security-Aware Error and Exception Handling

Checking for adequacy of exception and error handling should be a key focus of the GridStreamX Edgeware application software's design review. The GridStreamX Edgeware application software's detailed design should list all predictable faults — both exceptions and errors, no matter how obscure — that could possibly occur during the software's execution. For each fault listed, the design should define how the software will handle it as well as how the software will react if confronted with an unanticipated (undocumented) fault. Some "unanticipated" faults, especially seemingly obscure faults, can be identified through comprehensive threat modeling which focuses primarily on "exceptional cases of use" (or, more accurately, misuse and abuse). Developers could preempt additional faults during pseudo-coding by cautiously examining the logical relationships between software objects and developing "pseudo" exception handling routines to manage these faults. Reviews of pseudo-code should include checking for the presence and sufficiency of such pseudo-routines.

Perform Fault Propagation Analysis

Fault propagation analysis involves two techniques for fault injection testing of source code, extended propagation analysis and interface propagation analysis [18,19]. The objective of both techniques is not only to observe individual state changes as a result of faults in the GridStreamX Edgeware application but to trace the propagation of state changes that result from any given fault throughout a fault tree generated from the GridStreamX Edgeware application program's source code. Using a component's or application's source code rather than its design specification to generate the fault trees enables the tester to compare fault trees from different versions of source code, generated at different stages of development, to determine whether the software has become more or less vulnerable as it has evolved. It is also possible to compare a fault tree automatically generated from code with a tree manually generated from the design specification to determine whether assumptions made during design about what can or cannot lead to a security compromise were accurate (i.e., substantiating or disproving the original security hypotheses on which the design is based).

Security Fault Injection of Binary of the GridStreamX Edgeware Application Executables

The objective of security fault injection in the GridStreamX Edgeware application is to observe how an attack on a vulnerable execution environment component that results in an unanticipated output from that component will affect the GridStreamX Edgeware application software system that takes that unanticipated output as input and acts on it. For example, one fault injection technique that has proved useful for observing the GridStreamX Edgeware application software's behavior in the face of a DoS attack involves the application of the GridStreamX Edgeware application software wrappers to simulate the compromise of various environment resources that the targeted software relies upon. Security fault injection simulates such faults through data perturbation (i.e., alteration of the type of data the execution environment components pass to the software system, or if testing at the individual component level, that one of the software system's components passes to another). Performing fault injection at both levels can reveal the effects of security defects at each level on the behavior of the individual of the GridStreamX Edgeware application components and on the system as a whole.

Port Blocking on Devices for Secure Communications

The objective of a transport layer attack is to gain access to an organization's data and exfiltrate, manipulate, or destroy an organization's data. Since the GridStreamX Edgeware application exchanges data on the transport layer, this layer was used as the focal point for the cyber-attacks. The transport layer uses two network protocols: TCP and UDP. TCP is a reliable and connection-oriented protocol, which means it ensures data packets are delivered to the destination computer [20]. UDP is an unreliable, connectionless transport used for speed or real-time applications [20]. There are 65,536 TCP/UDP ports and all ports should not be open for use during a data transmission session. For example, the GridStreamX uses ports 135 and 445 to transmit data. This is a concern because ports 135 and 445 (Microsoft RPC and DS ports) are vulnerable to probing (which can yield a port map of the host) and reveal whether the host operating system is a Microsoft product leading to additional attacks. The mitigation strategy for port blocking should involve only using those ports through which the data needs to be transmitted (e.g., 22 for SSH/SCP, 443 for HTTP over SSL, and 989 for FTP over SSL) and the protection of application interfaces through application shielding (the use of a security wrapper tool to enforce input validation) and source code analysis (to scan the source code during testing to identify security flaws in protocols) to provide suggested corrections.

Deployment of Wireless Intrusion Detection Sensors

When deploying wireless intrusion detection sensors in a GridStreamX Edgeware application environment, the sensor may be integrated with the access point or provided as a standalone component (or both). While standalone sensors will be more expensive, they permit more flexibility as to where the sensor is positioned. This will allow greater control over the area that is monitored when compared to sensors that are integrated with an access point (as an access point will be located to maximize network visibility of clients, not optimal monitoring). Greater flexibility may also afford the opportunity to obtain higher-resolution location information as to the source of transmissions. The deployment of sensors will provide better coverage, than if the sensor components were integrated with the access points.

FUTURE RESEARCH

The GridStreamX Edgeware application continues to mature and is potentially integrated with an organization's operational environment, the mobile and wireless devices used to connect to both corporate and untrusted networks that the application uses should be considered highly vulnerable and potentially threatening to the security posture of the application itself and of the corporate network. As the devices using the GridStreamX Edgeware application under consideration are mobile and will be used to access networks in a range of environments, there is the potential that they may be inadvertently lost or stolen and the sensitive information contained on the device revealed. In the event that it is lost or stolen, the duration for which the organization is exposed can be minimized by disabling affected accounts or revoking access credentials until new credentials have been issued. Additionally, consideration could be given to protecting potentially sensitive data on the device from disclosure to unauthorized parties by adequate baseline configuration of the device, use of complex passwords, and disk encryption software.

Additionally, should the wireless interface of the mobile device be inadvertently left enabled, there is the potential that the device could, unbeknown to the user of the device, establish a connection to a rogue peer or network. Where possible, the device should be administratively configured to prevent connection establishment to arbitrary networks. Specifically, *ad hoc* modes of network should be disabled if not required. Likewise, the device should be restricted from connecting only to authorized networks (as identified by SSID and MAC addresses) using authorized authentication and link layer security protocols and algorithms. Where the device may be required to establish connections to arbitrary networks, a host-based detection capability may be warranted.

CONCLUSION

In closing, wireless grid Edgeware technology is an emerging technology, however, it needs time to mature before it's capable of meeting the full range of security requirements to become an operable and trusted application within a business environment. This research is the first step in a larger effort to help wireless grid Edgeware technology become more anticipative by developing more robust and future-oriented Edgeware defense strategies. If security experts can anticipate possible hacker reactions before implementing defenses for wireless grid Edgeware technology, they will be better prepared to manage and defeat hacker's strategies and tactics that evolve in response to defense measures. The range of threats facing wireless grid Edgeware technology, devices, and communications, when combined with the immaturity of Edgeware security, represents a real information security risk. Research must be taken to ensure that the potential increase in vulnerabilities in wireless grid Edgeware technology is suitably controlled and managed.

REFERENCES

[1] Wireless Grids Corporation (2013). Gridstream workplace as a service (WPaaS) edgeware product. http://wgrids.com/?page_id=28 (Accessed May 31, 2013).

[2] Li, G., Sun, H., Gao, H., Yu H., & Cai, Y. (2009). A survey on wireless grids and clouds. In *Eighth International Conference on Grid and Cooperative Computing, GCC'09* (pp. 261–267). IEEE.

[3] Rabinovich, M., Xiao, Z., & Aggarwal, A. (2004). Computing on the edge: A platform for replicating internet applications. In *Web Content Caching and Distribution* (pp. 57–77). Dordrecht: Springer Netherlands.

[4] Pang, H. & Tan, K. (2004). Authenticating query results in edge computing. In *20th International Conference on Data Engineering, Proceedings* (pp. 560–571). IEEE.

[5] Davis, A., Parikh, J., & Weihl, W. (2004). Edgecomputing: Extending enterprise applications to the edge of the internet. In *Proceedings of the 13th International World Wide Web Conference on Alternate Track Papers & Posters* (pp. 180–187).

[6] Goh, S., Pang, H., Deng, R., & Bao, F. (2006). Three architectures for trusted data dissemination in edge computing. *Data & Knowledge Engineering*, 58(3), 381–409.

[7] Markham, T. & Payne, C. (2001). Security at the network edge: A distributed firewall architecture. In *Proceedings DARPA Information Survivability Conference & Exposition II, DISCEX '01* (Vol. 1, pp. 279–286). IEEE.

[8] Rajanna, P. & Gyani, J. (2012). A comparative study of cloud and grid computing security solutions. *International Journal of Computer Science and Electronics Engineering*, 2(1), 1–8.

[9] Gruschka, N. & Jensen, M. (2010). Attack surfaces: A taxonomy for attacks on cloud services. In *2010 IEEE 3rd International Conference on Cloud Computing (CLOUD)* (pp. 276–279). IEEE.

[10] Van Cleeff, A., Pieters, W., & Wieringa, R. (2009). Security implications of virtualization: A literature study. In *International Conference on Computational Science and Engineering, CSE '09* (Vol. 3, pp. 353–358). IEEE.

[11] McKnight, L., Howison, J., & Bradner, S. (Guest Editors). Introduction: wireless grids — Distributed resource sharing by mobile, nomadic, and fixed devices. *IEEE Internet Computing*, 8(4), 24–31.

[12] Treglia, J., McKnight, L., Kuehn, A., Ramnarine-Rieks, R., Venkatesh, M., & Bose, T. (2011). Interoperability by 'Edgeware': Wireless grids for emergency response. In *44th Hawaii International Conference on System Sciences (HICSS)* (pp. 1–10), IEEE.

[13] McKnight, L., Anius, D., & Uzuner, O. (2002). Virtual markets in wireless grids: Peering policy obstacles. In *The TPRC 30th Research Conference on Communication, Information and Internet Policy* (pp. 1–23).

[14] McKnight, L., Marsden, J., Treglia, J., Nanno, E., Hameed, A., & Lu, Y. (2013). *Open Specifications for Wireless Grids Technical Requirements*, Version 0.2, 10.13140/2.1.2654.4646.

[15] Brooks, T. & McKnight, L. (2012). Securing wireless grids: Architecture designs for secure wiglet-to-wiglet interfaces. *International Journal of Information and Network Security (IJINS)*, 2(1), 1–16.

[16] Treglia, J., Ramnarine-Rieks, A., & McKnight, L. (2009), Collaboration in a wireless grid innovation testbed by virtual consortium. In *Networks for Grid Applications: Third International ICST Conference, GridNets 2009*, Athens, Greece, September 8–9, Revised Selected Papers 3 (pp. 139–146). Springer, Berlin, Heidelberg.

[17] Jajodia, S., Noel, S., & O'Berry, B. (2005). Topological analysis of network attack vulnerability. *Managing Cyber Threats*, 5(2005), 247–266.

[18] Voas, J. (1997). Building software recovery assertions from a fault injection-based propagation analysis. In *The Twenty-First Annual International Proceedings of Computer Software and Applications Conference, COMPSAC '97* (pp. 505–510). IEEE.

[19] Voas, J. (1997). Fault injection for the masses. *Computer*, 30(12), 129–130.

[20] Harris, S. (2007). *All in One Cissp Exam Guide* (Fourth Ed.). McGraw-Hill, Osborne.

Chapter 6

Secure the Edge? Understanding the Risk of Wireless Grids Edgeware Technology*

ABSTRACT

This chapter contributes to the foundational understanding of the security vulnerabilities and risks toward wireless grid Edgeware technology. Since communication networks and devices are subject to becoming the target of exploitation by hackers (e.g., individuals who attempt to gain unauthorized access to computer systems), these individuals are gaining ever-increasing knowledge of the often widely reported exploitable vulnerabilities in these types of innovative technologies; and thus are able to craft increasingly effective computer network attacks (CNAs) against such technologies. This research responds to the overall proposition: what security vulnerability enumerations would contribute to the degradation and risk in using a wireless grid Edgeware application in a virtualized cloud environment? Using supporting research pertaining to cyber-attacks and vulnerabilities towards a wireless cloud (e.g., the integration of cloud computing and a wireless grid architecture), security vulnerabilities in virtualization environments, and specific vulnerabilities exploited against a wireless grid Edgeware application, this

*Originally published as Brooks, T., Kaarst-Brown, M., Caicedo, C., Park, J., & McKnight, L. (2014). Secure the edge? Understanding the risk towards wireless grids edgeware technology. *International Journal for Internet Technology and Securea Transactions* (*IJITST*), 8, 5(3), 191–222.

research provides a greater understanding of the practical ways wireless grid Edgeware technology can be attacked and the risk in utilizing this technology.

INTRODUCTION

Complex computing architectures are an operational imperative and challenge throughout an organization. Evolving information systems and information technology (IT) architectures challenge existing approaches to information security. With the evolution and adoption of new and innovative forms of IT (e.g., virtualization, cloud computing, wireless grids, etc.), new architectures using this IT may render many existing information security techniques ineffective. As organizations adopt new enterprise computing business models with the integration of intelligent mobile devices (e.g., Smartphones, iPads, etc.) and social media (e.g., Facebook, Twitter, etc.), these architectures will become highly control-dependent on automated networks and systems with open, less secure architectures. Organizations seek to control these new systems and networks through the development and use of new technologies, including IT [39]. Often, support for these architectures requires the connection of IT for interoperability with varying degrees of threats (e.g., a negative event to cause harm to a computer system), vulnerabilities (e.g., weakness in computer networks/systems), and risks (e.g., the possibility of harm or loss) [27]. Such connectivity and interoperability are often done without a sound understanding of the hostile environment in which each system is operating, the vulnerabilities existing within each system, the additional vulnerabilities caused by the connectivity amongst the operating environment, or the full magnitude of the consequences to support operations that can result from a successful exploitation [41]. In short, the actual threats, vulnerabilities, and risks being incurred from these environments, whether autonomously or separately, are still not well understood.

"Distributed" computing, a computing methodology that harnesses the power of many machines linked together for a common purpose, gives unlimited computing power to individual users [62]. As complex computing environments increase, the nature of these distributed systems and their associated vulnerabilities are known to an increasing set of malicious individuals (e.g., hackers) who want to break into and exploit their vulnerabilities [64]. Today, access to these complex systems, exploitation tools, and the ability, or lack thereof, to detect exploitation are factors placing these information systems using IT at ever-increasing risks [64]. Because of the abundance of hardware, software, and computing devices needed for these multi-connected complex systems, the concept of end-to-end security becomes critical. Known as the "C-I-A" triad of information security, the major security issues of confidentiality (or loss of authorization), integrity (or loss of information accuracy), and availability (or uninterrupted use of information) for these types of environments also require an unprecedented dependence on secure information communication [3, 65]. One form of distributed computing through a dynamic virtual network that exists only while it's in use is known as a wireless grid.

Reference [46] defines wireless grids as an *ad hoc* dynamic sharing of physical and virtual resources among heterogeneous devices [see Figure 1(a)]. Wireless grid architectures and platforms enable heterogeneous resource discovery and sharing through the formation of wireless grid virtual networks [45]. The wireless grid or "Grid" is software-driven, serverless, infrastructureless (in the sense of dedicated infrastructure) and is made possible by the "Grid Core" which is a piece of software that is installed on any Grid-enabled device consisting of a common core library with binding for the local environment [67] [see Figure 1(b)]. Radio components support the connectivity for wireless grid, and also carry the

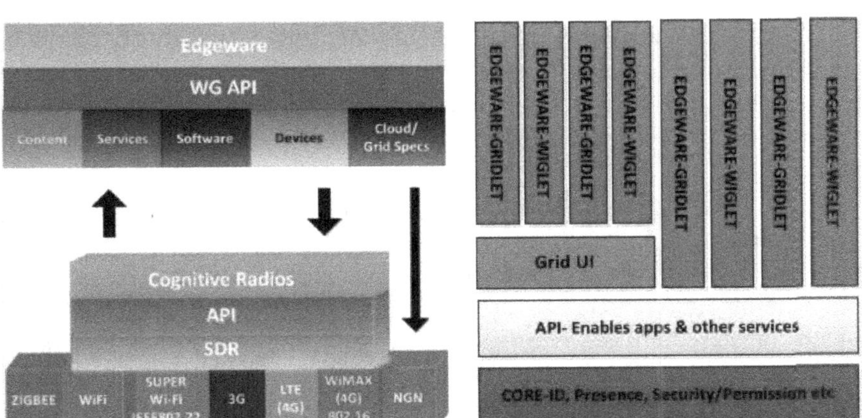

(a) (b)

Figure 1. **(a) WiGiT Open Framework. (b) Edgeware Grid Core**

information exchanging functionalities among heterogeneous nodes [47]. Each communication node has at least one radio and this radio provides the connectivity between the service request node and service nodes, or between the service request node and one access point (AP) to wired networks, which connects the service nodes [47]. The radio components may support both remote access (supported with cellular networks or Wi-Fi networks) and local access (supported with shorter-range wireless standards, such as Bluetooth and Zigbee) [47, 67]. *Ad hoc* or mesh networks are an option for connectivity when hierarchical systems are not available or a different option is preferred and coexistence mechanisms among multiple radios may be defined by each system [47]. Through the radio components, wireless grids can intelligently and dynamically interconnect users at multiple sites, transfer digital media, assume and respond to different equipment types, and adapt to low power conditions and diminished communications capabilities [45].

Edgeware is similar to "Edge computing", where the data and computing power is processed away from a centralized point to the edges of a network [43]. Edgeware is a new class of software applications enabling *ad hoc* connection of people, devices, software, and services in a personal cloud, supported by a personal cyberinfrastructure [67]. The vertical boxes, in Figure 1(b) represent "Edgeware" applications that reside on a user interface, which in turn reside on an application program interface (API), and may represent dozens or hundreds of different sorts of mini-programs that enable different kinds of resource sharing and functionality [66]. Edgeware technology is specifically designed for software applications deployed on wireless grids utilizing virtualization and cloud technologies and refers to the software capability to deploy network "edge" devices (e.g., nodes) without the dependency of a central server for processing [45].

Edge devices are routers, switches, routing switches, integrated access devices (IAD), multiplexers, and a variety of metropolitan area network (MAN)/wide area network (WAN) access devices that provide entry points into enterprise or carrier/service provider core networks which translate between one type of network protocol and another [61]. Edgeware applications can dynamically make use of content and resources present in devices — Smartphones, laptops, personal computers (PC), cameras, printers, screens, etc. — through connectivity via a wireless grid [45]. Edgeware applications are typically delivered as a service on wireless grid platforms and come in two primary varieties: GRiDLET's (i.e., proprietary Edgeware applications) and WiGLET's (i.e., non-proprietary open Edgeware applications).

This chapter presents the information security risk for implementing wireless grid Edgeware technology in an organization's virtualized cloud environment. Although highly innovative, this new information system model alters the security models of traditional security policies and presents a growing concern regarding the C-I-A triad threat to information security from hackers (e.g., individuals who attempt to gain unauthorized access to computer systems) gaining ever-increasing knowledge of exploitable vulnerabilities in this type of technology.

BACKGROUND

In today's hostile cyber environment, hackers are continuously evolving their attack methodologies and targets. With the increasing growth of these new and innovative technologies, such as cloud computing, virtualization, wireless grids, etc., dependency on the "the cloud" makes it an increasingly attractive target for hackers. Hackers are creating entirely new classes of attacks that are even more difficult to discover. Hackers opportunistically scan the Internet to find and infect computer systems that are mis-configured or lack current software security patches [79]. These new classes of attacks are emerging rapidly with the evolution of network technologies and with each new "killer" application that comes along. Since hackers have grown adept at a wide range of attacks, including theft of confidential information, implanting and remotely executing malicious code, and launching denial-of-service (DoS) attacks [72]. Highly skilled hacker's use automated tools that are also very sophisticated, and their effects are initially much more difficult for computer security staff and security technology products to detect [77]. Hackers are gaining ever-increasing knowledge of the often widely-reported exploitable vulnerabilities in innovative technologies and thus are able to craft increasingly effective attacks against these applications which incorporate these technologies.

Unfortunately, the unique properties of the cloud make it difficult to counter these attacks. The high processing speed and tight coupling of these systems enables attacks to progress much faster than humans can react; the large scale, coupled with the ability of hacker's to encrypt and hide sensitive information, makes it difficult to observe and attribute a hacker's activities. The process of running multiple services on the same servers and network elements (i.e., virtualization) means that compromising one (perhaps) less secure service enables hackers to attack another.

Through the cohesion of understanding the vulnerabilities of a wireless cloud, virtualization, and a wireless grid Edgeware application (i.e., GridStreamX), this chapter sets the foundation for discovering new compromises on wireless grid Edgeware technology and contributes to the foundational understanding of the technology and architecture of the vulnerabilities and risk towards potentially implementing wireless grids Edgeware technology in an organizational virtual cloud environment. By examining cyber-attacks, vulnerabilities, the likelihood of a hacker(s) attack, their potential impact, and countermeasures to mitigate this threat is also taken into consideration. In addition to the increase in complexity and availability of wireless grids Edgeware technology provides, today the risk of hackers being caught is relatively low and attacks are often not detected. The rapid proliferation of innovative technologies, such as virtualization, cloud computing, wireless grid Edgeware, etc., the increased availability of sophisticated tools, and the lack of sufficiently developed and deployed effective information security protections, make this architecture an increasingly lucrative target for hackers.

RELATED WORK

While there has been much work on detecting vulnerabilities and cyber-attacks in cloud, virtualization, wireless, and grid systems [14, 40, 44] research on the security of wireless grid Edgeware is beginning to increase [8, 10]. Like any complex system, wireless grid Edgeware networks are subject to mistakes in the form of implementation errors and misconfigurations of devices. All the vulnerabilities that exist in conventional wired and wireless networks will apply to wireless grid Edgeware technology as well. For example, hackers may gain unauthorized access in virtualized environments by simply installing a new version of the hypervisor on the client machine which copies all subsequent users' decrypted disk images to the attacker's machine [25]. Hackers may be able to gain connectivity to cloud-based infrastructure-as-a-service (IaaS) network management controls and thereby disable or disrupt operations [31]. Handheld devices used in wireless networks could be attached to the organization's network with malware, viruses, or other malicious code which may corrupt data on a device and subsequently be introduced into the network connection [55].

Cybercriminals' growing preference toward the use of low-volume, targeted attacks in wireless environments are stealing information and data from compromised devices [58]. These attack threats are concerning which still need to be addressed for leveraging wireless grid Edgeware as a secure data communications method.

Grid computing is often regarded as the predecessor of cloud computing and many authors claim that cloud computing and grid computing are quite similar [23, 24, 26]. Grid computing enables virtualization of distributed computing and data resources such as processing, network bandwidth, and storage capacity to create a single system image, granting users and applications seamless access to vast IT capabilities [21, 23]. Consequently, grids typically provide services to authenticate and authorize users to access resources on a remote set of machines on the same grid [22]. Grid computing can also be wireless or mobile where computing loads must be allocated dynamically to respond to changing conditions and information generated by required at critical nodes. Wireless grids are *ad hoc* dynamic sharing of physical and virtual resources among heterogeneous devices, which utilize "Edgeware", as a platform that enables heterogeneous resource discovery and sharing through the formation of wireless grid virtual networks [45]. Although the security research on wireless grids is fairly new, computer network attacks (CNAs) on grid and wireless sensor networks have been prevalent in the research literature for years [13, 56, 51].

Edge computing has emerged as an important technique for delivering web content, services and diverse service interfaces over the Internet and has its roots in content delivery networks (CDNs) that deliver content by moving it from centralized servers to the edge of the network, closer to end-users [43]. Using edge computing, parts of a Web application — and in some cases, the entire application — can be distributed across networks and many client requests can be processed completely at the edge, avoiding wide area network communication altogether [18]. In practice, pushing application logic to edge servers introduces a number of technical challenges which can lead to cyber-attacks, one of which is data security; for applications that run on a database, edge computing entails the distribution of (parts of) the database, to edge servers that perform query processing on behalf of the central database management systems (DBMS) [52]. Since the edge servers are not necessarily as secure as the corporate data center, the query results produced by them must be checked for integrity; specifically, a recipient must be able to verify that the values in his query result have not been tampered with and that no spurious tuples are introduced [52].

Although there has been research pertaining to Edge computing [18, 43, 52], there is not a significant body of related work towards CNAs against Edge computing (or Edgeware in general). Reference [28] performed research ensuring data security in an edge computing platform through three schemes that enable users to check the correctness of query results produced by the edge servers. Their research proposes two new schemes for verifying the query results produced by the unsecured edge servers. The schemes are based on the observation that if necessary a group of edge servers can be running different operating systems and protected by different security products, thus increasing the difficulty for attackers to compromise all the edge servers concurrently without being detected [28]. Reference [28] research is important because it shows that each scheme offers different security features (e.g., verifiability, unforgeability, identifiability, undeniability, and prevention of misuse) and imposes different demands on the edge servers, user machines, and interconnecting network.

With the new paradigms of cloud computing, virtualization, wireless grids, etc., these dynamics will cause certain key challenges to rise in prominence in protecting against certain CNA attacks. Reference [54] publication on cloud and grid computing security solutions identified CNA attacks consisting of cross-site scripting, structure query language (SQL) injections, DoS, internet protocol (IP) spoofing, address resolution protocol (ARP) poisoning, and physical access of hardware components. Reference [54] further researched the processing of data coming back from the cloud and how it may be vulnerable to certain types of CNA attacks. Reference [54] research is significant because it discusses how cloud computing offers its users services and applications, which are provided through the Internet, and thus, a large number of computers will be in the path of the data when the data is sent to the cloud for analysis which makes to data susceptible to attacks.

Reference [37] research on the technical security issues in cloud computing identified the various distinct web services technologies used to build cloud computing systems and depending on the type of cloud — either IaaS, platform-as-a-service (PaaS), or software-as-a-service (SaaS), the different security issues that pertain to those infrastructures. Reference [37] research identified CNA attacks on protocols using extensible markup language (XML) signature element wrapping, browser-based cloud authentication, cloud malware injection, metadata spoofing, flooding, and

DoS. The important aspect of this study is the threat of flooding attacks on cloud systems using IaaS, which also integrates virtualization and workplace-as-a-service (WPaaS) technologies. Neither [54] nor [37] research on the identification of cloud computing attacks and mitigation strategies for those attacks provide attack specifics regarding different cloud computing deployment models (e.g., SaaS, PaaS, IaaS) from the perspective of using virtualization technologies. Although an IaaS private cloud computing infrastructure utilizes the concept of virtualization and virtualization is important to the cloud, CNA attacks against virtualization technology itself is also a concern.

Virtualization can expand the utilization of existing computing infrastructures through the hypervisor (e.g., the software layer which allows multiple operating systems to be installed concurrently on the same machine with total isolation from each other; also known as a Virtual Machine Manager). Reference [57] research on a cloud platform which multiplexes many customers' virtual machines (VM) across a shared physical infrastructure identified the introduction of new vulnerabilities, such as cross-VM side-channel attacks (extracting information from a target VM on the same host machine) in third-party clouds. This research demonstrated how to penetrate the isolation between VMs (e.g., via a vulnerability that allows an "escape" to the hypervisor or via side-channels between VMs) to violate customer confidentiality. The importance of this research is that it shows how improperly protected end-user machines could spread malware to the VM, and in turn, spread to other users as they connect to the VM. It also emphasizes the importance of virtualization technologies in the context of cloud computing security; however, the research only states attacks resulting from virtualization technologies.

Another potential attack point within a virtualization environment is the communications link between VMs. Reference [68] research identified specific attacks on the VM in the form of VM hyperjacking, VM escape, VM hopping, VM monitoring, VM DoS, and VM mobility. Through a network testbed, these researchers identified the security impacts of these attacks when introducing such modern virtualization technologies into a network testbed environment. Their experiments showed that hypervisor-based virtualization technologies introduce a hypervisor to manage and control the resource allocation but make the hypervisor a new attacking target [68]. The testbeds showed that they were still vulnerable to attacks like VM hyperjacking, VM escape, VM hopping, VM monitoring, and VM DoS; and an attacker may try to obtain root access to the host operating system, in order to inject virus or malware and damage the fundamental requirements of the hypervisor-based virtualization [68]. Although highly relevant, their research does not discuss how these attacks affect the control of communications between VMs in compromising the confidentiality, integrity, and availability of data exchanged across a virtual network within an organization. As cloud users connect to resources distributed across multiple VMs, the use of grid, specifically, wireless grid computing will also create separation securing against the attacks of this new form of distributed computing.

THEORETICAL FRAMEWORK

Through the foundational theory of risk management and CNAs, the theoretical framework (see Figure 2) used for this research dealt with identifying the security implications to wireless grid Edgeware to address the overall research question — what security vulnerabilities enumerations would contribute to the degradation and risk in using a wireless grid Edgeware application in a virtualized cloud?. This research framework supports the identification of threats to and vulnerabilities towards wireless grids Edgeware technology and the potential impact resulting from the loss of information or capabilities of this technology. The framework also supports the practice of generating relevant risk-reducing countermeasures by balancing risk reduction against these attributes for implementing wireless grids Edgeware technology. As these attributes change over time, it is necessary to periodically revisit the current understanding

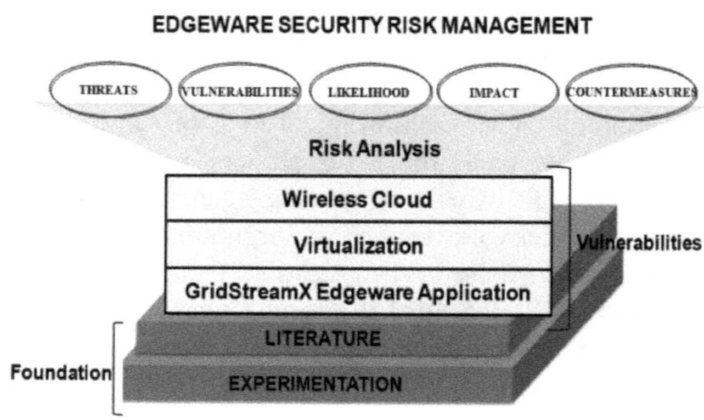

Figure 2. The Conceptual Edgeware Security Risk Framework

of the risks incurred within the current and projected operating environments and determine if a change in protection approach (e.g., technology, procedures, personnel) is warranted.

Additionally, the framework focuses on gaining insight into the risks that are being incurred (or will be incurred) based upon the operational usage of wireless grids Edgeware technology, future architectural designs, and hostile operating environments for wireless grids Edgeware technology. At the core of this approach is the underlying theory about the elements of risk management, its definition, and its relationship. In addition, this theoretical foundation was grouped into the following specific areas or factors: (1) threats (e.g., cyber-attacks targeting computer networks/systems), (2) vulnerabilities (e.g., weaknesses of an attack), (3) likelihood (e.g., probability of occurrence), (4) impact (e.g., impact from a cyber-attack), countermeasures (e.g., mitigating techniques against a cyber-attack) and overall risk (e.g., overall potential harm or loss). The overall risk takes all of these attributes into consideration. This framework influences the understanding of the information security risk to wireless grids Edgeware technology and is consistent with the theoretical elements of risk management.

The framework for this research supported the threat, vulnerability, likelihood, impact, and countermeasures research needed to provide insight and meaning to the information pertaining to the concept of a wireless cloud, virtualization technology, and data from a laboratory experiment regarding the degradation of the GridStreamX Edgeware application operating environment [6, 7, 8]. From the analysis of threats, the potential for a threat-source to exercise (accidentally trigger or intentionally exploit) a specific vulnerability was determined [36, 49].

This research determined which set of attacks hackers would more than likely invest in to attack wireless grids Edgeware applications. Vulnerabilities were identified for wireless grids Edgeware technology through the discovering of weaknesses that could be exploited by threats to its operational environment and technologies in order to determine the immediate objective of an attack (i.e., defeat of confidentiality, integrity or availability) [30, 49].

LITERATURE REVIEW

Risk Management

Discussions and research on wireless grids and Edgeware have been on the rise in academia [9, 10, 14, 47, 66, 67]. Although literature dates back decades in the areas of cloud computing, virtualization, wireless networks, and grid computing [5, 29, 22, 51], publications on wireless grids and Edgeware are beginning to increase. Recent research defines Edgeware as "a new class of software specifically designed for software applications deployed on wireless grids" [10, 47]. According to [66], "Edgeware" is software that resides beyond the cloud, across edge network devices (e.g., routers, switches, etc.), both wired and wireless. These definitions lead to the general purpose of the identification of cyber-attacks on wireless grid Edgeware with the consequence that there is a lack of clarity on the concept of a secure wireless grid Edgeware architecture. Nevertheless, a common understanding of the term Edgeware itself is beginning to emerge.

Risk, as defined in the American Heritage Dictionary, is the "possibility of suffering harm or loss". Risk is the net negative impact of the exercise of a vulnerability, considering both the probability and the impact of occurrence [49]. Risk management theory is described as the performance of activities designed to minimize the negative impact (cost) of uncertainty (risk) regarding possible losses [59]. The contributions of literature findings for this chapter first take into consideration risk management theory, in which several authors from academia could be attributed to identifying the origins of risk management theory [35, 48, 77]. The theory could also be attributed to publications from the *Journal of Risk Management and Risk Management* (formerly The National Insurance Buyer) from the 1950s to 1980s [17]. Reference [11] developed one of the earliest risk management approaches, which developed a structured methodology based on a set of concepts that subsisted in the later approaches, such as vulnerability analysis, threat analysis, risk analysis, and control implementation. These early researchers tended to agree that institutional specialization in risk management gave it a valued position in business education [59].

Risk management theory in the context of IT and information system security is not a new research domain [2, 20]. Reference [32] performed risk management in their research to identify the threat of criminal hackers performing cloud malware injection attacks, direct DoS attacks, and flood attacks in determining these as a significant concern to cloud environments. Reference [12] performed a comprehensive risk analysis of existing grid computing security issues identifying countermeasures to grid security issues at the host level (e.g., data protection, job starvation), architecture level (e.g., policy mapping, DoS, information security), and credential level. [73] Risk management research on computational grids, data grids, and service grids identifies specific types of vulnerabilities that could exist for each grid computing system. Reference [71] risk management research on virtualization environments identified how the threat of hackers could originate from security parameters from five different components using virtualization: (1) hardware, (2) other VMs, (3) the virtual machine monitor (VMM) (4) the virtual machine monitors' management (VMMMs) and (5) network. [31] identified four cloud-specific technology vulnerabilities — web applications and services, virtualization, and cryptography — which include such vulnerabilities as VM escape, session riding and hijacking, and insecure or obsolete cryptography through risk management analysis. These researchers were particularly instrumental in establishing the foundation for identifying risk in grids, clouds, and virtualization technologies.

Computer Network Attacks

Computer and network security aims to provide confidentiality, data integrity, and service availability [55]. Information security is the protection of information and the systems and hardware that use, store, and transit that information [75]. An important aspect of information security is to ensure the confidentiality, integrity, and availability of the data being processed as information [75]. In the early days of computing, the emphasis was on computer security because of the nature of the threats, such as physical theft of equipment, espionage against the products of the systems, and sabotage [72]. Developments in networking, software, engineering, and architecture changed all of this throughout the years and one of the biggest threats to information security became known as a CNA [78]. A computer attack may be defined as actions directed against computer systems to disrupt equipment operations, change processing control or corrupt stored data [78]. Computer attacks can be classified into three areas: (1) physical attacks, which involve conventional weapons directed against a computer facility or its transmission lines, (2) electronic attacks which involve the use of power of electromagnetic energy as a weapon (more commonly known as electromagnetic pulse — EMP) to overload computer circuitry and (3) CNA involving malicious code as a weapon to inject computers to exploit weakness [78]. Cyber as a prefix was used for the first time in the word "cybernetics", which was coined and used by Norbert Weiner in his book of the same name published in 1948 [60, 76].

Cyber, as defined in the American Heritage Dictionary, is a combining form meaning "computer", "computer network" or "virtual reality". A cyber-attack is an attack, via cyberspace (e.g., Internet) targeting an enterprise's use of cyberspace for the purpose of disrupting, disabling, destroying, or maliciously controlling a computing environment/infrastructure; or destroying the integrity of the data or stealing controlled information [16].

Cyber-attacks are performed through CNA consisting of five steps: reconnaissance (surveillance for data gathering), vulnerability scanning (discovery of a technical weakness), gaining access (inside the system), maintaining access (privilege escalation), and covering tracks (hiding evidence of intrusions or activities) [69]. Research has been written on CNAs throughout the 1970s [74], the 1980s [53], 1990s [4] and in the 2000s [33]. In the CNA literature, the major research findings for this research pertained to hackers/hacking [64] and the history of CNAs [70]. Hacking has existed, in various forms, since the late 1950s [64]. Hackers can be external (no access) or internal (authorized access) to the systems they plan to attack. Hacking is intrinsically linked with network security and the existence of hacking gave rise to the network security industry. Recently, the term hacker has taken on a new meaning as defined by [19] as someone who maliciously breaks into systems for personal gain. Technically, these criminals are "crackers" or "black hat" hackers (criminal hackers) who break into systems with malicious intent and are 'external' to the systems they are attempting to attack; are out for personal gain, fame, profit, and even revenge; and modify, delete and steal critical information often making other people miserable [19].

Hackers conduct CNAs on systems for a variety of reasons. Some hackers attack information systems simply for the challenge of penetrating an important system based on the value of the information within the network [34]. Other hackers attack information systems for the purpose of revealing vulnerabilities and weaknesses in popular software applications and hardware [73]. Lastly, some hackers may attack information systems out of a sense of financial or personal gain, effectively using their skills to steal money, or otherwise valuable data, which they can either sell or use to blackmail their victims [63]. Hackers accessing networks that are considered important (or regarded as difficult to penetrate) satisfies the egos of these hackers who determine their targets based on the degree of difficulty involved in performing CNA attacks [38].

The recent emergence of innovative technologies, such as cloud computing, virtualization, wireless grids, edge computing, etc., utilizing web applications/services to process information is common to CNAs. Reference [54] publication on cloud and grid computing security solutions identified CNA attacks consisting of cross-site scripting, SQL injections, DoS, internet protocol (IP) spoofing, address resolution protocol (ARP) poisoning, and physical access of hardware components. Reference [37] research on the technical security issues in cloud computing identified the various distinct web services technologies used to build cloud computing systems and depending on the type of cloud — either IaaS, PaaS, or SaaS, the different security issues that pertain to those infrastructures. [68] research identified specific attacks on the VM in the form of VM hyperjacking, VM escape, VM hopping, VM monitoring, VM DoS, and VM mobility. Reference [42] published a comparative study on the nature and complexities that grid computing introduces regarding the vulnerabilities in middleware, web services, and portals for grids. The relevance this literature has to wireless grids Edgeware technology is that by understanding the concept of CNA and how similar technologies are attacked, it's easier to understand methods and techniques to protect the application and its network against security loopholes.

CLOUD, VIRTUALIZATION, AND EDGEWARE VULNERABILITIES

Technology vulnerabilities take many forms and are fundamental failures in network and software designs meaning that the technology always will have a problem no matter how well it is implemented. Unmitigated vulnerabilities require risk management planning and analysis to deal with impacts to organizational assets. Whether the vulnerabilities are exploited intentionally (malicious) or unintentionally (non-malicious), the net result is that the confidentiality, integrity, and/or availability of the organization's assets may be impacted.

There are a number of known vulnerabilities documented throughout cloud, virtualization, and wireless grid Edgeware literature [8, 14, 40, 44, 79]. They range from the obvious (failure to authenticate) to the subtle (key management). When performing known vulnerability analysis, security engineers/specialists must consider the technology as it has been described in the artifacts that were reviewed for asset identification. Classifying vulnerabilities allows for pattern recognition of vulnerability types. This in turn may enable the security development teams to recognize and develop countermeasures to deal with classes of vulnerabilities by dealing with the vulnerabilities at a higher level of abstraction. For example, [9] detailed four cyber-attack classes for a wireless cloud (i.e., wireless grid, cloud computing, data-in-transit, insider) contributing to the identification of 37 specific vulnerabilities, such as inconsistent parameter validations, implicit sharing of privileged- confidential data, inadequate identification/authentication/authorization and exploitable program logic errors enabling circumvention of access control. Since the wireless cloud applications are device and location-independent and compatible with many device types (including mobile and nomadic devices, phones, tablets, laptops, and network computers), it's important to understand the vulnerabilities to this infrastructure. The wireless grid Edgeware applications will use cloud infrastructure to enable users to share and communicate with data wirelessly; however, managing security cyber-attacks and vulnerabilities in architecture assets are two fundamental challenges for any organization [50].

Additionally, the common exploits of security properties in virtualized computing environments and their security vulnerabilities from the perspective of cyber-attacks contribute to the combination of threats and vulnerabilities that Edgeware technology is exposed to. Research performed by [7] identified six virtualization cyber-attacks areas (i.e., footprinting, botnets, hypervisor, virtual code, virtual desktop infrastructure, and others) with 24 specific attacks towards virtualization technology contributing to the risks that involve unauthorized change and reception of malicious information stored in virtualized computing environments. This research recognized the importance of Hypervisor attacks, which could be especially devastating within the cloud if penetrated. A compromised hypervisor exposes all VMs on a single physical server to attack and hackers could use this as a launching point to access VMs; and initiate a DoS which could prevent a VM's access to host resources such as CPU, memory, and devices; and delete or disable VM's to prevent user access. Control of communications between VMs would compromise the confidentiality, integrity, and availability of data exchanged across a virtual network. Through the identification of the cyber-attacks and vulnerabilities to these virtualized computing environments, the impact of integrating wireless grid Edgeware technology with virtualization in a wireless cloud environment is realized.

Finally, CNA research performed by [8] identified nine major categories of vulnerabilities (e.g., authentication, misconfiguration, information disclosure, cryptographic, DoS, hijacking, race condition, infrastructure and input manipulation) and 55 specific security vulnerabilities in a wireless grid Edgeware application called the GridStreamX Edgeware application; which could compromise communications between the user and the wireless cloud provider and could allow hackers to intercept data (e.g., passwords, encryption keys, files); redirect web browsers to compromised sites (e.g., cross-site scripting [XSS], etc.); and impersonate applications on the virtual network (e.g., principal spoofing, etc.), thus inhibiting secure communications. The combination of threats and vulnerabilities illustrates the risks that this wireless grid Edgeware technology is exposed to. Since this technology plans to provide a more interoperable, scalable, and flexible approach to ways for intelligent devices to provide communication, the research performed by [6, 8] uncovered a significantly high risk due to the number of vulnerabilities and its increased dependence on cloud and virtualization technology making it an increasingly attractive target for hackers.

RISK ASSESSMENT

As stated in NIST SP 800-30, a risk assessment is used to "identify, estimate, and prioritize risk to organizational operations (i.e., mission, functions, image, and reputation), organizational assets, individuals, other organizations, and the Nation, resulting from the operation and use of information systems" [49]. To understand the risk that wireless grids Edgeware technology posed in a virtualized cloud environment, a thorough risk analysis on each threat category to define the likelihood of an attack occurring, along with the consequence of what will happen if the attack occurs, was performed. The NIST SP 800-30 assessment framework was used because it was clear, concise and contained a sound approach to performing risk assessments. Additionally, the framework was originally developed by the Joint Task Force Transformation Initiative Interagency Working Group with representatives from the Civil, Defense, and Intelligence Communities (i.e., U.S. Department of Defense (DoD), Office of the Director of National Intelligence, Committee on National Security Systems) in an ongoing effort to produce a unified information security framework [49]. This framework also provides a solid description of information system-level assessments and provides a succinct qualitative/quantitative nature in performing assessments during the risk management process for any organization and/or information system.

Using a qualitative and quantitative risk analysis approach, this research assessed wireless grid Edgeware technology from the identification of (1) threats, (2) vulnerabilities, (3) likelihood, (4) impact, and (5) countermeasures. The risk towards wireless grid Edgeware technology was expressed as a function of the likelihood of a given threat exploiting a given vulnerability, the magnitude of the impact should a threat successfully exploit a vulnerability and its data being attacked, and the adequacy and effectiveness of the security controls in place to protect the system. The adequacy of planned or existing security countermeasures was also accounted for when assessing the overall risk of a particular threat/vulnerability pair. If a potential threat was found to be likely to exploit an identified vulnerability, the wireless grid's Edgeware technology was subject to a certain level of risk. The assessment of the degree of that risk was based on the criticality of the wireless grid Edgeware technology is an organizational operating environment and the information that it would process and store and on the probability of loss of data or functionality due to the expected impact to the organization's operating environment.

Analysis

In addressing the overall research question for this research — what security vulnerabilities enumerations would contribute to the degradation and risk in using a wireless grid Edgeware application in a virtualized cloud? — this research acknowledged that the security vulnerabilities towards wireless grid Edgeware technology is not difficult to identify and analyze. This is due to the fact that the data needed for this analysis is not too complex or hard to come by with the right tools, although the technology may be constantly changing. The data needed for this risk assessment required an in-depth understanding of hackers, their goals, objectives and an appreciation of the types of attack tools they use to perform cyber-attacks and vulnerability enumerations (e.g., BackTrack5 r3). The results of this research needed to be considered along with the vulnerabilities, cyber-attacks and impact analysis in order to assess the overall risk in using wireless grids Edgeware technology. This coordinated analysis of risk, using all the risk components (e.g., threat, vulnerabilities, likelihood, impact, countermeasures) was accomplished by actively involving threat, vulnerability, likelihood, and impact analysis, as well as those who will eventually be responsible for deriving insights into the ways to protect against cyber-attacks and developing effective ways to provide the requisite responses to those attacks.

Having determined what threats are important and what vulnerabilities might exist to be exploited, it can be useful to estimate the likelihood and impact of the various possible risks. Likelihood determination indicates the probability that the vulnerability may be exercised given the threat and vulnerability and can be described as a rating of high, medium, or low [49]. In information security, "likelihood" is a qualitative estimate of how likely a successful attack will be, based on analysis and past experience. Independent of likelihood and controls, the risk's impact must be determined. That is, impacts are consequences that an organization must face if there is a successful attack. The operational impact of the loss of information (or services) is essentially determined, by several factors determined by threats and vulnerabilities, by looking at what the ultimate operational impact might be, given that attacks of various types by various threats are successful [49].

Therefore, the likelihood of successful exploitation is determined based on the resources required to exploit the vulnerability, the threat's motivation and opportunity to do so (i.e., willingness), and the adequacy of the planned or existing security safeguards to repel the exploitation attempt. The magnitude of impact should a threat successfully exploit a vulnerability is determined based on the expected impact that an attack could cause and the planned or current countermeasures that would mitigate the impact. Together, likelihood and impact provide the overall risk in determining the likelihood of a cyber-attack occurring and its predicted degree of harm if the attack is successful.

The findings from the wireless grid Edgeware application laboratory experiment further supported the research framework with the integration of the cyber-attacks identified from the wireless cloud and virtualization research [6]. The likelihood and impact analysis used a systematic analytical approach that provided a straightforward description of wireless grids Edgeware being analyzed and the risk of using the application in an organizational setting. Research of this kind is significant to information security specialists who will be responsible for implementing and securing wireless grids Edgeware technology within their organization. Understanding the threats and vulnerabilities will assist organizations in developing security policies to address this issue.

In all, [6] identified 116 cyber-attacks (i.e., wireless cloud — 37, virtualization — 24, GridStreamX Edgeware application — 55), which suggested that a cyber-attack will occur upon implementation of wireless grid Edgeware technology over a period of time or as a percentage change of occurrence. This research used a qualitative and quantitative method of data analysis. To facilitate the analysis, the likelihood and impact factors were based on a subjective analysis of the relative priority of specific threat's exploiting vulnerabilities from the researcher's extensive experience in analyzing cyber-attacks and performing vulnerability exploitations. The descriptive statistics, as displayed in Table 1, such as mean and standard deviation were used to describe the basic features of the data and to provide simple summaries about the risk from the data.

The sample of the likelihood and impact descriptive statistics displayed in Table 1 was calculated using IBM's statistical package for social sciences (SPSS) v20 software. From the analysis, the mean of likelihood was 6.91 (n = 116) with a mean standard error of 0.239. The measure of the dispersion of the likelihood in the study was determined through the range, minimum, maximum, standard deviation, and variance. The

Table 1. Descriptive Statistics from the Wireless Grid Edgeware Risk Assessment

Descriptive		Likelihood	Impact
N	Valid	116	116
	Missing	0	0
Mean		6.9138	6.9741
Std. Error of Mean		0.23918	0.24594
Median		8.0000	8.0000
Mode		8.00	8.00
Std. Deviation		2.57604	2.64891
Variance		6.636	7.017
Skewness		–0.909	–0.843
Std. Error of Skewness		0.225	0.225
Kurtosis		–0.373	–0.497
Std. Error of Kurtosis		0.446	0.446
Range		8.00	8.00
Minimum		2.00	2.00
Maximum		10.00	10.00

Note: These statistics are derived from the data used in this research.

range of the "likelihood" value in the study was 8 (high) with a maximum value of 10 (very high) and a minimum of 2 (low), whereas the standard deviation of the likelihood was 2.576 and a variance of 6.636 (see Figure 3). The distribution of the values of the likelihood is asymmetrical and negatively skewed with a long tail to the left with a value of –0.909 with a standard error of 0.225. The shape of the distribution is flatter as shown by the kurtosis statistic with a value of –0.373 and a standard error of 0.446.

On the other hand the mean of "impact" is 6.97 (n = 116) with a mean standard error of 0.246 (see Figure 4). The range of the impact in the study was 8 (high) with a maximum value of 10 (very high) and a minimum of 2 (low). The standard deviation of the impact is 2.649 and a variance of 7.017. The distribution of the values of the impact is asymmetrical and negatively skewed with a long tail to the left with a value of –0.843 with a standard error of 0.225. The shape of the distribution is flatter as shown by the kurtosis statistic with a value of –0.497 and a standard error of 0.446.

The analysis of descriptive statistics reveals that the mean interrelationship between the likelihood of the cyber-attack (6.91) and the mean

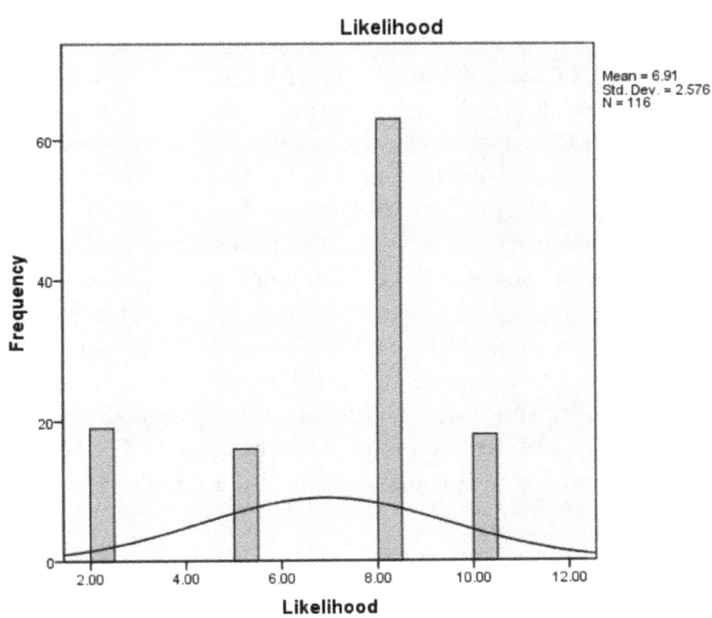

Figure 3. Likelihood Histogram

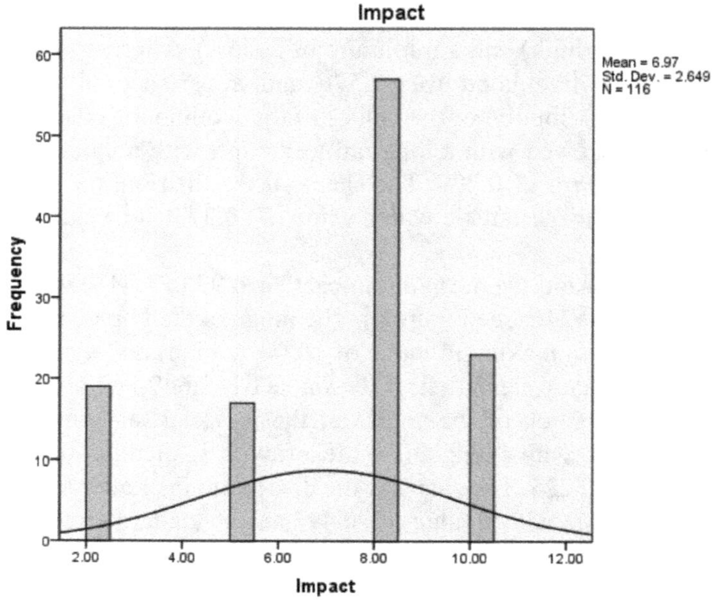

Figure 4. Impact Histogram

interrelationship between of the impact of the cyber-attack (6.97) to be positive when multiplied (48.16)[1] producing a "Moderate" risk determination from the NIST level of risk assessment scale. To explore this result further, the researcher compared means for the likelihood and impact across levels of risk. Starting with likelihood, the research shows its mean as being lower when evidence indicates the likelihood of discovering unintentional weaknesses leads to exploitable vulnerabilities. The reason is that risk is the net negative impact of the exercise of a vulnerability considering both the probability and the likelihood of occurrence. The impact should be greater since the level of impact on organizational operations (including strategy, functions, image, or reputation), assets, or individuals results from the likelihood of a cyber-attack. The likelihood of a cyber-attack occurring means it should be slightly lower when evidence

[1]Risk is a function of the likelihood of a threat event's occurrence multiplied by the potential adverse impact should the event occur, which can be computed as: Risk = Likelihood times Impact ($R = L*I$) (NIST, 2012). The 48.16 comes from the likelihood of the cyber-attack (6.91) × the impact of the cyber-attack (6.97).

indicates the likelihood of discovering unintentional weaknesses that can lead to exploitable vulnerabilities. In other words, the relationship between likelihood and impact is mutual.

Since the standard errors for both likelihood (0.239) and impact (0.246) are small, the statistical estimates derived from the data are reasonably good. Additionally, the variance of the likelihood (6.636) and impact (7.017) are at least three standard deviations away from their means and indicate that the values are close to their respective means and close to the range identified within this study. This relation also appears to hold for the skewness and kurtosis. The asymmetrical and negative skewness of the left skewed distribution for both the likelihood and impact indicating that most of the risk assessment values are concentrated on the right of the mean, with extreme values to the left. The asymmetrical and negatively skewed kurtosis platykurtic distribution of both the likelihood and impact produced a flatter than a normal distribution with a wider peak indicating that the probability for extreme risk values is less than for a normal distribution, and the risk values are wider spread around the mean. While the researcher did not hypothesize these differences, they are somewhat diagnostic of the form of the researcher's subjective judgment and provide a potentially fruitful area for future research.

The ultimate worst case scenario of any security risk could potentially be a catastrophic loss to any organization. However, such extreme worst-case scenarios are not those that are experienced by the vast majority of organizations that are the victims of such security incidents. Therefore, as displayed in Figure 5, the cyber-attacks for this research were assessed using a likelihood and impact graph grouped into four quadrants: (I) threatening, (II) high potential; not likely, (III) less risky and likely and (IV) likely; low potentially spanning four areas of consideration for alleviating the attacks: (1) mitigation, (2) manage, (3) monitor and (4) make do. Thus, it is appropriate to look at the 33 (28% of the total attacks identified) "threatening" cyber-attacks (those considered "very high [8]" and "high [25]") that need "mitigation" in order to avoid the realistic worst case losses that could be expected from these attacks. The obvious danger in overtly focusing on the threatening quadrant I attack is that 63 (54%) of "moderate" attacks, which need to be "managed", could be missed or given insufficient attention. The other 20 (17%) "less risky" cyber-attacks (those considered "low [2]" and "very low [18]") would not pose a significant threat to an organization. There is also an inherent difficulty in conceptualizing these threatening attacks. By their very nature they are

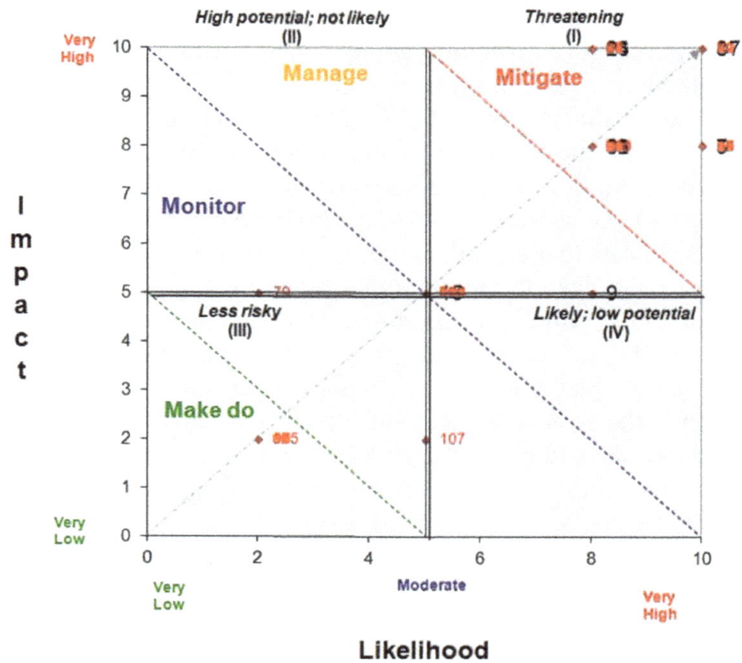

Figure 5. The Wireless Grid Edgeware Vulnerabilities Likelihood and Impact Graph

subjectively analyzed and should they occur, they could rapidly overwhelm most systems using wireless grids Edgeware technology. Also, human perception being what it is can also consider any security risk with potential safety or within the "manage" range as intolerable, where security controls could be less than effective.

The consequence of a security risk can usually be expressed as a measure of loss. Impacts derived as part of this assessment were used to inform the determination of overall risk consequences. In reality, risk tolerance for using wireless grids Edgeware technology is likely to be exhibited as a gradient, where the risk may become increasingly less tolerable as the risk level is elevated. The various risks that have been identified and characterized through this research as "threatening" or "moderate" must be considered for mitigation. Mitigation of a risk means changing the architecture of the software or the business in one or more ways to reduce the likelihood or the impact of the risk. The cyber-attacks considered in the areas of "mitigate" and "manage" should first be addressed. For example, changing authentication mechanisms from user identification (userid) and password to pre-shared public key certificates can make it far more difficult to impersonate a user. Reducing the period of time that a vulnerability is available for exploit is another way to reduce the likelihood of a risk. For example, if the GridStreamX Edgeware application sessions expire after 10 minutes of inactivity, then the window of opportunity for session hijacking is about 10 minutes long. Ensuring that proper cryptography is incorporated in the design can also help, for example, when applied correctly. It is easier to detect corruption in encrypted data than in unencrypted data, and encrypted data is harder for a hacker to use if they get it — even if they receive it via wireless communications. The high-level number of cyber-attacks identified within the "mitigate" and "manage" quadrants could also be mitigated through the proper countermeasure implementations.

Depending on the cost of making failure impossible through countermeasure correction, it may be much more cost-effective to enable wireless grid Edgeware technology systems to detect and repair failure(s) quickly and accurately. For example, some of the exploits identified for the GridStreamX Edgeware application identified that the application is very temperamental and can crash when provided bad input and (for the sake of argument) cannot be modified or replaced. A focus on correction would be to add business logic to validate input and make sure that the GridStreamX Edgeware application never received input that it could not handle. In contrast, a focus on correction would be to add monitoring or other software to watch for the module to crash and try to restart the module quickly with minimal impact. Mitigation is never without cost. The fact that remediating these cyber-attacks costs money makes the risk impact determination step even more important. Mitigations can often be characterized well in terms of their cost to the business: man-hours of labor, cost of shipping new devices with the improved software, delay entering the market with new features because old ones must be fixed, etc. This ability to characterize the mitigation's cost of wireless grid Edgeware technology, however, is of little value less the cost of the business impact is known.

The overall "Moderate" risk determination from this analysis would be applicable to those organizations utilizing this software in less data-sensitive environments where the communications and information that is transmitted would not be categorized as highly sensitive, confidential, and/or classified. However, those organizations whose information assets often take the form of databases, private credentials (e.g., social security numbers, userid, password, etc.), audit records, financial information (e.g., bank account numbers, etc.), intellectual property, and other vital business information (e.g., banks, investment firms, etc.), the same risk analysis would increase this risk determination to a "High" or "Very High" level of risk due to the target value of the data from a hacker's perspective and the numerous cyber-attacks identified within this research which could allow access to this data.

Since all organizations incur risks, it is imperative that financial organizations and those entities that deal with highly classified data assign priorities to risks, ensure adequate budgets have been allocated to address risks, and allow for the implementation as well as maintenance of appropriate risk-reducing controls. Risk management is not about eliminating and/or avoiding risks altogether, as this approach is typically cost-prohibitive as well as time-consuming, and thereby, not in the best interest of most stakeholders. The risks of this wireless grid Edgeware technology within these highly sensitive entities are inherent and/or inevitable; as such, the challenge stakeholders will have in implementing a risk management process to address this wireless grid Edgeware technology will be in finding the right balance between minimizing the impact of serious risks and accepting a level of risk that will not adversely affect or impact the cost, schedule, and performance of the organization. In the case of these types of organizations, confidentiality and integrity are very important, but if availability is negatively impacted via this technology, then the business impact may manifest in other ways, such as lost customers, failure to meet service level agreements (SLAs), compromised data records, stolen identities, etc.

In general, approaches to risk management for wireless grid Edgeware technology/systems and the development infrastructure that supports the production of those systems will have to focus largely on the implementation of security protocols and processes as reactive mechanisms in the operational virtualized cloud environment. Although those security technical mechanisms are evolving and becoming increasingly sophisticated, they are not sufficient to provide the strength of protection and resiliency that is needed in today's complex and highly interconnected wireless grid Edgeware domain. This risk assessment is designed to be applied iteratively, first at a high level during the requirements definition stage of a wireless grid Edgeware system acquisition and later at lower, more detailed levels during a wireless grid Edgeware system design, implementation, and operations. The result is a more proactive methodology that builds protective and resiliency mechanisms during acquisition and development. These mechanisms in turn provide increased assurance that the security features, practices, procedures, and architecture of a wireless grid Edgeware system are strong enough to mitigate all known operational risks, resulting in a residual risk that is small enough to be acceptable to the wireless grid Edgeware system and, ultimately, the intended users of this innovative technology.

DISCUSSION

The implications of wireless grids Edgeware applications are profound and will drive a shift in the fundamentals of new information systems design, operation, and management. This new technology will permit interoperability and connectivity between users and networks (e.g., the Internet, cloud, *ad hoc* multi-user networks private networks, etc.) by providing robust appliance interfaces permitting access to structured and unstructured data of every description. By adopting this new wireless grid Edgeware technology, organizations will become "dynamically flexible offering a higher degree of agility and responsiveness to emergent business requirements" [1]. However, in the wireless grid's Edgeware environment, hackers must be outmaneuvered rather than merely protected against. Organizations will need secure technology that blocks obvious access avenues and augments fixed safeguards with a more directed and dynamic defense. As a solution, one method is to ensure that the concept of "information assurance" exists throughout an organization looking to integrate wireless grid Edgeware applications.

Information assurance consists of measures that protect and defend information and information systems by ensuring their availability, integrity, authentication, confidentiality, and non-repudiation [16]. These measures include providing for the restoration of information systems by incorporating protection, detection, and reaction capabilities [16]. To address the information assurance component of "protection" of wireless grids Edgeware technology in a secure virtualized cloud environment, first, persons responsible for Edgeware applications, the mobile and wireless devices, and software/hardware for the virtualized cloud environment should undergo specific security awareness training. Protection means applying network protection techniques to protect the Edgeware application against attacks. This will support the identification of the risks and responsibilities associated with owning and operating the mobile devices using the application. Next, mobile and wireless devices running wireless grids Edgeware applications should undergo specific basic input/output system (BIOS) and operating system hardening procedures (e.g., remote connectivity to the device should be disabled where possible, and only ports the application uses should be open, etc.). Firewalls and antivirus software should be installed and maintained on the device(s) running the wireless grid Edgeware application. Any credentials stored on the device(s) using wireless grid Edgeware applications should be encrypted, or all remote access from the device(s) to the enterprise wireless cloud network should be mediated via two (or three) factor authentication. This will minimize the opportunity for an unauthorized person in possession of a hacking device to be able to remotely access the network.

Additionally, an intelligent platform management system should be incorporated within the wireless cloud network environment for further protection of device(s) and data. An intelligent platform management system would provide the automatic monitoring of performance indicators through wireless sensor data objects and the automatic selection of data routes for processing information. The potential of thousands of devices using wireless grid Edgeware applications distributed on various wireless cloud platforms is conceivable. As it is not possible to effectively monitor and manage these devices manually, an intelligentized platform management system could be employed to carry out automatic monitoring and management of the devices through wireless sensors. This way device failures and potential attacks in the environment could be detected and diagnosed immediately to ensure the stability of the system. Furthermore, in the wireless cloud, there could be sufficient routes for point-to-point transmissions of data, but because of the instantaneous requirement for information transmission, there is a need for high-speed selection of routes for data processing, which is impossible to accomplish manually. This could be achieved through an automatic selection based on real-time monitoring of the quality of the various routes for faster data processing also using an intelligent platform management system. Since there could be a huge amount of information to transmit in a limited number of bandwidths, the system could also have the capability of allocating bandwidths automatically according to the state of the flow of information.

In regard to the "detection" of wireless grids Edgeware technology in a secure virtualized cloud environment, responsive capabilities using an intrusion detection system (IDS) should be performed. Detection means to make a forecast of an issue warning against cyber-attacks. When intrusions are detected, the IDS will raise an alert and optionally implement some responsive action. Such action may involve the paging of a security administrator, reconfiguration of network devices, or performing a DoS attack against the attacking device (e.g., rogue AP for example). The incorporation of a responsive capability must be given careful consideration. If the IDS itself is to mount the response, it will advertise the presence of the detection system to a hacker. Likewise, if the response is initiated by the IDS, but via another network infrastructure component (e.g., the AP) for example, a hacker may leverage the responsive capability to target legitimate clients. For example, a hacker could spoof the media access control (MAC) of a legitimate client running the wireless grid Edgeware application and operate in AP mode; the responsive capability may then launch a DoS attack against that MAC address-effectively denying service to a legitimate client in the wireless cloud network. Additionally, intrusion detection components can be incorporated into deployed wireless grid Edgeware application devices. Incorporation of the detection system components within the wireless cloud would give the detection system access to a rich set of information, over and above that available to a separate, passive monitoring component. For example, a passive sniffer (or set of sniffers) that is capable consideration of the number and location of passive sniffers required to ensure the area of interest is adequately covered and techniques that are capable of effectively detecting wireless intrusions in a fully passive manner are required. A major disadvantage of incorporating the detection system components within the devices themselves is that updates, reconfiguration, and initial enrollment carry a significant management burden.

Finally, for "reaction", once a malicious entity (e.g., device, software, authorized user, etc.) or rogue AP has been detected from within the wireless grid Edgeware application and has gained access to the operational virtualized cloud network, an intrusion response system (IRS) may attempt to prevent the malicious entity from communicating with the network; or in the case where the intruder had deployed a rogue AP, prevent any legitimate stations from connecting to that device. Reaction means the capability of stopping or preventing the cyber-attack from spreading when the wireless Edgeware application is under attack. Once an intrusion (that is a violation of a security policy) has been detected, the IRS may wish to take responsive action to limit the capability of the intrusive behavior to impact the wireless grid Edgeware application and its operating wireless cloud network. Responsive actions are designed to disable the attacking station or to prevent the progression of its intrusion. The most basic and crude method for disabling an intruder is to flood the target radio frequency with noise (e.g., radio jamming) or mount an attack on the clear channel assessment algorithm used by wireless stations (reference). In addition to low-level responses, the coordination protocols of the MAC layer can also be manipulated. In particular, the virtual carrier sensing protocol employed by IEEE 802.11 devices can be exploited. By setting large media reservation values in ready-to-send (RTS) clear-to-send (CTS) exchanges, the network allocation vector (NAV) values of associated stations can be inflated and stations prevented from transmitting. Typically such responses would, however, result in DoS conditions for all wireless grid Edgeware application devices configured to use that frequency or channel.

A board range of information assurance techniques and procedures will be needed to secure the wireless grid Edgeware application and its operating environment. The information assurance approaches identified here are to prevent or mitigate all threats towards wireless grid Edgeware applications, combined with concerns that implementation or configuration errors may diminish the effectiveness of the remaining security services and motivate the requirement to supplement these preventative measures with a capability to detect and respond to security-relevant events. These security-relevant events include not only cyber-attacks but other violations of wireless security policies such as detecting when a mobile device leaves a wireless cloud active while simultaneously connecting to an otherwise secured wired network. Such a monitoring capability could also be used to provide assurance that the deployed wireless cloud was only adverting and using approved protocols and algorithms. Numerous wireless intrusion detection/response techniques will utilize sensor data to attempt to triangulate and locate the point from which a wireless hacker is operating. The accuracy of such techniques, given the vagaries of wireless communications, is a matter of debate. Given the highly dynamic nature of a wireless grid Edgeware applications and there virtualized operational environment, the use of a single information assurance parameter is unlikely to be reliable. Only when multiple techniques are combined can the number of cyber-attacks being attempted be constrained.

From a risk management/security perspective, wireless grids Edgeware technology presents a unique set of challenges. First, compared to traditional network systems, the roles of the various components of a wireless grid are somewhat burred. For example, the Grid user interface [UI] (which provides a user interface for access to certain "GRiDLET" programs) might in turn act as a requestor of another service (e.g., the CORE platform which manages the connectivity, security/permissions and communications between nodes on the network) that it relies on; it's not well understood if the two components can both be requesters and provide to each other, and so on. Vulnerabilities tend thus to relate to the uncontrolled or careless interaction between components rather than to the behavior of a well-bounded piece of software that can be monitored using standard techniques. A second difficulty typical of wireless grid Edgeware systems lies in the nature of the communications between components. Precise details of the protocols used become largely irrelevant. A cyber-attack exploits poorly defined or ambiguous semantics of the requests, erroneous parsing, lack of security checks, etc. Such exploits can only be possibly detected using payload analysis (e.g., deep packet inspection) which is computationally intensive and presents numerous issues on its own.

Additionally, the wireless devices with Edgeware technology will be portable and will invariably be exposed to untrusted wireless environments. Monitoring and recording the types of interactions such a device enters into while it is away from its main environment is important. Depending on the nature of the interactions that the device is exposed to in those untrusted environments, it may be pertinent to restrict its capabilities when it returns to its main environment until some degree of trust in the state of the device has been established. In this case, the risk of the environment not being capable of monitoring the events taking place over its wireless interface would not provide a detailed history of the interactions that the device has performed. Depending on the circumstances, the monitor may provide information about the identity of the communicating parties; the particular protocols and algorithms used; and the volume of traffic, for example. By sharing the collected information about the interactions of the wireless device which occurred in untrusted environments with the main network (upon its return), the wireless grid Edgeware devices can provide an indication of its trustworthiness which may necessitate additional measures prior to the device being allowed to re-establish full functionality on its main network.

Wireless grids Edgeware technology reliability and trustworthiness, including its network, operating systems and end-user protection, would also be a substantial concern. However, proper implementation of wireless grids Edgeware applications would depend on the accurate implementation of the countermeasures identified, the application's ultimate purpose within an organization, how that purpose ties into the organization's business activities, and the proper development of security policies and procedures for the application. The continued use of literature and vulnerability exploitations would provide a constant process that regularly reevaluates the risks throughout an Edgeware application's use. To this end, the current state of information assurance efforts with respect to wireless grid Edgeware technology was developed. This revealed that there are a number of security mechanisms available and that the need for wireless monitoring (i.e., IDP, IRS, intelligent development platforms, etc.) is needed to detect threats and cyber-attacks against wireless grids Edgeware technology.

FURTHER RESEARCH

No prior research had been performed on wireless grid Edgeware technology developed by Syracuse University's WIGIT specifically focusing on the challenges associated with the security vulnerability exploitations of this technology within an operating environment. This is a field ripe with potential for further investigation into specific analysis techniques capable of interpreting and reconstructing the potentially complex scenarios that might be realized by cyber-attacks in future environments. In particular, the dynamic bindings which arise due to security discoveries and subsequent invocations of wireless grid Edgeware technologies make such analysis non-trivial.

A number of unmitigated threats and significant challenges remain to be addressed within wireless grids Edgeware technology and its devices operating in wireless cloud environments in general. Because of the erosion of traditional "secure" perimeters or network boundaries (e.g., de-perimeterization) of the wireless cloud networks, the demand for enforcing security is moving away from the network to the system and applications that run on it. The focus of hackers and security experts has moved away from just protecting the infrastructure to focusing on applications. This increases the requirements for secure end-points and methods for establishing mutual "trust" between Edgeware technology systems, as well as establishing the requirement for secure applications and mobile application code.

The need for trust is because future wireless grids Edgeware technology users will not require their wireless cloud provider(s) to adopt their specific security policies, procedures, and security software (e.g., scanning tools). The issues arise around multi-tenancy because this requires strong security isolation technologies be used to separate different customers' processes and data. The need for encryption arises because wireless grid Edgeware technology represents the dissolution of standard network perimeters and will require organizations to encrypt all data-at-rest and in-transit. Critical to the success of wireless grids Edgeware technology will be the ability to answer the following questions as related to information security for leveraging the technology in a wireless cloud environment:

- When it comes to wireless grid Edgeware technology to be secure, those systems using the technology not only have to be attack-resistant, but they will also have to be "attack-resilient" (e.g., recoverability); therefore, should wireless grid Edgeware systems be able to recover from cyber-attacks, resuming operation at or above a minimum level of service, as soon as the source of the attack has been isolated and blocked, and the damage has been contained?
- In determining how wireless grid Edgeware technology defects can be exploited to compromise its execution environment, can penetration testing complement black box security fault injections, which are used to determine how execution environment defects can be exploited to compromise the software?
- Comparing how wireless grid Edgeware technology tolerates real-world style attack patterns vs. injected faults designed to trigger specific insecure behaviors, how likely is the level of sophistication a hacker would have to have to successfully compromise wireless grid Edgeware technology? and
- In determining what additional countermeasures or mitigations could reduce the frequency of cyber-attacks against wireless grid Edgeware technology, rather than its attack surface, would this significantly increase the level of sophistication or resources a hacker would need to launch a successful cyber-attack against the technology?

Each device operating the wireless grid Edgeware technology should apply organizational policies (e.g., for routing, access control, packet scheduling, mobility, etc.), customized to the needs of its applications and users. Each wireless cloud utilizing wireless grid Edgeware technology should run independently, without interfering with the operation of other networks the system is not accessing. Therefore, improvements to the wireless grid Edgeware devices and the wireless cloud will be a continual process. Not only do the underlying intrusion detection techniques themselves have to evolve but also the integration of these techniques into host-based wireless grid systems deployment must be considered. Traditional intrusion detection techniques are challenged by the fact that typical network development frameworks and approaches privilege very high-level programming languages and make intensive use of software abstractions, which is in direct opposition with the assumptions used by host-based detection techniques. Simultaneously, these systems are stateful (e.g., defined operational time) and the legitimacy of, or potential risks associated with a particular request, can only be evaluated in the context of a given system state. The state space and the possible transitions of wireless grid Edgeware systems tend to be extremely complex, which tends to render analysis-based techniques particularly difficult to implement in this research.

Therefore, these proposed future research directions are independent but interrelated. While each can be conducted in isolation, they will each produce research outcomes that will be useful inputs into wireless grid Edgeware technology and future operating environments:

"Black Box" Security Testing for Wireless Grid Edgeware Technology

"Black box" tests should be performed on the binary executable of wireless grid Edgeware software, and in essence "poke at" the software from the outside in order to observe its outputs and behaviors, in addition to examining the actual code that implements it. This method of testing ensures that the parts of a wireless grid Edgeware application that will be exposed to a user actually work correctly and securely. For acquired and reused black box components (e.g., the functionality of a wireless grid Edgeware application), black box tests would be considered highly useful. However, they are also valuable for testing executables (from scratch or open source) compiled from source code because they enable the tester to see the software "in action", in order to confirm assumptions about a given component's behavior when it receives various inputs from other components, its environment, or its users.

Black box testing would also enable a tester to observe the wireless grid Edgeware software's behavior in response to a wide variety of user inputs and environment configuration and state changes, including those that indicate potential cyber-attack patterns. These kinds of interactions between the wireless grid Edgeware software and its external environment and users are impossible to achieve during normal testing. Black box test data should be generated based on the wireless grid Edgeware software's specifications (i.e., specified variables) and from the cyber-attack patterns indicated in the wireless grid Edgeware software's future threat models, attack trees, or abuse/misuse cases (e.g., exploits identified from this research). Black box testing should exercise as many inputs as possible, both valid and invalid. Testing should include observation of memory usage by the wireless grid Edgeware software when it is subjected to as many and widely varied unique valid and invalid sequences of inputs.

Identity-Based Architecture for Wireless Grid Edgeware Technology

De-perimeterization has happened, is happening, and is inevitable; relying only on network-based protection is increasingly ineffective. This does not suggest giving up on perimeter protections but implies that security designs must realize host systems are susceptible to attack no matter where they are located. The central tenant of an identity-based architecture (IBA) utilizing Edgeware technology is that the network is inherently untrustworthy and data is unsecure. A fully envisioned IBA for wireless grid Edgeware technology would utilize a combination of technologies to identify the system and users, prove that the system has not been modified from its approved state, and validate any requested communications through a combination of identity and context. The future of this process integrates the onboard trusted platform module (TPM) chip common in modern systems to uniquely identify the system and establish a hash of system configuration items including static operating system file components, running processes, and hardware architecture. The TPM contains an endorsement private key (EK) that uniquely identifies the TPM (thus, the physical host), some cryptographic functions that cannot be modified and the respective manufacturers sign the corresponding public key to guarantee the correctness of the chip and validity of the key. The stored hashes are compared during communication handshakes to attest that the system has not been modified and that it is still secure. The chip allows systems to not only uniquely identify the endpoints of a communication channel but also allows systems to authorize access on configuration status and connectivity context as well as simple user-defined roles.

Unfortunately, because of a lack of supporting protocols and infrastructure, a fully mobile context-aware IBA using wireless grid Edgeware technology is currently visionary. However, some of the key concepts could currently be implemented: certificate-based user and system authentication, encrypted tunnels between devices, and policy control points both at the desktop and at the secure zone perimeter. Certificates for authentication and encryption and the associated key management infrastructure are expensive, but well-established technologies. Policy control points are still developing and include network or client-based network access control mechanisms, for example, SSL VPN technologies that utilize transient scanning software to validate system configuration and software patching, as well as physical architecture separation.

Secure Wireless Inadvertently Enabled Remote Access

Where a wireless capable device is connected to wireless grid Edgeware technology, via a remote wired network, there is the potential that the wireless interface of the device is enabled concurrent with the wired connection into the main network. If this situation arises, there is the possibility that a bridge between the wireless interface and the broadband interface providing connectivity to the main network could allow anyone within the wireless range of the device, to connect to the main network. To counter this threat, further research on how the devices should be restricted via group policy, host-based wireless security software, or some other administrative control from bridging interfaces is needed. If possible, the device should be configured in such a way that the simultaneous activation of the wired and wireless interface is not possible.

The concurrent activation of both wired and wireless interfaces on a device connected to the main network introduces the possibility of a wired network being made accessible via the wireless interface (e.g., network bridge). The countermeasures for mitigating remote access bridging threats must be researched and implemented to prevent local access bridging. In the local environment, however, this can be supplemented by the detection system monitoring, and raising alerts when a device is detected on both the wired and the wireless network segments. Such a capability requires research on the integration of both wired and wireless detection technologies in order that the wireless grid Edgeware technology and the wireless cloud it's operating in will have the situational awareness to make such observations.

Additionally, the wireless connectivity in this scenario will also have to address the threats posed by a mobile device that has been roaming and has now returned and wants to establish a wireless or wireless connection to the main network. Prior to allowing a device to reconnect to the main network after roaming to untrusted environments, the device should be quarantined and evaluated. Such an evaluation may be as simple as updating antivirus and antispyware software on the device and forcing a scan prior to reconnection to the network. More complex interactions with host-based monitoring software may also be required. An important aspect in such an environment is the capability to detect connections from devices that have not undergone the requisite health checks to the unrestricted main network. This will require the system to have knowledge of which devices have been roaming, which have been assessed as healthy, and those devices currently connected to the main network. An alert should be raised whenever a roaming device, reconnects to the network without having undergone the requisite health checks.

Improved Host-based Configuration Control and Intrusion Detection in a Wireless Cloud

Within a wireless cloud environment utilizing wireless grid Edgeware technology, both network and host devices must be protected. Improved protection of host devices requires research in two major areas: (1) host-based configuration control and environment; and (2) host-based intrusion detection capabilities for wireless grids Edgeware technology and wireless clouds.

Further research on wireless grid Edgeware technology on improved host-based configuration control can ensure that the vulnerability surface of devices is minimized within a wireless cloud environment. The role of trusted computing hardware, specifically trusted platform modules (TPM) and mandatory access control frameworks [e.g., security enhances Linux (SE Linux)], in enforcing wireless-related security policies warrants investigation. The use of these techniques to enforce security boundaries in Edgeware devices should also be researched and investigated to determine the extent to which they can mitigate device driver vulnerabilities (through domain separation) that can potentially be exploited to gain remote access to wireless grid Edgeware devices.

The incorporation of host-based intrusion detection capabilities into wireless grid Edgeware roaming devices should be researched to understand how the technology permits the monitoring of intrusion while associated with foreign networks. As with network-based wireless intrusion detection techniques, however, host-based techniques are immature. The applicability of emerging detection techniques for wireless grid Edgeware (as applied in network-based wireless intrusion detection systems) and wireless cloud should be investigated and techniques specifically for host-based, wireless grid Edgeware/wireless cloud systems developed. Such integration may allow the resolution with which areas of the wireless grid Edgeware and wireless clouds are monitored to be dynamically determined. For example, with appropriately configured wireless cloud infrastructure, alerts raised by a wireless grid Edgeware network-based intrusions detection systems could be corroborated by the view that portion of the wireless cloud network is assessed by malicious mobile hosts currently active in a specific location.

It is envisioned that when combined with trusted computing technologies the use of host-based intrusion detection systems, specifically for wireless grid Edgeware technology and wireless clouds, could simplify the assessment and establishment of trust in devices that wish to connect and reconnect to a wireless cloud after roaming. The secure storage of host-based logs could conceivably allow the measurement and attestation of the integrity, or compromise, of wireless grid Edgeware devices in a wireless cloud. Research in the area of wireless grid Edgeware and wireless cloud host-based configuration control, assessment, and intrusion detection will impact the utility of alert correlation and dynamic event investigation strategies. Finally, advances in wireless grid Edgeware and wireless cloud host-based techniques will contribute to the security of communication nodes in Edgeware devices and wireless cloud deployments.

Dynamic Intrusion Correlation with Heterogeneous Sensors

To maintain a holistic view of wireless grid Edgeware and wireless clouds, network events integrated alerts from multiple sources including wired intrusion detection systems; wireless intrusion detection systems; host-based systems; and network-based systems should be researched and developed. While alerts raised by each of these systems could be reviewed independently and correlated by security experts, this would be manually intensive, time-consuming, and error-prone. The automated analysis, correlation, and fusion alerts from multiple sensors within a wireless cloud, or across sensors from different wireless clouds could support security analysts by directing their attention to the most critical events.

Future research in two broad areas is required to optimize wireless grid Edgeware and wireless cloud intrusion detection sensor deployments and their integration with other detection and monitoring systems. First, research challenges related to wireless grid Edgeware and wireless cloud intrusion detection system sensor deployments that need to be considered include the optimal placement of wireless sensors (both location and density); the evaluation and correlation of physical layer parameters; and the assignment of confidence weights, based on current noise and interference levels. Further, the effectiveness of integrating host-based detection systems with statically deployed infrastructure as a mechanism for dynamically reconfiguring the range or granularity of wireless cloud intrusion detection system sensor coverage must be evaluated. Secondly, once various detection technologies have been integrated, effective algorithms and techniques should be researched to enable the correlation of outputs from the various component systems. Alert correlation, which is an emerging field in wired intrusion detection, must be researched for wireless grid Edgeware and wireless cloud technologies and the integration of wireless alerts for wireless cloud architectures will likely introduce additional research challenges that must be addressed.

Power Constrains in Wireless Clouds and Edgeware Devices

Wireless cloud deployments, in which wireless grid Edgeware devices and potentially mobile devices communicate directly with each other, are particularly appealing in environments where there is limited or no pre-existing communication infrastructure available — in disaster recovery scenarios, for example. The range of threats to communications and devices in wireless grid Edgeware and wireless cloud modes of deployment, while sharing a number of similarities with infrastructure-based modes of deployment, present unique challenges. The additional challenges that must be addressed in wireless grid Edgeware and wireless cloud environments include the fact that nodes in a wireless cloud environment are likely to be powered by batteries and therefore are power-constrained. A reliance on a finite power source introduces a new avenue of cyber-attacks, in which an attacker may attempt to drain the power of one or more nodes in a wireless cloud network by having them unnecessarily transmit information. Another challenge with wireless cloud architectures is that, unlike infrastructure networks where all frames are directed to the AP, in wireless grid Edgeware and wireless cloud architectures, nodes need to maintain routing information. Not only do they need to maintain this information, but it is dynamically changing. This introduces the potential for hackers to manipulate and interfere with the routes over which frames are transmitted.

Additionally, the absence of a centralized authentication server (all nodes are responsible for authenticating their peers) and the requirement that all management traffic (including intrusion detection alerts) must be communicated in-band, over the same wireless cloud channels that may be the target of a cyber-attack. Establishing the provenance of alerts that may originate from compromised or malicious sources is an open problem. Applying heuristic and corroborative techniques to evaluate the reliability of alerts from given wireless grid Edgeware device sensors presents a significant research challenge. Isolation of devices from a wireless cloud architecture also makes the process of updating intrusion detection signatures and the correlation of alerts problematic. As a more proactive step, security personnel will try to develop methods for finding the vulnerabilities within wireless grid Edgeware and wireless cloud environments before hackers do. Research to develop heuristic methods of detecting malicious behavior for this technology and architecture activities where perhaps no security exists yet is needed. The challenge for defenders is that hackers have a seemingly infinite number of possible options available to mutate their attack vectors. Hackers will adapt their attack using the most efficient and low-cost modification of their original method.

Host-Based Logs for Edgeware Application Mobile Devices

The threats towards mobile devices using the GridStreamX Edgeware application or wireless grid Edgeware technology are also a sufficient security concern. Specifically, the process of allowing a roaming device to reconnect to an organization's network will require detailed device assessments. Mobile devices with trusted computing capabilities may be able to store host-based logs in a secure and tamper-resistant manner. This information could then be used to expedite the process of re-establishing a connection with the organization's network. For example, if such capabilities could be used by the device to provide verifiable attestations that the roaming device had only established connections with other trusted networks the vetting process associated with reconnection to the main network could be simplified. Such capabilities, however, remain a research challenge.

The role of host-based security countermeasures and detection techniques is more obvious as the devices to be protected are expected to operate outside of the protective perimeter of the main network. Integration with wired intrusion detection will be required to ensure that roaming devices do not connect to the main network's unrestricted network prior to undergoing a health check assessment. Integration of wired and wireless intrusion detection systems can be used to provide assurance that wireless and wired interfaces of devices are not simultaneously active, creating a bridge between the wired and wireless networks. However, a number of threats will remain unmitigated. As the mobile devices roam and access foreign networks, information about the devices [wireless device driver information and previously associated network service set identifier's (SSID) for example] will be leaked. The process of re-establishing the trustworthiness or health of a roaming device prior to allowing reconnection to a trusted network is complex and assumes that the software making the assessment of the host is free from errors and faults in both its design and implementation. Such assurance is typically gained through independent evaluations. As products implementing network access protection/network admission control are only just emerging on the market, evaluated products are unlikely to be available in the short term.

All the approaches discussed in this section could potentially be transferable to wireless grid Edgeware devices and wireless cloud networks. Once the expected behavior of nodes has been specified, nodes using this specification should not require further updates to detect non-compliant behaviors. Further research would be required, however, to determine the feasibility of using specification-based approaches in wireless grid Edgeware-based wireless cloud networks. It is anticipated that the knowledge and techniques identified would, in part at least, be transferable to infrastructureless modes of wireless grid Edgeware device deployment, but a gap analysis would need to be undertaken to determine the outstanding research challenges.

CONCLUSION

In closing, this research observed at the start of this thesis that in addition to identifying the security vulnerabilities for a secure cloud-to-Edgeware technology via the GridStreamX Edgeware application; there are the ongoing threats of hackers, which are every day coming closer to merging into a more complex problem for this new type of technology. But perhaps the greatest threat posed by hacking is to the fundamental integrity of the Internet as a communications platform. As the hacking industry continues to grow unabated, security vulnerabilities have the potential to undermine any new technology's capability to provide trust in the confidentiality, integrity, and availability of information traversing in innovative technologies such as wireless grids Edgeware applications or wireless devices. Even with sound security policies, standards, practices, and procedures, a steady flow of vulnerability exploitation catastrophes towards the wireless grid's Edgeware technology could over time lead many to stop trusting the wireless grid Edgeware platform altogether.

This research considers security to be an integral part of the wireless grid Edgeware technology strategy, considering that in many cases the infrastructure may (or may not) be actually owned or controlled by the organization using the technology. Thus more research is needed to clearly understand the following:

- Information security must be designed into the fabric of wireless grid Edgeware technology and the wireless cloud infrastructure. Security is systemic to any future enterprise architecture leveraging wireless grid Edgeware technology and the wireless cloud, and organizations need to consider security at all steps in creating and deploying the core architecture.
- Wireless grid Edgeware technology and the wireless cloud is basically an outsourcing model — the question is whether the wireless cloud provider will live up to their security obligations, and understanding the

security models offered by the wireless cloud providers is key to having a successful security strategy.

- Where wireless grid Edgeware technology and the wireless cloud provider responsibilities start and stop, and thus organizations should define a clear security model considering the points of demarcation, and establish SLAs to ensure that the security approaches and mechanisms provided by the wireless cloud provider are a solid part of the chain of security mechanism that cover all points of the deployed architecture.
- For confidence in a wireless grid Edgeware technology and the wireless cloud implementations, the need to have sufficient visibility to see who was doing what and how across the infrastructure is paramount. This means the use of governance, or the ability to monitor, manage, and control, all aspects of the architecture, including the ability to trace issues with security down the sources of the problems.

The modern hacker is more likely to be supported by large criminal organizations or rogue states and fueled by a thriving underground exploit market, where zero-day exploits (e.g., system vulnerabilities where no countermeasure or mitigation currently exist) are sold for tens of thousands of dollars each. The greater organization and collaboration are also evident in the tools used by the hacker. The cyber-attacks used today exhibit unprecedented sophistication and stealth and display evidence of professional software development lifecycles with auto-updating capabilities and the ability to identify and adjust to different system architecture, protocols, and security patch levels.

Understanding that wireless grid Edgeware technology and the wireless cloud create risks and require a rethinking — but not reinvention — of security controls and architecture. Many of the existing security models may not work with wireless grid Edgeware technology and the wireless cloud, and this research is advocating the reinvention of new security methods, in the context of wireless grid Edgeware technology and wireless cloud computing. Organizations should consider the nature of wireless grid Edgeware technology and the wireless cloud, and the need to place data, processes, applications, and services on systems that organizations do not own, nor control. However, with some forethought and planning, wireless grid Edgeware technology and wireless cloud-based systems can be just as secure, if not more secure, as traditional systems.

REFERENCES

[1] Armbrust, M., Fox, A., Griffith, R., Joseph, A. D., Katz, R., Konwinski, A., Lee, G., Patterson, D., Rabkin, A., & Stoica, I. (2010). A view of cloud computing. *Communications of the ACM*, 53(4), 50–58.

[2] Bandyopadhyay, K., Mykytyn, P. P., & Mykytyn, K. (1999). A framework for integrated risk management in information technology. *Management Decision*, 37(5), 437–445.

[3] Bernard, S. & Ho, S. (2008). Enterprise architecture as context and method for designing and implementing information security and data privacy controls in government agencies. *Advances in Government Enterprise Architecture*, 340–370, IGI Global, Hershey, Pennsylvania.

[4] BloomBecker, B. (1990). *Spectacular Computer Crimes: What They are and How They Cost American Business Half a Billion Dollars a Year!* Dow Jones-Irwin, Homewood, IL.

[5] Borden, T., Hennessy, J., & Rymarczyk, J. (1989). Multiple operating systems on one processor complex. *IBM Systems Journal*, 28(1), 104–123.

[6] Brooks, T. (2014). *Edgeware Security Risk Management: A Three Chapter Thesis on Cloud, Virtualization and Wireless Grid Vulnerabilities.* Unpublished doctoral thesis. Syracuse University, Syracuse, New York.

[7] Brooks, T., Caicedo, C., & Park, J. (2012). Security vulnerability analysis in virtualized computing environments. *International Journal of Intelligent Computing Research*, 3(1/2), 277–291.

[8] Brooks, T., Kaarst-Brown, M., Caicedo, C., Park, J., & McKnight, L. (2013). A failure to communicate: Security vulnerabilities in the gridstreamx edgeware application. In *Proceedings of the IEEE 8th International Conference for Internet Technology and Secured Transactions (ICITST-2013)*, pp. 521–528.

[9] Brooks, T., Robinson, J., & McKnight, L. (2012). Conceptualizing a secure wireless cloud. *International Journal of Cloud Computing and Services Science*, 1(3), 89–114.

[10] Brooks, T. & McKnight, L. (2013). Securing wireless grids: Architecture designs for secure wiglet-to-wiglet interfaces. *International Journal of Information and Network Security (IJINS)*, 2(1), 1–16.

[11] Campbell, R. P. & Sands, G. A. (1979). A modular approach to computer security risk management. In *Proceedings of the National Computer Conference* (Vol. 48, pp. 293–303).

[12] Chakrabarti, A. (2007). *Grid Computing Security.* Springer-Verlag, Berlin, Heidelberg, New York, NY.

[13] Chan, H. & Perrig, A. (2003). Security and privacy in sensor networks. *Computer*, 36(10), 103–105.

[14] Chen, Y., Paxson, V., & Katz, R. (2010). *What's New About Cloud Computing Security?* University of California at Berkeley, UCB/EECS-2010-5.

[15] Cody, E., Sharman, R., Rao, R. H., & Upadhyaya, S. (2008). Security in grid computing: A review and synthesis. *Decision Support Systems*, 44(4), 749–764.

[16] Committee on National Security Systems (CNSS) (2010). *National Information Assurance Glossary*, CNSS Instruction No. 4009. http://www.cnss.gov/Assets/pdf/cnssi_4009.pdf (Accessed June 15, 2010).

[17] Crockford, G. (1982). The bibliography and history of risk management: Some preliminary observations. *The Geneva Papers on Risk and Insurance*, 7(23), 169–170.

[18] Davis, A., Parikh, J., & Weihl, W. E. (2004). Edgecomputing: Extending enterprise applications to the edge of the internet. In *Proceedings of the 13th International World Wide Web Conference on Alternate Track Papers & Posters* (pp. 180–187).

[19] Farsole, A. A., Kashikar, A. G., & Zunzunwala, A. (2010). Ethical hacking. *International Journal of Computer Applications (IJCA)*, 1(10), 14–20.

[20] Fenz, S., Ekelhart, A., & Neubauer, T. (2011). Information security risk management: In which security solutions is it worth investing? *Communications of the Association for Information Systems*, 28(1), 329–357.

[21] Foster, I. (2002). What is the grid? A three point checklist. *GRIDtoday*, 1(6), 1–4.

[22] Foster, I., Kesselman, C., Nick, J. M., & Tuecke, S. (2003). *Grid Computing: Making the Global Infrastructure a Reality.* John Wiley & Sons, Inc., Hoboken, NJ.

[23] Foster, I., Kishimoto, H., Savva, A., Berry, D., Grimshaw, A., Horn, B., Maciel, F., Siebenlist, F., Subramaniam, R., Treadwell, J., & Reich, J. V. (2006). *The Open Grid Services Architecture,* version 1.5. Global Grid Forum.

[24] Foster, I., Zhao, Y., Raicu, I., & Lu, S. (2008). Cloud computing and grid computing 360-degree compared. In *Proceedings of the IEEE Grid Computing Environments Workshop (GCE '08)* (pp. 1–10).

[25] Garcés-Erice, L. & Rooney, S. (2012). Secure lazy provisioning of virtual desktops to a portable storage device. In *Proceedings of the 6th International Workshop on Virtualization Technologies in Distributed Computing Data* (pp. 45–52).

[26] Garfinkel, S. (2007). Commodity grid computing with Amazon's S3 and EC2. *USENIX*, 32(1), 7–13.

[27] Gelbstein, E. & Kamāl, A. (2002). *Information Insecurity: A Survival Guide to the Uncharted Territories of Cyber-Threats and Cyber-Security.*

United Nations ICT Task Force and the United Nations Institute for Training and Research (Vol. 1), New York, NY.

[28] Goh, S., Pang, H., Deng, R., & Bao, F. (2006). Three architectures for trusted data dissemination in edge computing. *Data & Knowledge Engineering*, 58(3), 381–309.

[29] Goldberg, R. (1973). *Architectural Principles for Virtual Computer Systems.* Ph.D. Dissertation, Harvard University, Massachusetts.

[30] Gortney, W. E. (2012). Joint publication 1-02: Department of defense dictionary of military and associated terms. U.S. Department of Defense.

[31] Grobauer, B., Walloschek, T., & Stocker, E. (2011). Understanding cloud computing vulnerabilities. *IEEE Security & Privacy*, 9(2), 50–57.

[32] Gruschka, N. & Jensen, M. (2010). Attack surfaces: A taxonomy for attacks on cloud services. In *Proceedings of the IEEE 3rd International Conference on Cloud Computing (CLOUD 2010)* (pp. 276–279).

[33] Hansman, S. & Hunt, R. (2005). A taxonomy of network and computer attacks. *Computers & Security*, 24(1), 31–43.

[34] Hartmann, B., Doorley, S., & Klemmer, S. R. (2008). Hacking, mashing, gluing: Understanding opportunistic design. *IEEE Pervasive Computing*, 7(3), 46–54.

[35] Horrigan, W. (1969). *Risk, Risk Management and Insurance.* Withdean Publications, Hove.

[36] Jajodia, S., Noel, S., & O'Berry, B. (2005). Topological analysis of network attack vulnerability. *Managing Cyber Threats*, 5(2005), 247–266.

[37] Jansen, W. A. (2011). Cloud hooks: Security and privacy issues in cloud computing. In *Proceedings of the 2011 44th Hawaii International Conference on System Sciences (HICSS '11)* (pp. 1–10).

[38] Jordan, T. & Taylor, P. (1998). A sociology of hackers. *The Sociological Review*, 46(4), 757–780.

[39] Kaarst-Brown, M. L. & Robey, D. (1999). More on myth, magic and metaphor: Cultural insights into the management of information technology in organizations. *Information Technology & People*, 12(2), 192–218.

[40] Kotsovinos, E. (2010). Virtualization: Blessing or curse? *Queue*, 8(11), 40.

[41] Lang, B., Foster, I., Siebenlist, F., Ananthakrishnan, R., & Freeman, T. (2006). A multipolicy authorization framework for grid security. In *Proceedings of the Fifth IEEE International Symposium on Network Computing and Applications (NCA '2006)* (pp. 269–272).

[42] Lee, W., Squicciarini, A. C., & Bertino, E. (2011). Detection and protection against distributed denial of service attacks in accountable grid computing systems. In *Proceedings of the 2011 11th IEEE/ACM International Symposium on Cluster, Cloud and Grid Computing (CCGrid '2011)*, pp. 534–543.

[43] Lin, Y., Kemme, B., Patino-Martinez, M., & Jimenez-Peris, R. (2007). Enhancing edge computing with database replication. In *Proceedings of the 26th IEEE International Symposium on Reliable Distributed Systems (SRDS 2007)* (pp. 45–54).

[44] Löhr, H., Ramasamy, H. G., Sadeghi, A. R., Schulz, S., Schunter, M., & Stüble, C. (2007). Enhancing grid security using trusted virtualization. *Lecture Notes in Computer Science, Autonomic and Trusted Computing*, 4610, 372–384.

[45] McKnight, L., Bose, T., Marsden, J., Nanno, E., Treglia, J., Volos, H., Chen, X., Sharma, P., & Ma, X. (2012). In McKnight, L. (Ed.), *Open Specifications for Wireless Grids Technical Requirements, Version 0.1* (pp. 1–22). Syracuse University.

[46] McKnight, L. W., Howison, J., & Bradner, S. (2004). Guest editors' introduction: Wireless grids — Distributed resource sharing by mobile, nomadic, and fixed devices. *IEEE Internet Computing*, 8(4), 24–31.

[47] McKnight, L., Marsden, J., Treglia, J., Nanno, E., Hameed, A., & Lu, Y. (2013). In McKnight, L. (Ed.), *Open Specifications for Wireless Grids Technical Requirements, Version 0.2* (pp. 1–45). Syracuse University.

[48] Mehr and Hedges (1963). *Risk Management in the Business Enterprise.* Irwin Publishers, Homewood, IL.

[49] National Institute of Standards and Technology (NIST) (2012). *Guide for Conducting Risk Assessments.* NIST Special Publication, http://csrc.nist.gov/publications/drafts/800-30-rev1/SP800-30-Rev1-ipd.pdf (Accessed September 11, 2012).

[50] Onwubiko, C. & Lenaghan, A. P. (2007). Managing security threats and vulnerabilities for small to medium enterprises. In *Proceedings of the 2007 IEEE Intelligence and Security Informatics* (pp. 244–249).

[51] Padmavathi, D. G. & Shanmugapriya, M. (2009). A survey of attacks, security mechanisms and challenges in wireless sensor networks. *International Journal of Computer Science and Information Security*, 4(½), 1–9.

[52] Pang, H. & Tan, K. L. (2004). Authenticating query results in edge computing. In *Proceedings of the 20th IEEE International Conference on Data Engineering* (pp. 560–571).

[53] Perry, T. S. & Wallich, P. (1984). Can computer crime be stopped? *IEEE Spectrum*, 21(5), 34–45.

[54] Rajanna, P. & Gyani, J. (2012). A comparative study of cloud and grid computing security solutions. *International Journal of Computer Science and Electronics Engineering*, 2(1), 1–8.

[55] Raymond, D. R. & Midkiff, S. F. (2008). Denial-of-service in wireless sensor networks: Attacks and defenses. *IEEE Pervasive Computing*, 7(1), 74–81.

[56] Rehana, J. (2009). *Security of Wireless Sensor Network*. University of Technology, Helsinki, TKK-CSE-B5.

[57] Ristenpart, T., Tromer, E., Shacham, H., & Savage, S. (2009). Hey, you, get off of my cloud: Exploring information leakage in third-party compute clouds. In *Proceedings of the 16th ACM Conference on Computer and Communications Security* (pp. 199–212).

[58] Saha, S., Jamtgaard, M., & Villasenor, J. (2001). Bringing the wireless Internet to mobile devices. *Computer*, 34(6), 54–58.

[59] Schmit, J. T. & Roth, K. (1990). Cost effectiveness of risk management practices. *Journal of Risk and Insurance*, 57(3), 455–470.

[60] Sen, B. (2004). Cybermetrics-meaning, definition, scope and constituents. *Annals of Library and Information Studies*, 51(3), 116–120.

[61] Sheldon, T. (2012). Edge devices. Linktionary.com

[62] Sloman, M. (1994). Policy driven management for distributed systems. *Journal of Network and Systems Management*, 2(4), 333–360.

[63] Smith, A. D. & Rupp, W. T. (2002). Issues in cybersecurity; understanding the potential risks associated with hackers/crackers. *Information Management & Computer Security*, 10(4), 178–183.

[64] Thomas, D. (2003). *Hacker Culture*. University of Minnesota Press, Minneapolis, MN.

[65] Tipton, H. F. (2010). *Official (ISC)^2 Guide to the CISSP CBK* (Second Edition). Auerbach Publications, Boca Raton, FL.

[66] Treglia, J., Ramnarine-Rieks, A., & McKnight, L. (2010). Collaboration in a wireless grid innovation testbed by virtual consortium. *Networks for Grid Applications*, 139–146.

[67] Treglia, J. V., McKnight, L. W., Kuehn, A., Ramnarine-Rieks, A. U., Venkatesh, M., & Bose, T. (2011). Interoperability by 'edgeware': Wireless grids for emergency response. In *Proceedings of the 2011 44th Hawaii International Conference on System Sciences (HICSS)* (pp. 1–10).

[68] Tsai, H. Y., Siebenhaar, M., Miede, A., Huang, Y., & Steinmetz, R. (2012). Threat as a service? Virtualization's impact on cloud security. *IT Professional*, 14(1), 32–37.

[69] Tutănescu, I. & Sofron, E. (2003). Anatomy and types of attacks against computer networks. In *Proceedings of the Second RoEduNet International Conference* (pp. 265–270).

[70] Tyagi, N. K. & Vyas, A. (2008). Data security from malicious attack: Computer virus. In P*roceedings of the BVIM Indiacom2010 (Track 2: Web Technologies, Computer Networks & Information security [G-III]) National Conference* (pp. 1–10).

[71] Van Cleeff, A., Pieters, W., & Wieringa, R. (2009, July). Security implications of virtualization: A literature study. In Paper presented at the *2009 International Conference Computer Science Engineering*, Las Vegas, NV.

[72] von Hippel, E. & Paradiso, J. A. (2008). User innovation and hacking. *IEEE Pervasive Computing*, 7(3), 66–69.

[73] Wallner, J. (2008). *Cyber Risk Management*. Encyclopedia of Quantitative Risk Analysis and Assessment. Wiley Online Library.

[74] Whiteside, T. (1978). *Computer Capers: Tales of Electronic Thievery, Embezzlement, and Fraud.* Crowell, New York, NY.

[75] Whitman, M. E. & Mattord, H. J. (2011). *Principles of Information Security.* Course Technology Learning, Boston, MA.

[76] Wiener, N. (1948). *Cybernetics*. Hermann, Paris.

[77] Williams and Heins (1964). *Risk Management and Insurance.* McGraw Hill, New York, NY.

[78] Wilson, C. (2003). *Computer Attack and Cyberterrorism: Vulnerabilities and Policy Issues for Congress*. In E. Linden (Ed.), *Focus on Terrorism*, Volume 9, pp. 1–42.

[79] Yi, S., Naldurg, P., & Kravets, R. (2001). Security-aware *ad-hoc* routing for wireless networks. In *Proceedings of the Second ACM International Symposium on Mobile Ad Hoc Networking & Computing (MobiHoc'01)* (pp. 299–302).

Chapter 7

Edge Computing and Cyber Warfare: Strategies for Future Operations in a Wireless Grid SDN-Enabled World

ABSTRACT

Cyber warfare has become an increasingly prominent threat in the modern world and with the rise of Edge computing, the nature of cyber warfare is evolving. The emergence of Edge computing introduces new vulnerabilities and attack vectors that can be exploited by cyber attackers. Leveraging 5G architectures, Edge platforms are essentially designed to take advantage of cloud-native concepts — the ability to leverage self-contained functions within or across cloud data centers, communicate in a micro-services type environment, and work together to deliver services and applications. Overlays are formed on top of these often unreliable Edge networks, permitting the virtualization of networks that can appear to be more reliable, hence a new type of architecture. The concepts for this type of Edge computing platform is drawn from the rich base of software-defined network (SDN) and network functional virtualization (NFV) concepts used in cloud computing, except that they must be optimized for the heterogeneous and rapidly changing nature of the basic substrate network formed opportunistically by Edge networks. This chapter explores the concept of cyber warfare at the Edge, focusing on the unique challenges and opportunities presented by Edge computing, and proposes the beginning strategy for a new infrastructure for performing future operations on an Edge platform integrating an SDN approach.

It examines the potential impact of cyber-attacks on Edge devices and the Edge infrastructure, as well as the implications for the overall security of networks and data. Additionally, this chapter discusses the key strategies and technologies that can be leveraged to enhance the security of Edge computing environments and mitigate the risks of cyber-attacks. Finally, the chapter provides insights into the evolving nature of cyber warfare and the critical role of Edge computing in shaping the future of cybersecurity.

INTRODUCTION

In recent years, cyber warfare has emerged as a major threat to global security, with a growing number of nation-states and non-state actors utilizing cyber-attacks to achieve their strategic objectives. As computing technology continues to advance, so too does the complexity of cyber threats, and the rise of Edge computing is no exception. Edge computing, which involves processing data closer to the source of its creation, offers a range of benefits, including reduced latency, improved performance, and increased reliability [10]. However, it also introduces new security risks, as Edge devices and infrastructure are vulnerable to a range of cyber-attacks. In this chapter, we explore the evolving landscape of cyber warfare at the Edge, highlighting the unique challenges and opportunities presented by this emerging technology. We examine the potential impact of cyber-attacks on Edge computing environments, as well as the strategies and technologies that can be employed to enhance their security. Ultimately, this chapter aims to provide a comprehensive overview of cyber warfare at the Edge and to inform stakeholders about the critical importance of securing this technology in the face of an ever-evolving cyber threat landscape.

In "Cyber War", Richard Clarke explores the growing threat of cyber-attacks on national security and offers strategies for defending against them [4]. Drawing on his experience as a former White House advisor on cybersecurity, Clarke argues that cyber-attacks are becoming more sophisticated and can cause significant damage to critical infrastructure, including power grids, financial systems, and communication networks [4]. Alongside the informatization of weapons and equipment, cyber warfare operations will inevitably permeate every area of the battlefield, thus cyberspace is extremely large. At the same time, the cyber warfare operation will begin before the commencement of a campaign and run through the whole battle. In particular, the reconnaissance of information and the protection of information systems are to continue throughout the course of the whole campaign and are clearly marked by the characteristic of a full span of time. The diversified composition of the cyber warfare operation force, a fast-changing situation on the battlefield, and the vast operation space together present numerous factors that will affect the use of a new Edge platform. Processing data from a Cloud out to the Edge of a network can drastically increase performance and productivity. To make flexible use of the Edge platform, requirements are needed to adapt systems and the ever-changing situation of cyber warfare operations.

Fog computing and related approaches, e.g., mobile Edge computing (MEC), are situated close to the Internet of Things (IoT) and mobile devices. These types of software-defined fog networks referred to as "SDFN", support the creation of information convergence devices that seek connection with other peers to form basic mobile edge networks. Leveraging 5G architectures, these SDFNs are essentially designed to take advantage of cloud-native concepts — the ability to leverage self-contained functions within or across data centers (the cloud), communicate in a micro-services type environment, and work together to deliver services and applications. Overlays are formed on top of these often unreliable Edge networks, permitting the virtualization of networks that can appear to be more reliable, hence a new type of SDFN. The concepts for this type of SDFN are drawn from the rich base of software-defined network (SDN) and network functional virtualization (NFV) concepts used in cloud computing, except that they must be optimized for the heterogeneous and rapidly changing nature of the basic substrate network formed opportunistically by Edge networks.

To address the inherent drawbacks of cloud computing, Fog computing has emerged as a promising solution. Fog computing, a term put forward by Cisco in 2012, has emerged as a promising technology that can bring cloud applications closer to the physical IoT devices at the network edge [14] (see Figure 1). The main purpose of Fog computing is to bring computational resources closer to end users as well as reduce the amount of data needed to transfer to the cloud for processing and storage [1]. Fog computing aims to reduce cloud involvement in data processing by filtering and preprocessing data produced by the rising number of sensors and other IoT devices connected to the fog computing environment [13]. This improved utilization of edge resources leads to faster communication and task execution.

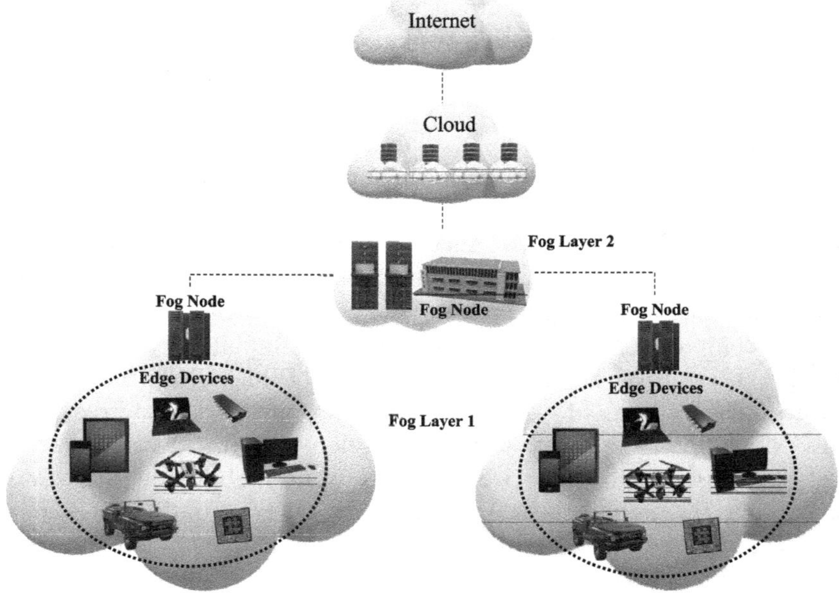

Figure 1. Fog-to-Cloud Architecture (F2C)

A particular research challenge is to provide mechanisms for the decentralized processing of data and for virtualized resource provisioning in fog landscapes for capabilities [1]. To address this challenge, a dynamic software environment, i.e., SDN, is required. This architecture and the communication in an edge environment have to provide the functionality to execute capabilities, monitor, and analyze IoT services in addition to the deployment and migration of the virtualized IoT resources. Furthermore, in case of failure or violated service constraints, the framework has to be able to reconfigure the fog landscape for continued functionality.

Another idea regarding the architecture and communication in an Edge environment is using NFV in combination with SDN at the Edge of the network. SDN is an emerging paradigm that promises to change this state of affairs, by breaking vertical integration, separating the network's control logic from the underlying routers and switches, promoting (logical) centralization of network control, and introducing the ability to program the network (see Figure 2) [17]. NFV is a novel paradigm that enables scalable and flexible deployment of network services on Edge or

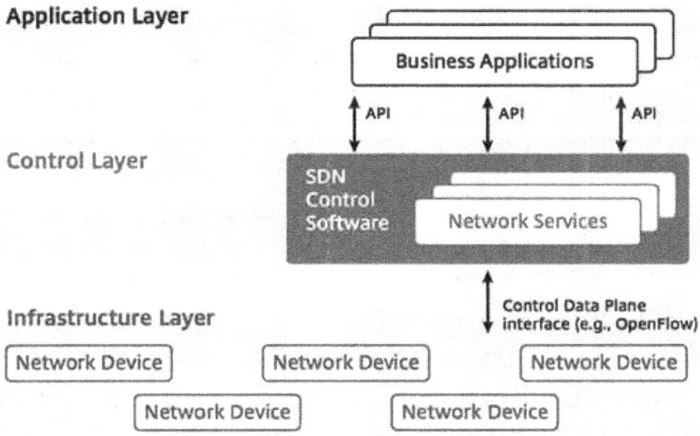

Figure 2. Simplified View of an SDN Architecture

cloud infrastructure [17]. This suggestion aims at improving the flexibility and dynamic behavior of network services, as well as user services. NFV is a technology to virtualize network resources and to provide them according to the current demand. Hence, network resources such as firewalls, databases, and routers can be deployed on demand [17]. The SDN is needed to create virtual networks and run software services on the deployed devices. This technique leads to a major flexibility improvement at the Edge of the network. Besides the adapted architecture, the authors address the topic of distributed management of devices in Edge clouds.

Within this topic, the machine-to-machine (M2M) communication, between the devices in an Edge cloud and between Edge clouds, is mentioned. Additionally, privacy is a critical issue, and fog computing leads to a crucial change concerning this topic. Fog computing enables a new privacy approach by not transferring critical data to a centralized device but to a device located at the Edge of the network. Furthermore, the concept of using NFV in combination with SDN can create an architecture consisting of the following layers (bottom to top): 5G wireless, fog computing, NFV, and cloud computing [17]. The bottommost layer emphasizes mobile technologies such as 5G and Wi-Fi. The structure of the network and the participating network devices are managed using an SDN approach. This enables the managing component located in the cloud to have a global network overview and to adapt the devices and services according to the current demand.

Edge computing constitutes a new concept in the computing landscape as the technology brings the service and utilities of cloud computing closer to the end user and is characterized by fast processing and quick application response time (see Figure 3) [16]. Edge computing refers to locating applications — and the general-purpose computing, storage, and associated switching and control functions needed to run them — relatively close to end users and/or IoT endpoints [16]. This greatly benefits application performance and associated quality of experience (QoE), and it can also improve efficiency and thus the economics depending on the nature of the specific application. Edge computing is also important for the localization of data and efficient data processing. Industry and Government regulations may require localization of data for security and privacy reasons. Certain application scenarios may pose restrictions on

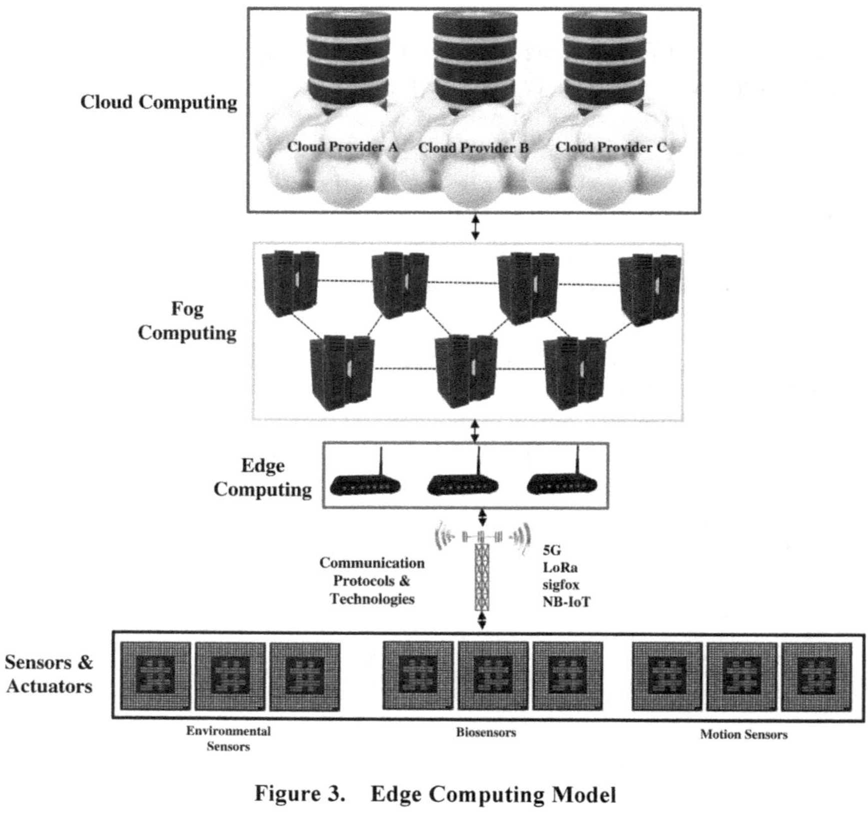

Figure 3. Edge Computing Model

the use of excessive transport bandwidth or may require transport to external sites to be scheduled by time of day, requiring local storage or caching of information. Additionally, there may need to be local processing of information to reduce the volume of traffic over transport resources. An example of this type of computing is called MEC.

MEC is based on a comparable idea as Fog computing but places an emphasis on mobile devices at the Edge of the network [2]. The key features of the entire MEC environment are task sharing between mobile devices and task offloading to the cloud. The mobile devices are able to intercommunicate and take task requests from each other. Additionally, so-called MEC servers are located at the Edge of the network responsible for connecting mobile devices to the cloud [2]. In this approach, the Edge of the network is the Edge of the radio access network (RAN). Hence, the base stations of the RAN represent the MEC servers, i.e., the fog cells in Fog computing. These MEC servers are owned by telecommunication companies and are able to process task requests. Due to the fact that most of the communication takes place in the RAN, the emphasized communication technologies in MEC are the cellular communication generations 3G, 4G, and especially 5G [2].

While the adoption of wireless devices such as laptops and personal digital assistants provides increased flexibility and mobility to the manner in which networked information can be accessed and processed, the adoption of wireless devices exposes the information that is stored and processed on those devices to increased threats. Additionally, the network resources being accessed are also at greater risk.

The major threats posed by the adoption of mobile devices include, but are not limited to:

- Loss or theft of the device, resulting in disclosure of sensitive information, or impersonation of a legitimate user/device to the network.
- Incorrectly configured device may act as a gateway to an otherwise secured network.
- Inadequately protected devices may be a source of malicious code (trojans or viruses) that affect the secure network.

In order to address the increased threats, wireless devices must be configured to minimize risks from these threats as far as is practicable. The specific configuration settings adopted must be based on documented security policies, but general guidelines that should be addressed include

(*NOTE*: this is not meant to represent an exhaustive list, but merely provide an indication as to the types of configuration settings that will need to be considered):

1. **Operating system security:** The mobile device must be configured with an approved and hardened operating system with the latest security patches applied. Internet connection sharing and file-sharing features should be disabled. Screensaver passwords should be enabled.
2. **Applications:** The mobile device should have antivirus, personal firewall, and intrusion detection software correctly installed and configured with the latest definitions and updates. The firewall should provide both inbound and outbound filtering and alerts. File or disk encryption should be implemented by a third-party application if not implemented by the operating system. All unapproved applications should be removed from the device. VPN software should be configured to use only approved algorithms and routing between the VPN interface and other interfaces should be disabled, preventing the routing of Internet or LAN traffic to the VPN.
3. **Access control:** BIOS-level password protection should be enabled if supported to prevent low-level configuration changes to the device. Operating system login should be based on strong passwords, certificates, or two-factor authentication.
4. **Wireless network interface card:** *Ad hoc* mode should be disabled and the wireless NIC should be configured to only associate with known networks. Unsupported authentication (EAP) methods and encryption modes (e.g., WEP) should be disabled to mitigate security rollback attacks. Infra-red and Bluetooth devices should be disabled.

As the next generation of wireless technology, 5G differs starkly from previous wireless generations. Where previous wireless generations were designed to connect people to people and to connect people to the Internet, 5G extends even more broadly. The 5G architecture is essentially designed to take advantage of cloud-native concepts — the ability to leverage self-contained functions within or across data centers (the cloud), communicate in a micro-services environment, and work together to deliver services and applications [10]. Disaggregation and virtualization are two key elements of 5G cloud-native architecture. The use of SDN and NFV basically allows the disaggregation and virtualization of many of the telecommunications and mobility functions like serving/public gateway (S/P-GW), mobility management entity (MME), RAN central unit/ distributed unit (CU/DU), traffic detection function (TDF), internet protocol (IP) routing, and ethernet encapsulation/switching [10].

These functions are hosted as software services and dynamically instantiated in different parts of the network segments; thus, the overall 5G network is designed to be software-configurable. Consequently, networks are evolving to primarily utilize SDN, NFV, and cloud-native architectures to enable disaggregation and virtualization of primary functions. This leads to the separation of the control plane and user plane and introduces capabilities such as network slicing and MEC. 5G also shifts to a services-based architecture (SBA), which moves from a response-request method of communication to a producer-consumer type model.

MOTIVATION

With the new service provisioning requirements posed by 5G (i.e., the ultra-low latency and massive machine-type communication) urge the functionalities offload from the network core to Edge. The various demands of the quality of service (QoS) guarantee cast by the diverse services make the SDN an essential enabler of Edge network capabilities evolution involving a new virtualization scenario and functions compared to the traditional SDN scenario [5]. However, 5G network performance and network slicing significantly enhance SDN functional and architectural viability [5]. To date, most of the existing SDN research focuses on the core network to provide a better data plane and control plane performance.

At first glance, the solution is far from perfect for performing operations on an Edge platform integrating an SDN approach. These SDFNs create a complexity of multiple networks that must be tested and implemented, with different footprints of various types of equipment and associated logistics and of course different provisioning, security architectures, and interfaces. They are not usually seamlessly integrated, making it difficult to move across networks when one is not available (e.g., network outages, weather, etc.). In Edge networks, these difficulties place a heavy burden on preserving the connectivity necessary for cyber operations. The explosion of options for communications, though imperfect, combined with the increasing complexity have led to a seemingly reasonable desire to unify the communications apparatus as a whole.

Due to the increased use of 5G and Edge computing, the deployment of massive IoT infrastructures in urban areas and industrial verticals are currently being implemented (e.g., smart city and Industry 4.0) [5]. IoT infrastructures are expected to be highly pervasive and composed of millions of heterogeneous physical devices distributed through multiple sites or domains with each domain being connected to application platforms hosted in cloud computing or metropolitan data centers [4]. Therefore, from a perspective against our adversaries, such complex infrastructures will be a critical task dealing with important issues of fault, configuration, accountability, performance, and security. As a result, the adopted distribution strategy of IoT platforms between cloud and Edge points using multi-access Edge computing nodes can reduce delay and avoid bottlenecks not only in the data plane but also in the control or management plane. This is due to the fact that each node can host device management functions and control a subset of IoT devices for a wireless sensor network (WSN). Nevertheless, there is still room for improving existing single-domain literature solutions regarding multi-domain or multi-edge deployments where several WSNs require management. To this end, SDN technologies can enhance operations in multi-domain IoT deployments, as SDN improves control plane, device mobility, and device resiliency.

This chapter identifies a SDFN, supporting the creation of information convergence devices that seek connection with other peers to form basic mobile Edge networks to support cyber operations. In a crude analogy, we consider each communications option like a node in which, like an access point (AP), are the bits of communications flow. Each communications option, whether a point-to-point link or a complex, enterprise service, is simply treated as a different node. The framework employs planes on each end for the nodes, which are added in parallel, as many as we can find to connect devices. As in the case of communication flow, so long as one node is "operational", communication can flow, and if more nodes are clear, the communication flow can be better.

Even by this description of the SDFN, we seem to be solving one problem (the problem of "communication layers"), but not effectively addressing the sprawl of equipment, and perhaps exacerbating the problem by adding more "things". In the near term, we believe the gains more than offset the disadvantages, since unified solutions allow for competition and improved solutions over time and in recapitalization activities. We suggest that several technologies, such as cognitive radios, 5G cell towers, reconfigurable antennas, smart devices, and software-defined radios (SDRs) can provide a longer-range solution by replacing "boxes" at first and eventually entire suites of equipment with a single, configurable system. Such a system would eventually mimic any communications architecture through software virtualization, analogous to the way virtual machines in data centers can mimic any processor and any network through network virtualization. In time, legacy systems would be replaceable by capabilities that could be installed in a single black box reconfigurable transceiver, replacing large accumulations of equipment (i.e., palettes of boxes). In this approach, the full power of the SDN can be brought to bear, and, as in the case of cloud data centers, the need to maintain dozens of legacy equipment clusters will fade over time.

This chapter is organized as follows. In next section, Software-Defined Security Threats, we briefly discuss the commonly known threats to an SDN architecture. The Full Converge of the Edge Platform section provides the SDFN that could potentially be used for capabilities. The Software Defined Fog Network Architecture section addresses various concepts for security operations that the SDFN could use in the future. Finally, the Future Research section details future research work required for the concept of an SDFN to develop into reality.

SOFTWARE-DEFINED SECURITY THREATS

Threats on SDNs can be classified based on SDN major functional components described earlier in Figure 2 and the type and nature of attacks that each component can be subjected to during these attacks. Attacks on SDNs can be also classified based on the type of assets or resources a typical SDN may have. For example, attacks can be focused on switches' flow tables where those flow tables include information related to network management, switching, routing, and access control [2]. Attacks can be also focused on the controller as the central location for management and control. The channel between the controller and the switches is another major attacks target where such a channel involves important messages that can be hijacked. At the top level, the controller communicates with high-level applications using a standard interface (e.g., REST). Such an interface can be also attacked in order to trick the controller to allow malicious applications to join the network and interact with the controller, the network, and its traffic. Some additional major attacks on SDN environments are as follows.

Spoofing refers to a process where network information [e.g., IP, media access control (MAC), address resolution protocol (ARP), etc.] is forged intentionally to hide the actual identity of the traffic originator or attacker. For example, users may use spoofed IP addresses to access network resources. Spoofing is often part of a larger attack, such as SYN flooding, Smurf, and domain name service (DNS) amplification [15]. Spoofed addresses can also be part of a botnet or a zombie network to launch distributed denial-of-service (DDoS) attacks. Currently spoofing threats in SDN primarily include ARP spoofing and IP spoofing. ARP spoofing involves linking an attacker's MAC address to a legitimate IP address. The original purpose of ARP is to resolve IP to MAC addresses. The ARP spoofing attack may cause traffic to be hijacked from the original intended receiver and, as a result, a legitimate user or host is knocked out of the network. IP to MAC mapping tables can be used to detect ARP spoofing. In OpenFlow, ARP poisoning is possible between the controllers and switches if the optional SSL encryption is not used. ARP cache poisoning occurs when an attacker is located in the same subnet of the victim's computers & security network (e.g., internal attacks).

ARP spoofing involves linking an attacker's MAC address to a legitimate IP address [6]. The original purpose of ARP is to resolve IP to MAC addresses. The ARP spoofing attack may cause traffic to be hijacked from the original intended receiver and, as a result, a legitimate user or host is knocked out of the network. IP to MAC mapping tables can be used to detect ARP spoofing. ARP spoofing attacks can be countered with packet-level information. Low-resolution attacks require information at the flow, not the packet level. Packet-level details are only required at high-resolution level attacks. For example, attacks like DoS and domain name server (DNS) amplification can be handled with information at the flow level details. On the other hand, ARP spoofing and cache poisoning attacks require information at the packet level.

IP spoofing is usually used as an opening to other types of security attacks, such as DNS tampering or amplification [15]. A DNS is a directory that associates IP addresses with domain names. To reroute traffic to illegitimate websites, an attacker may manipulate the DNS directory. What all spoofing methods have in common is that they try to redirect traffic to illegitimate hosts. They can also be considered to achieve man-in-the-middle (MiM) attacks. Spoofing can be mitigated by a proper authentication scheme. Spoofing or forged IP addresses may occur from within the network. Based on the nature of IP address forging, source address validation from within the network can be difficult to detect. In general, an SDN approach may not need a dedicated router where routing functionalities are included in the OpenFlow controller and switches.

Tampering is the deliberate and unauthorized modification or destruction of network information, such as topology, flows in flow tables, policies, and access lists [3]. For example, an intruder may try to inject flow rules that will cause network misbehavior. They may inject flow tables or firewall rules that will deny legitimate hosts or allow illegitimate hosts. Intruders may also try to tamper with topology information and consequently cause some traffic to be hijacked. In SDN controller distribution, different controllers communicate important information. It is very important to secure this communication channel from being hijacked or tampered. As flow-based traffic management, SDN can help prevent unintended traffic tampering. Packets can be inspected before they go on the wire for their destination for some integrity attributes. Validation results can be carried out with the traffic to be checked at the destination point. Tampering can be mitigated by distributing auditing and monitoring across several network points. If one point is attacked, the rest of the network points can be used to detect and correct such tampering. To protect against tampering, the controller should manage and routinely check encryption methods and legitimate connections. Another related issue is controller failure modes (fail safe and fail secure modes). It is possible to compromise integrity or confidentiality when the controller or switches are pushed to switch to one of those failure modes.

Information disclosure attacks have no direct intention to destroy or disrupt the network but to spy on its information [8]. In addition to the sensitive information that attackers try to get, they will initially try to sniff network information such as topology, nodes' features, or communication details among nodes. The impacts of SDN architecture on scanning attacks can be mixed. The controller is a central location for control of all network switches. Being able to invade the controller, the attacker can have tremendous network access. On the other hand, data is isolated from the controller, unlike traditional switches where control is co-located with the data inside the switch. In SDN, flow rules exist in switches' flow tables. If intruders succeed in accessing those switches directly, they can tamper with flow rules and cause traffic to go to the wrong destinations. If they succeed in disconnecting a switch from communicating with the controller, they can assume control and cause a significant traffic misdirection. If they can hijack traffic from a legitimate host, they can impersonate that host and join the network as a spy. To protect private information, there are other actions to consider. Whitelisting and blacklisting can be used to filter traffic. White- and blacklistings in traditional networks are defined based on IP and MAC addresses.

FULL CONVERGE OF THE EDGE PLATFORM

The procedures of and sequence of targets in cyber-warfare operations have evolved. Although cyber — warfare operations are not particularly well suited as costly signals of resolve or capabilities in the context of coercive diplomacy, they have a distinct utility for signaling to manage escalation risks. From the original attacking pattern of carrying out cyber-attacks, step-by-step from the front to the back based on the progress of the campaign fighting, into the in-depth attacking pattern of hackers. Whereby, fatal attacks are launched on most vital network parts, for instance, the central node in the Command, Control, Communications, Computers [C4] Intelligence, Surveillance, and Reconnaissance [ISR] system, and the weapon control system. Within the scope allowed in the cyber battlefield, the focus is laid on the whole situation of the campaign, and the need to hit the target, to weaken or completely eradicate the adversary's combat capabilities is imperative [5]. With the invisible and silent rivalries of the cyber warfare operation, the war is manipulated in an even more mysterious, constantly changing, and unpredictable manner. Quick response is an important pre-requisite in defeating the adversary and attaining victory in cyber warfare operations [7].

In the command of cyber warfare operation, the Edge platform must be able to respond swiftly and flexibly, alter the tactics of operation at any time in accordance with the changes in the situation of the adversary, and mobilize the reserve force or activate the new information warfare weapons decisively at the critical moment (see Figure 4). However, we can firmly grasp the initiative of the cyber warfare operation only when we are able to rapidly deploy manpower and weapons. Cyberspace allows us to quickly get hold of the situation of cyber warfare operation on the battlefield, swiftly formulate and determine countermeasures, make corresponding changes in response to every change initiated by the adversary, implement changes more skillfully than the adversary does, move without losing control, and act without lacking tactics [6].

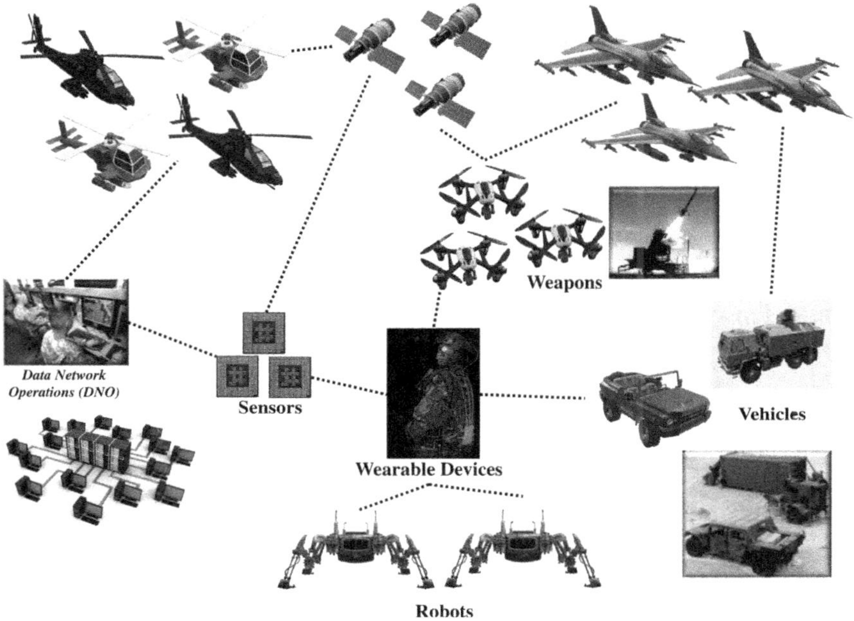

Figure 4. The Internet of Military/Battlefield Things

Edge computing has emerged as the solution to the continuously increasing numbers of Internet-connected devices and to the ever-increasing amounts of data transmitted by them using advanced algorithms and hardware components; it allows sensor data processing at the source and reduces the volumes of data transmitted within the network [12]. Edge computing can potentially play a crucial role in enabling military/battlefield applications by increasing the number of ubiquitous sensing and computing devices worn by military personnel and embedded within military equipment (combat suits, instrumented helmets, weapon systems, etc.) Reference [3] As far as fighting space is concerned, the objective of this chapter is to begin to form a comprehensive, three-dimensional Edge platform covering the cyber-space underground, underwater, air, and outer space. In cyber warfare operations, there is no boundary to this fighting space, which can extend to anywhere on the ground and in the air of belligerent parties in cyberwar [9]. Therefore, the total coverage of the platform is not only confined to the actual battlefield with soldiers and weapons but should also involve the whole dimensions of the strategies or the whole territory of the cyberspace arena as well.

In this three-dimensional fighting space, the main modes of transmission of information entail optical information transmission for underground operation, long waves for underwater information transmission, medium waves, short waves, ultra-short waves, and microwaves for information transmission in the air, and satellite transmission in space. In terms of fighting functions, the Edge platform must combine six sub-systems of cyber warfare operation namely: the reconnaissance system, attack system, defense system, command and control system, comprehensive support system, and security and confidentiality system into one single entity. Each of these sub-systems not only can act separately and independently in a particular time segment, stage, and area during the cyber warfare operation but can also be integrated to form a single operation system. Hence, the Edge platform not only has to cover and connect the various subsystems in the cyber warfare operation system but should also be able to separate or realign the various components based on the changes in the combat power.

With respect to the network for information flow, the Edge platform should cover the sensor network, information network, and engagement network, so that the three networks can work together as a whole. That is to merge an intelligence information detection network, information transmission network, information-processing network, and requisition information networks into the various cyber warfare operation units and weapon platforms. Furthermore, the Edge platform must ensure full network coverage and linkage in all the areas where information has to be reached. Likewise, with regards to the level of warfare operation, the Edge platform should achieve the integration of different levels, essential elements, and processes such as the integration of strategies, campaigns, and tactics, the integration of systemic power, unit power, and element power, the integration of command personnel, combat personnel, and weapon platform as well as the integration of the processes of warfare operation preparation, planning, organization, implementation, and effectiveness assessment.

As a new architecture, Edge computing can expose both new security opportunities and challenges. Attackers will eventually investigate Edge's strengths and weaknesses and will try to maximize exploits based on vulnerabilities. For example, zero-day attacks refer to attacks committed based on newly discovered vulnerabilities. A significant amount of such attacks are expected to be exposed in the coming years impacting Edge computing. In this section, we discuss the concept of an Edge as an evolution of basic communication concepts for future capabilities.

Notwithstanding the features identified above, Edge systems by their very nature, have a number of general vulnerabilities due to their method of operation. Some of these include the following:

- **Invasion and resource stealing:** To invade an Edge network, the attacker will first try to determine the access parameters for that particular network. Hacking techniques such as MAC spoofing may be used to attack an Edge network. For example, if the underlying network uses MAC-address filtering of clients, all an intruder has to do is find out the MAC address and the assigned IP address for a particular client. The intruder will wait till that client goes off the network and then start using the network and its resources while appearing as a valid user.
- **Denial-of-service (DoS):** In a general DoS attack, an intruder can attempt to disrupt the network operation by generating excessive interference, such as is produced by a microwave oven or some sort of broadband signal generator. A more specific DoS attack would be when an intruder sends an IEEE 802.11 disassociate message to the target Edge node to disconnect it.
- **Stealth DoS:** If an adversarial node continually requests a connection with an Edge node, no matter if the target agrees or not, it is possible to drain power by forcing the node to continually respond (regardless of whether or not the node accepts the connection).
- **Hijack attack:** Abuse of routing protocols to allow eavesdropping on victims out-of-range of the attacker by detouring the traffic through corrupted Edge nodes within the transmission range of both victim and attackers.
- **Rogue access points:** A rogue AP is one that is installed by an attacker (usually in public areas like shared office space, airports, etc.) to accept traffic from wireless Edge clients to whom it appears as a valid authenticator. Packets thus captured can be used to extract sensitive information, or for launching further attacks by, for example, modifying the content of the capture packet and re-inserting it into the Edge network.

Node-to-Node Communications

In the most basic case, we wish to establish communications between two separated nodes. We can do this using a secure wireless (or wired) communication medium (as displayed in Figure 5), and the communication signal introduced on one end appears at the other end. Abstractly, this can be a conduit of not only electrons, bits, bytes, etc. (as would be conveyed in the conductor of a secure wire), but it could also be implemented with varying degrees of certainty that third parties cannot intercept what is being communicated. This could also be denoted as a "Trusted Path" that would utilize a trusted platform management (TPM) network.

There will always be physical limitations — especially if the communication is wireless. In contemporary communications, these include the limitations of electronic equipment, the ambient physical medium, the geometries of communications, and the barriers/impairments between communications modes. For example, wireless signals between Nodes A and B are often facilitated through waveform and signaling conventions that are implemented by AP (Figure 6).

These APs are intended to make the best use of the limited physical channel, often incorporating simultaneous connections, authentication and authorization, traffic movement, and encryption protocols that are to

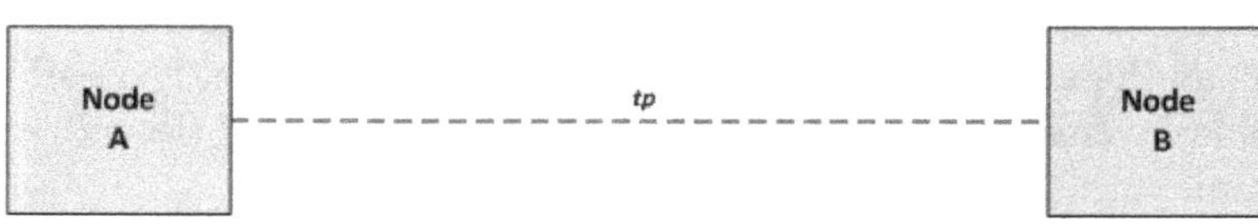

Figure 5. Communications Between Nodes A and B Secure Communications

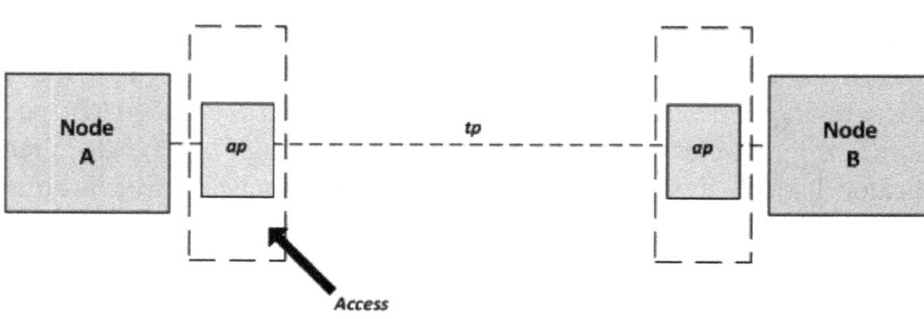

Figure 6. Waveforms Through Access Points

achieve the most efficient and reliable approximation of the "trusted path" possible. In the present state of the art, the closest approximation of a trusted path in this scenario, for example, might be a wireless sensor node platform utilizing Bluetooth radio transceivers in order to achieve high bandwidth data communication, a coarse wavelength division multiplexing (CWDM) or dense wavelength division multiplexing (DWDM) system (Figure 3) impressed onto a single mode fiber optic strand, which can support as much as 20 terabits/sec [11]. Even so, this feed would be difficult to realize with a single electrical channel (i.e., CWDM/DWDM employs nearly 200 parallel channels to achieve this effective bandwidth rate). To add capacity and resilience, and to step more in the direction of the trusted path, we can add several copies of Figure 7 node chain.

To simplify the splitting of a single signal into two channels in dealing with the differences in reliability, latency, and data rate, we implement an Edge intelligent manager in the control processor (*cp*) that ideally manages the different connections seamlessly as displayed in Figure 8.

In principle, this should be able to accommodate any number of these parallel chains which we shall call "communication flows". The concept is analogous to multi-path TCP, but the concept is not limited to TCP. The communication flows can be fundamentally different in nature, as suggested in Figure 8, with some being based on a line-of-sight connection (i), or formed from two different taps in a proprietary cloud network (ii) (perhaps using a commodity satellite communication [SATCOM] service, etc.), as Edge nodes in a mobile *ad hoc* network (iii), or even as hops in a temporally disjoint transport concept (iv) such as an accumulated batch transmission in a delay tolerant network [DTN] [15].

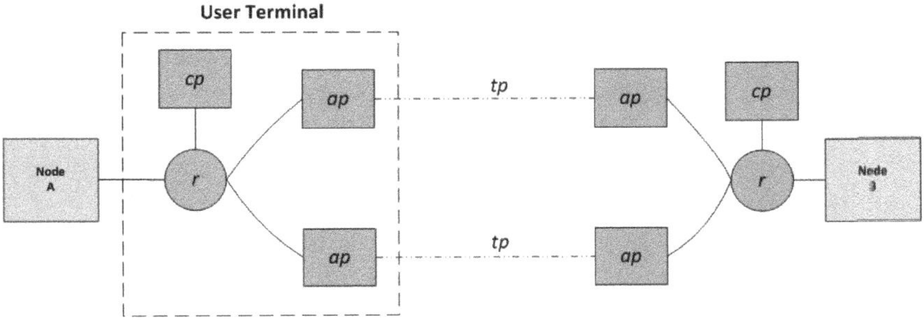

Figure 7. Trusted Communication Flow Paths (*tp* — Trusted Path, *r* — Router, *cp* — Control Processor, *ap* — Access Point)

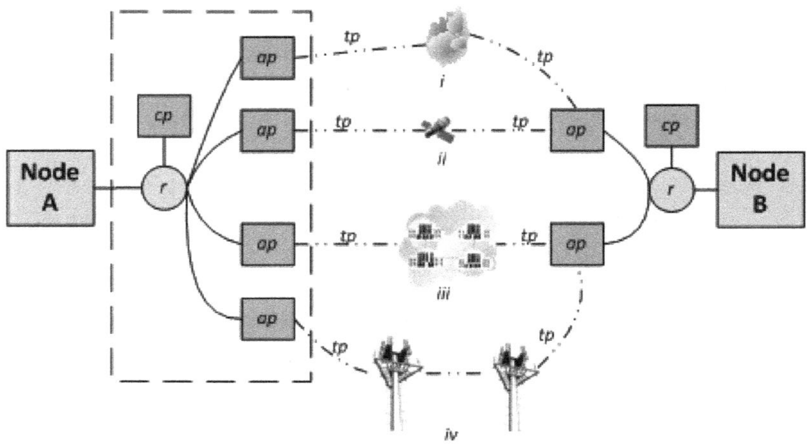

Figure 8. Extended Multiple Communication Flows Including (1) Point-to-Point Radio Frequency, (2) Use of a Cloud-Like Proprietary SATCOM Service, (3) As Edge Nodes of a Mobile *Ad Hoc* Network, (4) Depiction of Delayed, 5G Hopping Network

THE SOFTWARE DEFINED FOG NETWORK ARCHITECTURE

SDN technology can facilitate flexibility, security, and efficient resource sharing, particularly within Fog and IoT infrastructures. Flexibility, demanded by numerous applications concerning interdomain mobility, M2M communications, and addressing, is a noteworthy attribute of SDN. SDN controllers offer a unified network perspective, thereby enabling the provision of device mobility, adaptable M2M communication, and device address management [14]. Consequently, by integrating an SDN controller, infrastructure and device management can be significantly streamlined. A paramount challenge for extensive IoT infrastructures is to ensure secure data routing and device provisioning [2]. Researchers have examined an SDN architecture aimed at securing data routing by deploying a centralized verification mechanism within the SDN controller [8].

The SDN controller assumes a critical role in network resource sharing or slicing, and in the overall efficient utilization of network resources. As detailed in [10], SDN controllers are deployed within the fog infrastructure to enable network sharing between smart devices. However, the employment of a centralized SDN controller introduces the potential risk of a single point of failure or attack [8]. Furthermore, the large volume and diversity of IoT devices, in terms of capabilities and application requirements, hinder the scalability and performance of centralized control. Hence, the deployment of multiple controllers is essential to ensure resiliency and to address scalability and performance issues [8]. This framework incorporates software-defined routing and control for extensive fog deployments. Yet, it also considers multi-edge deployments to tackle the multidomain IoT device management problem for applications. The placement of multiple SDN controllers in clusters can be executed either dynamically or statically to minimize latency and resource usage or to maximize efficiency [8]. As a consequence, the management of devices and networks within IoT infrastructures, combined with the placement of multiple SDN controllers, can facilitate load balancing, fine-grained traffic forwarding, and enhance bandwidth availability [2].

This proposed SDFN architecture is predicated on a multidomain network setup, with each domain integrated into Layers 2 and 3 of an SDN. By leveraging SDN's topology detection and flow control over each network site, the SDFN can construct a global network view while simultaneously isolating the device management procedures at the MEC appliance nodes. These MEC appliance nodes could potentially host applications or capabilities for operations. Consequently, an SDFN architecture can be divided into four primary building blocks, three of which are deployed at the MEC appliance nodes, while the remaining one is deployed to the cloud. The comprehensive SDFN architecture is illustrated in Figure 9.

The three main Edge building blocks are described as follows.

(1) The **Provisioning Component (PC)** serves as the capability uploading element within the Edge platform. By maintaining a whitelist of MAC addresses, the device can cross-validate the whitelist with the SDFN topology, thereby facilitating zero-touch device provisioning for capabilities and tools designated for distribution at the Edge for operations.

(2) The **Software-Defined Monitor (SDM)** monitors the bytes of incoming packets and applies rules concerning the maximum allowed bandwidth in order to increase the performance of the toolset. SDM is the element that reads service level agreements (SLA) and applies them over a specific number of devices. Therefore, control signals for enabling or disabling devices are also part of SDM. The business logic integrates at this point, by deploying multiple descriptors

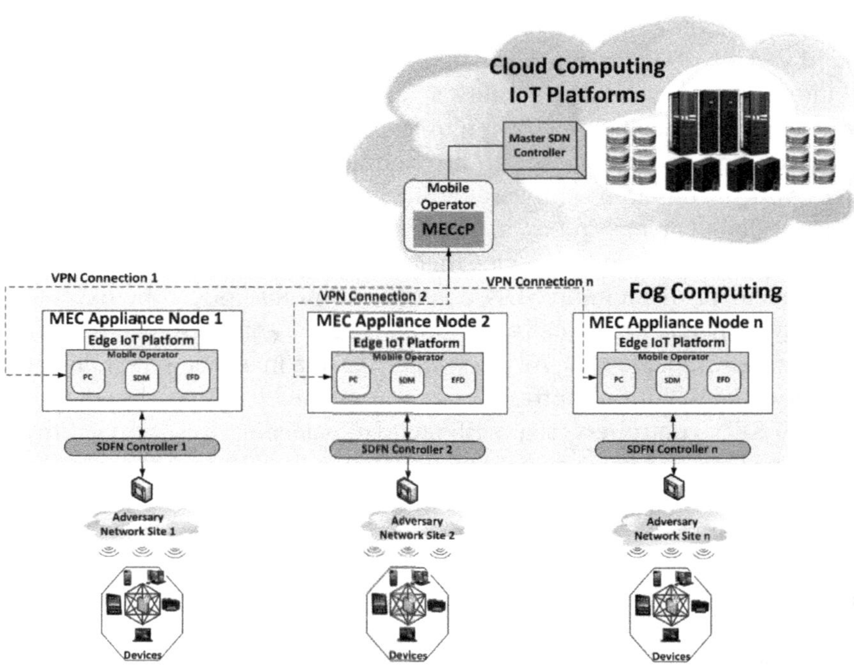

Figure 9. Software-Defined Fog Network (SDFN)

describing SLAs with different requirements that are mutable over time.

(3) The **Edge Fault Detector (EFD)** detects failures in M2M communications by validating the MAC address of each frame with a whitelist in real-time. EFD is able to detect three types of operational failures: (1) unavailability of data due to an inactive device, (2) unauthorized devices to avoid intrusions, and (3) application security faults.

The aforementioned architecture elements are placed on each MEC appliance node and are connected to the cloud elements through a dedicated virtual private network (VPN) link. The VPN connectivity is used for controlling plane traffic of mobile operators and for data traffic generated by Edge IoT platforms and applications (e.g., big data). From the cloud, three elements are deployed:

(1) The **Master SDFN Controller** that uses the aggregated topology information from the MECcP to enable cloud SDN.

(2) The **MEC Controller Platform (MECcP)** provides a global view of the IoT deployment to a master SDN controller, by aggregating all the topology information for each of the domains.
(3) The **MEC Appliance** provides direct interaction with the tools against the devices under operations.

This proposed framework is primarily based on the Fog, Edge computing paradigms, and SDN technology. More precisely, leveraging lightweight device management services that can be implemented as containers on very constrained MEC devices, hence eliminating the handshake and control signals exchange with the cloud, would be ideal. This results to faster response times compared to centralized device management. Therefore, by multidomain device management, the task becomes less complicated, and the idea of device management decentralization leads us to utilize SDN to its fullest extent. SDN can provide a global view of networks, as a result, it can provide multidomain information that allows multidomain monitoring and control.

Given that the SDFN is designed to solve logically centralized bottlenecks and utilize both Edge and cloud services; the mobile operator, MECcP, and MEC Appliance are used to create an enclave that forms the SDFN that directly supports the platform for all capabilities/tools and applications as displayed in Figure 10. For now, it will suffice to indicate that each SDFN attempts to optimize its connection with others, through any means possible (i.e., through one or more of the available communication flows).

The proposed SDFN architecture is predicated on a multidomain network setup, with each domain incorporating functionalities of Layer 2 and Layer 3 of SDN. By leveraging SDN's topology detection and flow control over a network site, SDFN can construct a comprehensive global network view. Concurrently, it can isolate any device management procedures at the MEC appliance nodes to facilitate tighter coordination for operations. Consequently, an SDFN architecture can be categorized into four primary building blocks, three of which are deployed at the MEC appliance nodes, and the fourth is deployed in the cloud. The complete architecture, as presented in Figure 7, is divided into four key procedures: the provisioning component (PC), the Edge Fog director (EFD), the software-defined monitor (SDM), and the MEC central processor (MECcP). These procedures interact with all the network elements constituting end-to-end IoT applications, including devices and APs, the MEC appliance

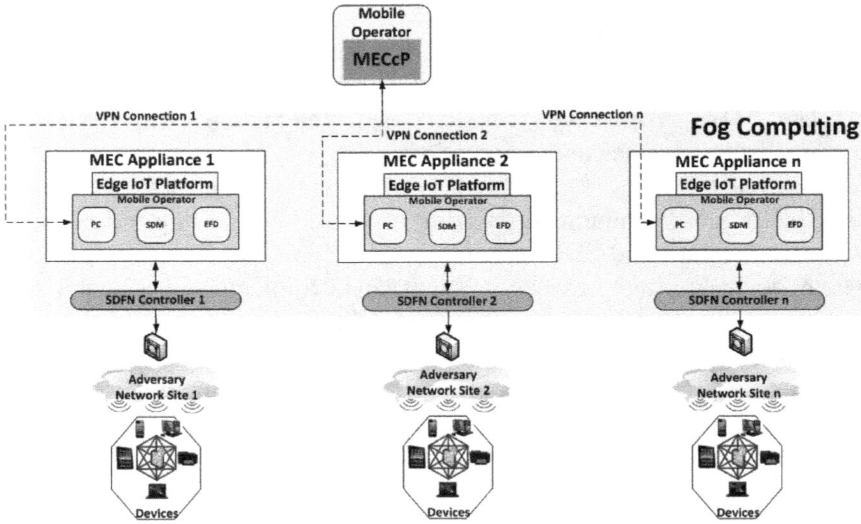

Figure 10. Components of the SDFN

(which is a requirement of the SDFN controller, both domain and cloud), and the Fog/Edge platforms. Figure 10 introduces a sequence diagram of the provisioning procedure, and all SDFN procedures are briefly described in the subsequent sections.

(1) **Procedure 1 (Access):** Upon a device's connection to an AP, the SDFN controller requests network/device information. The PC then matches rules for the devices based on source MAC addresses and the Edge IoT platform's destination IP address. Subsequently, the PC component requests the topology of devices connected to the AP from the AP's application programming interfaces (APIs). By leveraging the AP API, the PC can update the SDN controller's link layer discovery protocol (LLDP) inventory and reconstruct the SDN topology. Consequently, the SDFN controller retains the topology information and is capable of adding flow rules over each device or group of devices. This process, based on MAC and IP address filtering, proves more efficient compared to IP layer control messaging, particularly for large-scale sensor networks, as verified by our evaluation results. Utilization of LLDP significantly reduces computational overhead.

(2) **Procedure 2 (PC):** The device provisioning is based on two main loops presented in Figure 11. The first loop is defined as the

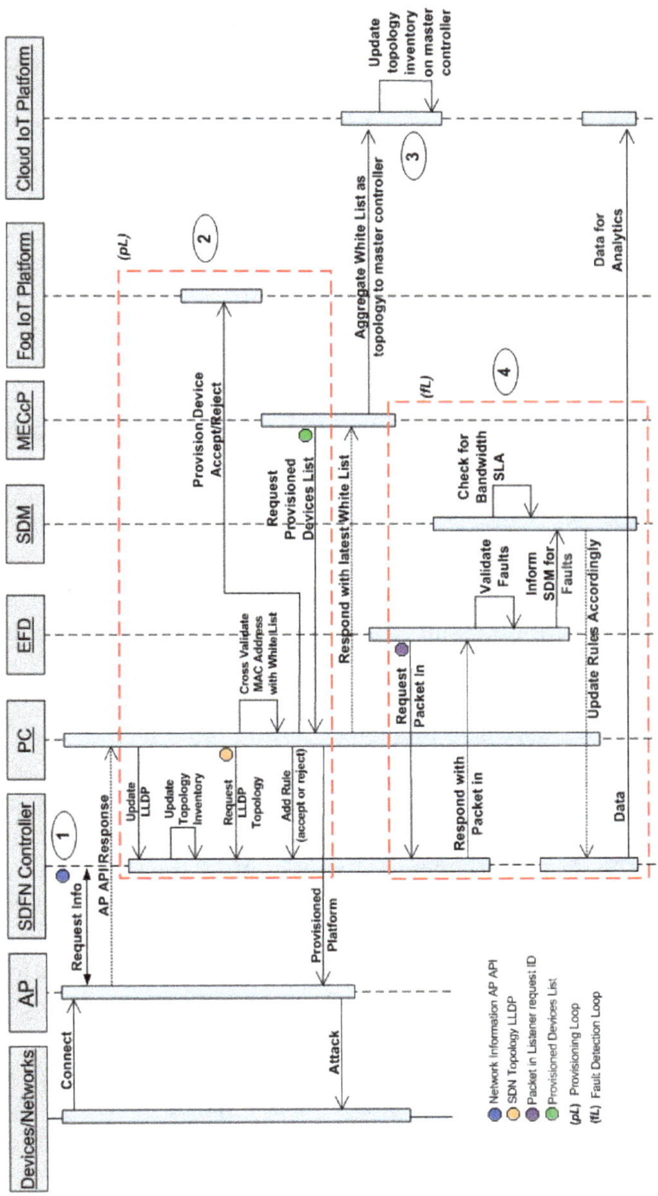

Figure 11. Provisioning Diagram

provisioning loop (*pL*). Considering that the access topology is integrated at the SDFN controller, the PC is able to operate the provisioning. Provisioning happens by cross-validating the MAC addresses currently connected at the APs with a whitelist of MAC addresses, this process runs again if the access topology is updated. The cross-validation is implemented based on Algorithm 1. Algorithm 1 utilizes the binary search which has a known time complexity of $O(log\ n)$, where n is defined as the number of devices to be provisioned. Furthermore, a for-loop is used to assess the status of each device. The for-loop has a time complexity of $O(w)$, where w represents the elements of the whitelist. Considering the binary search is executed as many times as possible the algorithm checks for the device status, and the total complexity of Algorithm 1 is: $O(log\ n) * O(w)$. This results to $O(n * log\ w)$ time complexity for Algorithm 1.

(3) **Procedure 3 (MECcP Topology Aggregation):** MECcP constructs the global multidomain network view by integrating the topology inventory of all SDFN controllers. During the setup period, each SDFN controller of the APs subscribes to the cloud master SDFN controller, and the inventory aggregation is automatically updated. Therefore, the master SDFN controller gathers all the topology information, which allows cloud SDFNs. MECcP is dynamic and incorporates new network topologies on the fly.

(4) **Procedure 4 (EFD):** The EFD component is the main loop faults loop (fL). This procedure is implemented as an event that monitors incoming packets from the SDFN switches (packet ins) and targets operational faults (e.g., detection, counterattacks, etc.). Additionally, to enhance the fault detection procedure, a SDM component is developed. The SDM is implemented by monitoring the byte count of each device and accordingly adds a flow rule to the switch. Furthermore, EFD implements Algorithm 2, the time complexity is not very different from Algorithm 1, due to the similar binary search use. However, in the fault detection case, the algorithm will check the packet in messages from the SDFN controller. To this end, the for-loop complexity will be $O(p)$, where p is given by the following: $p = Df * N$. So, for the algorithm worst case time complexity we have: $O(p) * O(logw)$ resulting in $O(p * logw)$. All data analytics are sent to the cloud platform for further processing and storage.

In Figure 11 abstraction above, of a pure connection between two points with a perfect cable, the only protocols involved are those

Algorithm 1: Device Provisioning/Blacklisting Algorithm

```
Data: SDFN Topology S, White list W, Provisioned Devices P,
      OpenFlow Rules SDFN, Edge Platform Address IIP, Black List B
while ! S.updated() do
    If SDFN topology is updated start again
    W ← getwhitelist();
    foreach device ∈ S do
    if
      (BinarySearch(device.MAC ≠ P.MAC)
      AND
      (BinarySearch(device.MAC ∈ W.MAC) then
          P ← device.MAC;
          SDFN.addrule(Accept, IIP ← device.MAC);
          W.MAC.remove(device.MAC);
          P.MAC.remove(device.MAC);
          remove MAC address until offensive topology gets updated
      else
          B ← device.MAC;
          SDFN.addrule(Accept, IIP ← device.MAC); black listing the
          device using SDFN
      end
    end
end
```

impressed upon the wire or channel. Any bits impressed upon one are conveyed to the other end after a time-of-flight delay. There is no notion of a control plane, negotiation for provisioning access to the pool of bandwidth, etc. In almost every other case, additional protocols are required to achieve effective connectivity across physical channels, a particular network or service, and the combination of all networks and services. If we consider the scaled implementation involving thousands of copies of Edge nodes, then we furthermore need to consider the type of management (centralized, distributed, or some combination) or provisioning, since limited resources must be efficiently brokered to the individual nodes.

Even in the case of a single AP (Figure 8), the free space channel often requires adaptive modulation, forward error correction, and other mechanisms to achieve reliable operation. Military communications, as well as

Algorithm 2: Edge Fault Detection Algorithm

```
Data: SDFN Topology S, White list W, Provisioned Devices P,
      OpenFlow Rules SDFN, Edge Platform Address IIP, Black List B,
      Edge Detection Frequency Df
ExpectedDevices ← emptylist();
creating expected devices list for cross validation Nsize ← P.size();
while Df.NotChanged() do
    If SDFN topology is updated start again
    for i ∈ [0, |Nsize|] do
        Fault ← BinarySearch(SDFN[i].MAC, P[i].MAC);
        if Fault then
            ExpectedDevices[i].MAC ← P[i].MAC
        else
            Fault Detected B ← SDFN[i].MAC;
            SDFN.addrule(Reject, IIP ← SDFN[i].MAC);
        end
    end
    if ExpectedDevices.Size() ≠ P.Size() then
        ReportFaults (ExpectedDevices)
    end
end
```

contemporary commercial ones, can employ sophisticated frequency hopping and spread spectrum techniques [16]. The cues for which adjustments are to be made are usually baked into the protocol design, though in some cases adjustable "knobs" are exposed that can be managed during the communications process. These amount to a rudimentary control plane established over the air between the modems, and usually the user does not have to be extensively involved, and these control plane functions did not appear in the data sent from Nodes A to B.

As we extend the complexity to the Edge-based communications concept, more control plane complexities are introduced. Some of the key linkages are depicted in Figure 12 for a real-world type of implementation. For the present discussion, we shall separate these categories into "modes" of internal communications. They are effectively meta-channels, perfectly isolated from each other, meaning that the bits that flow in channels of "Mode 1" will not appear in the bits that flow in "Mode 3".

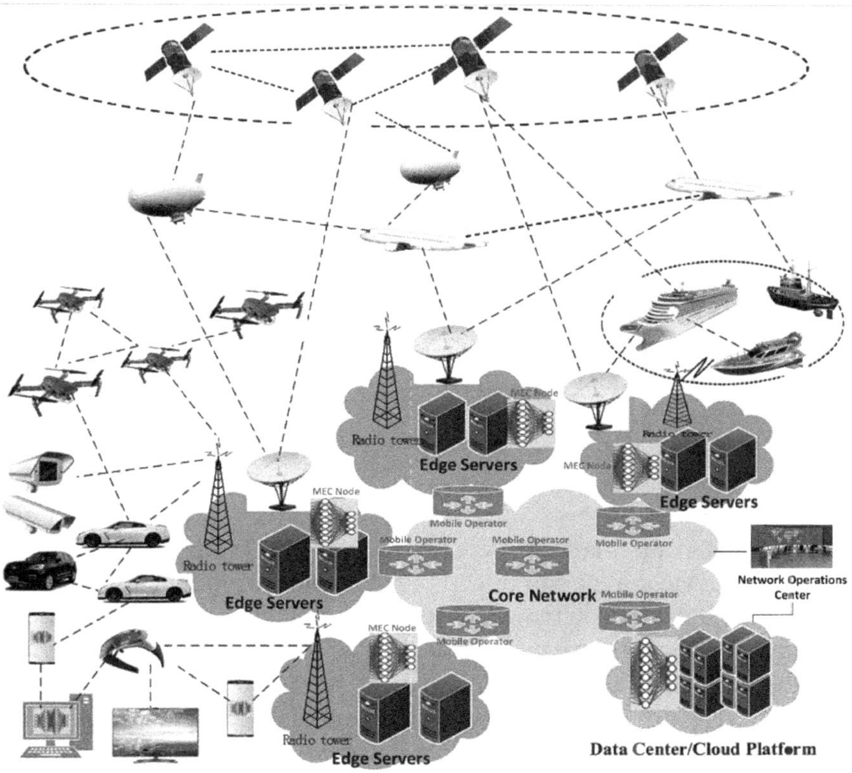

Figure 12. Depiction of Edge Multi-Modem Interactions and Different Types of Communications that Can Take Place in Edge Computing Enclaves

Furthermore, there can be several channels of the same type, and these are also isolated from each other.

The scenario we shall focus on involves the communications between four Edge enclaves involving four adversarial networks/devices as identified in Figure 12. It is necessary for two Edge nodes to be operational, perhaps to employ a SATCOM AP, for additional services.

Mode 1: Established communication channels — Mode 1 channels refer to the desired primary communications channels, the only ones that would appear when an electrical signal bearing information is impressed upon a physical cable. In the case of an actual physical electrical cable, there can only be a single Mode 1 channel. It is possible to establish conventions for multiple Mode 1 channels in this physical medium, and these correspond to the concepts of time division multiple access (TDMA), frequency division multiple access (FDMA), and code division multiple access (CDMA) as examples. In this case, it is always necessary to apply additional concepts that allow the superimposed individual (virtual) channels to be combined in the physical medium and effectively separated. For example, in the case of TDMA, bits from different Mode 1 channel are time sequenced in the same physical medium, and conventions must be agreed upon to correctly separate particular bits as belonging to particular Mode 1 channel. In other cases, such as wavelength division multiplexing (WDM), channels are treated as effectively being a series of spatially separated channels, as though there were multiple physical cables.

Mode 2: Edge service endpoints — Mode 2 communications refer to the entire category of platform-internal communications, in particular, those channels within the platform between an EDGE Control Processor and a physical device that do not directly appear over the medium negotiated by compatible devices on two different platforms. This is a very important category of communication, associated with the "care and feeding" of devices, and there may be a rich variety of Mode 2 messages. Also, you could differentiate Mode 2 communications to denote hierarchy within a physical device. For example, an optical modem may have an internal wireless system, etc., that can be managed by commands from the Edge central controller. Examples could include (1) wholesale provisioning and configuration of a physical device using serverless computing, (2) access to device measurands (e.g., temperatures, current/voltage, error rates), (3) operations necessary to establish pointing, channel selection, and (4) security-related preparation (e.g., key exchange, security protocol selection).

Mode 3: Channel management — Mode 3 communications pertain to the meta-exchanges and/or "baked in" conventions necessary for M2M communications. The information in Mode 3 communications does not "escape" the physical device, meaning that for example, the meta-data passed between devices do not appear in the user's expected (Mode 1) data stream. Examples of "baked-in" conventions include remote frequency hopping patterns of a particular protocol that do not change. More sophisticated meta-exchanges include the means by which adaptive protocols negotiate settings, such as bit rate, modulation time, dynamically changing frequency hopping patterns, etc. in a complex dense wavelength division multiplexing (DWDM) scheme, a Mode 3 communication might be used to explain the wavelength plan as devices come into contact. For cognitive radios, Mode 3 communications might be essential for coordinating changes in different operating parameters.

Mode 4: Edge-to-global (hierarchy-spanning) — Mode 4 interactions are "unrestricted", whereas these interactions take place between nodes that are subordinated to some notion of a hierarchy/control plane above the level of particular Edge nodes. For example, if we are concerned with provisioning many Edge nodes for capabilities, we would need to construct something like a network operations center (NOC), to manage entire groups of Edge nodes in a uniform, scalable way. Mode 4 communications are simply a specialized form of Mode 4 communications. For example, a NOC would likely appear to be a well-known destination (e.g., IP address, phone number, interest topic, etc.) to Edge nodes, but the mechanism for access/interaction between hierarchical levels might otherwise be indistinguishable from the unrestricted case.

It is easy to be confused by the mixture of virtualized communications channels with physical (real-world channels). For example, between two physical devices (each being on a separate EDGE NODE), we can over the same physical channel pass several Mode 1, Mode 3, and Mode 4 communications streams. Furthermore, in the case of communication flows, we might distribute Mode 1 and Mode 4 flows in some mixture across different communication flows (but Mode 3 information flows are confined to particular communication flows). Furthermore, some things cannot be readily virtualized. For example, precision timing transfer between an EDGE and a physical device might require more precise determinism than is available over a traditional Ethernet connection. Analog signals, such as those involving antenna remoting, involve a single Mode 1 "flow" (in this case an analog/microwave continuously varying signal) that cannot intermingle control plane/metadata traffic.

TRANSMISSION OF INFORMATION AT HIGH SPEED WITH STABILITY

In the ever-changing information warfare, the rapid, accurate, secure, and uninterrupted transmission of information is an important guarantee of ensuring smooth and efficient command, capturing a favorable position in cyber information, and gaining the initiative on the battlefield [9]. It is therefore necessary to maintain an advanced and stable Edge information transmission system to satisfy the requirement of providing high-capacity, high-speed, and stable information transmission in modern cyber warfare operations.

High-capacity, high-speed transmission of information, and full compatibility in various formats. To meet this requirement, first, the Edge platform should be able to provide many different methods of transmission. Various transmission modes and methods should be used in combination, and in particular, great effort should be put into the development of optical cables and satellite systems with high capacity and capability for long-distance transmission. Second, the band of transmission must be wide; various frequencies such as high frequency (HF), very high frequency (VHF), super high frequency (SHF), and extra high frequency (EHF) should be utilized rationally and scientifically with the bandwidths allocated automatically according to the properties of the information transmitted. Furthermore, the system should have high compatibility, which can handle various formats of information such as voice, data, images, and multi-media documents at the same time including the following:

- **Uninterrupted transmission at any time and under any circumstances:** It is only through generalization, systematization, and integration of information transmission facilities, and through standardization of transmission regulations, transmission agreements, and the various connections that uninterrupted transmission of information in various systems, combat units and cyber warfare operation weapon platforms can be achieved. Capability in transmission in multiple modes. The system should have the capability of providing fixed transmission, mobile transmission, hidden transmission, and transmission under harsh conditions to satisfy the requests for information by various combat units and weapon platforms under different circumstances. A stable and reliable Edge system with strong anti-damage and anti-jamming abilities and with good defense capability. In the cyberwar dominated by information and information technology, information networks, nodes, and information processing are certainly the major targets of reconnaissance and attack by the two sides and are the first targets to attack during the cyberwar. Their survival in the cyberwar is subject to serious challenges, thus reliability is an important indicator of the system.

- **Automatic monitoring and correction of deviation in transmission quality:** Automatic monitoring of transmission quality includes two aspects: first, it performs quality control over the transmitted information and monitors any loss, miscoding, and leak of information during transmission; second, it carries out quality control over the transmission channels and detects such failures as channel congestion, interference, short-circuit and disconnection in a timely manner. Correction of deviation also consists of two parts: the first part deals with the recovery of and supplement to miscoded information and the repair of the defect of leakage of information; the second part is the timely adjustment of information with falling quality and automatic switching to the best routing by making use of the multi-directional routing feature of the transmission system.
- **Synchronous control at multiple nodes:** Spatially, the reconnaissance system, information attack system, information defense system, comprehensive support system, information security and confidentiality system, and the cyber warfare operation command system of cyber warfare operation are distributed in the three-dimensional space between the ground and outer space; and in terms of networking, the above systems are located at the different nodes of the network. It is necessary for the Edge platform to ensure the connection, communication, and mutual operation among the various levels and systems to enable the various combat units, weapon platforms, and commanders at all levels to obtain complete and accurate information in time when required.
- **A "random access" function:** Should also be available at each of the Edge nodes of the information network using the Edge system. This is so every combat unit, weapon platform, or command system can gain access to the network at any Edge node of the three-dimensional battlefield. The Edge system should recognize them right away and provide them with the corresponding identities and statuses, thereby enabling them to obtain the necessary operation information and support, as well as connecting them to other units that have logged onto the system and allowing them to upload the relevant information for sharing.

AUTOMATIC MANAGEMENT OF EDGE SYSTEM

The Edge platform is a complex system. It comprises many pieces of high-tech equipment, has a wide coverage and involves a very broad scope of content. It works in a special environment and demands a high standard of time-effectiveness, accuracy, stability, and confidentiality. Thus, the operation and management of the system itself is very complicated, and a function of automatic management is indispensable.

Automatic management of information is imperative in the Edge platform, and it is mainly manifested in the following areas. The first one is the automatic filtering of information. For information collected by the Edge information reconnaissance system, the system should be able to automatically identify and classify the various parameters like the source, nature, properties, status, position, and distribution of the information, to discard the false and dross but retain the true and essential information, and to clean up junk information automatically.

Information being processed in this manner will thus become useful information. The second one is the automatic address searching. After classifying the collected information, the Edge system should proceed with its allocation. First, the system should be able to perform auto-searching, providing a fast and convenient method to look for information. Second, it should automatically search the addresses as required by the sub-systems and send the relevant information to them. The third aspect is the automatic display of information. Based on the need of leadership, the information can be displayed in various formats such as text, voice, image, and multi-media, and can be fed into the various monitor terminals of the combat units, operation elements, and command systems. The fourth aspect is the remote control of information at distant parallel networks. Authorization can be obtained at any node of the system when necessary, so that information at any other nodes can be viewed, utilized, and redirected.

Automatic management of the physical platform refers to the automatic management of the physical structure of the Edge platform. The first aspect is the automatic monitoring of performance indicators. There are thousands of weapon platforms, network facilities, and terminals, which will be widely distributed on the Edge platform. As it is not possible to effectively monitor and manage them manually, an intelligentized management system must be employed to carry out automatic monitoring and management, which must be performed at different levels. Only in this way can failures in the system be detected and diagnosed immediately to ensure the stability of the system. The second aspect is the automatic adjustment of the structure. In the battlefield, reconnaissance systems, which are the sources of information, will be subjected to substitutions within different facilities and spaces in different timeframes.

There will also be constant realignments and changes of the combat units and consequential changes in the flow of information and the shift of focus of command. Therefore, the structure of the Edge platform has to be modified accordingly. The third one is the automatic selection of routes. In the Edge network system, there are sufficient routes for point-to-point transmission, but because of the instantaneous property of information transmission, there is a need for high-speed selection of routes, which is impossible to accomplish manually. This can only be achieved through an automatic selection based on real-time monitoring of the quality of the various routes. The fourth feature is the automatic allocation of bandwidths. This is one of the important measures to make use of the Edge system resources scientifically. In modem warfare, there is a huge amount of information to transmit in a limited number of bandwidths. This requires the use of technology scientifically, and the system to have the capability of allocating bandwidths automatically according to the state of flow of information.

Automatic safety management is a fundamental requirement of modern Edge platforms. The first aspect is the automatic recognition of identity. The second feature is the automatic monitoring of the environment. Because of the availability of "random access" function in the Edge platform and the heavy utilization and mutual penetration of various kinds of modern cyber warfare operation measures, the system must possess a function of automatic identity recognition. First of all, the Edge system should automatically recognize and verify the identities of the facilities that have gained random access to the system; second, it should be able to distinguish whether the information that has entered the system is true (positive) or false (negative), or whether it comes from our side or the adversary.

The environment surrounding the hardware around the Edge platform could be extremely harsh. There are many environmental factors posing tremendous threats to the safety of the Edge platform, such as super-strong electromagnetic interference and radiation, excessive dosage of nuclear, chemical, and biological contaminations, serious erosions due to wind, sand, rain, and snow, which can all seriously affect the functions of the system and even its existence. Therefore, the Edge system should be able to monitor the environmental parameters automatically and issue warnings in time. The third aspect is the automatic linkage of Edge systems. When the outside attack, which is threatening the safety of the Edge system has escalated to a certain level to reach safety coefficient values, the system, should be able to carry out an evaluation of the level of safety automatically. While issuing warnings automatically, the safety management system should also be able to connect to the corresponding counterattack systems or defense systems in accordance with the safety level, to give protection to the Edge platform system and to launch effective counterattacks.

COMPONETS OF THE EDGE PLATFORM

If classified according to the systemic structure in Figure 11, the Edge platform mainly has three core functions: operation, information, and management. In terms of the function of command of information, its major roles are as follows: obtaining information on the status and the positions in the battlefields of the various combat units and main weapon platforms; transmitting situational information of the battlefields to the various command elements, combat units, and weapon platforms. Giving guiding information to various mobile weapon platforms, the Edge platform will also have to transmit information for identifying the target of attack and providing feedback information on the effect of operations. In terms of the function of command of operation, the Edge platform comprises the following:

- **Command and decision-making Edge system:** The command and decision-making Edge system is the core of the Edge platform, as well as the core of the entire cyber warfare operation. It is mainly made up of the command personnel, staff officers, engineering and technical personnel, and the various technical facilities used in the command during the warfare operation. Backed by the information Cloud network system, the command and decision-making Edge system keeps abreast of the real-time situation in the information warfare battlefields, making assessments based on the intelligence information, planning the actions of the various combat units, drawing up plans for cyber warfare operations and plans for support, and choosing the rational and scientific mode of command, thereby implementing effective control of cyber warfare operations and the battlefields and exercising control and management of the command system.

- **Edge information detection system:** The information detection system is the component of the Edge platform that captures the source of information and is the source of all information used in the command of operation. Its main tasks are the detection, identification, surveillance, tracking, and location of all acoustic, optical, electrical, magnetic, and mechanical signals in the information warfare battlefields, which are performed mainly by means of the following measures and methods: use of electronic reconnaissance satellites, image reconnaissance satellites, ocean surveillance satellites, missile early-warning satellites, and manned reconnaissance spacecrafts in information detection in outer space. Additionally the use of early-warning aircraft system, manned reconnaissance aircraft, unmanned reconnaissance aircraft, air-drifted reconnaissance system, and so on in information detection in the air; use of optical reconnaissance system, wireless communication reconnaissance system, radar reconnaissance system, ground (sea) surface sensor reconnaissance system, and so on in information detection on ground (sea) surface; and use of acoustic sensor system and non-acoustic sensor system in underwater information detection.
- **Edge information transmission system:** The Edge information transmission system is the brain of the Edge platform and is the foundation, which integrates the various forces of information warfare into a single power system. The wide application of modern information technology has turned the information transmission network into an unobstructed, grid-style entity with revolutionary changes in transmission methods, modes, and volume alike. In terms of physical structure, the Edge information transmission network includes 10 types of networks namely: satellite network, microwave relay network, scatternet, ultra-short-wave network, short wave network, long wave network, mobile network, wired network, optical transmission network, and computer network. An interconnected grid network is built up which consists of various types of networks such as the star network, ring network, bus network, and compound network, so that information can be transmitted in various forms including sound, word, image, and multimedia.
- **Edge information processing system:** The Edge information processing system is mainly responsible for the screening, identification, computation, assessment, classification, encryption, storage, distribution, and backup of original information. The development of modern

computer technology has provided the information processing system with the capability of high-speed operation, massive storage, and parallel processing. Intelligence information obtained by digital sensors can be fed directly into the computers for computation or storage without the need of a change of codes, but non-digital information has to be encoded to become digital information before it can be processed.

- **Edge auxiliary decision-making system:** Auxiliary decision-making function is an indispensable function of the future Edge platform and is an important tool in making scientific and rapid decisions, racing against time for operation, and attaining initiative in battles. First, using simulation technology, the Edge auxiliary decision-making system should provide simulated warfare operations for practice so that drills on various schemes and plans can be carried out, thereby enabling the schemes and plans to be optimized. Second, it should provide a specialist system, furnishing the command personnel with consultation and assistance in decision-making, to minimize errors in decision-making. Third, it should provide an automatic operating system, which can solve such problems as lack of precision and retardation in decision-making as seen in the manual operating systems.
- **Edge management and control system:** The Edge management and control system performs automatic management of the entire system of the Edge platform, thus ensuring the whole system is running in good condition. The first function is account management. It performs the identification, authorization, level setting, and system setting for all logged-in accounts, and provides services to the users. The second aspect is network management. Based on the need of the warfare operation command and changes in battlefield situation, it is to make timely adjustments to the network structure, implement quality control to the network, and select routes for information transmission. The third area is data management. It carries out general control of the parameters, flow, and change of data in the system. The fourth role is facility management. It executes categorized quality control and management of the devices and facilities logging onto the system.
- **Edge security and confidentiality system:** In informatized warfare, the security and confidentiality of the Edge platform will be faced with very harsh conditions, and the related task is extremely arduous. Therefore, the Edge system should be able to resist various security threats such as hacking of the network, electromagnetic attacks, theft of

information, disruption by special attacks, hard destructions, and harsh environment, and be able to integrate into one single entity the functions of system monitoring and control, display, issue of warning, and launch of counterattack.

- **Edge target indication and guiding system:** It mainly serves three functions. The first one is navigation and positioning. It gives guiding information to our own combat units and weapon platforms so that they can move accurately along their selected tracks or towards their targets. The second one is friend or foe identification. It should be able to provide all-weather, over-the-horizon, rapid, accurate, and reliable friend-or-foe identification of all kinds of targets. The third one is to provide information on the target. Information concerning the category, position, and characteristics of the target is to be supplied to the appropriate cyber warfare operation units so that they can carry out interference, suppression, and attack on the target and feedback on the results to the system.
- **Edge command information countermeasure system:** In modern cyber warfare operations, the use of the Edge platform as a weapon is a natural development, and the command information itself should possess the capability of information countermeasure. Command information countermeasure means disrupting or obstructing the adversary in obtaining, transmitting, managing, and using the command information while ensuring our personnel are able to do so in a normal manner, thereby safeguarding the security and superiority of our command information.
- **Integrated information support system:** The Edge platform is a huge and complex system and requires support from many facilities and information to operate reliably. The main supportive facilities include survey and mapping support, support, geographical information support, power support, frequency spectrum support, and other auxiliary supportive facilities.

SECURITY COUNTERMEASURES OF CYBER-INFORMATION EDGE WARFARE OPERATIONS

The future platform for command of cyber-information Edge warfare operations will be operating in a very harsh environment. There are serious threats to its safety, which mainly include threats to its network security, information security, and physical security, and it is necessary to adopt appropriate countermeasures against the threats to secure the initiative in confronting the adversary. The primary measures to be taken include: using different kinds of technical defense measures, strengthening the security design of the information facilities and undertaking research and production of our own facilities, using the Edge platform as a weapon, enhancing the regenerating power of the platform in battlefields, and so on.

- **Technical defense measures:** The technical defense measures are the basic ways and means in responding to security threats, playing a crucial role in strengthening the security level of the platform. They mainly involve the following technologies. The first one is the new technology in information transmission. If technologies such as direct-sequence spread-spectrum technology, frequency hopping technology, adaptive technology, burst communication technology, and diversity reception technology are employed, the capability of the system to resist interference during information transmission is greatly increased. The second one is the information encryption technique. Information encryption is a very effective technique in ensuring the secure processing and storage of information on the Edge platform.

  Technologies that can be adopted include cryptographic technique systems that have a high level of security, operational efficiency, and adaptability and are easy to operate with passwords, and digital security terminals, which can carry out link-by-link and end-to-end encryption among the users. The third kind of technology to be used is network firewall technology. The primary function of this technology is to set up access control to the network to separate and deny the access of unauthorized and illegal users, thereby safeguarding the internal network and information. The network firewall technology can be classified into IP packet filter firewalls, link-level firewalls, application-level firewalls, and comprehensive firewalls in accordance with their features. The fourth one is the anti-virus technology. It includes anti-virus cards and software, which can promptly detect and remove viruses in the system.
- **Platform design and research and development measures:** Unlike the general platforms used by civilians, the Edge platform presents a much higher degree of risk and instability and a much higher chance of

being attacked. Hence, it is necessary to consider security as an important indicator and to take the appropriate measures right at the initial stages of network design, hardware production, and software development. First, we should insist on using physical isolation measures in network design, separating the Edge platform from the information networks used by civilians, and separating the Edge platform used during wartime from the platforms used for training, management, and support during peacetime.

Second, for key hardware and chips, we must insist on the use of domestic products, preventing our adversary from installing components such as defective chips, which will lead to serious security issues such as breakdown of the system, theft of information, and failure of the chips at critical moments. Third, we must persevere in the development of important operating software by ourselves, precluding our adversary from pre-setting hidden attacks, loopholes, and virus programs, thus avoiding grave potential threats to our system.

- **Turning an Edge platform into a weapon:** Weaponization of the Edge platform is an objective requirement of modern information warfare and is also the most important way to deal with the threats to the platform. The development goal of weaponization of the Edge platform should focus on enhancing the three capabilities in dealing with security threats, namely, the capability of regional electronic protection, the capability of information counterattack, and the capability of self-defense.
- **Enhancement of the regenerative power of the Edge platform in the battlefields:** No matter how comprehensive the security measures are, damage to the Edge system at war is inevitable and exists objectively. Hence, enhancing the regenerative power of the Edge platform has become an important element in eliminating security threats and ensuring the proper running of the system, and the keys to enhancing the regenerative power of the system on the battlefield are the technical supportive measures that are scientific, rational, timely, and accurate. The first requirement is that technical support should be standardized, which includes the standardization of allocation of technical support forces, standardization of the provision of technical equipment and facilities as well as the standardization of the operative processes of technical support. Second, the technical support should be provided in an integrated manner.

During cyber warfare operations, the Edge platform is the unified platform for cyber services, field and station armies as well as operation tactics and strategies. Therefore, technical support has to be set up in an integrated mode, eliminating the barriers between different armed services, breaking free from the various subordinating relations within the organizational systems, and not being confined by having only one single system of equipment. Third, technical support should be regionalized. The principle of "the big protecting the small, the equipped supplying the deprived" should be adopted in the technical support in cyber battlefields, and support should be provided across the regions with the levels of support being reduced, the efficiency of support being increased, and resources being shared. Fourth, there should be networkization of the Edge technical support. Every functional unit of the Edge platform is constituted by multiple channels, multi-regional devices, and multi-system facilities. All the links in the system are intertwined, interdependent, and inseparable from one another, thereby forming an interconnected entity. Thus, technical support should be changed from the single facility support in the past to comprehensive support through networkization, providing distant technical information inquiry, fault diagnosis, and technical support.

FUTURE RESEARCH

This proposed Edge platform for capabilities is still in a hypothetical and theoretical stage which needs further detailed and defined research for implementation into an operational environment. More advanced algorithms, mechanisms/tools, and mitigation approaches are needed to address this effort and hence we envisage developing a closed networking standard-based framework for supporting this initiative. In traditional networks, traffic monitoring is typically done close to routers or middleboxes, with the collected information being reported to a central collector where the network management applications are running. In modern dynamic networks, numerous security-monitoring systems based on programmable Edge networks are available, but it is difficult to evaluate how they perform, especially in large-scale networks.

Research is needed to investigate applications, which can utilize a distributed Edge security-monitoring framework. For the Edge traffic security monitoring, we are proposing to develop a system that decouples monitoring from forwarding, a fine-grained network flows monitoring, which is an important capability for effective real-time detection of security threats attacks against this platform. This should offer flexible, dynamic, and fine-grained flow-based monitoring that integrates well with an Edge architecture. The role of this framework will be to provide monitoring and security at each layer and interface along with providing security operations. The key security aspects include access control, data protection, and detection of network attacks such as Denial-of-Service, Spoofing, session hijacking, network protocol poisoning, topology tampering and information disclosure scanning, etc.

Furthermore, in this proposed future work, machine-learning techniques for accurate detection of behavioral patterns, fingerprinting, attack flows and anomalies in the Edge-based networks need to be developed. These machine learning/deep learning-based anomaly detection algorithms can be employed in the Edge control plane for behavioral analysis and traffic-based anti-spoofing techniques or monitoring the communication channels in the Edge architecture. Research to develop reference hardened secure Edge-stack, security application modules, and conduct experiments. The measurement of the efficacy of this framework in terms of network resources, metadata flow database, acceptable memory and computational overhead for analytics, latency, and other resource usage during attack time also demonstrates the capabilities, in real-world network management needs to also be developed.

Additionally, research on a fraudulent network with the same network topology and endpoints of the Edge, using the same IP addresses of corresponding endpoints on an operational network must be performed. When we detect a compromise on the operational network where the tools resided in the Edge, we transfer the communications between the compromised PC and the operational network endpoints to the ones between the compromised PC and the fraudulent network while keeping the communications between the compromised PC and the command and control (C2) server intact. That is achieved by using OpenFlow's flow tables for matching and rewriting packets. Researching that we can contain the compromised PC without the adversary observing any difference before and after the cyber fraud and that the session remained intact during and after the transfer should be performed. Furthermore, the implementation and evaluation of this Edge cyber fraudulent architecture for IPv6 must be taken into consideration.

CONCLUSION

This chapter proposes the beginning strategy for a new infrastructure for performing future operations on an Edge platform. This document has outlined a modular distributed network architecture that seeks to bind effective security constructs that are fundamentally necessary for this Edge platform, and this is an area where excessive creativity can render much of these concepts attainable. These future Edge technologies can enhance operations in multi-domain IoT deployments, as Edge computing improves control plane, device mobility, and device resiliency for capabilities. Developing new Edge system theories is the soul of the reform of modern cyber-warfare. Developing theories on the theoretical basis of cyberwar operations to meet the need for secure operations is the inevitable demand of organizations in anticipation of the challenges posed by the new threats to computing. It is also the necessary preparation for winning the future high-tech cyber wars, and the basic route to seize the commanding point of Edge theories.

The principle of attacking the critical points means that in cyber operations, the Edge systems should focus the attacks on the critical places and the key points of the adversary to paralyze its system of the adversary until the adversary loses all capabilities. Consequently, the aim of cyber operations is no longer the destruction of the viable force and the group of the adversary, but rather the paralyzing and the sabotaging of the system of the adversary composed of the system, scouting and early-warning system, high-tech weapons control system, airports, ports, roads, bridges, electric and energy facilities, and key military installations. The principle of real-time reaction means in commanding cyber operations, the Edge has to endeavor to master and understand the situation in real-time, make resolutions in real-time and dispatch resolute disposals timely. The Edge should strive to achieve the "seamless connection" of understanding the situation, making resolute disposals, and giving protection to malicious activities. This is because cyber operations happen without warning. It moves fast and the operation time is short. The opportunity to attack may vanish quickly and every minute and every second on the cyber battlefield and may influence the outcome of the cyber war.

The completeness, stability, and anti-destructiveness of the whole Edge platform, like its sophistication, directly affect the outcome of the cyber operation. Therefore, developing an Edge platform for cyber operations will play an important role in guiding the construction of an Edge platform, the efficient functioning of cyber activities, and the seizure of the initiative in the cyberspace domain. The Edge platform joins the five-dimensional (land, sea, air, outer space, and electronic field) operation commands together and combines the battles and combat commanding into one body. This may overcome the shortcomings existing in past commands (such as dissection into isolated bits, excessive levels and tiers, and duplication of efforts) to enhance the time-effectiveness of operation commands and satisfy the demand for precision operations at the Edge. Integrated Edge computing is the product of the revolutionary development of computing around the world. It is an innovation that meets the need for precision cyber operations, and the inevitable trend of the development of theory for information wars.

REFERENCES

[1] Abbasi, B. Z. & Shah, M. A. (2017, September). Fog computing: Security issues, solutions and robust practices. In *2017 23rd International Conference on Automation and Computing* (*ICAC*) (pp. 1–6). IEEE.

[2] Atiqur, R., Wu, G., & Liton, A. M. (2020). Mobile edge computing for internet of things (IoT): Security and privacy issues. *Indonesian Journal of Electrical Engineering and Computer Science* (*IJEECS*), 18(3), 1486–1493.

[3] Castiglione, A., Choo, K. K. R., Nappi, M., & Ricciardi, S. (2017). Context aware ubiquitous biometrics in edge of military things. *IEEE Cloud Computing*, 4(6), 16–20.

[4] Clarke, R. A. (2010). *Cyber War: The Next Threat to National Security and What to Do About It.* HarperCollins, New York, NY.

[5] Haas, M. C. & Fischer, S. C. (2017). The evolution of targeted killing practices: Autonomous weapons, future conflict, and the international order. *Contemporary Security Policy*, 38(2), 281–306.

[6] Jasper, S. (2020). *Russian Cyber Operations: Coding the Boundaries of Conflict.* Georgetown University Press, Washington, DC.

[7] Lin, H. & Zegart, A. (Eds.) (2019). *Bytes, Bombs, and Spies: The Strategic Dimensions of Offensive Cyber Operations.* Brookings Institution Press, Washington, DC.

[8] Lonergan, E. D. & Lonergan, S. W. (2022). Cyber operations, accommodative signaling, and the de-escalation of international crises. *Security Studies*, 31(1), 32–64.

[9] Maathuis, C. (2022, March). On explainable AI Solutions for targeting in cyber military operations. In *International Conference on Cyber Warfare and Security* (Vol. 17, No. 1, pp. 166–175).

[10] Maciocco, C. & Sunay, M. O. (2020). Edge cloud: An essential component of 5G networks. *5G Verticals: Customizing Applications, Technologies and Deployment Techniques*, 169–210.

[11] Nebeling, M. & Thiele, H. J. (Eds.) (2018). *Coarse Wavelength Division Multiplexing: Technologies and Applications.* CRC Press, Boca Raton, FL.

[12] Sântejudean, T. V., Mois, G. D., Sanislav, T., & Folea, S. C. (2022, June). Edge computing in wireless sensing applications. In *2022 11th Mediterranean Conference on Embedded Computing (MECO)* (pp. 1–4). IEEE.

[13] Singh, S. P., Nayyar, A., Kumar, R., & Sharma, A. (2019). Fog computing: From architecture to edge computing and big data processing. *The Journal of Supercomputing*, 75(4), 2070–2105.

[14] Tordera, E. M., Masip-Bruin, X., Garcia-Alminana, J., Jukan, A., Ren, G. J., Zhu, J., & Farré, J. (2016). What is a fog node a tutorial on current concepts towards a common definition. arXiv preprint arXiv:1611.09193.

[15] Tsuru, M., Cahyo, W. N., & Brastama, P. A. (2020, July). Performance of delay tolerant network protocol in smart city scenario. In *Journal of Physics: Conference Series* (Vol. 1569, No. 2, p. 022056). IOP Publishing.

[16] Wang, X., Wang, J., Xu, Y., Chen, J., Jia, L., Liu, X., & Yang, Y. (2020). Dynamic spectrum anti-jamming communications: Challenges and opportunities. *IEEE Communications Magazine*, 58(2), 79–85.

[17] Yousaf, F. Z., Bredel, M., Schaller, S., & Schneider, F. (2017). NFV and SDN — Key technology enablers for 5G networks. *IEEE Journal on Selected Areas in Communications*, 35(11), 2468–2478.

Chapter 8

Developing a CyberAssurance Multiple Adversary Risk Model for Wireless Grids Edgeware

ABSTRACT

A good adversary model should have sufficient detail to provide insight into the underlying risk and be simple enough to minimize assessment resources. Gathering computer network attack data to one adversary is resource-intensive. Data is sparse or non-existent and often requires elicitation from experts. To simplify the problem, analysts frequently aggregate adversaries into adversary classes, for example, combining the many types of criminals into an "organized crime" group. Often, the initial reaction of the risk assessment team is to model every possible adversary. Once the group realizes the amount of additional data required, conservatively about 20% more time is required for each additional adversary, the team quickly reduces the range of potential adversaries to the group that is seen to be the most formidable — a foreign intelligence service (FIS). The question often left unanswered is how much inaccuracy has been introduced into the analysis by simplifying the adversary model. For this chapter, the author defines an adversary as a hostile individual or organization that is motivated to attack a United States (US) commercial wireless grid information system for the purpose of illegally viewing data, i.e., attacking the system's confidentiality. Non-malicious events, such as incompetent users or natural disasters, are beyond the scope of this study. Furthermore, we assume that an adversary is limited to computer network attacks as authors did not examine physical attacks or those involving social engineering.

INTRODUCTION

CyberAssurance encompasses the concepts of recognition, fortification, reestablishment, and survivability capabilities to defend systems and networks against cyber-attacks [1]. In short, it's the justified confidence that networked systems are adequately secure to meet operational needs, even in the presence of attacks, failures, accidents, and unexpected events [1]. The main purpose of this study is to identify the most appropriate methods for combining the effects of multiple adversaries on a specific computer network in a CyberAssurance risk model. A good adversary model should have enough detail to provide insight into the underlying risk and yet be simple enough so that resources spent on the model-building process are maintained at a reasonable level. Gathering computer network attack data to any adversary is resource-intensive. Data are usually sparse or nonexistent. Lengthy data elicitation by experts is often required. To simplify the problem, analysts frequently aggregate adversaries into adversary classes, for example, combining several foreign intelligence services (FIS) into one group, or combining the many types of criminals into a group called "organized crime". Often, the initial reaction of the risk assessment team is to model every possible adversary. Once the group realizes the amount of additional data required, conservatively about 20% more time is required for each additional adversary, the team quickly reduces the range of potential adversaries to the group that is seen to be the most formidable — FIS. The question often left unanswered is how much inaccuracy has been introduced into the analysis by simplifying the adversary model.

For this chapter, we define an adversary as a hostile individual or organization that is motivated to attack a United States (US) commercial wireless grid information system for the purpose of illegally viewing data, i.e., attacking the system's confidentiality. Non-malicious events, such as incompetent users or natural disasters, are beyond the scope of this study. Furthermore, we assume that an adversary is limited to computer network attacks. The authors did not examine physical attacks or those involving social engineering. However, there is no reason to believe that the results of this analysis do not extend to these types of events. To apply decision analysis techniques to this problem, we also assume that our adversaries behave rationally with respect to their own preferences [5]. Even adversaries that do not appear "rational" to the average employee, such as a suicide terrorist, can demonstrate rational planning in relation to their preferences. Reference [10] states that "most adversaries are rational within their frames of reference" and "if the adversary is paying attention, he will choose an attack that minimizes his costs and maximizes his benefits". This model assumes a rational adversary that will analyze a portfolio of computer network attacks and wisely choose attacks that are most beneficial to their cause, that is, have a high probability of success, are not very detectable, and do not require excessive resources.

The range of potential adversaries in the literature is intimidating. Reference [4] in his foundational information system classification scheme, including hoodlums, gang initiates, reporters, and nature. A full enumeration of possible adversary groups from different references is included in Appendix A, and the definitions of these classes are provided in the next section. In general, all references agree on a basic set of adversaries; they differ in how specific adversary subsets can be partitioned from a superset.

Therefore, we believe that these adversaries can generally be divided into nine major adversary classes:

1. Foreign Intelligence Services
2. Information Warriors
3. Cyber Terrorists/Activists
4. Hackers/Crackers/Script Kiddies
5. Malicious Insiders
6. The Press
7. Organized Crime/Lone Criminals
8. Law Enforcement
9. Industrial Competitors

In this analysis, the authors do not consider four of the nine adversary classes: Press, Organized Crime, Law Enforcement, and Industrial Competitors. The authors did not believe that the press was a valid adversary of a US commercial wireless grid information system. The press already seems to have a reasonably large number of human sources of information that have access, are inexpensive, and are knowledgeable.

Organized crime was considered because of their apparent motivation to attack commercial wireless grid information systems, but was not included. Intuitively, drug dealers would seem to be motivated to attack government databases for many reasons, including gathering information on counter-narcotic surveillance missions. However, open-source data on drug dealers do not seem to support this conjecture. Perhaps, they perceive too much risk for very little gain. In the US, law enforcement works closely with commercial companies and shares a large amount of information. This fact, coupled with the demonstrated ethical behavior of the US law enforcement community, makes a US law enforcement attacker unlikely. Foreign law enforcement organizations can arguably be considered part of an adversary's foreign intelligence apparatus.

Industrial competitors, both US and foreign, are definite concerns. However, contractor systems seem to be more attractive targets than the government because contractor information systems can be less secure than the government and the anticipated retribution from a discovered attack appears to be less severe. The large number of potential targets outside of government information systems and trusted business relationships among industrial competitors seem to make government contractors far more attractive victims. With such a large number of contractor information systems, the adversary has a far greater opportunity to find a vulnerable system.

Therefore, the authors limited the scope of this assessment to analyze the best ways to combine the effects of the following adversary classes:

- Foreign intelligence services;
- Information warriors;
- Cyber terrorists;
- Hackers;
- Malicious insiders.

ADVERSARY CLASS DESCRIPTIONS

Foreign Intelligence Services

Foreign intelligence services (FIS) are considered to be well-funded and risk-averse entities that are highly motivated to gain access to classified national defense information. They have spent several years investing resources in developing advanced computer attack tools and techniques [6]. They prefer to remain undetected in their activities, as follows:

- avoid possible negative consequences of attack attribution,
- avoid the potential loss of sophisticated tools and techniques if their attack is detected,
- ensure that the target does not realize that their information has been compromised and take steps to mitigate the importance of the loss, and
- prevent the target from patching an exposed vulnerability or remove a back door implanted by the FIS.

The FIS may use less sophisticated tools and techniques to reduce the possibility of correct attribution by masquerading as another adversary class so that they can save more advanced tools to be used in times of crisis.

Information Warriors

Reference [3] describes the Information Warrior as "a military adversary who tries to undermine his target's ability to wage war by attacking the information or network infrastructure". They are more risk tolerant, as many of their attacks will occur in times of war and are quite noticeable by definition. The Information Warrior may have the funds of a FIS at their disposal but may not be as technically savvy as their FIS counterparts, especially if the Information Warrior is part of a military unit and cannot easily practice their craft in peace. For the purpose of this analysis, the authors will consider the information warrior to be a military unit in time of war that is interested in gaining intelligence on a US commercial wireless grid infrastructure to facilitate a future network-oriented or physical denial of service attack. The information warrior differs from a FIS in that their attacks are often more focused on the modification of data or denial of service attacks.

Cyber Terrorists

There may be some debate as to whether there exists a credible threat to a US commercial wireless grid computer system from a terrorist organization today. The argument is that if there are Cyber Terrorists, why have we not seen them? There have been many examples in the press of "hacktivism" where attacks against government and civilian servers were made by activists or politically outraged hackers.[1] These attacks have been limited to denial-of-service (DoS) attacks and web page defacement. For the purpose of this chapter, the authors assume that there exists a terrorist organization possessing hacker-level skills and moderate funding that is motivated to attack a US commercial information system. Their goal is to discover what intelligence the organization has on the terrorist organization and what sources are used to collect intelligence. Cyber Terrorists are modeled to possess moderate skill levels and are not risk averse.

Hackers

Reference [2] defines a hacker as "a person who enjoys learning the details of computer systems and how to stretch their capabilities — as opposed to most users of computers, who prefer to learn only the minimum amount necessary; one who programs enthusiastically or who enjoys programming rather than just theorizing about programming". For this chapter, the author is not interested in the recreational hacker, who is unlikely to attack our hypothesized system, or the "script kiddie", who is unlikely to possess the skills required. Instead, we are mostly concerned with the malicious "cracker" who has moderate skills and a desire to compromise a network for their own malicious purposes, or on another's behalf [3]. Crackers do not generally have large financial resources but often have access to a great deal of computing power by hijacking other machines, such as a research network or computers at an educational institution. They seem to have one limitless resource, time. Given sufficient time, they will generally find a system vulnerable to attacks. Some of them are risk-averse and tread gingerly around the edges of the law, but others have no fear of prosecution and engage in illegal activities without considering the risks involved [10]. In this study, we focused on the latter. They are bold enough to attack a US commercial wireless grid information system and are confident enough that any successful attack cannot be attributed to the individual.

[1] https://www.sciencedirect.com/topics/computer-science/hacktivist.

Malicious Insiders

Malicious insiders come in many varieties, ranging from those with a great potential for harm, such as the disgruntled system administrator, to others that are dangerous based only on their physical access, such as the angry janitor who denied medical benefits [3]. Malicious insiders are dangerous because they are already trusted to some degree by the organization. They possess the organizational knowledge and computer access that other adversary classes hope to achieve. Malicious insiders are also dangerous because they are difficult to detect. They do not have to beat a firewall, an intrusion detection system, or other boundary protection systems, because they are already inside. They also have a certain degree of plausible deniability if their attacks are detected. Because of their intimate knowledge of the organization, they are more likely to cause harm than external adversaries and will do so more efficiently. Malicious insiders can work for their own benefit (such as disgruntled employees) or collude with an external adversary (such as a traitor purchased by an FIS). In our model, we consider a Malicious Insider as a disgruntled employee with user-level access.

ADVERSARY CAPABILITY MATRIX

Table 1 provides a high-level view of the capabilities of the various adversary classes. This information is used to determine the attractiveness of various attacks to each adversary and will help develop weights. In this chart, we consider the following characteristics of an attacker:

- Technical expertise,
- Risk tolerance,
- Resources available,
- Starting access,
- Attack goal.

We qualitatively evaluate each of these parameters for each adversary. Technical Expertise describes an attacker's computer attack skills. Risk Tolerance describes the extent to which an adversary fears detection, attribution, and subsequent consequences. Resources Available rate the financial and technical resources available to the adversary. Starting Access describes what the network accesses an adversary at the beginning of an attack on a "new" network.

Table 1. Adversary Capabilities Matrix

	Capabilities				Motivations
	Technical Expertise	**Resources Available**	**Starting Access**	**Fear of Detection**	**Attack Goal**
FIS	Very High	Very High	None	Very High	Gather intelligence; Insert back doors for Info Warrior
Info Warrior	Medium–High	High	None	Low–High	Disrupt war effort (infrastructure)
Cyber Terrorist	Low-Medium	Medium	None	Very Low	Disrupt infrastructure, deny terrorist intelligence collection, embarrass target
Hackers	Medium	Low	None	Medium	Gain access to a restricted network
Insiders	Low	Very Low	User-Level	High	Alter data, deny availability, embarrass the company, gain financially

The defender develops and deploys countermeasures to mitigate the effectiveness of the attacker. Countermeasures can:

- increases the probability of detection, thus increasing the risk to the attacker and allowing the defender to block an attack that would otherwise succeed (e.g., an intrusion detection system),
- make the attack less likely to succeed by adding complexity to the attack (such as the insertion of a firewall) or by completely mitigating an attack by removing a vulnerability (such as the application of a patch), and
- increase the resources required to complete the attack by requiring a large amount of money or time (such as encryption).

In Table 2, we converted the qualitative labels above with ordinal ranking to help determine the dominance of one adversary over another. A higher number indicates that the US is worse off in that characteristic than if the adversary has a lower number; however, at this point, we make no claim as to how much worse off the US is.

Table 2. Alternate View of Adversary Capabilities Matrix

	Capabilities				Motivations
	Technical Expertise	Resources Available	Starting Access	Fear of Detection	Attack Goal
FIS	5	5	1	1	Gather intelligence
Info Warrior	3–4	4	1	4	Disrupt infrastructure, cause chaos
Cyber Terrorist	2–3	3	1	5	Enable physical attacks, disrupt infrastructure, deny intelligence collection
Hackers	3	2	1	3	Gain access
Insiders	2	1	5	2	Alter data, deny availability, embarrass the company, gain financially

A quick inspection of Table 2 shows that if one adversary class "dominates" another class, the adversary is at least as good in a particular category, or better, than another adversary. If dominance exists, and assuming that the countermeasures that we would apply to the network affect the dominated adversaries in a similar manner to the dominating adversaries, then we might be able to remove the dominated adversary from consideration. In this situation, there are two interesting cases based on the uncertainty of our data. Both the information warrior and cyberterrorist can dominate the hacker. Because the Information Warrior is considered to have a score of at least "Medium" for technical expertise, the hacker is dominant. Since we only see the information warrior in times of crisis, we could possibly say that the attacker can be removed from a wartime analysis because any countermeasure applied to the Information Warrior will affect the Hacker in a similar way. Similarly, if we believe that Cyber Terrorists possess a "Medium" skill level instead of "Low" skills, we can also eliminate "Hacker" Hacker' as an adversary class. The results indicate that Hacker had little to no effect on the model. We used the dominance concept to create a "Super FIS" adversary that dominated all other "outsiders".

The Model

To test various adversary combination techniques, we require a model. The authors developed the following CyberAssurance Risk Model

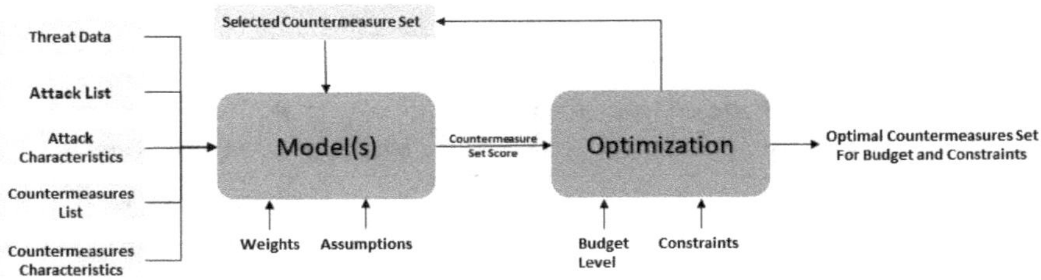

Figure 1. High-Level View of the CaRM Model

(CaRM): CaRM is a value-based risk model that scores computer attacks against a system based on an adversary's preferences, vulnerabilities inherent in the system, and the resulting impact of a successful attack. The model then evaluates various combinations of countermeasures or architectural choices that mitigate the attacks on the decision maker's satisfaction. A high-level view of the CaRM model is shown in Figure 1.

The CaRM model is a suite of tools and techniques that can be tailored to a specific problem or accommodate different management desires and assumptions. The model translates inputs into common value measures. Some techniques used by CaRM include the following.

- Bayesian belief nets to model adversary behavior.
- Attack tree software to enumerate network attacks.
- Multi-attribute value models to score adversary attacks and measure countermeasure effectiveness.
- Optimization models to determine the best "sets" of countermeasures to be applied to a network.
- Cost-benefit analyses to evaluate the trade-offs between the positive (security-enhancing) and negative (mission degradation) features of countermeasures.

In this analysis, the author opted for simplicity rather than completeness to meet our objectives. Instead of creating a fully developed adversary model using Bayesian belief nets, the author developed a simpler qualitative model using open-source information and presented it in tabular form. Instead of creating complex attack trees, the author simplified the attacks into larger classes and assessed them directly. However, we created an adversary value model for each attack. Each attack was scored based on several measurable traits. This scoring considers the technical capabilities and risk aversion of each adversary and weights the importance of each parameter separately for each adversary. For example, an FIS might place a higher weight on the "detection" category than the Information Warrior. A Hacker might place more emphasis on the resources required instead of the probability of success, as this data is different for each adversary class.

The heart of the model is a mathematical formulation used to score each attack. In this case, we use an additive value model with single-dimensional value functions [8]. The value model uses the following equation to calculate the value of each alternative.

$$v(x) = \sum_{i=1}^{n} w_i v_i(x_i) \tag{1}$$

where
$v(x)$ is the value of the alternative;
$i = 1$ to n is the number of the value measure;
x_i is the score of the alternative on the ith value measure;
$v_i(x_i)$ = is the single-dimensional value of a score of x_i;
w_i is the weight of the ith value measure;
and $\Sigma_{i=1}^{n} w_i = 1$ all weights sum to one.

A full attack mitigation analysis using CaRM would also consider the disutility that a countermeasure would impart onto the system, in addition to the gain in security. The negative traits that a countermeasure set could impart include making the information system less easy to use, less functional, less interoperable, and slower. For this analysis, we only considered the positive, security-enhancing traits of the countermeasures. The impact of a successful attack was simplified by applying higher weights to adversaries believed to be the most important. We made this simplification because the attacks have the same end result: the defeat of the confidentiality of the network.

The basic steps of the CaRM process are:

Step 1: Identify attacks and countermeasures.
Step 2: Develop value functions and weights for each adversary class.
Step 3: Score each attack according to the value function of each adversary in the baseline network before countermeasures are added.

Step 4: Characterize the effectiveness of individual countermeasures and countermeasure sets for the attacks.
Step 5: Aggregate the adversary values for a portfolio value.
Step 6: Optimize the set of countermeasures for adversary sets.

Step 1: Identify Attacks and Countermeasures

The Network

To determine what attacks adversaries can use, we need a target. In this case, we assume that the adversaries attack a Linux server running an older version of Solaris for multiple Windows clients on a wireless grid. The operating system does not have the most current vendor patches and does not update the virus definitions regularly. They have to go through a long approval process to obtain the patches approved because of potential conflicts with their poorly designed enterprise applications. They do not use firewalls, filtering routers, or wireless intrusion detection systems. In addition, the server provides multiple services for the user, including web browsing, email, application server, and file transfer protocol (FTP) services. The only protection provided by the server is password protection and Internet protocol (IP) address filtering to only trusted sites, both internal and external to the network.

The Attack Classes

We define an attack as the sequence of steps required to defeat the confidentiality of the network successfully. These attacks could be intrusive, such as attacking the network directly, or passively, such as sniffing packets, as messages leave the server for the Internet. For simplicity, we aggregated the individual attack steps into larger classes. The attacks used in the model are listed in Table 3 [9].

The Countermeasures

Countermeasures were applied to the network to mitigate the attacks listed above. Countermeasures can include technical solutions (such as firewalls) or policy mandates (such as minimum password length). Our model evaluates the effectiveness of several countermeasures to enhance network security. The countermeasures used are as follows: Countermeasure

Table 3. The Attacks

Attack Name	Attack Description
Password Attack	Attempting to gain access to the computer system by guessing or capturing user logons and passwords.
Buffer Overflow	Causing the system to exceed the buffer memory storage allocated for the program, allowing the attacker to then execute a file of his choice with root privileges.
Capture and Read Traffic	Intercepting communications between two parties and reading the data contained in the packets.
Execute a Core Dump	Exploiting the fact that sensitive data located in random access memory (RAM), such as hashed passwords, are written to the computer's hard drive when an execution error occurs.
Exploit NFS Sharing	Exploiting vulnerabilities in the Network File System (NFS) that might allow the attacker to remotely mount the file system.
Exploit Symlink Vulnerabilities	Exploiting symbolic links associated with easily accessible "junk" files in order to escalate privileges using the file that the "junk" file points to.
Racing Attack	Hijacking a process that is executed with higher privileges for short periods of time in order to become privileged too.
World Writable Files	Exploiting poorly configured system files so that the attacker could return a privileged shell to another user by modifying the Set User ID (SUID) bit.

descriptions were taken from the authors' experience and several sources, as noted below. Cost data are notional and should not be considered authoritative. Many other countermeasure options exist and can range significantly in terms of cost. For example, implementing a firewall can be as simple and inexpensive as activating a built-in firewall that ships with Microsoft® Windows 11. The countermeasures listed in Table 4 should be considered as a subset of a larger class of countermeasures [9].

Step 2: Developing Value Functions and Weights for Each Adversary Class

As a part of the CaRM model process, we want to determine the fundamental objective of the adversary. In this case, the fundamental objective for the adversary is to "determine the best attack". We then need to define

Table 4. The Countermeasures

Countermeasure Name	Countermeasure Description	Cost
Auditing	The independent examination of records and activities to ensure compliance with established controls, policy, and operational procedures, and to recommend any indicated changes in controls, policy, or procedures.	$10K
Good Password Policies	Enforcing strong passwords, enabling password aging, running password cracking to verify strength, and properly protecting password files.	$5K
Encryption (In-Line Encryptor)	A hardware and software point-to-point device that encrypts all data traffic on a line. Often associated with a government product authorized for "Type 1" encryption.	$35K
Encryption (SSL/IPsec)	Software that provides authentication and encryption over the Internet. Secure Sockets Layer (SSL) secures two applications and is typically built into the Web browser. Internet Protocol Security (IPsec) secures everything in the network and requires a client installation.	$5K
Establishing User Access Control Lists (ACLs)	Mechanism implementing discretionary and/or mandatory access control between subjects and objects.	$5K
Filtering Router	A router or system is used to check the source and destination network addresses of data packets, and either permits or denies the packet passing through.	$20K
Firewall	A system that helps to prevent outsiders from obtaining unauthorized access to internal information resources. The firewall enforces the access control policy, i.e., permit or deny, between two networks.	$35K
Virtual Private Network (VPN)	Protected IS link utilizing tunneling, security controls, and end-point address translation giving the impression of a dedicated line which includes SSL/IPsec.	$35K
Network-Based Intrusion Detection System	Software that detects an attack on a network or computer system. A network intrusion detection system (IDS) is designed to support multiple hosts.	$35K

Table 4. ***(Continued)***

Countermeasure Name	Countermeasure Description	Cost
Limit Core Dumps	Limiting the display or printout of the contents of memory. When a program abends (sic), a memory dump can be taken to examine the status of the program at the time of the crash.	$5K
Minimize Exported File Systems	Minimizing the use of Linux's Network File Systems (NFS). NFS exports files to a remote system and allows that client to access the files, so any user on the client can access the files.	$5K
No-Stack Execution	Disabling "Stack Execution" of programs in which certain programs are allowed to run on system memory (the "stack") which can reduce the chance of a memory buffer overflow.	$5K
Restrict SUID	Disallowing computer processes to run with the Set User ID (SUID) bit on. Certain processes with the SUID bit on run for a short while as root allowing an attacker to hijack the process and obtain root privileges.	$5K
Review and Restructure Permissions	Removing world-writable files and directories; limiting read privileges to those with a need to know; these are often initialization files, startup files, and critical configuration files.	$5K
Select Robust Shell Environment	Strengthening the shell (command interpreter) environment that remote users can use to gain interactive shell access.	$5K
Timely Patches	Installing software patches to operating systems and applications in a timely manner.	$5K
Host-Based Wireless Intrusion Detection System	Software that detects an attack on a network or computer system. A Host WIDS is set up to detect illegal actions within the host.	$5K

the objectives of the attacks that make them more or less desirable to an adversary. The descriptive labels that we assign to various levels of value satisfaction within an objective will be called "value measures" [7]. For this simplified analysis, we determined three objectives for an adversary when choosing an attack. They want to maximize their probability of successfully completing the attack, minimize the probability of detection

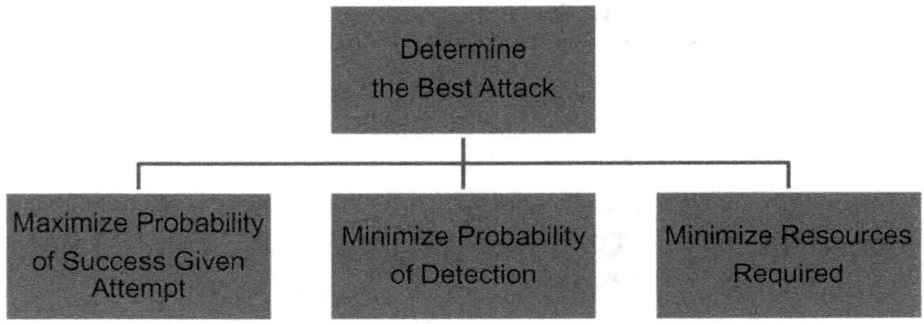

Figure 2. Adversary Value Hierarchy

given an attempt, and minimize the resources required to execute the attack. For simplicity, we refer to these as the probability of success, probability of detection, and resources required, respectively. These objectives form a value hierarchy, as illustrated in Figure 2.

A properly constructed value hierarchy is collectively exhaustive, mutually exclusive, operable, and the smallest possible size [7]. To be mutually exclusive, each goal must be independent of the others. To achieve independence in our value hierarchy, we must define the probability of a successful goal by assuming that the attack was not detected. Furthermore, we assume that each adversary has the same value hierarchy. The adversaries differ in the value they place on the scores and weights they assign across the objectives. For each objective, we developed a table of qualitative measures to score attacks and then assigned a quantitative value to each measure using a single dimensional value function. Some examples follow the complete data provided in Appendices B and C.

Probability of Success

The probability of success describes the likelihood that the attack will succeed once the adversary executes the attack. Many variables can affect this parameter; however, for this analysis, we leave this parameter at a coarse level of granularity. Ideally, we would like to use the actual probability of success as the scale. However, experience has shown that these data are not readily available and experts are either reluctant or unable to provide valid estimates. Instead, we built a scale using descriptive measures to score each attack, as shown in Table 5.

For each adversary, we develop a value function to measure the level of satisfaction of the adversary for each measure of each objective.

Table 5. Constructed Scale for Probability of Success Value Measure

P(Success)	Description	Example
Very Low	Highly complex or difficult; no past history of success	A cryptanalytic attack against strong encryption
Low	Complex or difficult attack with little history of success	Developing a life cycle attack against a bus controller
Medium	Somewhat complex or difficult; uses known techniques in new ways; previously used with mixed success	Developing a unique attack script against off-the-shelf software or developing special-purpose hardware
Medium–High	Fairly simple, but still has some tricky parts; requires multiple sequential steps to gain the required access	Exploiting multiple vulnerabilities on multiple systems
High	Very simple; will work if vulnerabilities are present; frequently used successfully in the past	Exploit known vulnerabilities with off-the-shelf scripts or cracking an 8-character password
Very High	Nearly certain of success	Guessing a weak password or using a default account

For simplicity, we used a discrete single-attribute value function (SVF). As a rational adversary, FIS prefers attacks that are more likely to succeed. However, an FIS has many resources, including time and money, and may still find value in an attack that is less likely to succeed. Similarly, the hacker has an almost limitless amount of time to conduct attacks. They can afford to try many attacks with low probabilities of success because they know that they may eventually beat the odds and find an attack that works. On the other hand, information warriors must complete their military objectives within a certain timeframe. Therefore, they place less value on attacks with a low probability of success. The FIS SVF for the probability of success is shown in Figure 3. We constructed the scale so that the most desirable trait from the adversary's perspective scores a "1" and the least attractive scores a "0". The value number for a particular alternative gives the proportion of the distance, in a value sense, that the alternative is from the alternative with an overall value of "0" and the alternative with an overall value of "1" [8].

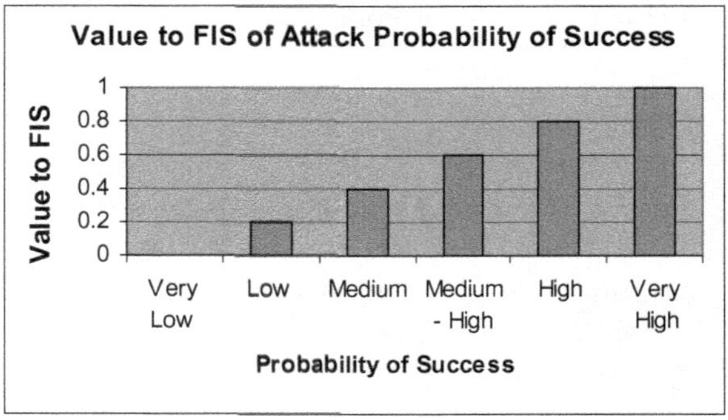

Figure 3. Single Attribute Value Function of FIS for Probability of Success

Table 6. Constructed Scale for Probability of Detection Value Measure

P(Detection)	Description	Example
Very Low	Passive attack with no footprint.	Passively collecting traffic off a microwave link.
Low	Leaves a footprint but no detection mechanism is looking for it.	Installing a sniffer on a network in receive-only mode.
Low-Medium	Leaves a footprint; the detection mechanism is looking for it but will typically miss it.	Detecting malicious software installed during the software development life cycle.
Medium	Leaves a suspicious footprint, but may be attributed to normal behavior.	Several unsuccessful login attempts.
High	Leaves an audit trail, readily identifiable as anomalous behavior.	Logging in as System Administrator during unusual hours.
Very High	Sets off an alarm; readily identifiable as an attack.	Network flood attack.

Probability of Detection

The probability of detection measures the likelihood that a network owner will detect an attack in progress. As with the probability of success, we would prefer to use the actual probability as a natural scale, but we simply do not have that data. Table 6 lists the measures of the probability of the detection goal.

The SVF for the FIS is shown in Figure 4. The FIS is very risk-averse. Attacks that are "Very Low" in detectability are scored the highest. Other

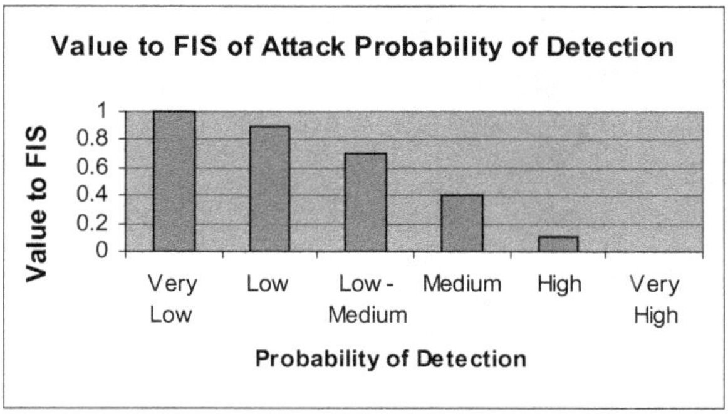

Figure 4. Single Attribute Value Function of FIS for Probability of Detection

Table 7. Constructed Scale for Resources Required Value Measure

Resources Required	Definition	Example
Very Low	Less than $10,000	Attack requires only common tools and requires days to weeks.
Low	$10,000–$100,000	Attack requires commercially available special hardware and software and takes months to set up.
Medium	$100,000–$500,000	Attack requires some specialized equipment and requires multiple staff for months to set up, test and run.
High	$500,000–$1,000,000	Attack requires the development of specialized hardware and software, and extensive staff.
Very High	Over $1,000,000	Attack requires very sophisticated tools and techniques and substantial staff for years.

attacks lose their attractiveness from a value perspective. An attack scoring "High" on the scale, for example, might only be attempted if that attack scores well on all other parameters.

Resources Required

The resources required to measure the financial cost of conducting an attack on each adversary (see Appendix D for value functions for each adversary group). The FIS has the resources of a nation-state. Rational

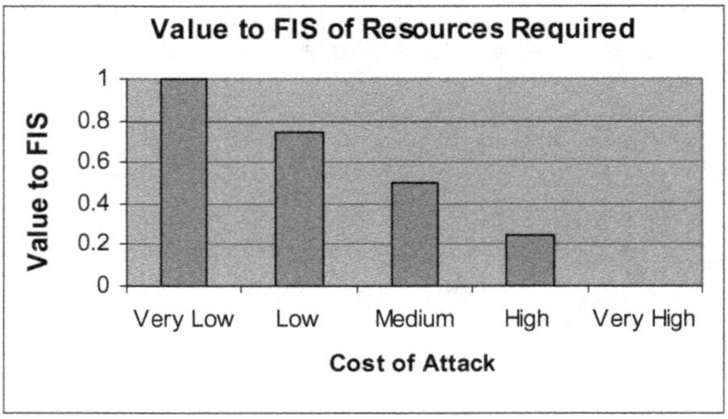

Figure 5. Single Attribute Value Function of FIS for Resources Required

adversaries prefer attacks that cost less. However, they obtain more value from a higher-cost attack than an adversary with limited resources, such as the hacker. Table 7 lists the measures for the required resources.

The SVF of the FIS for the required resources is shown in Figure 5. The FIS has nearly limitless resources but prefers less expensive attacks over more expensive attacks. However, if the only attack that exists against the system is "Very High", the FIS would probably have enough research money to fund the development of one of these attacks.

Weights

Each adversary has a different importance (weight) applied to each objective to demonstrate their preferences, as shown in Table 8. A FIS might place a higher weight on the probability of the detection objective compared to the resources required objective. To develop the weights, we used the balance beam method of swing weight elicitation by a panel of experts [11]. The balance beam method measures the importance of changing (swinging) from the worst possible measure on an objective (such as Very Low) to the best possible measure (such as Very High). This method poses a series of preference questions to a data provider. For example, an expert might hypothesize what an FIS would prefer: an attack that is undetectable, but not likely to succeed, and very expensive OR an attack that is very detectable, but guaranteed to succeed and free. The expert then selects which attack is preferable, using the balance beam as a visual aid.

Each adversary has a level of importance for the US to mitigate based on the assumed impact of a successful attack. For this model, the FIS and

Table 8. Weights for Individual Adversaries

Adversary	Probability of Success	Probability of Detection	Resources Required
FIS	0.3	0.6	0.1
Information Warrior	0.6	0.3	0.1
Cyber Terrorist	0.5	0.2	0.3
Hacker	0.3	0.1	0.6
Insider	0.6	0.3	0.1

Table 9. Impact Weights for Individual Adversaries in Order of Importance to Mitigate

Adversary	Weight
FIS	0.3
Insider Information	0.3
Info Warrior	0.2
Cyber Terrorist	0.1
Hacker	0.1

Insider were considered to be the most damaging adversaries. The FIS and Insider were each considered to be one and a half times more important than the information warrior. The information warrior is considered twice as important as either a Cyber Terrorist or Hacker. Table 9 lists the weights.

Step 3: Score Each Attack According to the Value Function of Each Adversary for the Baseline Network

Each attack is scored based on its attractiveness to the adversary class under consideration. In general, attacks that are likely to be successful are difficult to detect, and accomplishing the goal of the adversary scores very highly. Attacks that are deficient in any of these areas receive lower scores based on the value function of that particular adversary.

Each attack is described according to its probability of detection, probability of success, and resources required for an attacker starting outside of the network. With a baseline network, there are many excellent choices for attacks. The results are presented in Table 10.

Table 10. Attack Scores for an Outsider on the Baseline Network

Attack Name	Probability of Detection	Probability of Success	Resources Required
Password Attack	Low–Medium	Medium–High	Very Low
Buffer Overflow	Low	Very High	Very Low
Capture and Read Traffic	Very Low	High	Low
Execute a Core Dump	Low	Medium	Very Low
Exploit NFS Sharing	Low	Medium–High	Very Low
Exploit Symlink Vulnerabilities	Low	High	Very Low
Racing Attack	Low	Low	Very Low
World Writable Files	Low	High	Very Low

Table 11. Attack Scores for the Insider on the Baseline Network

Attack Name	Probability of Detection	Probability of Success	Resources Required
Password Attack	Very Low	Low	Very Low
Buffer Overflow	Low	Low	Very Low
Capture and Read Traffic	Low	Very Low	Very Low
Execute a Core Dump	Low	None	Very Low
Exploit NFS Sharing	Low	Low	Very Low
Exploit Symlink Vulnerabilities	Low	Low	Very Low
Racing Attack	Medium–High	Low	Very Low
World Writable Files	Low	Low	Very Low

A similar table was created for the insider. Their baseline values will be greatly different than an "outsider". This is because they already have a level of access to them as users and are much harder to detect. Table 11 presents the results.

Step 4: Characterize the Effectiveness of Individual Countermeasures and Countermeasure Sets on the Attacks

Countermeasures have one positive trait — they make it harder to complete successfully and thereby help ensure mission accomplishment in a

Table 12. CM Attack Scores for the "Outsider" on the Baseline Network

Attack/ Countermeasure Effect Matrix	Probability of Detection	Probability of Success	Adversary Resources Required	Cost to US to Implement Countermeasure
Password Attack Baseline — Outsider	**Low–Medium**	**Medium–High**	**Very Low**	**N/A**
CM#1 Auditing	High			$10,000
CM#2 Good PW Policies	Medium	Medium		$5,000
CM#7 Install Firewall	Medium	Low	Low	$35,000
CM#8 Install VPN	Medium	Low	Low	$35,000
CM#9 Install IDS	Very High			$35,000
Combined Effect of all Countermeasures	**Very High**	**Very Low**	**Low**	**N/A**

hostile environment. They do this by making the attack harder to detect, less likely to succeed, or more costly. Countermeasures have two negative traits — they usually cost money and they may hinder mission accomplishment by increasing manpower requirements, making the system harder to use, and reducing bandwidth, interoperability, and functionality just to name a few. For this analysis, we only considered the security-related benefits and financial costs of the countermeasures.

In Table 12, we examine one attack on the system — the brute-force password attack from an outsider. In the first row, we score the attack on the baseline in terms of the probability of detection, probability of success, and resources required from the adversary. The second through sixth rows characterize the effects of individual countermeasures if they are applied to the network. For example, if we choose to implement Countermeasure #1 (Auditing), we increase the probability of detection from the baseline score of "Low-Medium" to the new value of "High". The last column lists the financial cost of the countermeasure to the network owner, which is used in the optimization as a constraint. We see that some countermeasures affect every one of the adversaries' objectives, whereas others only affect certain objectives. For example, an intrusion detection system only increases the risk of detection but does not mitigate the probability of success. A second countermeasure is needed to work in concert with the intrusion detection system to mitigate the probability of success. A gray box with no data indicates that the countermeasure has no effect on the adversary objective. The complete data table is provided in Appendix E.

The last line of the chart lists the maximum security benefits to the network if all countermeasures are in place. This parameter is used to demonstrate diminishing returns to the scale of the additional countermeasures. It is also used to identify superior countermeasures that can completely mitigate an attack objective. Mathematically, the Countermeasure Benefit (CB) for any chosen countermeasure *set* against any *objective* of attack j is defined as

$$CB_j = CMax_j + \frac{\left(\sum_{i \in I} y_i C_{ij}\right) - CMax_j}{\left(\sum_{i \in I} C_{ij}\right) - CMax_j} \times (DMax_j - CMax_j) \qquad (2)$$

where

I = set of Countermeasures (CMs) indexed by i;
J = set of Attacks indexed by j;
CB_j = benefit score for the current CM set against Attack j;
$CMax_j$ = maximum benefit provided by the "best" selected CM against Attack j;
y_i = binary decision variable {0,1} indicates whether a particular CM is included in the current CM set;
C_{ij} = benefit of Countermeasure i against Attack j;
$DMaxi$ = maximum benefit achieved from implementing all countermeasures.

In other words, this equation determines the benefit of any possible countermeasure set by approximating the proportion of benefits achieved between a well-defined lower and upper bound. The lower bound ensures that the benefit gained from any countermeasure set is at least as good as the "best" countermeasure (CMax term). The upper bound is the benefit of implementing every possible countermeasure (DMax term). The resulting benefit of any countermeasure set is the proportion of the benefit gained by moving from the single best countermeasure to the upper bound.

Step 5: Aggregate the Adversary Scores for a Portfolio Score

At this point, the model translates the qualitative scales into an initial attack score for each adversary in the baseline system without any countermeasures. To optimize the performance of every set of countermeasures against each attack, we require a metric to maximize or minimize. For this model, we minimized the sum of the individual attack scores. The optimization model minimizes the value of the portfolio to the adversary and therefore increases the security of the US commercial wireless sector. However, there are some problems with this optimization objective. For example, the optimization might reduce an adversary's portfolio value by 90%, giving the impression of iron-clad security. However, several attacks that are perfect against the system still exist. To help with this problem, we need to translate portfolio value into a verbal description of risk that is more useful to the decision-maker.

Table 13 shows the baseline, optimized, and best possible attack values against our hypothesized network along with the qualitative risk description for the FIS. The "optimized" column shows the resulting attack values from minimizing the risk subject to our financial constraints. The "best possible" column gives the attack values if we are able to implement every possible countermeasure at our disposal without regard to financial constraints. Figure 6 shows the constructed scale used to

Table 13. FIS Baseline, Optimized, and Best Possible Values

Attack Name	Baseline Attack Value	Optimized Attack Value	Best Possible Attack Value
Password Attack	0.70	0.13	0.08
Buffer Overflow	0.94	0.07	0.06
Capture and Read Traffic	0.94	0.24	0.24
Execute a Core Dump	0.76	0.05	0.05
Exploit NFS Sharing	0.82	0.24	0.11
Exploit Symlink Vulnerabilities	0.86	0.05	0.05
Racing Attack	0.65	0.07	0.07
World Writable Files	0.88	0.07	0.05
Portfolio Value	6.55	0.92	0.71
Risk Level	**Very High**	**Very Low**	**Very Low**

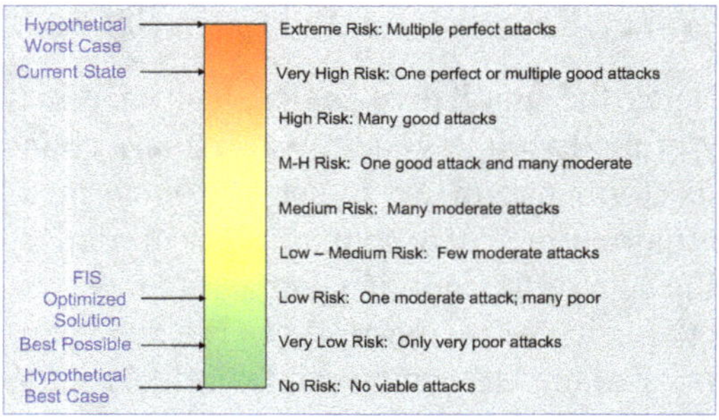

Attack Score Range	Attack Description
.9-1	Perfect Attack
.6-.9	Good Attack
.4-.6	Moderate Attack
.2-.4	Poor Attack
0-.2	Unviable Attack

Figure 6. Constructed Scale to Determine Attack Portfolio Risk Level and Translation Table for Attack Values to Risk Labels

determine the Risk Level. This Risk Level is based on the number and quality of available attacks. The quality of the attack is translated from a quantitative value to a qualitative description using the table in Figure 6. In this case, both the Optimized Attack Value and the Best Possible Attack Value have the same relative risk level. The small difference in the Portfolio Values of "0.92" and "0.71" are practically meaningless from a system view.

Step 6: Optimize the Set of Countermeasures for Adversary Sets

Once we develop our scales, we can determine the optimal set of countermeasures for each adversary scenario. The optimization of this model is a non-smooth binary integer program. For optimization, the FrontlineSolvers® OptQuest Solver Engine was used.[2] In other words, the optimization requires the model to find the best set of countermeasures that work together as a group to minimize the adversary's ability to attack within the budget constraints of the defending organization. Figure 7 shows the model outputs for the FIS. Countermeasures preceded by a "1" and highlighted in blue on the left were selected as part of the best set. In this case, the amount expended is equal to the budget ($100,000).

---

[2] https://www.solver.com/optquest-solver-engine.

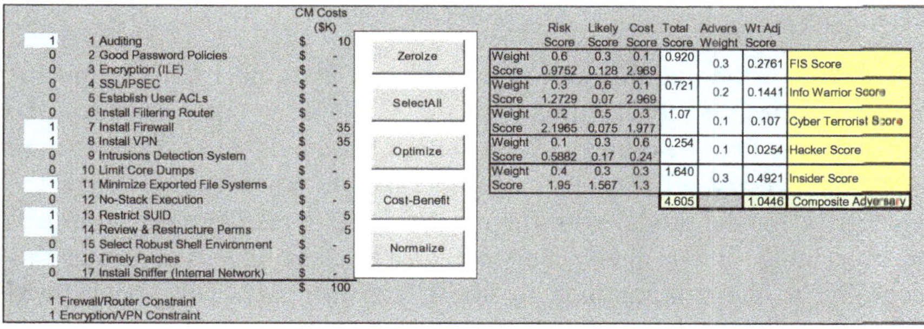

Figure 7. Screen Shot of the Model for the FIS Only Scenario

If we were only interested in mitigating one adversary, we would ask for optimization to minimize the sum of the portfolio attacks available to that adversary. For multiple adversaries, we would minimize the sum of each adversary's portfolio. If adversaries are not of equivalent importance to the US, we can weigh the values of the more dangerous adversaries higher to have a greater mitigation effect on them. The result in the multiple adversary model is a set of countermeasures that may not be optimal for any one adversary but will be optimal for the group of adversaries under consideration. These countermeasure portfolio recommendations and the resulting security values can be quantitatively compared to show the differences in the resulting security from multiple methods of combining adversaries. We run the optimization routine using various combinations of adversaries and weights. The authors tested the following six methods of combining adversaries:

- **Method 1:** Using only the most formidable adversary (FIS) as a proxy for all adversaries.
- **Method 2:** Using a hypothetical worst-case adversary (Super FIS — a combination of the most dangerous traits of the FIS and Information Warrior) as a proxy for all adversaries.
- **Method 3:** Using the FIS and the Insider as a proxy for all adversaries.
- **Method 4:** Using the Super FIS and the Insider as proxies for all adversaries.
- **Method 5:** Using all adversaries and giving them equal importance.
- **Method 6:** Using all adversaries and giving more weight to the more formidable adversaries.

RESULTS

The results of the optimization runs are listed in Table 14. The rows list the adversaries and the columns list the available countermeasures. An "X" indicates that the optimization solution included that countermeasure for that adversary set. The Weighted Composite adversary serves as the benchmark for the model with the most favorable results because it uses the most data. It considers every adversary class and assigns weights according to their importance for the US to mitigate. The Unweighted Composite adversary also considers every adversary class but treats each adversary class as equally important. The FIS, information warrior, cyber-terrorist, hacker, and insider were considered independent of each other, that is, optimized for each adversary as if they were the only adversary in existence. The "FIS & Insider" is a hybrid case that considers only two adversaries — the FIS as the most formidable and the Insider as the most capable of catastrophic damage. The "Super FIS" hypothesizes the existence of an adversary with the skills and resources of a nation-state and the risk tolerance of the Information Warrior. The "Super FIS and Insider" is a hybrid case that uses the Super FIS and Insider to represent all other adversaries. The results were grouped into similar solutions.

Table 14 provides only a comparison of which countermeasures were chosen to counter each adversary. At this point, we can say that any adversary group that selects the same countermeasure set as the benchmark provides the same level of security. We do not know whether the security provided by the benchmark is "good enough" or how much worse another solution will perform as this is discussed in the next section. However, an analysis of Table 14 provides some insightful results for this case. These results cannot be generalized for all possible computer networks and countermeasure sets.

***Insight #1*:** The only adversary under consideration that performed identically to the benchmark was the "Super FIS & Insider". Because the benchmark provides the best security and uses the most resources, we can say that the "Super FIS & Insider" has the same value as the benchmark from a security standpoint and uses fewer resources.

***Insight #2*:** The unweighted composite, FIS, super FIS, information warrior, and cyber-terrorist all provided the same countermeasure

Table 14. Optimization Results of Countermeasures to Adversary Classes

Adversary Class	Auditing	Good Password Polices	Encryption (INE)	SSL/ IPsec	Establish User ACLs	Install Filtering Router	Install Firewall	Install VPN	Network Based IDS	Limit Core Dumps	Min Exported File Systems	No-Stack Execution	Restrict SUID	Review & Restructure Perms	Robust Shell Environment	Timely Patches	Host-Based IDS
Weighted Composite Adversary	X						X	X		X			X	X		X	
Super FIS & Insider	X						X	X		X			X	X		X	
Unweighted Composite Adversary Policies	X						X	X			X		X	X		X	
FIS	X						X	X			X		X	X		X	
Info Warrior	X						X	X			X		X	X		X	
Cyber Terrorist	X						X	X			X		X	X		X	
Super FIS	X						X	X			X		X	X		X	
Insider	X	X			X			X		X	X	X	X	X	X	X	X
FIS & Insider	X	X				X		X		X	X		X	X		X	X
Hacker		X					X	X			X	X	X	X		X	

recommendations. The implication is that one of these groups can be used to represent the rest of the group.

Insight #3: The countermeasures recommended by the groups listed in Insight #2 differed from the benchmark in two ways. The countermeasure “Limit Core Dumps” was included in the benchmark and excluded from the groups above. The countermeasure “Minimize Exported File Systems” was excluded from the benchmark, but included with the groups listed above. This is because of the insider’s effect on the benchmark. The Insider is very different from all other adversaries, as shown by the countermeasure choices in Table 14. The Weighted Composite adversary includes the insider and gives the insider more importance through a higher weight (0.3) than the Unweighted Composite adversary (0.2). Note that assigning no weights and assigning equal weights to the five adversaries (0.2 each) are mathematically equivalent.

Insight #4: Countermeasure choices seem to make intuitive sense. Some countermeasures are inexpensive and effective and are therefore recommended across all adversaries under consideration. These include restricting SUIDs, reviewing and restructuring permissions, and providing timely patches. Also selected for every countermeasure set. The VPN was one of the most expensive countermeasures but was also modeled as one of the most effective.

Insight #5: Several countermeasures are never selected for any adversary. These include the in-line network encryption (INE), SSL/IPsec, and Wireless Intrusion Detection System (WIDS). The encryption concerns of the network are handled by selecting the VPN (which includes SSL/IPsec). INE is just as expensive as VPN but handles fewer attacks. The IDS is very effective at increasing the probability of the detection objective but does not mitigate the adversaries’ other two objectives (probability of success and resources required). A WIDS is one of the most expensive countermeasures. Thus, the model has to make tough resource allocation choices and select countermeasures that most effectively mitigate the attack portfolio of the adversary. This does not mean that the countermeasures are ineffective. All the models state that the recommended group of countermeasures as a whole would score worse if WIDS was added, and other countermeasures were taken out in order to fulfill the budget constraint. If we had an unlimited budget and if we ignored the burden that countermeasures impart to the system, then we would pick every countermeasure.

SECURITY AND RISK IMPLICATIONS OF ADVERSARY CLASSES

So far our analysis shows that the Weighted Composite Adversary and "Super FIS and the Insider" have the same value. Because the Weighted Composite considers all adversaries and weighs their importance, it should provide the best composite security solution. However, how much security did we obtain from the Weighted Composite adversary and how much better is it than any other combining method? To answer these questions, we must examine the individual attack values before and after the application of countermeasures. Figure 8 shows a graph of the five basic adversary classes. Each bar represents the level of risk of a particular adversary. Each bar was scaled from "0" to "1". If all attacks against the network were perfect, then the risk would be extreme and valued at "1". If every attack were completely ineffective, the risk would be non-existent and valued at "0". The risk in the practical world is between.

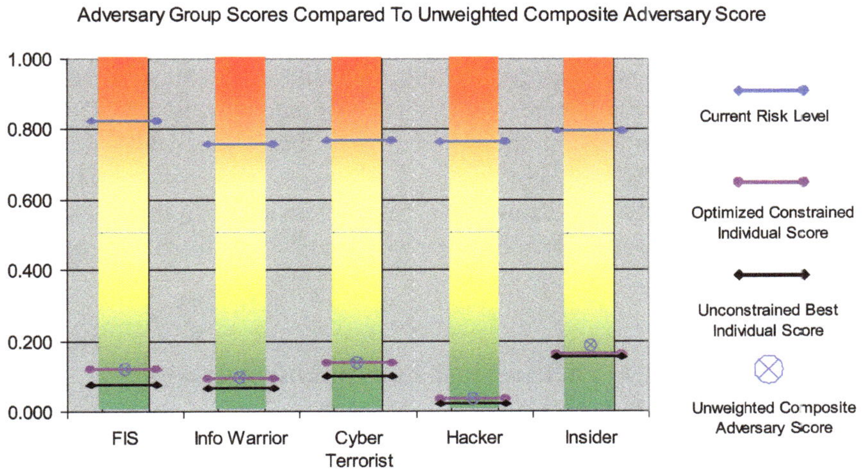

Figure 8. Comparison of the Unweighted Composite Adversary Against Every Adversary Class

Each bar contains four markers. The top blue line shows the risk level to the network from the adversary before any countermeasures are applied. In this hypothetical network, the risk is very high. The middle purple line shows the level of risk for each adversary if we run the optimization only for that adversary. This is the best that we can realistically achieve if we are only concerned about the adversary. The lower black line shows the best results if we had unlimited resources and decided to implement every possible countermeasure. The difference between the middle and low lines is the risk that we can possibly mitigate, but have decided to accept it because of budget limitations. The blue circle with the "X" shows the level of risk that we have if we consider all adversaries and try to maximize security across the entire rogue's gallery using the Unweighted Composite method. Clearly, the optimal for all adversary classes may not be optimal for any individual. In the chart below, we see that the risk level for each adversary under the "Optimized Constrained Individual" and the "Unweighted Composite" is nearly equivalent for every adversary except for the insider.

Figure 8 provides an intuitive visual sense of the risk level, but still lacks a critical piece of data. We lost some resolution in the data by normalizing the attack scores. We get an "average" view of risk but do not have any information on the extreme values of any one attack. The risk level for 10 attacks that each score "0.1" is very different from 1 attack that scores "1" and 9 attacks that score "0". Table 15 gives us some insight into these data by showing each individual attack score from Figure 9 for the FIS. These data were aggregated into a qualitative risk level, as shown in Figure 7. The Unweighted Composite score and Optimized FIS score are identical, meaning that the Unweighted Composite works well for mitigating attacks by the FIS.

Table 16 shows the same data for the insider. In this case, the Unweighted Composite leaves a possibly unacceptable level of risk (medium–high).

Method 1: Using Only the Most Formidable Adversary as a Proxy for All Adversaries

Method 1 hypothesizes that the risk model will give good results compared to the benchmark if only the FIS is considered an adversary. This method has been used in past risk assessments to minimize the data collection

Table 15. Attack Scores for the FIS Compared with the Unweighted Composite Adversary

Attack Name	Baseline Attack Score	Unweighted Composite Score	Optimized Attack Score	Best Possible Attack Score
Password Attack	0.70	0.13	0.13	0.08
Buffer Overflow	0.94	0.07	0.07	0.06
Capture and Read Traffic	0.94	0.24	0.24	0.24
Execute a Core Dump	0.76	0.05	0.05	0.05
Exploit NFS Sharing	0.82	0.24	0.24	0.11
Exploit Symlink Vulnerabilities	0.86	0.05	0.05	0.05
Racing Attack	0.65	0.07	0.07	0.07
World Writable Files	0.88	0.07	0.07	0.05
Portfolio Value	6.55	0.92	0.92	0.71
Risk Level	**Extreme**	**Very Low**	**Very Low**	**Very Low**

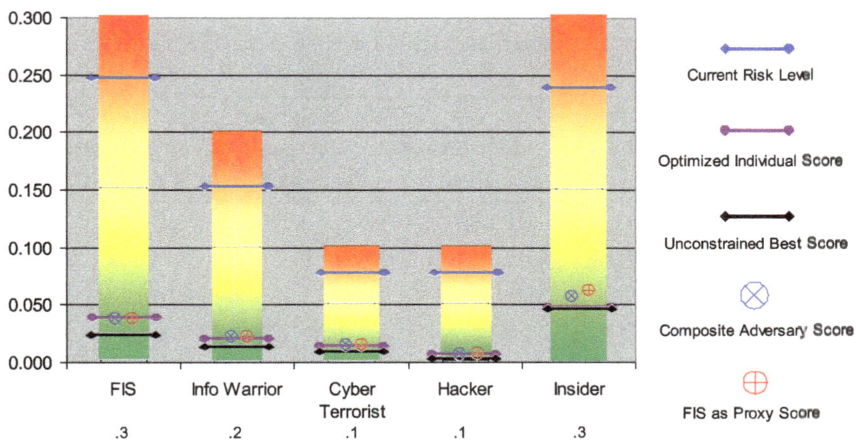

Figure 9. Adversary Group Scores Compared to FIS as a Proxy for All Adversaries

required, and it uses the fewest resources of all methods because it only requires one adversary. To test the effectiveness of this method, we optimized the countermeasure set for the FIS and examined how the "FIS set" mitigated all other adversaries. This method has the effect of slightly

Table 16. Attack Scores for the Insider Compared with the Unweighted Composite Adversary

Attack Name	Baseline Attack Score	Unweighted Composite Score	Optimized Attack Score	Best Possible Attack Score
Password Attack	0.84	0.60	0.53	0.53
Buffer Overflow	0.81	0.12	0.08	0.08
Capture and Read Traffic	1.00	0.08	0.04	0.04
Execute a Core Dump	1.00	0.61	0.40	0.40
Exploit NFS Sharing	0.84	0.06	0.04	0.04
Exploit Symlink Vulnerabilities	0.60	0.04	0.04	0.04
Racing Attack	0.39	0.04	0.04	0.04
World Writable Files	0.84	0.09	0.04	0.04
Portfolio Value	6.32	1.64	1.21	1.21
Risk Level	**Extreme**	**Medium–High**	**Low–Medium**	**Low–Medium**

Table 17. Attack Portfolio Scores and Risk Levels for the FIS as a Proxy and Benchmark

Adversary	FIS as Proxy Portfolio Score	FIS as Proxy Risk	Weighted Composite Portfolio Score	Weighted Composite Risk
FIS	0.92	Very Low	0.97	Very Low
Info Warrior	0.72	None–Very Low	0.77	None–Very Low
Cyber Terrorist	1.07	Very Low	1.15	Very Low
Hacker	0.25	None	0.37	None
Insider	1.64	Medium–High	1.49	Low/Low–Medium

increasing the security against non-insider classes and moderately decreasing the security against insiders. The level of risk against the Insider has increased from "Low/Low–Medium" to "Medium–High" as shown in Table 17. Figure 9 does not seem to show this because the values in the graph are averages and may miss the importance of extreme attacks. Therefore, this technique may be worthwhile if the insider is not a major concern. However, if the insider is a large portion of the risk, then this may not be the best method.

Method 2: Using a Hypothetical Worst Case Adversary (the Super FIS — A Combination of the Most Dangerous Traits of the FIS and Info Warrior) as a Proxy for All Adversaries

Method 2 expands on Method 1. Method 2 uses the "Super FIS" to represent a technically savvy adversary with minimal fear of detection (see Figure 10). This method may be a way to aggregate the list of non-insiders into a dominant composite group. This is a new method for treating an adversary and has never been tested before. In this model, the Super FIS scored identically to method 1. Because it scores as well as the FIS, it is difficult to say if it can outperform Method 1. Perhaps there would be some differentiation between the two methods if the dataset was larger or if the key assumptions were different. This is a good area for further studies (see Table 18).

Method 3: Using the FIS and the Insider as a Proxy for All Adversaries

Method 3 builds on Method 1 and hypothesizes that the risk model will give good results compared to the benchmark if we consider both the FIS & the

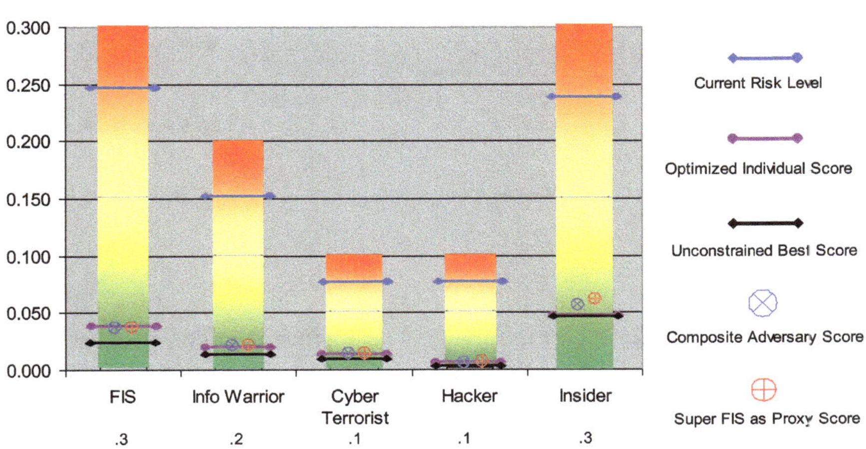

Figure 10. Adversary Group Scores Compared to Super FIS as a Proxy for All Adversaries

Table 18. Attack Portfolio Scores and Risk Levels for the Super FIS as a Proxy and Benchmark

Adversary	Super FIS as Proxy Portfolio Score	Super FIS as Proxy Risk	Weighted Composite Portfolio Score	Weighted Composite Risk
FIS	0.92	Very Low	0.97	Very Low
Info Warrior	0.72	None–Very Low	0.77	None–Very Low
Cyber Terrorist	1.07	Very Low	1.15	Very Low
Hacker	0.25	None	0.37	None
Insider	1.64	Medium–High	1.49	Low/Low–Medium

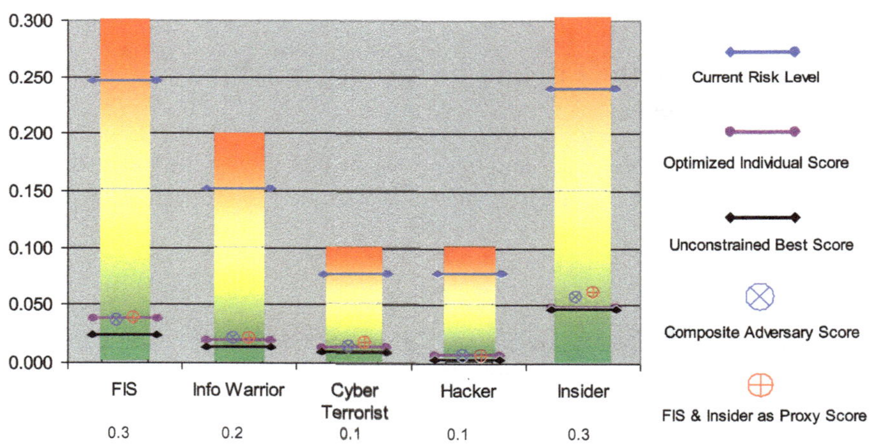

Figure 11. Adversary Group Scores Compared to FIS & Insider as a Proxy for All Adversaries

Insider as adversaries (see Figure 11). The Insider is added because it is very different from all of the "outsiders". The net effect of Method 3 is to slightly degrade the security scores from the benchmark for FIS, information warriors, and cyber terrorists. This is because these groups have lost some importance since the FIS only represents the un-modeled "outsiders". The security score for the hacker decreased slightly, but the risk level increased slightly because of one attack that is now much more attractive.

Table 19. Attack Portfolio Scores and Risk Levels for the FIS & Insider as a Proxy and Benchmark

Adversary	FIS & Insider as Proxy Portfolio Score	FIS & Insider as Proxy Risk	Weighted Composite Portfolio Score	Weighted Composite Risk
FIS	1.12	Very Low	0.97	Very Low
Info Warrior	0.95	None–Very Low	0.77	None–Very Low
Cyber Terrorist	1.31	Very Low	1.15	Very Low
Hacker	0.31	None–Very Low	0.37	None
Insider	1.27	Low	1.49	Low/Low–Medium

The overall security score for the insider was better than that for the benchmark. However, all of these changes were relatively small and did not significantly change the level of risk compared to the benchmark (see Table 19).

Method 4: Using the Super FIS and the Insider as a Proxy for All Adversaries

Method 4 builds off Method 3 and hypothesizes that the risk model will provide good results compared to the benchmark if we consider both the Super FIS & the Insider as the adversary (see Figure 12). In short, Method 4 scored identically to the benchmark, while using fewer resources (using this dataset and assumptions). This appears to be an excellent way to combine adversaries in resource-constrained environments (see Table 20).

Method 5: Using All Adversaries and Giving Them Equal Importance

This method is essentially the same as the benchmark, except that all adversaries are considered equally important for mitigation (see Figure 13). This technique is identical to Methods 1 and 2. This Method increases the risk from the Insider from Low/Low–Medium to Medium–High. Because this method scores as well as Methods 1 and 2 and uses more resources, this method cannot be recommended for decisions with constrained resources (see Table 21).

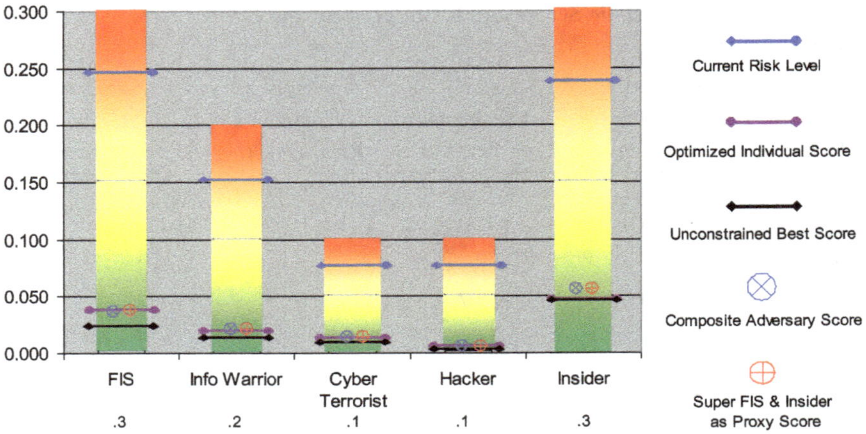

Figure 12. Adversary Group Scores Compared to Super FIS & Insider as a Proxy for All Adversaries

Table 20. Attack Portfolio Scores and Risk Levels for the Super FIS & Insider as a Proxy and Benchmark

Adversary	FIS & Insider as Proxy Portfolio Score	FIS & Insider as Proxy Risk	Weighted Composite Portfolio Score	Weighted Composite Risk
FIS	0.97	Very Low	0.97	Very Low
Info Warrior	0.77	None–Very Low	0.77	None–Very Low
Cyber Terrorist	1.15	Very Low	1.15	Very Low
Hacker	0.37	None	0.37	None
Insider	1.49	Low/Low–Medium	1.49	Low/Low–Medium

Method 6: Using All Adversaries and Giving More Weight to the More Formidable Adversaries

Method 6 is the benchmark used to compare all other methods. The data for Method 6 is an inherent part of the previous charts in Methods 1–5, and will not be repeated here. Method 6 scored the best from a security standpoint, tying with Method 4, and used the most resources.

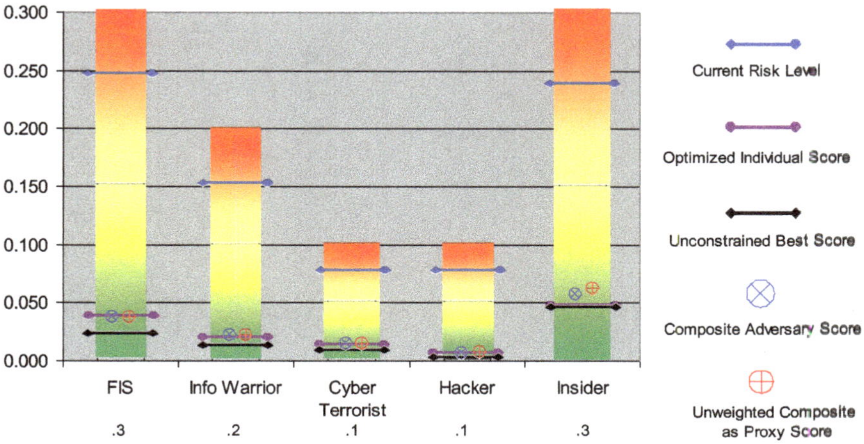

Figure 13. Adversary Group Scores Compared to Unweighted Composite as a Proxy for All Adversaries

Table 21. Attack Portfolio Scores and Risk Levels for the Super FIS & Insider as a Proxy and Benchmark

Adversary	FIS & Insider as Proxy Portfolio Score	FIS & Insider as Proxy Risk	Weighted Composite Portfolio Score	Weighted Composite Risk
FIS	0.92	Very Low	0.97	Very Low
Info Warrior	0.72	None–Very Low	0.77	None–Very Low
Cyber Terrorist	1.07	Very Low	1.15	Very Low
Hacker	0.25	None	0.37	None
Insider	1.64	Medium–High	1.49	Low/Low–Medium

CONCLUSIONS

The main purpose of this study is to identify the most appropriate methods for combining the effects of multiple adversaries on a specific computer network in an information assurance risk model. If one had unlimited time and resources, then there would be no problem — just modeling everything. In this chapter, we looked at several different ways to combine adversaries and examined their performance. Figure 14 presents a brief

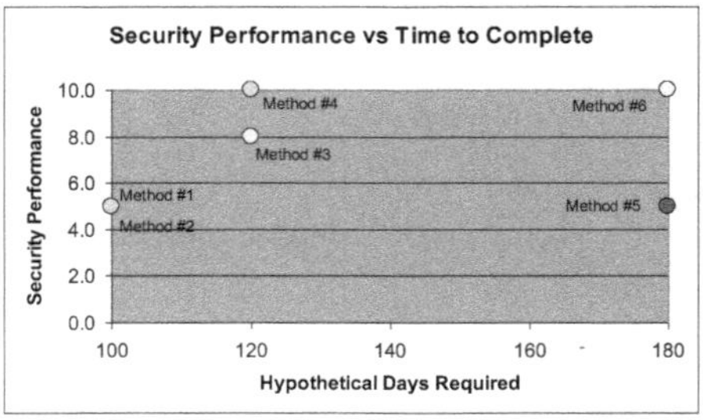

Method	Days to Complete	Security Performance
Method 1	100	5
Method 2	100	5
Method 3	120	8
Method 4	120	10
Method 5	180	5
Method 6	180	10

Figure 14. Plot and Data Chart of Method Security versus Resources Required in Days

summary of the data obtained using the most conservative case. Each Method is represented as a dot on the plot. The horizontal axis shows how long a risk assessment may take in days, assuming that a full risk assessment using all adversaries will take 180 days. The vertical axis provides a subjective indication of the solution quality. Methods 4 and 6 scored the best from a security perspective. They mitigated both the portfolio of attacks available to the adversary and the risk resulting from extreme attacks left in the portfolio. Method 3 also performed well from a security standpoint. It mitigated the risk of extreme attacks very well but did not do as well as mitigate the entire portfolio. It was subjectively scored as 80%, as in Methods 4 or 5. Methods 1, 2, and 5 effectively mitigated the portfolio but left large amounts of risk with the Insider. They were scored 50% as good as those in Methods 4 and 5.

The green points on the plot "dominate" other points. Method 4 dominates Methods 3, 5, and 6 because it scores as well as, or better than each other method on both the security and resources required. Methods 1 and 2 are equivalent and both dominate Method 5 in terms of the resources required. The yellow points (Methods 3 and 6) dominate Method 5.

Based on the data and analysis thus far, we can make some initial recommendations. However, it is important to test these conclusions with larger and more varied datasets and assumptions before these conclusions can be considered valid for decision-making.

When time and manpower permits, Method 6 (the weighted composite adversary) is the preferred way of combining multiple adversaries. Method 6 uses the most data and provides the best results for multiple adversary groups. This method was used as a benchmark for testing all other methods. This method considers the diversity of adversaries, their preferences, and their importance to mitigate from a US perspective. Method 6 also uses the most resources by doubling the time required to conduct a risk assessment over a single adversary model. The resources required for Method 6 can be reduced by excluding the attacker as an adversary class. The Hacker (as modeled) was dominated by most other adversaries and had no noticeable effect on the model. The Hacker should be included in commercial or non-sensitive government network risk assessments that may not be of interest to the FIS or Information Warrior. In this study, Method 4 dominated Method 6 because it provided equivalent results with fewer resources. However, in a comprehensive national security study, Method 6 offers more assurance that the model recommendations are valid because all adversaries are considered.

If short on resources, Method 4 (the Super FIS and the Insider) is the preferred way of combining multiple adversaries. Creating a hypothetical Super FIS and Insider produced *identical* countermeasure recommendations as Method 6 using 33–50% of the resources. A Super FIS becomes a composite of the FIS, information warrior, cyber-terrorist, and hacker. The Insider is included because it is significantly different from the rest. The Insider already has access that is unaffected by many boundary protection devices, such as network-based firewalls or routers, that might be recommended for the FIS. Not considering the Insider has the effect of marginally increasing security against the "outsiders" but leaves significant Insider risk.

If time is critical, Method 2 (the Super FIS only) is the preferred way of combining multiple adversaries. Even Although Methods 1 and 2 scored equivalently, it is thought that Method 2 will outperform Method 1 with a larger set of data. Although you are considering a hypothetical adversary, Super FIS is a composite of all adversaries that start their attack outside the network. The Super FIS security solution will produce results that a decision-maker can feel comfortable using to make risk-management decisions. The security solution will not be as good as a more rigorous analysis, including the insider, but will be very close. This method uses the same resources as Method 1, but helps account for a broader range of outsiders than just the FIS.

AREAS FOR FUTURE STUDY

Although this chapter sheds light on many different ways to model multiple adversaries in an information assurance risk model, there are still many other questions that remain unanswered. Eight of these are listed below:

Research Area #1 — Testing with More Data

Past logic suggests that you can either do a risk assessment can be performed quickly or correctly. This appears to be true in the case of simplistic automated tools that simplify risk assessments into one equation: Risk = Threat ∗ Vulnerability ∗ Impact. Often, this equation forces the user to perform mathematical operations on ordinal numbers, does not account for countermeasure dependencies, does not account for the negative traits of countermeasures, and cannot be optimized over a limited budget. However, there may be techniques that can speed up the process such that simplifying methods do not need to be developed, including:

- Development of a risk assessment framework that can be easily tailored by weight and value function changes in each situation.
- Development of risk teams who can operate on economies of scale.
- Data repositories that leverage off previous work.
- Automated tools that can reduce the burden of data collection.
- Pre-approved risk metrics that management understands and uses.
- Standardized weights that are representative of an organization's core values.

A good first question is how well the conclusions hold for other systems and datasets. The dataset used in this model is the only one available in the open literature. This data should be validated by computer network attack experts. New data, possibly randomly generated, should be used to test the conditions under which the results remain valid.

Research Area #2 — The Use of Influence Diagrams

A more probabilistic approach to information system risk assessment can be implemented using influence diagrams. An influence diagram is a graphic representation of the elements in a decision problem and the relationships between them. In the influence diagram shown in Figure 15, we modeled the attacking groups, attacks against the network, and different computer networks as yellow squares. These represent decisions in the

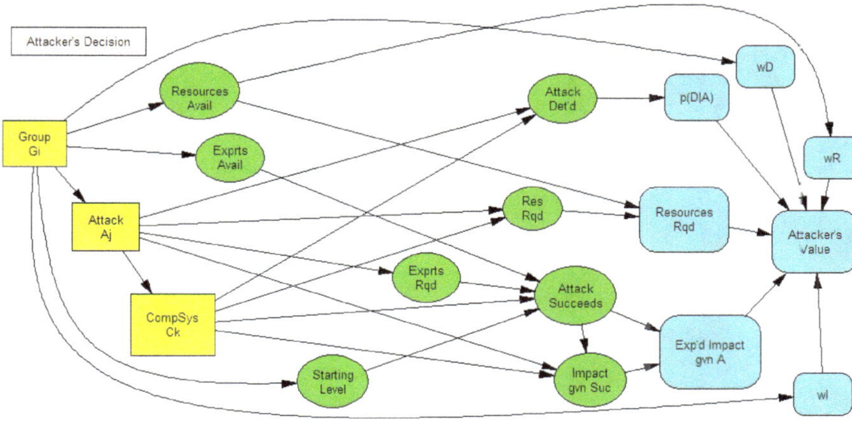

Figure 15. Attackers Influence Diagram

Gi	Ck	A1	Aj	AJ
1	1			
	2			
	3			
2	1			
	2			
	3			
...	...			
I	K			

Numbers reflect relative likelihood Gi will choose Aj against Ck

Figure 16. Adversary Attack Likelihood Chart

influence diagram. Green ovals represent uncertainties, such as the resources available to the attacker, probability of success, impact, and starting access. The blue blocks represent the values and formulae required to calculate them.

This influence diagram produces a chart of the relative likelihood that Adversary *Gi* chooses Attack *Aj* against network C_k as shown in Figure 16.

Now, the defender can create their own influence diagram and score the countermeasures based on the attack mitigation aspects of the countermeasures as well as the mission support parameters, as shown in Figure 17.

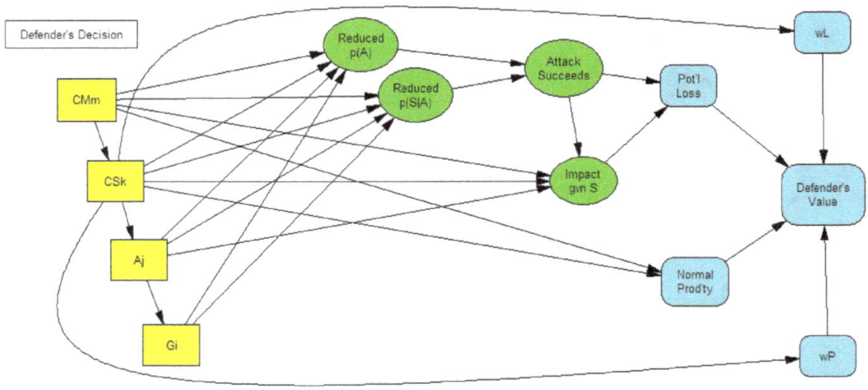

Figure 17. Defender's Influence Diagram

Finally, countermeasure strategies can be evaluated using decision trees created from the influence diagram, as shown in Figure 18.

Research Area #3 — Difference Scoring Algorithms

This study introduces the concept of translating quantitative attack values into qualitative risk assessments to provide a better picture of the actual risk level of a system from the perspectives of average portfolio risk and extreme attack risk. These ideas need to be debated and refined, and should eventually be formalized within an organization. This model used a combination of scoring techniques, including the summation of individual attack values into a portfolio that was minimized by an optimization model. There are many different ways to combine individual attack values into a portfolio and optimize the set to obtain the best security, one of which is described in Research Area #2. Other techniques might perform "better" from a customer perspective or may be more efficient, allowing the optimization of larger problems.

The concept of CyberAssurance entails not only the current level of security of a system but also how much we know about the level of security. For example, we might have a vendor who says their firewall is "unbeatable". However, we know nothing about its security because the vendor is maintaining its capabilities propriety. On the other hand, we may have a government-produced firewall that is only "pretty good", but

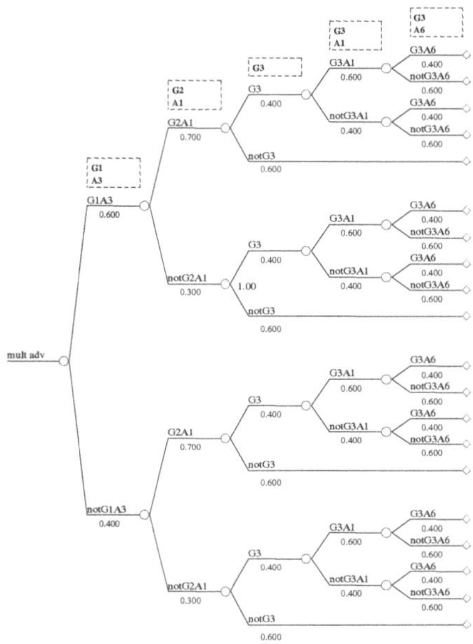

Attacks by Group

P	G1A1	G1A3	G1A6	G2A1	G2A2	G3A1	G3A4	G3A6	G3A7
P = 0.040	Y	Y	Y	Y	Y	Y	Y	Y	Y
P = 0.060	Y	Y	Y	Y	Y	Y	Y	N	Y
P = 0.027	Y	Y	Y	Y	Y	N	Y	Y	Y
P = 0.040	Y	Y	Y	Y	Y	N	Y	N	Y
P = 0.252	Y	Y	Y	Y	Y	N	N	N	N
P = 0.017	Y	Y	Y	N	Y	Y	Y	Y	Y
P = 0.026	Y	Y	Y	N	Y	Y	Y	N	Y
P = 0.012	Y	Y	Y	N	Y	N	Y	Y	Y
P = 0.017	Y	Y	Y	N	Y	N	Y	N	Y
P = 0.108	Y	Y	Y	N	Y	N	N	N	N
P = 0.027	Y	N	Y	Y	Y	Y	Y	Y	Y
P = 0.040	Y	N	Y	Y	Y	Y	Y	N	Y
P = 0.018	Y	N	Y	Y	Y	N	Y	Y	Y
P = 0.027	Y	N	Y	Y	Y	N	Y	N	Y
P = 0.168	Y	N	Y	Y	Y	N	N	N	N
P = 0.012	Y	N	Y	N	Y	Y	Y	Y	Y
P = 0.017	Y	N	Y	N	Y	Y	Y	N	Y
P = 0.008	Y	N	Y	N	Y	N	Y	Y	Y
P = 0.012	Y	N	Y	N	Y	N	Y	N	Y
P = 0.072	Y	N	Y	N	Y	N	N	N	N

Figure 18. Countermeasure Decision Tree

we are 100% certain of its vulnerability and strength. What would the decision-maker prefer? How much should be spent on testing to ensure that a product does what it is supposed to, and nothing less (or nothing more!).

This chapter introduces the simple notion that you want to prioritize risk-mitigation efforts based on what is important to you. This is the essence of the weighting objectives. New research would be helpful in developing better ways to elicit weights from at-risk participants. A formal study on this technique and software instantiation could be very helpful.

CONCLUSION

The purpose of this study was to identify the most appropriate methods for combining multiple adversaries against a computer network in an information assurance risk model. This is a very difficult problem that is even more challenging because of the lack of data. This lack of data increases the resources required to perform resource-intensive information system risk assessment. Insights into ways of combining multiple adversaries can increase the accuracy of our risk models and potentially reduce the amount of resources required.

To gain insight into this problem, we hypothesized the existence of a new and relatively unprotected government network that is of interest to multiple adversary groups. We identified attacks against the system and scored them from an adversary's perspective using parameters such as the probability that the attack would succeed and the resources required for the attack. We then created a list of possible countermeasures and quantified their benefits in terms of each adversary's preference.

We then constructed an optimization model that maximized the security of the network constrained by a limited budget. We ran this optimization against adversaries using various combinations of techniques and weights. We determined which countermeasure sets were preferred by each set of adversaries and quantified and compared the security benefits of each approach. We then analyzed how the selected countermeasure sets differed, using various combinations and weighting techniques.

The results of this analysis were promising. Some techniques for combining the effects of multiple adversaries yield identical results to those of more detailed techniques. However, there is no proof that these techniques can be extended to other networks, adversaries, assumptions, or countermeasures. For this particular model, it appears that the creation of a composite adversary can provide results similar to those of a more complex model. However, this conjecture needs to be tested with more datasets and different assumptions. It appears that if a group of adversaries is somewhat homogenous and the countermeasures affect the adversaries in a similar manner, then the composite adversary might work. Finally, we suggest that further research is needed to shed more light on shadows obscuring adversarial behavior.

REFERENCES

[1] Brooks, T. T. (Ed.) (2017). *Cyber-Assurance for the Internet of Things*. John Wiley & Sons, Hoboken, New Jersey.

[2] Brooks, T. (2022). The Professionalization of the Hacker Industry. *International Journal of Computer Science & Information Technology* (*IJCSIT*), 14(3), 87–99.

[3] Chng, S., Lu, H. Y., Kumar, A., & Yau, D. (2022). Hacker types, motivations and strategies: A comprehensive framework. *Computers in Human Behavior Reports*, 5, 100167.

[4] Cohen, F. (1997). Information system attacks: A preliminary classification scheme. *Computers & Security*, 16(1), 29–46.

[5] Gomez, M. A. & Whyte, C. (2022). Cyber uncertainties: Observations from cross-national war games. In *Cyber Security Politics* (pp. 111–127). Routledge, Milton Park, Abingdon, Oxfordshire.

[6] Kaňák, P., Piškula, J., & Dvořáková, J. (2022). Transforming the Czech (oslovak) foreign intelligence service 1990–1994. *International Journal of Intelligence and CounterIntelligence*, 35(2), 374–395.

[7] Keeney, R. L. (2008). Applying value-focused thinking. *Military Operations Research*, 13(2), 7–17.

[8] Kirkwood, C. W. (1997). *Strategic Decision Making* (p. 149). Duxbury Press, London SW1A 1NT, England.

[9] McClure, S., Scambray, J., & Kurtz, G. (2003). *Hacking Exposed: Network Security Secrets and Solutions* (Fourth Edition). McGraw-Hill/Osborne, London SW1A 1NT, England.

[10] Schneier, B. (2000). *Secrets & Lies: Digital Security in a Networked World.* Wiley, New York, NY.

[11] Watson, S. R., Buede, D. M., & Buede, D. M. (1987). *Decision Synthesis: The Principles and Practice of Decision Analysis.* Cambridge University Press, Cambridge, England.

APPENDIX A: LIST OF ADVERSARIES

Information Source Adversaries	Cohen
Foreign Intelligence Services	X
Information Warriors	X
Terrorists	X
Organized Crime	X
Other Criminals	X
The Press	X
Industrial Competitors	X
Malicious Insider	X
Hackers	X
Police	X
Crackers	X
Drug Cartels	X
Domestic Extremist/Activist	X
Private Investigator	X
Consultants	X
Vendors	X
Customers	X
Club Initiates	X
Cyber Gangs	X
Tiger Teams	X
Maintenance People	X
Professional Thieves	X
Hoodlums	X
Vandals	X
Crackers for Hire	X
Deranged People	X
Government Agencies	X
Economic rivals	X
Nation States	X
Global Coalitions	X
Military Organizations	X
Paramilitary Groups	X
Infrastructure Warriors	X
Extortionists	X

APPENDIX B: VALUE FUNCTIONS FOR EACH ADVERSARY GROUP MINIMIZE PROBABILITY OF DETECTION OBJECTIVE

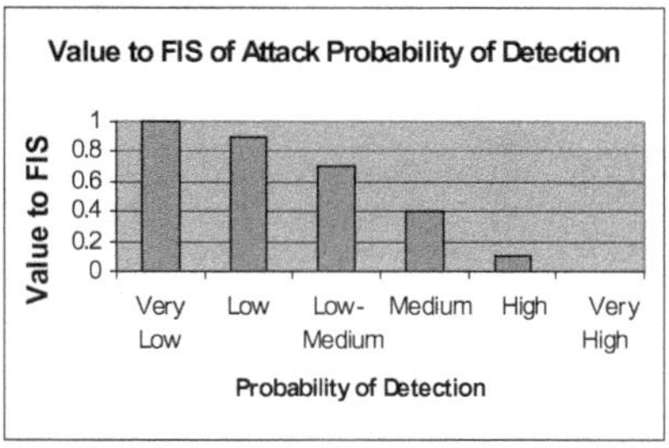

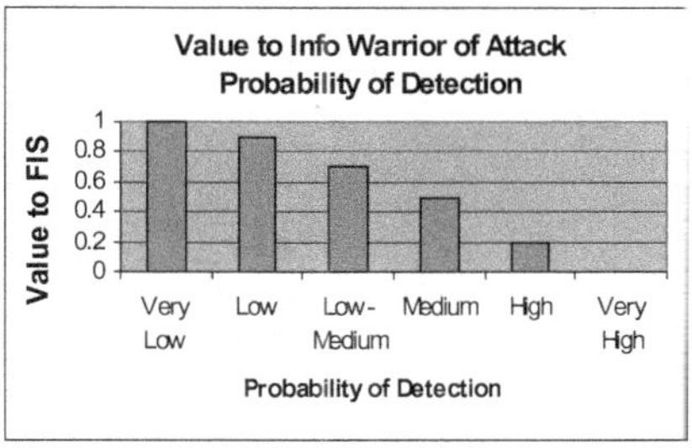

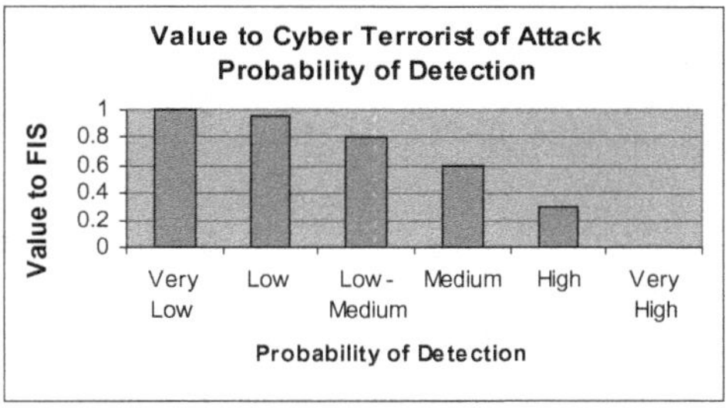

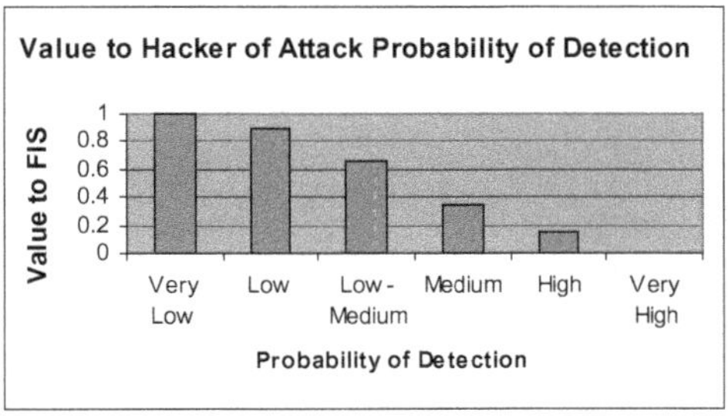

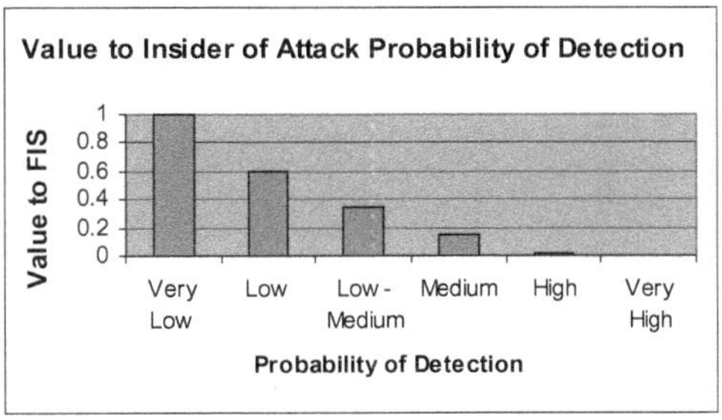

P(Detection)	Description	Example
Very Low	Passive attack with no footprint	Passively collecting traffic off a microwave link
Low	Leaves a footprint but no detection mechanism is looking for it	Installing a sniffer on a network in receive-only mode
Low-Medium	Leaves a footprint; the detection mechanism is looking for it but will typically miss it	A hook installed in software during a life cycle attack
Medium	Leaves a suspicious footprint, but may be attributed to normal behavior	Several unsuccessful login attempts
High	Leaves an audit trail, readily identifiable as anomalous behavior	Logging in as Sys Admin during unusual hours
Very High	Sets off an alarm; readily identifiable as an attack	Network flood attack

APPENDIX C: VALUE FUNCTIONS FOR EACH ADVERSARY GROUP MAXIMIZE PROBABILITY OF SUCCESS OBJECTIVE

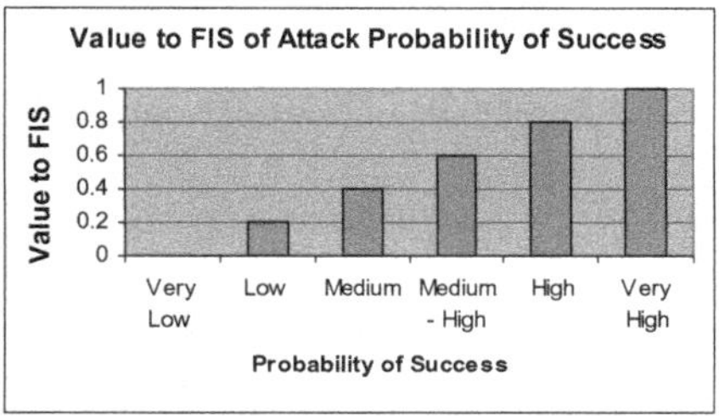

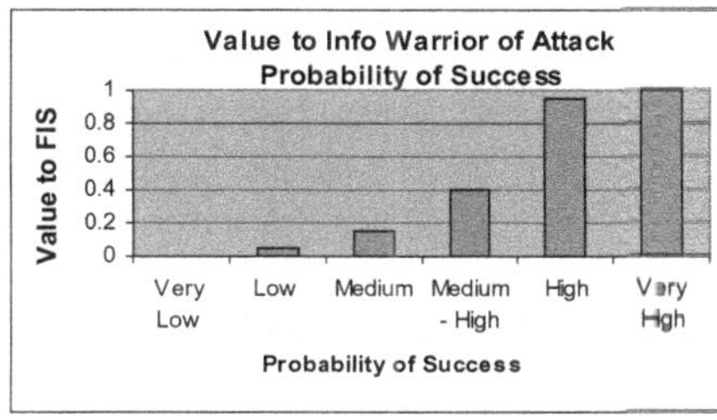

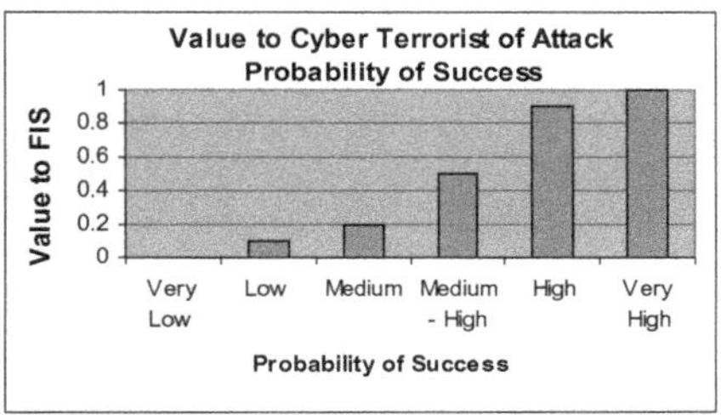

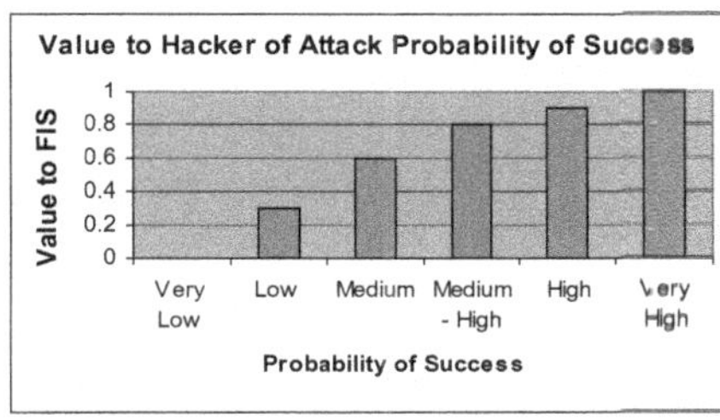

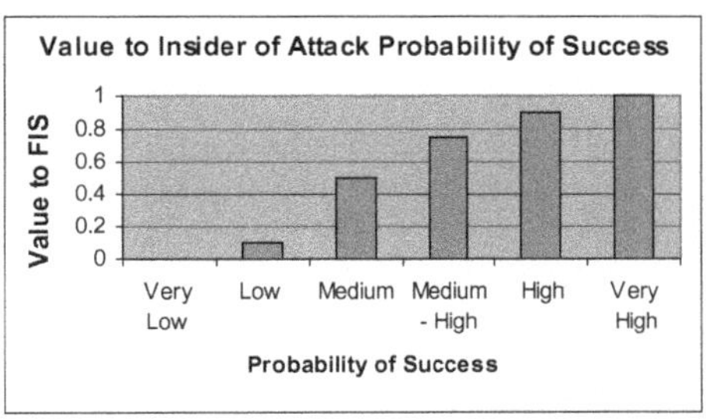

P(Success)	Description	Example
Very Low	Highly complex or difficult; no past history of success	A cryptanalytic attack against strong encryption
Low	Complex or difficult attack with little history of success	Developing a life cycle attack against a bus controller
Medium	Somewhat complex or difficult; uses known techniques in new ways; previously used with mixed success	Developing a unique attack script against off-the-shelf software or developing special-purpose hardware

(Continued)

(*Continued*)

P(Success)	Description	Example
Medium–High	Fairly simple, but still has some tricky parts; requires multiple sequential steps to gain the required access	Exploiting multiple vulnerabilities on multiple systems
High	Very simple; will work if vulnerabilities are present; frequently used successfully in the past	Exploit known vulnerabilities with off-the-shelf scripts or cracking an 8-character password
Very High	Nearly certain of success	Guessing a weak password or using a default account

APPENDIX D: VALUE FUNCTIONS FOR EACH ADVERSARY GROUP MINIMIZE RESOURCES REQUIRED OBJECTIVE

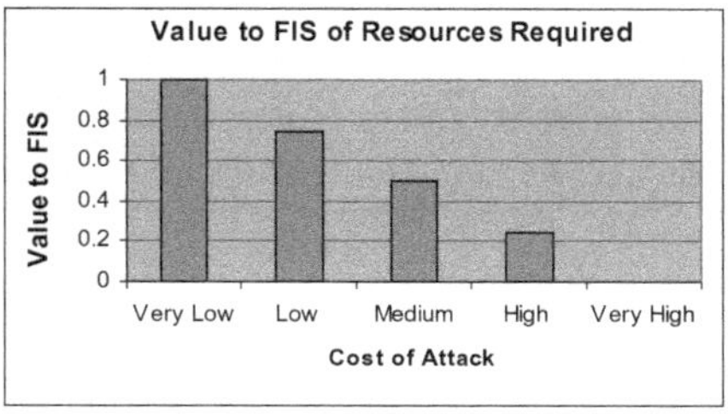

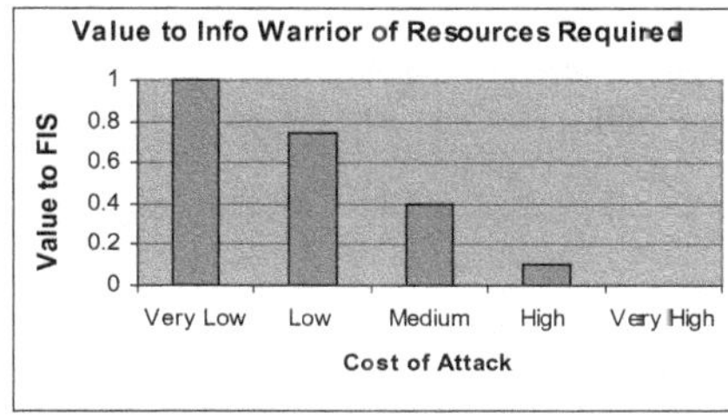

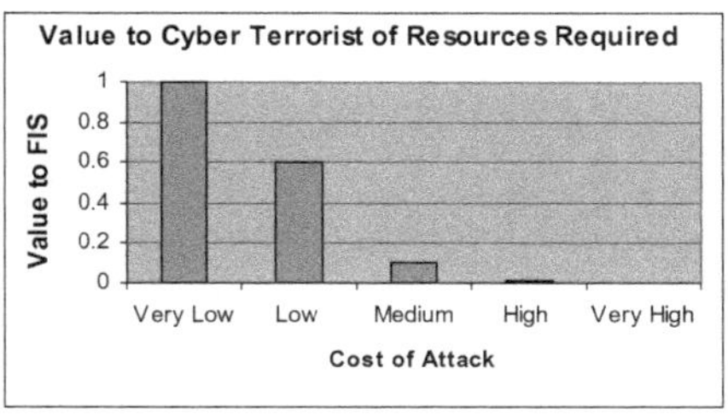

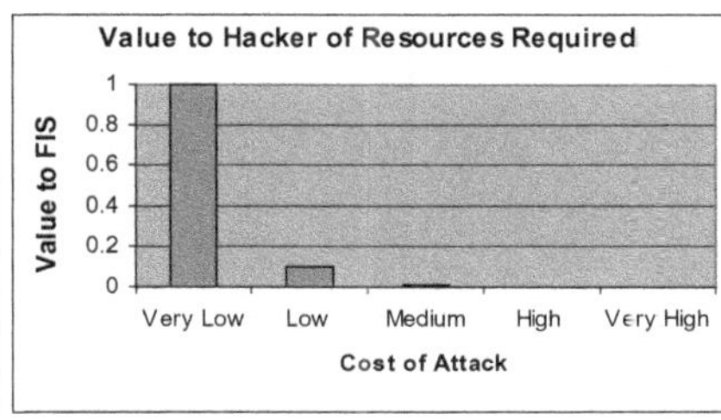

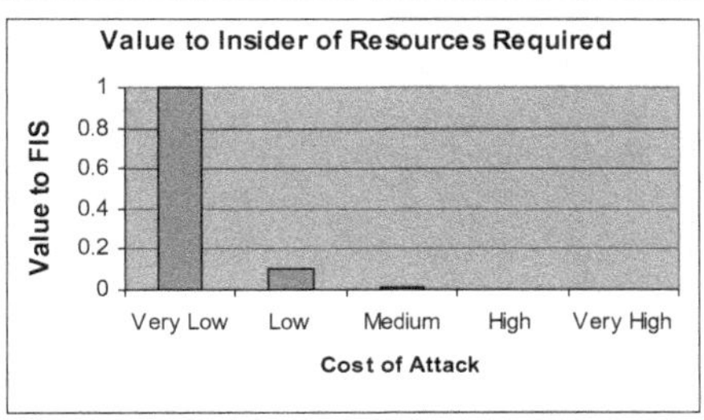

Resources Required	Definition	Example
Very Low	Less than \$10,000	Attack requires only common tools and requires days to weeks
Low	\$10,000–\$100,000	Attack requires commercially available special hardware and software and takes months to set up
Medium	\$100,000–\$500,000	Attack requires some specialized equipment and requires multiple staff for months to set up, test, and run

(*Continued*)

(*Continued*)

Resources Required	Definition	Example
High	\$500,000–\$1,000,000	Attack requires the development of specialized hardware and software, and extensive staff
Very High	Over \$1,000,000	Attack requires very sophisticated tools and techniques and substantial staff for years

APPENDIX E: COUNTERMEASURE MITIGATION DATA FOR ADVERSARIES

"Outsiders"

	Outsider Attacks Attack Name and Number	Probability Detection	Probability Success	Resources Required
	1 Brute Force Password Attack	Low-Medium	Medium-High	Very Low
CM	1 Auditing	High		
CM	2 Good Password Policies	Medium	Medium	
CM	7 Install Firewall	Medium	Low	Low
CM	8 Install VPN	Medium	Low	Low
CM	9 Intrusions Detection System	Very High		
	Combined Effect of all CMs	Very High	Very Low	Low
	2 Buffer Overflow Attacks	Low	Very High	Very Low
CM	6 Install Filtering Router	Medium	Medium	Medium
CM	7 Install Firewall	High	Low	Medium
CM	8 Install VPN	High	Low	Medium
CM	12 No-Stack Execution		Low	Low
CM	13 Restrict SUID		Low	Low
CM	14 Review & Restructure Perms	Medium	Low	Low
CM	16 Timely Patches		Low	Low
	Combined Effect of all CMs	Very High	Very Low	High
	3 Capture and Read Traffic with a sniffer	Very Low	High	Very Low
CM	3 Encryption (ILE)	Low	Very Low	Very High
CM	4 SSL/IPSEC	Medium	Low	High
CM	8 Install VPN	Medium	Very Low	Very High
	Combined Effect of all CMs	Medium	Very Low	Very High
	4 Execute a Core Dump	Low	Medium	Very Low
CM	6 Install Filtering Router	Low-Medium	Very Low	Medium
CM	7 Install Firewall	Medium	Very Low	Medium
CM	8 Install VPN	High	Very Low	Medium
CM	10 Limit Core Dumps		Low	Low
CM	16 Timely Patches		Low	Low
	Combined Effect of all CMs	Very High	Very Low	High
	5 Exploit Network File System	Low	Medium-High	Very Low
CM	1 Auditing	Medium		
CM	9 Intrusions Detection System	Medium		
CM	11 Minimize Exported File Systems		Low	Low
CM	14 Review & Restructure Perms	Low-Medium	Low	Low
CM	16 Timely Patches		Medium	Low
	Combined Effect of all CMs	High	Very Low	Medium
	6 Exploit Symlink Vulnerabilities	Low	High	Low
CM	13 Restrict SUID	High	Very Low	Medium
CM	14 Review & Restructure Perms	High	Low	Medium
	Combined Effect of all CMs	Very High	Very Low	Medium
	7 Race Conditions/Privileges	Low	Low	Medium
CM	6 Install Filtering Router	Medium	Very Low	
CM	7 Install Firewall	Medium	Very Low	High
CM	8 Install VPN	Medium	Very Low	High
CM	13 Restrict SUID		Very Low	
CM	14 Review & Restructure Perms		Very Low	High
	Combined Effect of all CMs	Very High	Very Low	Very High
	8 World Writable Files	Low	High	Very Low
CM	1 Auditing	Medium	Very Low	
CM	5 Establish User ACLs	Low	Medium	Low
CM	6 Install Filtering Router		Medium	
CM	7 Install Firewall	High	Low	Medium
CM	8 Install VPN	High	Low	Medium
CM	9 Intrusions Detection System	Medium		
CM	11 Minimize Exported File Systems		Low	Low
CM	13 Restrict SUID		Very Low	Low
CM	14 Review & Restructure Perms		Low	Low
CM	15 Select Robust Shell Environment		Medium	Low
	Combined Effect of all CMs	Very High	Very Low	Medium

"Insiders"

	Insider Attacks Attack Name and Number	Probability Detection	Probability Success	Resources Required
	9 Brute Force Password Attack	Low	Very High	Very Low
CM	1 Auditing	Very High		
CM	2 Good Password Policies	High	Medium-High	
CM	9 Intrusions Detection System	Very High		
	Combined Effect of all CMs	Very High	Low	Very Low
	10 Buffer Overflow Attacks	Low	High	Very Low
CM	12 No-Stack Execution		Low	Low
CM	13 Restrict SUID		Low	Low
CM	14 Review & Restructure Perms	Medium	Medium-High	Low
CM	16 Timely Patches		Low	Low
	Combined Effect of all CMs	Medium	Very Low	Medium
	11 Capture and Read Traffic with a sniffer	Very Low	Very High	Very Low
CM	3 Encryption (ILE)	Low	Low	Very High
CM	9 Intrusions Detection System	High		Medium
CM	4 SSL/IPSEC	Medium	Low	High
CM	8 Install VPN	Medium	Very Low	Very High
	Combined Effect of all CMs	High	Very Low	Very High
	12 Execute a Core Dump	Very Low	Very High	Very Low
CM	10 Limit Core Dumps		Medium	Low
CM	16 Timely Patches		Medium	Low
	Combined Effect of all CMs	Very Low	Very Low	Medium
	13 Exploit Network File System	Low	Very High	Very Low
CM	1 Auditing	Medium		
CM	9 Intrusions Detection System	Medium		
CM	11 Minimize Exported File Systems		Low	Low
CM	14 Review & Restructure Perms	Medium	Low	Low
CM	16 Timely Patches		Medium-High	Low
	Combined Effect of all CMs	High	Very Low	Medium
	14 Exploit Symlink Vulnerabilities	Low	Very High	Low
CM	13 Restrict SUID	Medium	Low	Medium
CM	14 Review & Restructure Perms	Medium	Low	Medium
	Combined Effect of all CMs	High	Very Low	Medium
	15 Race Conditions/Privileges	Low	Medium	Medium
CM	13 Restrict SUID	Medium	Low	
CM	14 Review & Restructure Perms	Medium	Low	High
	Combined Effect of all CMs	High	Very Low	High
	16 World Writable Files	Low	Very High	Very Low
CM	1 Auditing	Medium	Low	
CM	5 Establish User ACLs	Low-Medium	Medium	Low
CM	9 Intrusions Detection System	Medium		
CM	11 Minimize Exported File Systems		Low	Low
CM	13 Restrict SUID		Low	Low
CM	14 Review & Restructure Perms		Low	Low
CM	15 Select Robust Shell Environment		Medium-High	Low
	Combined Effect of all CMs	High	Very Low	Medium

Notes 1: The yellow line indicates the baseline values for each adversary objective before any countermeasures are implemented;

Gray boxes indicate that the countermeasure has no effect on the adversary objective;

The combined effects of all countermeasures indicate their effect on the adversary objective if every possible countermeasure is implemented. This provides a benchmark for the most attack mitigation that can be achieved.

Chapter 9

An Internet Control Device Embedded Sensor Agent (IcdESA) for Wireless Grids*

ABSTRACT

The Internet of Things (IoT) is playing a critical role in transitioning traditional application stovepipes toward an innovative Internet paradigm that facilitates processes and services in an ever-changing environment. The IoT consists of billions of Internet-connected devices (ICDs), or "things", each possessing the ability to sense, communicate, compute, and potentially actuate. These ICDs, which may include sensors, radio frequency identification (RFID) devices, social media platforms, clickstreams, business transactions, actuators, and laboratory instruments, can exhibit intelligence, multimodal interfaces, and physical/virtual identities and attributes. Wireless grid applications have become instrumental in driving the IoT ecosystem, extending connectivity from the cloud to the edge. However, the IoT faces numerous technology challenges. These include leveraging and integrating existing systems and technologies, achieving interoperability with IPv6 networks, and enabling rapid responses to malicious events and comprehensive analysis of accumulated malicious information. Moreover, the challenges

*Originally published as Brooks, T. (2020). An internet control device embedded sensor agent. *International Journal of Internet of Things and Cyber-Assurance*, 1(3–4), 267–290.

include minimizing new IoT system deployments. New IoT networks, with their inherent vulnerabilities, can be exploited by cybercriminals to pose serious threats to the IoT infrastructure. As organizations and individuals increasingly rely on information dependent on IoT systems, these systems become more susceptible to exposed cyber-attacks. As the IoT continues to amalgamate new transmission and processing technologies (e.g., satellite and mobile communications networks) into one highly integrated network, many access points become easy targets for hackers. Often, pinpointing the source or location of these cyber-attacks is complex, making it difficult to determine the intent of the attack accurately. Consequently, once IoT devices and networks are attacked and neutralized, their processing capabilities can be severely compromised. This chapter delves deeper into the details of an ICD-embedded sensor agent for IoT architectures and discusses the area of Cyber-Assurance. This domain is critical as a means for IoT smart devices and networks to autonomously secure themselves against security threats. The concept of cyber-assurance must ensure embedded security within these IoT devices to allow these new networks to function correctly, even when subjected to a cyber-attack.

INTRODUCTION

Our nation's security, from the battlefield to the homeland, is increasingly dependent on the security of Cloud computing, a rapidly emerging platform for running networked services [46]. Unfortunately, our increasing dependence on "the Cloud" makes it an increasingly attractive target for adversaries. Our nation's enemies have grown adept at a wide range of cyber-attacks, including theft of confidential information, implanting and remotely executing malicious code, and launching denial-of-service (DoS) attacks [32]. Unfortunately, the unique properties of Fog computing and the Cloud make it difficult to counter these attacks [19]. The high processing speed and tight coupling of these systems enable attacks to progress much faster than humans can react. The large scale, coupled with the ability of adversaries to encrypt and "hide" sensitive information, makes it difficult to observe and attribute an adversary's activities; running multiple services on the same servers and network elements means that compromising one (perhaps less secure) service enables adversaries to attack another.

However, achieving these dynamic capabilities today with Cloud computing is difficult because existing networking technology is surprisingly brittle [5]. Traditional network protocols do not allow us to run multiple copies of networks, manipulate their speed, or retain fine-grained control over their execution. The root of the problem is that network logic is tightly coupled with the physical network equipment. In contrast, virtualization has been widely studied in the context of individual server machines [6]. Virtual machines (VMs) enable tight control over software execution, strong isolation between different software instances, and migrating of running software from one physical location to another [6]. The plan is to develop a new Internet-connected device embedded sensor agent (IcdESA) through a previously published *Recognition, Fortification, Reestablishment, and Survivability* (R^2FS) process — that enables the automatic construction and manipulation of logically independent and self-contained virtual cyber domains.

DEPLOYMENT MODELS

The definition of cloud computing is:

> "… is a model for enabling convenient, on-demand network access to a shared pool of configurable computing resources (e.g., networks, servers, storage, applications, and services) that can be rapidly provisioned and released with minimal management effort or service provider interaction."[1]

Moving information assets to cloud computing offers the potential for reduced costs, on-demand self-service, ubiquitous network access, location-independent resource pooling, rapid elasticity, and measured service for the cloud user. At its essence, cloud computing is a pay-per-use model for enabling available, convenient, on-demand network access to a shared pool of configurable computing resources (e.g., networks, servers, storage, applications, services) that can be rapidly provisioned and released with minimal management effort or service provider interaction.

The four deployment models for cloud services are listed and defined in Table 1. Any cloud, regardless of its service deployment or architecture,

[1] Please see http://csrc.nist.gov/groups/SNS/cloud-computing/index.html.

Table 1. Types of Cloud Computing

Type of Cloud	Definition
Private Cloud	The cloud infrastructure is owned or leased by a single organization and is operated solely for that organization.
Community Cloud	The cloud infrastructure is shared by several organizations and supports a specific community that has shared concerns (e.g., mission, security requirements, policy, and compliance considerations).
Public Cloud	The cloud infrastructure is owned by an organization selling cloud services to the general public or to a large industry group.
Hybrid Cloud	The cloud infrastructure is a composition of two or more clouds (private, community, or public) that remain unique entities but are bound together by standardized or proprietary technology that enables data and application portability.

Note: Currently the public model is not considered appropriate for public sector use, in part due to security concerns. However, it is possible that some use for a public cloud will be determined in the future.

can be internal or external: internal clouds reside *inside* an organization's network security perimeter while external clouds reside *outside* the same perimeter. The Federal government will likely use some combination of the deployment models described below, with the likely exception of the public model.

The three delivery models used within cloud computing are listed below, and also depicted in Figure 1 are:

- **Software-as-a-Service (SaaS):** The capability provided to the consumer is to use the provider's applications running on a cloud infrastructure and accessible from various client devices through a thin client interface such as a Web browser (e.g., web-based email). The consumer does not manage or control the underlying cloud infrastructure, network, servers, operating systems, storage, or even individual application capabilities, with the possible exception of limited user-specific application configuration settings.
- **Platform-as-a-Service (PaaS):** The capability provided to the consumer is to deploy onto the cloud infrastructure consumer-created applications using programming languages and tools supported by the provider (e.g., java, python, .Net). The consumer does not manage or control the underlying cloud infrastructure, network, servers,

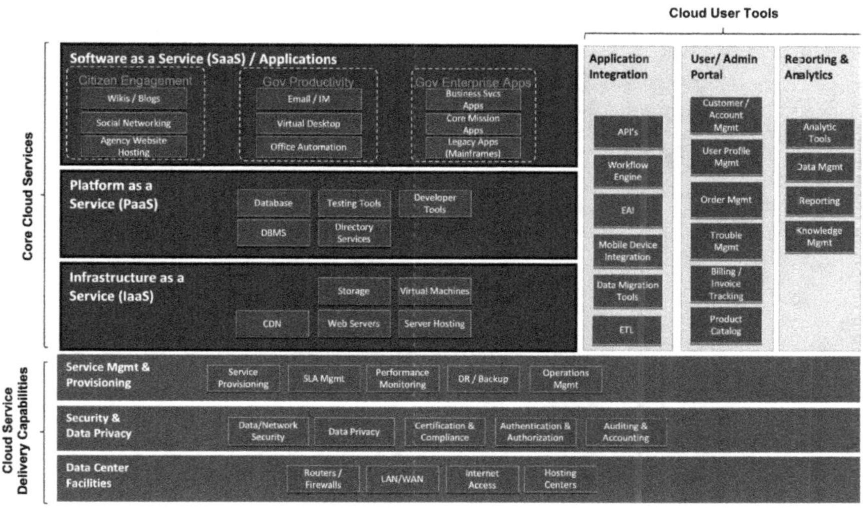

Figure 1. A Cloud Computing Framework

operating systems, or storage, but the consumer has control over the deployed applications and possibly application hosting environment configurations.

- **Infrastructure-as-a-Service (IaaS):** The capability provided to the consumer is to rent processing, storage, networks, and other fundamental computing resources where the consumer is able to deploy and run arbitrary software, which can include operating systems and applications. The consumer does not manage or control the underlying cloud infrastructure but has control over operating systems, storage, deployed applications, and possibly select networking components (e.g., firewalls, and load balancers).

A wireless grid refers to a network infrastructure that enables the interconnection and communication of multiple devices or systems through wireless connections (see Figure 2) [6]. It is a distributed network that allows devices to seamlessly exchange data, share resources, and collaborate without the need for physical cables or wired connections and the devices can be mobile or stationary and can range from sensors, actuators, and smartphones to computers, appliances, and other IoT-enabled devices. These devices communicate with each other using wireless communication technologies such as Wi-Fi, Bluetooth, Zigbee, or cellular networks.

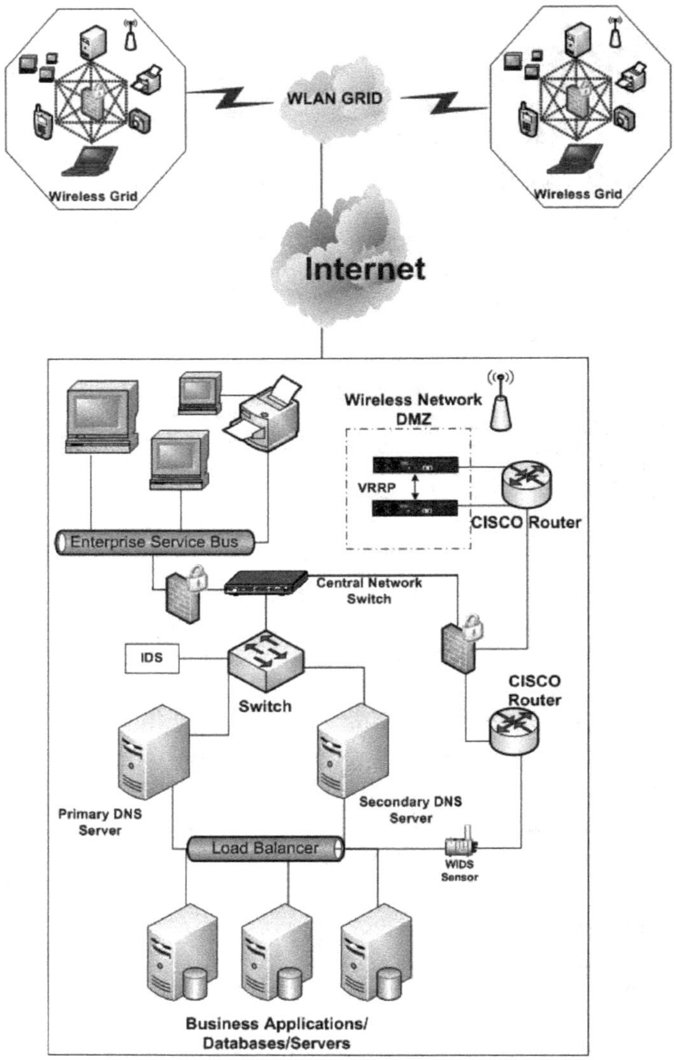

Figure 2. Basic Wireless Grid

The wireless grid infrastructure provides the necessary connectivity and networking capabilities to facilitate data transmission and exchange between devices.

Wireless grids are commonly deployed in various domains, including smart cities, industrial automation, healthcare systems, transportation, and

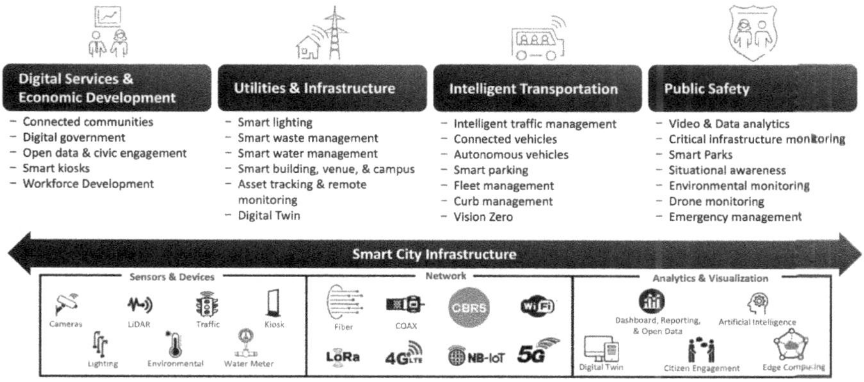

Figure 3. Sample Smart City

public safety (see Figure 3). They enable the integration of diverse devices and systems, allowing for real-time data collection, analysis, and decision-making. By leveraging wireless grid technology, organizations can create interconnected ecosystems that optimize resource utilization, enhance operational efficiency, and enable innovative applications. The concept of a wireless grid goes beyond traditional wireless networks by emphasizing the integration of multiple devices and systems into a cohesive and intelligent network. It enables devices to operate collectively, leveraging each other's capabilities and resources, thereby creating a more efficient and adaptable network infrastructure.

RECOGNITION, FORTIFICATION, REESTABLISHMENT, AND SURVIVABILITY (R²FS)

The robustness of cyber-assurance to the subversion of the IoT security methods is critical since the threat of information systems subversion presents a significant risk [3]. Information assurance (IA) for IoT networks is reliant on the security of its backbone architecture and the smart ICD providing networked services [40]. In order to perform successful cyber-assurance techniques, the process itself that carries it out must be trusted. This requires that the process itself be robust and resistant to the type of cyber-attacks that may be leveled against it. As a result, the level of trust associated with the cyber-assurance process must be evaluated in light of the assumed threat profile, which may be different for each individual ICD and/or IoT network. The detection of any alarm condition should immediately initiate steps to protect all information and resources that are being protected by the ICD. Although the security processor chips do contain hardware devices intended to monitor these indicators and raise an alarm if any out-of-bound condition is detected, this is typically not the case for other ICDs in this type of environment.

RECOGNITION

Due to the wireless nature of the IoT, ICDs in use will autonomously power up and participate in data transactions. An ICD may (or may not) have an integrated power source but instead rely upon readers, authenticators, etc., between other ICDs or cloud computing environments. Using gateway portals to radiate an antenna field that is able to detect the transmission of another ICD, the ICD may convert the signal to a radio frequency identification (RFID)/electrical current and store it in a capacitor [7, 24]. When the capacitor reaches a threshold level, it will discharge thereby powering the ICD and its transmitter to send data to other ICDs or Fog-cloud computing environments in IoT networks as displayed in Figure 4. Upon detecting the ICD, these readers, authenticators, etc., will have to detect valid RFID/electrical currents to perform IoT-defined shared-secret challenge-response protocols with other ICDs or IoT devices to establish a secure session or tunnel for data communications.

Recognition includes the identification of a cyber-attack being performed leading to the fortification of smart ICDs before gaining access to IoT networks and systems. Because of the availability of random access

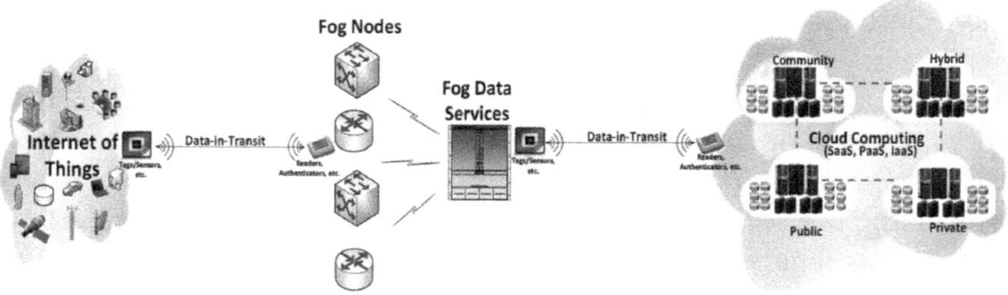

Figure 4. IoT Data-in-Transit

functions in the IoT, its devices and networks must possess a function of automatic malicious identity recognition. The ICD design efforts should focus on determining whether and how a given ICD's insecure security behaviors can be reconciled with the required security properties and behaviors of the IoT system as a whole. At a more concrete level, the ICD design should focus on determining whether the ICD sensor agent (i.e., a central embedded microprocessor) has been implemented within the integrated/assembled system with whatever countermeasures (e.g., security wrappers, virtual machines/sandboxes, application-level firewalls, etc.) are necessary to protect it from detrimental effects of any insecure standards and technologies used in that ICD sensor agent's development.

The ICD sensor agent should automatically recognize and verify the identities of malicious activities (e.g., virus, worms, trojan horses, attack scripts, logic bombs, etc.) that is trying to gain random access to the IoT system through automatic detection techniques and should be able to distinguish whether the information that is trying to enter the IoT Fog-Cloud system is valid or malicious. Through self-monitoring when an outside attack is threatening the safety of the system, an ICD sensor agent should be able to connect to the corresponding defense fortification process.

To defend against cyber-attacks amongst ICDs and IoT networks, identification of the cyber-attack through an embedded ICD sensor agent, as shown in Figure 5, is installed for operations in ICDs and IoT network environments. These ICD sensor agents should be designed in ICDs and IoT networks consisting of several components that can form resistors and be connected as voltage dividers on ICD motherboards/chips.

As data originates within IoT networks in the higher layers of the Open Systems Interconnection (OSI) model, the protocols at these layers pass the data down to lower layers for transmission and it will take the form of discrete messages. Upon data receipt, each lower-level protocol takes the entire contents of the message received and encapsulates it into its own message format, adding a header and possibly a footer that contains important control information through encapsulation.

This is an adaptation of Figure 6, a very similar drawing for the OSI Reference Model as a whole, showing specifically how data encapsulation is accomplished in Transmission Control Protocol/Internet Protocol (TCP/IP). As displayed, an upper-layer message is packaged into a TCP/User Datagram Protocol (UDP) message. This then becomes the payload of an IP datagram, which is shown here simply with one-header things, and can get a bit more complex than this. The IP datagram is then passed down to

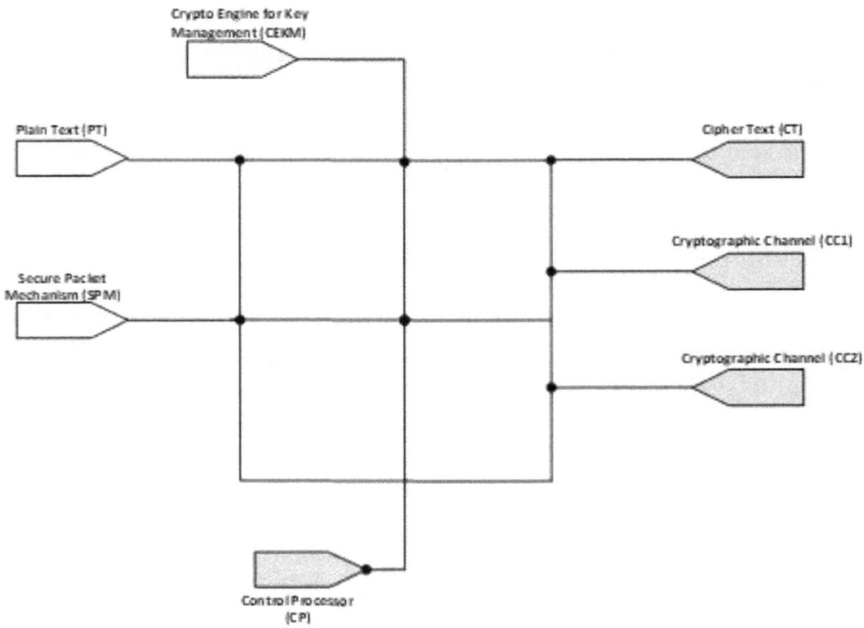

Figure 5. ICD Embedded Sensor Agent

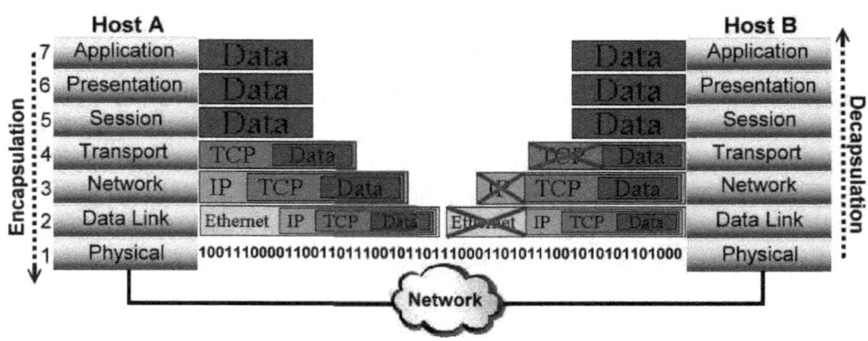

Figure 6. Data Encapsulation

layer 2 where it is in turn encapsulated into some sort of local area network (LAN), wide area network (WAN), or wireless local area network (WLAN) frame, then converted to bits and transmitted at the physical layer.

Currently, after data is encapsulated into an IP datagram, it is passed down to the data link layer for transmission across the current "hop" of the internetwork. There, it is of course further encapsulation, IP header and all, into a data link layer frame such as an Ethernet frame. An IP datagram may be encapsulated into many such data link layer frames as its routed across the internetwork; on each hop, the IP datagram is removed from the data link layer frame and then repackaged into a new one for the next hop. The IP datagram, however, is not changed (except for some control fields) until it reaches its final destination.

Due to the prominence of TCP/IP, the IP is one of the most important places where data encapsulation occurs on modern networks. However, as new IoT protocols such as infrastructure (e.g., 6LowPAN, IPv4/IPv6, etc.), identification (e.g., EPC, uCode, IPv6, URIs), communications/transport (e.g., Wifi, Bluetooth, LPWAN), discovery (e.g., Physical Web, mDNS, DNS-SD), data protocols (e.g., MQTT, CoAP, AMQP, Websocket, Node, etc.), device management (e.g., TR-069, OMA-DM), semantic (e.g., JSON-LD, Web Thing Model) and multi-layer (e.g., Alljoyn, IoTivity, Weave, Homekit) are developed and implemented, the encapsulation, formatting and processing of data will still exist at the bit level [45].

Once data is processed from a device to an IoT Fog-Cloud network/ system at the bit level, the following process occurs simultaneously:

Step 1: The ICD sensor agent receives a data packet (e.g., IPv4, IPv6, wireless, wired, etc.) and sends the data to a **custom cryptographic channel processor (CCP)** designed to support high-performance cryptographic algorithms (e.g., elliptic curve cryptography, field programmable gate arrays, etc.); for performing operations for cryptographic applications and a bus for connecting each processor to central processing unit (CPU) [18, 24]. These [future] algorithms will be designed, developed, and implemented using a Crypto domain-specific language (DSL), a language designed from the development of cryptographic algorithms for the protection of all data [2, 28].

Step 2: The ICD sensor agent processes any plain and cipher text using a **plaintext (PT)** and **cipher text (CT)** interface processors that buffer the input/output (I/O) between the crypto processors.

Step 3: The **secure packet mechanism (SPM)** initiates countermeasures to confine data and stop processing if malicious activity is found amongst the PT and CT. Malicious data is sent to the control processor and the control processor revokes any attempt to obtain a token since the data is identified as malicious. The SPM is connected to the ICD Senor Agent Voltage Ladder displayed in Figure 4.

Step 4: The **crypto engine for key management (CEKM)** purpose is the support the key management functions in support of the custom crypto processors [31, 39, 47]. The CEKM is a general-purpose processor with a multi-level operating system offering significant assurance of separation between tasks and providing key management functions in support of the custom crypto processors [17, 31, 38, 47]. The CEKM runs a secure operation system, which provides tasks and object separation, and the ICD agent, should support at least 1024 simultaneous channels [17, 31, 38].

Step 5: The ICD sensor agent provides two kinds of separation between the **cryptographic channels (CC)**. The CC are supported by several processors that form the lower part of the ICD sensor agent. The CC combines to support up to 1024 separate CCs. The **secure control processor (SCP)** ensures that the CCs and the I/O processors (PT and CT) perform in a manner that provides channel separation between the active channels flowing through the ICD sensor agent. The CC also supports cryptographic channel separation through its support of fast context switching between the channels. Each channel has a (possibly different) cryptographic algorithm and key. When a channel is swapped out in favor of another channel, the algorithm and key are swapped out of the memory used by the CC1 or CC2. The channel can be swapped out to RAM on board the ICD sensor agent or to external memory. When it is swapped to external memory, it is stored in encrypted format. The support for context switching ensures that channel algorithms, keys, and states are kept separate even for inactive channels. The SPM initiates countermeasures to confine data and stop processing if malicious activity is found. Data is then sent to the SCP and the SCP revokes any attempt to obtain a token since the data is malicious.

By installing these embedded ICD sensor agent tracers within different ICDs and changing the traces (e.g., configuration) depending on the ICD type, an intrusion could be detected if the traces are broken or shorted together. For example, a three-channel circuit can be configured by providing a voltage between nodes A through D. Nodes B, D, and E would each have a voltage of ½ positive-voltage supply (Vcc) with respect to ground if all the resistive elements are equal. If a resistor on a single channel is broken then the node voltage will become Vcc or ground. If both resistors were broken, then the node would float. To detect this, a pull-down resistor is required for each channel.

Shorting two resistors together will change the two node voltages to be either 2/3 Vcc or 1/3 Vcc. Finally, shorting Vcc to Ground (Gnd) can also be detected since all node voltages would then become 0V. To detect all the possible changes on each node, a circuit will need to be able to determine if the voltage of a node moves outside of an accepted operating window. To accomplish this, each channel requires two comparators, one to detect if the node voltage goes above a reference and one to detect if the node voltage goes below a reference. For the 3-channel sensor example, six comparators are required and the outputs are wired together as open drains to pull a detection signal low.

A voltage ladder is used to provide the high and low reference voltages as displayed in Figure 7. For the example above using standard resistor values, Ref_1 would be approximately 60% of boosted power supply voltage (BVCC) and Ref_2 would be 40% of BVCC. These voltage references can be shared between all three comparators if they have high-impedance inputs. The window is wide enough to detect some drift and noise, but still detect the tamper conditions described previously. Sharing the references and using the open-drain comparators helps to minimize component count.

Filtering is required on each channel node to maintain reliable operation. Malfunctions from the power supply of electromagnetic interface (EMI) could cause a false positive. This problem is made worse by the fact that the current at each node is very small. Filtering capacitors help to maintain the node and reference voltage. Unfortunately, this filtering causes delays in the response time of the detection signal. If a mesh trace is broken, it will take time for the voltage across the node filtering capacitor to change. This change could take several seconds to be detected by the comparators. The worst case is if two resistors are broken and a node is left floating, then the time to discharge the filtering cap will be dependent on the pull-down resistance for the node. To minimize current consumption, this resistance is very high.

Integrating the tamper circuit into a single ICD will reduce the board component count, power consumption, and cost. The example design uses six Maxim 9120 comparators each drawing 350 milliamps (mA). This pushes the power requirements for the design to over 2 microamperes (uA).

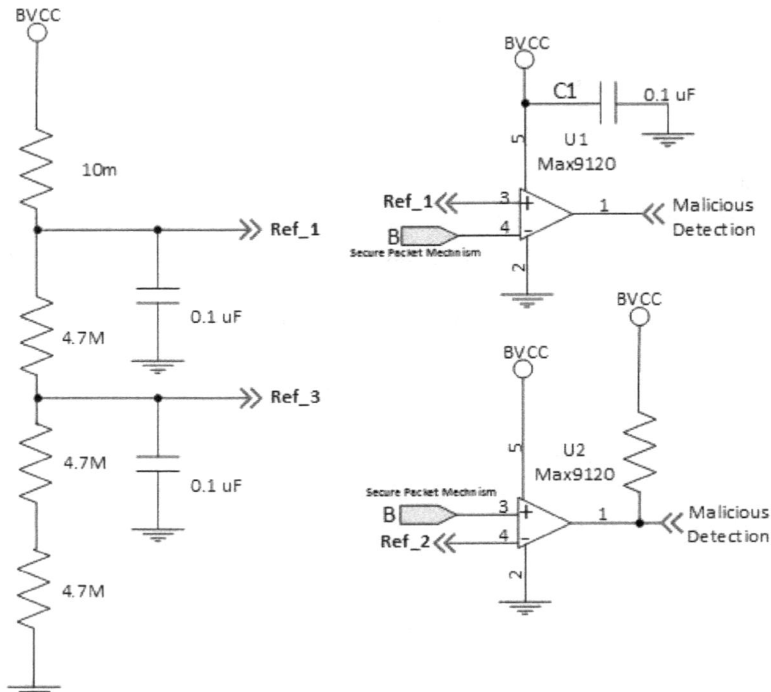

Figure 7. ICD Sensor Agent Voltage Ladder

not including the pull-down resistors and the voltage dividers created by the sensor. This current consumption is also in addition to any required real-time clocks and battery-backed random-access memory (RAM). The actual operating current is closer to 4 uA. Using a 180-milliampere-hour (mAh) battery would yield 5 years of reliable operation if left unpowered. When active, the sensor circuit is powered from the main supply, bypassing the battery.

To detect any malicious tamper the ICD sensor agent would constantly change the value on the output port. The input port would then be read and if the values match, then the traces are intact. If a trace is broken, then it would be detected when it is pulled high during a sequence. If a trace is shortened, it will be driven by an adjacent trace. The response time of this design depends on the number of signals and how fast a pattern can be applied and detected. In addition, the pattern should be random and hard to predict by an attacker. The main advantage of this design is the integration of the ICD sensor agent microcontroller with the necessary comparators to monitor the ICD which may be running at all times, it offers a higher degree of integration to reduce component and board count and needs increased performance to run fast enough to detect a malicious condition. Confining data to a single machine, either by physically disconnecting the machine or by leveraging access controls, can severely limit usability or prevent the sharing of information inside a secure network.

The ICD sensor agent needs to simplify the problem of virtual-link embedding by allowing the IoT networks to map a virtual link to multiple paths with a flexible path-splitting ratio for ICDs [10, 11, 41]. In addition, for efficient handling of online requests, the ICD needs to allow the ICD data to periodically re-optimize the mapping of existing virtual links, by either selecting new underlying paths or adapting the splitting ratios for the existing paths [10, 11, 41]. Flexible path splitting is realizable in practice without disrupting the basic properties of a link — such as predictable bandwidth, propagation delay, and in-order packet delivery [10, 11, 41]. Flexible path splitting allows the ICD to map virtual links to the IoT in polynomial time while making much more efficient use of IoT bandwidth and increasing robustness to IoT failures. This feature allows the ICD embedding algorithm not to assume any special capabilities from the network.

RECOGNITION ICD EMBEDDING ALGORITHM FOR DATA PROCESSING

The notations of the recognition ICD embedding problem can be defined as [8, 54]:

G^s = Fog-Cloud IoT network;
N^s = Nodes of Fog-Cloud IoT network;
L^s = Links of Fog-Cloud IoT network;
A_N^s = Node attribute of Fog-Cloud IoT network;
A_L^s = Link attribute of Fog-Cloud IoT network;
P^s = Paths on Fog-Cloud IoT network;
G^v = Virtual Fog-Cloud IoT network;
N^v = Nodes of virtual Fog-Cloud IoT network;
L^v = Links of virtual Fog-Cloud IoT network;

C_N^v = Node constraint of Fog-Cloud IoT network;
C_L^v = Link constraint of Fog-Cloud IoT network;
R_N = Resources allocated for virtual Fog-Cloud IoT network nodes;
R_L = Resources allocated for virtual Fog-Cloud IoT network links.

The IoT network is denoted by an undirected graph $G^s = (N^s, L^s, A^s{}_N, A^s{}_L)$, where N^s and L^s refer to the set of nodes and links, respectively. Use superscript to refer to IoT virtual network (VN), and use subscript to refer to nodes or links, unless otherwise specified. IoT nodes and links are associated with their attributes, denoted by $A^s{}_N$ and $A^s{}_L$, respectively. For the ICD embedded sensor agent, consider CPU capacity and location for node attributes, and bandwidth capacity for link attributes. Also, denote by *Ps* the set of all loop-free paths in the IoT network. The numbers near the links represent available bandwidths and the numbers in rectangles are the available CPU resources at the nodes as displayed in Figure 5.

Denoted by an undirected graph $G^v = (N^v, L^v, C_N^v, C_L^v)$ for a VN request, a VN request typically has link and node constraints that are specified in terms of attributes of the IoT network. C_L^v and C_N^v the set of link and node constraints, is denoted respectively. Figure 8 depicts two VN requests: the VN request 1 requires the bandwidth 20 over the links (*a*, *b*) and (*a*, *c*), and the CPU resource 10 at all nodes, *a*, *b*, and *c*; the VN request 2 is: connect two nodes $d, e \in N^v$ with constraints that node *d* should be in Location 1 (where nodes D & G are located), and node *e* should be in Location 2 (where node E & I are located), with 10 units of bandwidth on the virtual link between them.

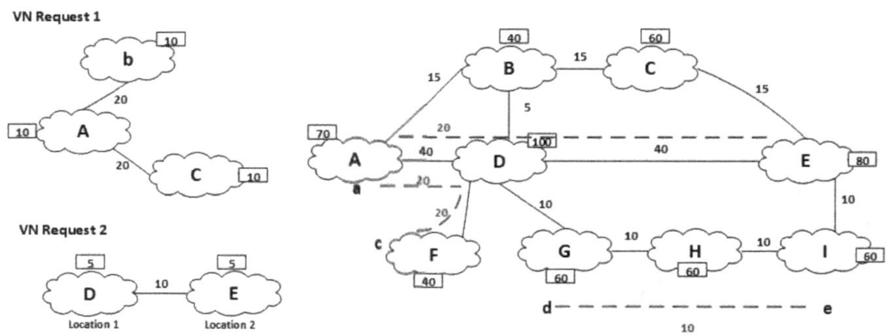

Figure 8. ICD Recognition Embedding

A virtual network embedding for a VN request is defined as a mapping M from G^v to a subset of G^s, such that the constraints in G^v are satisfied, i.e., [8, 54]

$$M: G^v \rightarrow (N', P', R_N, R_L) \quad (1)$$

where $N' \subset N^s$ and $P' \subset P^s$, and R_N and R_L are the node and link resources allocated for the VN requests. The VN network embedding can be naturally decomposed into node and link mapping as follows [8, 54]:

$$\text{Node Mapping: } M^N: (N^v, C_N^v) \rightarrow (N', R_N) \quad (2)$$

$$\text{Link Mapping: } M^L: (L^v, C_L^v) \rightarrow (P', R_L) \quad (3)$$

The right side of Figure 8 shows the VN embedding solutions for the two VN requests. For example, the nodes a, b, and c in VN request 1 are mapped to the IoT nodes A, E, and F, and the virtual links (a, b) and (a, c) are mapped to the IoT paths (A, D, E) and (A, D, F) with the CPU and bandwidth constraints all satisfied. A similar mapping occurs for VN request 2.

The main interest is to propose an efficient embedding algorithm for the recognition problem when a cyber-attack occurs, where VN requests arrive and depart over time. From the IoT network provider's point of view, a natural objective of an online embedding algorithm would be to maximize the revenue. The introduction of the notion of revenue that corresponds to the economic benefit of accepting VN requests is denoted by $R(G^v(t))$ the revenue of serving the VN requests at time t. Then, the objective is to maximize the long-term average revenue, given by the following [8, 54]:

$$\lim_{n\to\infty} \frac{\sum_{t=0}^{T} R(G^v(t))}{T} \quad (4)$$

The revenue can be defined in various ways according to economic models. In this design, the focus is on bandwidth and CPU as the main IoT network resources. Then, a natural choice of the revenue for a VN request would be the weighted sum of revenues for bandwidth and CPU, each of which is proportional to the amount of the requested resources. Thus, for a VN request G^v, revenue $R(G^v(t))$ is defined at any particular time t that the virtual network G^v is running as [8, 54]:

$$R(G^v(t)) = \sum_{l^v \in L^v} bw(l^v) + \propto \sum_{n^v \in N^v} \text{CPU}(n^v) \quad (5)$$

where bw(l^v) and CPU(n^v) are the bandwidth and CPU requirements for the virtual link l^v and the virtual node n^v, respectively. It's noted that the bandwidth revenue [i.e., the first term in Equation (5)] is not affected by the IoT paths that the virtual links are mapped to, in particular, physical distance or the number of hops of the mapped paths. This seems to be reasonable since VN requests only care about the satisfiability of their constraints in the IoT network and may not pay for longer distances.

To achieve the goal in Equation (5), it is crucial to embed incoming VN requests efficiently to determine malicious or non-malicious activities, such that the IoT resource is minimally occupied. This is because an inefficient embedding of a virtual network at time t may restrict the IoT's ability to accept future requests. Therefore, this simple embedding algorithm does not exploit any special capabilities from the IoT network. This algorithm collects a group of incoming requests during a time window and then tries to identify if the data is malicious or not and then allocates IoT resources to satisfy the constraints required by the requests to continue data processing. Some requests may be deferred due to lack of bandwidth or CPU resources in the IoT network and returned to the request queue. The requests in the queue are dropped if they cannot be served within some delay, which, specified by a request, corresponds to the time that a request is willing to wait. The requests in the request queue are processed again in the subsequent time windows.

Fog-Cloud IoT virtual networks may have strict requirements that preclude path splitting. As such, the following algorithms should handle a mix of all kinds of VN requests that are authorized for processing. As illustrated in Figure 9, when ICD requests are received in the IcdESA, first apply Algorithm 1 to determine if the data can continue to be processed. Continue to Algorithm 2 for link mapping, Algorithm 3 for requests for path splitting, and Algorithm 4 for path multiplicity. Unfortunately, node-remapping is difficult to perform for the unsplittable virtual links since the embedding algorithm processes one virtual link at a time. For the collection of virtual links that fail to find a suitable path, it may not be easily identified as the most congested link in a computationally efficient manner. To maintain computational simplicity, do not consider node-remapping for these requests.

The ICD embedded sensor agent processes all VN requests arriving within the time window as well as in the request queue, in decreasing order of their revenues. It then maps virtual nodes onto the IoT network for all the considered VN requests, and then maps the virtual links for the

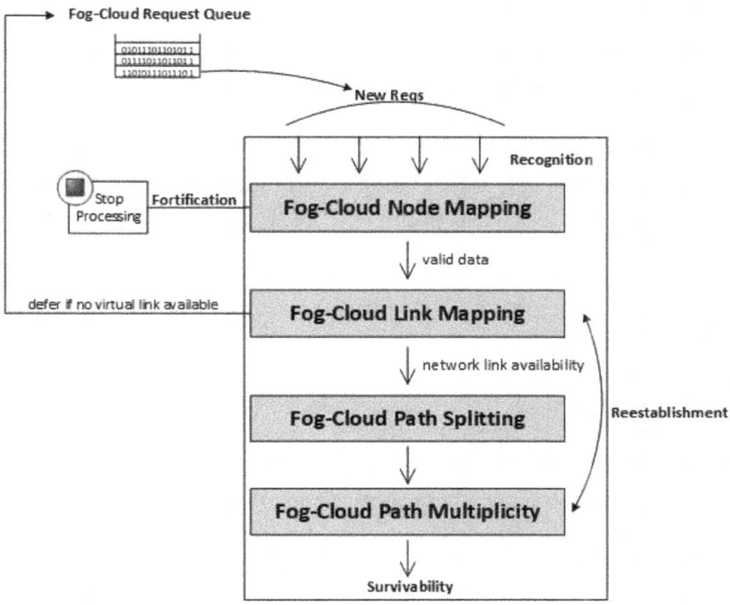

Figure 9. ICD Embedded Sensor Agent Algorithms

Algorithm 1. Fog-Cloud Node Mapping Algorithm

1: Determine malicious data from the device: $G^s = (N^s, L^s, A^s_N, A^s_L)$,
2: If malicious, stop the request and begin fortification.
3: If not malicious, sort the request according to its revenues.
4: If no request is left, stop.
5: Take one request with the largest revenue: $G^v = (N^v, L^v, C_N^v, C_L^v)$.
6: Find the subset G^v of IoT nodes that satisfy restrictions and available CPU capacity (larger than that specified by the request). If $G^v == \emptyset$, store this request in the queue, and GOTO Step 4.
7: For each virtual node, find the IoT node in G^s with the "maximum available resources" $R(G^v(t)$ (defined in Equation (4)), and GOTO Step 4.

requests that successfully finish the node mapping stage. The goal is to map the nodes and links of one request first, before mapping the other requests. In Algorithm 1, the IoT Node Mapping Algorithm method produces a similar mapping result, but this method is more efficient because of batch processing in the node/link mapping stage.

This baseline IoT VN embedding algorithm heuristically tries to achieve the goal in Equation (4) over each time window. Indeed, the algorithm contributes to instantaneous revenue maximization by giving higher priority to the requests with more revenue and accepting as many requests as possible in the node mapping. Additionally, the algorithm tends to make efficient utilization of the IoT bandwidth resources by mapping virtual links to the shortest paths in the IoT network, leaving more resources for future requests.

FORTIFICATION

Once the recognition of a cyber-attack has been identified from the recognition process, the fortification process takes place. Fortification means applying automatic embedded network protection techniques in ICD devices to protect IoT devices and networks during a cyber-attack. Fortification may include additional key hardware and chips installed as smart chips with embedded tokens for failure points and covert theft of information with general techniques all relying on code instrumentation and runtime assertion checking. Specific technical detail varies depending on the programming language used for the implementation of the ICD.

Once a cyber-attack has been identified through recognition, the embedded ICD SPM initiates a countermeasure to confine the signal containing the data package and stop processing the data (see Figure 10).

If the IoT signal containing packet data is valid, the ICD sensor agent will invoke its token security services. The token security services should define the interfaces to access the ICD secure packet sensor mechanism, which will have to be designed, developed, and implemented. Compared with existing direct authentication models using asymmetric key

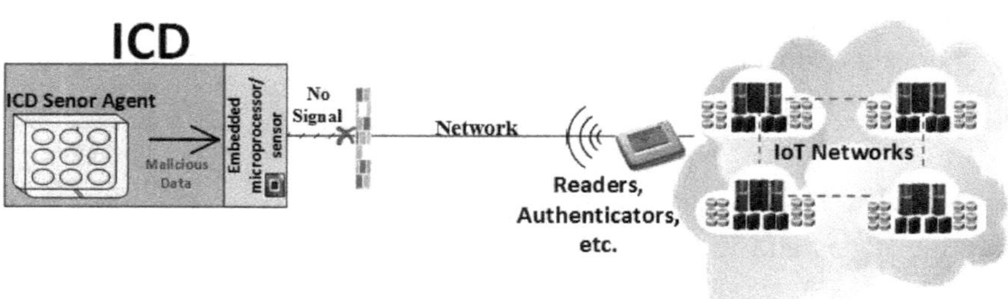

Figure 10. Fortification

exchange specified in [16, 52, 58], this method should be performed by removing redundant per-message authentication. The interfaces to access ICD sensor agent tokens will be based on IoT authentication mechanisms, such as those in wireless sensor networks like the Elliptic Curve Menezes-Qu-Vanstone (ECMQV) implicit certificate scheme and Elliptic Curve Diffie-Hellman (ECDH) key exchange protocol [22, 39].

That said, it is the intention of cyber-assurance to keep the authentication/authorization aspect of the process implementation-agnostic, and here to merely define how the decisions would be exchanged. For example, IoT-open authorization (OAuth) is an open protocol, which allows secure authorization in a simple and standardized way from third-party applications accessing online services, based on the representational state transfer (REST) web architecture [15]. The OAuth protocol provides an authorization layer for hypertext transfer protocol (HTTP)-based service application programming interfaces (API), typically on top of a secure transport layer, such as HTTP-over-transport layer security (TLS) (i.e., HTTPS) [14, 15]. IoT- OAuth architecture is meant to be flexible, highly configurable, and easy to integrate with existing services for the IoT by delegating the authorization functionality by (1) lower processing load with respect to solutions, where access control is implemented on the smart object; (2) fine-grained (remote) customization of access policies; and (3) scalability, without the need to operate directly on the device [14].

Therefore, to keep track of the available node/link resources of the IoT network, note that for an IoT node $n^s \in N^s$, do not use CPU(n^s) alone as the metric of available resources, because we not only want to make sure that there is enough CPU capacity available but also consider bandwidth capacity to prepare for the subsequent link mapping stage. Therefore, we define the amount of available resources for an IoT node n^s by

$$H(n^s) = \mathrm{CPU}(n^s) = \sum_{l^s \in \mathrm{L}(n^s)} bw(l^s) \tag{6}$$

where $L(n^s)$ is the set of all adjacent IoT links of n^s, CPU(n^s) is the remaining CPU resource of n^s, and bw(l^s) is the unoccupied bandwidth resource for the IoT link l^s. The definition in (6) is the number of virtual links and nodes used to measure the resources, not the actual amount of CPU and bandwidth resources. With this definition, for a virtual node, we find the IoT node with the maximum available resources (Step 5) of Algorithm 2.

Algorithm 2. Fog-Cloud Link Mapping Algorithm

1: Sort the request that successfully completed the node-mapping stage by their revenues.
2: If malicious data is identified, stop processing.
3: If non-malicious, take one request with the largest revenue.
4: For each virtual link of the request, search the *k*-shortest paths for increasing *k*, and stop the search if we find one with enough bandwidth capacity.
5: If fail in Step 3 for some virtual link, then defer this request, and store it in the request queue.
6: GOTO Step 4.

When the IoT nodes are selected for mapping, map the virtual links to specific IoT links. Finding an optimal mapping from a virtual link to a single IoT path with fixed node mapping reduces the Unsplittable Flow Problem (UFP), which is non-deterministic polynomial-time hardness (NP-hard) [21, 22]. Therefore, use the *k-shortest path algorithm* as an approximation approach in order to minimize bandwidth consumption by the virtual network [12, 20]. Then, search the *k*-shortest paths for increasing values of *k,* until a path is found which has enough bandwidth to map the corresponding virtual link [12, 20]. The *k*-shortest-path link-mapping algorithm can be solved in $O(M + N \log N + k)$ time in a IoT network with N nodes and M links [12, 20]. Both for computational efficiency and efficient use of IoT resources, *k* should be kept small.

To further support fortification, the ICD token will generate a random challenge, send it to the host, and the host will sign it and send it back for verification, using a certificate (or a least a public key) signed by a trusted entity. The trusted entity is yet to be determined but its credentials must have been previously loaded on the token so that validation of the host credentials can be anchored to a known trust point. Now it should be noted that there are issues involved in certificated path validation on small microprocessors and the longer the path, the longer this process will take. In addition, access to current certificate revocation lists (CRL) to perform certificate revocation checking should also be problematic. May low assurance systems solve these problems by off-loading this processing to the host. However, the host is not yet trusted until after this authentication has been performed. If the host fails its validation by the token, access to the token should be blocked. No information has been compromised at this point so the token should not be zeroized but at the same time, the token should not be considered available for use.

After the host has been successfully authenticated, the token must be authenticated to the host. The host will generate a random challenge, send it to the token and the token will sign it, using a per-token key that is signed by a trusted entity, and send it back for verification. As in the previous step, the trusted entity is yet to be determined but verification should be much easier for the host since it should have greater access to certificates and CRL. In this case, if the token's signature fails, the host must refuse further communication and log off the token. The occurrence of this condition most likely indicates that a nearly successful impersonation attack has been performed. If it is caught at this point, at least no sensitive data, other than authentication values, has been compromised, but it should be considered an important enough condition that occurrence is reported. As a result, the host should have a provision for creating an audit trail and collecting forensic evidence. After both the token and the host have been successfully authenticated to each other, then and only then, should the process be considered completed. At this time, the token can be made available for full use by the ICD.

REESTABLISHMENT

Reestablishment is a means to return the ICDs to their operational condition after the cyber-attack through remapping to a different route since the ICD was under attack (see Figure 11). In traditional network virtualization, a virtual network has a static mapping to the underlying physical network. Yet, remapping a virtual network is useful to (i) transparently recover from physical failures, (ii) reprovision physical resources to "make room" for a new virtual network and (iii) thwart adversaries trying to launch DoS or side-channel attacks on a virtual network.

Techniques such as embedded virtualization supporting multiple virtual networks — each consisting of a host, links, nodes, and switches — on a shared physical infrastructure could be applied [26, 44, 55]. Each IoT network may apply its own policies (e.g., for routing, access control, packet scheduling, mobility, etc.) for operating but needs to improve resiliency by allowing ICDs to dynamically change a virtual network mapping to the underlying physical hardware. As displayed in Figure 8, once authenticated, an ICD sensor agent is granted access control to an

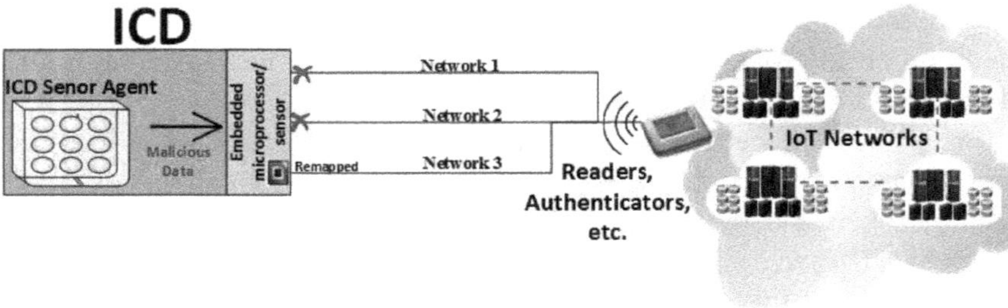

Figure 11. Remapping ICD to the IoT Network

IoT network. Since each ICD sensor agent needs a network resource in the IoT physical infrastructure (including servers, wireless nodes, bandwidth links, and virtual switches and routers), the ICD sensor agent runs an embedding system algorithm in the embedded processor to identify whether and where the ICD sensor agents should execution in the IoT network. The IoT will need to keep track of existing ICD allocations and run an optimization-embedded algorithm to compute efficiency by allowing a single ICD to span multiple IoT networking paths.

An embedding algorithm's use of multiple physical paths in Algorithm 3 offers a natural way to recover from link failures — simply splitting a virtual link's traffic over the remaining physical paths. More generally, the ICD sensor agent can completely remap a virtual network onto a different collection of physical switches and links, by re-running the embedding algorithm, installing a second copy of the packet-handling rules in the new locations, and cutting traffic over to the new virtual network — all without disrupting the controller application and the data traffic. In addition to remapping the (virtual) network elements, the ICD sensor agent can remap the end hosts by assigning new IP or MAC addresses, or by performing virtual machine migration to move (virtual) servers to a new physical location.

To correlate monitored traffic with other data sources, association rule-based approaches are traditionally used. However, the problem is more challenging in this case. Indeed, one of the advantages of IoT systems is their greater flexibility, but because of the open and loosely coupled nature of such systems, they tend to be subject to a great variety of usage scenarios (even if operated entirely within a single institution. Consequently, the global behavior of such as system, and therefore a global view of transactions, tends to be difficult to predict; in extreme cases, the global behavior might be emergent rather than expected

Algorithm 3. Fog-Cloud Algorithm for Requests with Path Splitting

1: For all requests with splittability, construct linear constraints on the commodities for each IoT link.
2: Solve Multicommodity Flow Problem (MFP).
3: If feasible, GOTO Step 5.
4: If infeasible, find the "bottleneck" IoT link.
5: Randomly choose one virtual link that is originally mapped at the bottleneck link, pick one end of the virtual link, and map it to another IoT node with maximum remaining resource H (defined in Equation (3)). Then GOTO Step 2 with new linear constraints.
6: If remapping of virtual nodes for T_{try} times does not produce a feasible solution, eliminate one of the VN requests having the "largest" impact on infeasibility.
7: Then, construct the linear constraints only with the remaining requests, and GOTO Step 2.

and predefined. It is thus correspondingly more difficult to model in terms of association rules. As virtual smart ICDs decouple servers from physical hardware, the IoT network will have to decouple entire networks from physical networks. Once a cyber-attack has been recognized and fortified, the dynamic association of smart ICDs, their IP addresses, and locations, will have to transpose back to a stable system. By changing the placement of smart ICD routing information and IP addresses will help defend against cyber-attacks.

The link mapping algorithm-supporting path splitting to enable efficient solutions is located in Algorithm 3. In Step 1, first construct linear constraints for the virtual links. For simplicity, consider a request with only one link l^v with the capacity constraint C, where two end nodes of l^v are denoted by $n^v{}_1$ and $n^v{}_2$. Denote by $M^N(n^v{}_1) = n^s{}_1$ and $M^N(n^v{}_2) = n^s{}_2$ the IoT nodes chosen for $n^v{}_1$ and $n^v{}_2$, respectively, by the node-mapping algorithm 2. The pair of IoT nodes $(n^s{}_1, n^s{}_2)$ is a commodity, and finding multiple IoT paths for l^v is equivalent to finding flows from source $n^s{}_1$ to destination $n^s{}_2$ in the IoT network with available bandwidth on the IoT links.

Thus, a group of, say r, virtual links generates a group of r commodities. The algorithm tries to find all the paths for r commodities based on the following linear constraints:

$$\forall l^s \in L^s, \sum_{i=1}^{r} fc_{i,} l^s \leq bw(l^s) \tag{7}$$

where $f(c_i, l^s)$ is the bandwidth on the IoT link l^s that we allocate to commodity c_i, or its corresponding virtual link. After generating the r commodities and the linear constraints, solve the resulting multicommodity flow problem (Step 2) multiple commodities (flow demands) between different sources and nodes. which can be solved in polynomial time.

Even with flexible path splitting, the MFP problem may not have a feasible solution because one or more IoT links do not have enough available capacity. The algorithm revisits the node-mapping decisions for these virtual links (Steps 4, 5, and 6). The failure in the MFP computation implies that one or more IoT links violate the linear constraints in Equation (4). Fortunately, the MFP algorithm can easily output the IoT links that violate the constraint, as well as the extent of the violation. The node-remapping stage focuses its attention on the IoT link with the largest violation (*bottleneck link*), i.e., the $l^s \in L^s$ with the highest value of $^{\mathrm{Pr}}{}_{=1} f(c_i, l^s) - \mathrm{bw}(l^s)$.

The ICD sensor agent will randomly choose one virtual link that is originally mapped to the path including the bottleneck link, and map one end of this virtual link to another IoT node with maximum remaining resource H (defined in Equation (3)), in order to avoid occupying this bottleneck link. The node remapping revisits the node mapping decision for the new requests. However, the remapping process does not change the resource allocation for virtual networks already running in the IoT. We try this node remapping for a pre-defined number of times T_{try} and make sure each time we choose a different bottleneck link. If the MFP is still infeasible after T_{try} trials, we defer the request that requires the most bandwidth on the bottleneck IoT link and return it to the request queue, and then try to solve the MFP with the remaining requests again. Larger values of T_{try} increase the computational overhead but improve the likelihood of finding a successful embedding.

In practice, some virtual networks may have strict requirements that preclude path splitting As such, I envision this algorithm to handle a mix of both kinds of VN requests. As illustrated in Figure 7, first apply Algorithm 2 for requests that do not allow path splitting, before applying Algorithm 3 for requests that allow path splitting. Unfortunately, node-remapping is difficult to perform for the unsplittable virtual links since the embedding algorithm processes one virtual link at a time. For the collection of virtual links that fail to find a suitable path, we cannot easily identify the most congested IoT link in a computationally efficient manner. To maintain computational simplicity, do not consider node-remapping for these requests. In the evaluation, we quantify the benefits of path splitting, with and without the node-remapping step.

Through path multiplicity, the ICD sensor agent can combine resources from multiple network paths to improve scalability, reliability, and security [25]. By network redirecting or remapping, an ICD will be useful to transparently recover from physical failures and mitigate adversary attacks. For example, if a physical ICD link is malicious and happens to pass through the recognition and/or fortification processors, the ICD sensor agent can map one or more ICDs to alternate physical paths, shielding the IoT network from processing the malicious packet.

To motivate IoT support for path migration, consider the example in Figure 5. Initially, IoT networks run a single virtual network with three nodes (mapped to physical nodes A, E, and F) and two virtual links that each require 20 units of bandwidth (mapped to the paths (A, D, E) and (A, D, F)). Now, suppose a new VN request arrives with a single virtual link that requires 30 units of bandwidth. Unfortunately, no pair of nodes in the IoT network can accommodate the new request, even if path splitting is permitted. For example, in the left side of Figure 5, nodes D and E have a path (D, E) with 20 units of bandwidth, a path (D, B, C, E) with 5 units of bandwidth, and a path (D, A, B, C, E) with 0 units of bandwidth — not enough to support a virtual link requiring 30 units of bandwidth. However, migrating some of the traffic for the first virtual network to a different path would enable the IoT to accept the new request. In particular, the IoT could carry half of the traffic for the virtual link (a,b) on a new path (A, B, C, E) to free up additional capacity on the IoT link (D, E). Then, the second virtual network can have a link (d,e) mapped to the IoT path (D, E).

In the migration algorithm described in Algorithm 4, this is fixed on the node mapping of the virtual networks already running on the IoT. By performing path migration, the rerunning of the link-mapping algorithm with requests that allow path splitting (Algorithm 3) is performed. Path migration is performed by either changing the splitting ratios for the existing paths or selecting new underlying paths. If only adjusting the splitting ratios is allowable rather than setting up any new paths, we have to make sure that the flows coming from a commodity only traverse the IoT paths originally taken in the link mapping stage. Thus, we add the following linear constraints to the constraints in Equation (8), Step 2 of Algorithm 4:

$$f(c_i, l^s) = 0, \quad \forall l^s \in L^s, \quad \forall ci, l^s \notin P^s(c_i) \tag{8}$$

Algorithm 4. Fog-Cloud Path Multiplicity Algorithm

For all the served requests,

1: Select the request set S whose durations are larger than a threshold T_{dur}.

2: If only changing the splitting ratio is allowed, add linear constraints (Equation (8)), so that each virtual link is forced to be mapped to the paths it originally took in the link-mapping step.
If setting up a new path is also allowed, skip this step.

3: Rerun the link-mapping algorithm with path splitting, and migrate the related paths.

4: Continue processing on a virtual network.

where $P\ s(ci)$ is the set of original IoT paths the virtual link (or corresponding commodity ci) was mapped to. Then we solve the MFP problem again with the new constraints of both Equations (7) and (8). If allowed, we can select a remap of the end hosts by assigning a new IP or MAC address or performing virtual machine migration to move virtual servers to a new physical IoT location, installing additional packet-handling rules in new IoT network locations, and moving traffic to the new IoT network without disrupting the IoT traffic. Additionally, APIs for specifying the desired frequency of changes to the physical IoT mappings must be dynamically triggered in response to suspected attacks or intrusions. The embedded SPM in the ICD sensor agent can completely redirect an ICD onto a different collection of IoT network routers, switches, and nodes, by re-running the embedding algorithm on the network.

Path migration allows the ICD to (periodically) treat the online embedding problem as an offline problem, to capitalize on the efficiency gains that are possible when handling a large collection of requests together. As such, I expect the benefits of path migration to be highest when the time window (for grouping requests) is small, and less significant as the window grows larger.

In practice, migrating paths introduce overhead to establish new paths, switch the traffic onto the new paths, and tear down the old paths. As such, the benefits of path migration should be weighed against the overheads. To illustrate this, I expect that VN requests would be quite diverse in their durations, which corresponds to their running time in the IoT network, ranging from a few months to several hours. As an example, a content distribution network like Akamai [1] may run infinitely, whereas an impromptu conference or video game may last for a few hours. The algorithm should not migrate short-lived virtual networks that are likely to exit the system soon after the migration completes. Thus, this algorithm only considers the requests whose durations are larger than some threshold T_{dur} (Step 1). Fortunately, migrating long-running virtual networks should offer ample benefits in practice since many short-lived virtual networks will come and go while they run. Virtual-network requests would indicate their likely duration, or we can infer that a virtual network that has run for a long time is likely to continue running for a long time, analogous to previous research on migration in the context of job scheduling [17].

SURVIVABILITY

When IoT technologies are used as part of mission-critical systems, these services should be survivable in order to support important missions. Reference [37] define survivability as the capability of an entity to continue its mission even in the presence of cyber-attacks, internal failures, or accidents [35, 36]. An entity ranges from a single component (object), with its mission in a distributed computing environment, to an information system that consists of many components to support the overall mission. An entity may support multiple missions and it identifies the static and dynamic models.

The static survivability model is based on redundant components (e.g., multiple copies of a critical component), prepared before the operation, to support critical services continuously in a distributed computing environment. Redundant components can be located in the same machine or in different machines in the same domain or even different domains. The same service can be provided by identical components (e.g., copies of the original component) or by diverse components that are implemented in various ways. Isolated redundancy (in different machines or domains) usually provides higher survivability because the replaced component can be running in an unaffected area. For instance, if the redundant components are distributed in different places of the network, the services provided by those components can be recovered in the event of primary network service failures. However, if there is a successful attack on a component, replacing that component with an identical copy is not a fundamental solution, because identical components are vulnerable to the same exploit used in the previously successful attack.

In the dynamic survivability model, unlike the static model, there are no redundant components. The components that have failed or are under the control of malicious codes are replaced by dynamically generated components on the fly and deployed in runtime when they are required. Furthermore, this model allows the replacement of malicious components with immunized components if possible, which enables it to provide more robust services than the static model. If we do not know the exact reason for the failures or types of malicious codes, or if it is hard to recover components against known failures or from the influence of malicious codes, we can simply replace the affected component with a new one — thereby creating in a renewed service. We call this a generic immunization strategy, which can be effective against cyber-attacks. If a component (a machine or a whole domain) is under attack, the generic immunization strategy suggests generating a new copy of the component and deploying it in a new environment that is safe from the attack. Although the generic immunization strategy supports service availability continuously, the new component might still be susceptible to the same failures or attacks.

Path splitting can be implemented in the IoT network without significant overhead. When the virtual node directs a packet over the virtual link, the IoT network sends the packet over one of the paths based on the target-splitting ratio. Path splitting may cause out-of-order packet delivery. Some virtual networks do not care about out-of-order packets; or they can reorder the out-of-order packets by themselves, e.g., those applications with only UDP flows. This can also make the virtual networks oblivious to the traffic splitting by preventing the disruptions of out-of-order packets in the IoT, e.g., using hash-based splitting.

Shifting the addresses, locations, and IoT network paths for an IoT service requires ICDs to share a secret numeric key with the IoT network. Similar to previous work on frequency hopping in wireless networks, the key modulates the changing of the IP addresses of the service [43]. The ICD and IoT need to change the server addresses by rewriting packet headers in routers and switches. Using network devices with anti-spoofing functionality, such as unicast reverse path forwarding (uRPF), can reduce network vulnerability conditions (e.g., denial of service, etc.), as the ICD verifies the validity of a source IP address and discards the traffic if the source IP address is not valid or is spoofed [21]. For example, virtual machines [VM] will be migrated from one physical server to another and the remapping of virtual links to IoT network paths through virtual switches and links to different physical locations will also take place [41].

Remapping IoT network paths does require coordination with end devices (e.g., Cloud servers, etc.), allowing the ICD to make these changes frequently to avoid sharing a physical server or link with other virtual networks, including response to suspected attacks. The ICD will trigger changes in VM addresses and locations and the remapping of virtual switches and links will travel over a special management virtual local area networks (VLANs).

One issue with reestablishment could entail misconstrued information. From past research in the intrusion detection field, log data obtained tends frequently to be incomplete, ambiguous, or otherwise unreliable [42]. The research community increasingly acknowledges this difficulty and the problem of log correlation in the presence of incomplete or unreliable data has received research attention [1, 27, 29]. In the context of the IoT, this problem is in fact related in certain cases to the emergent behavior problem: since emergent behavior has by nature no definition *a priori*, it follows that the precise corresponding correlation rules are also unknown or probabilistic, as opposed to discrete. Furthermore, evaluating a moving target defense within a single data center by changing IP addresses (within an existing block), VM locations, and virtual network embeddings, while continuing communication remote uses must be performed. Additionally, evaluating a defense where a virtual network moves from one data center to another, where the end-user accesses the service from an IP address in a different address block will also be required where the main performance metric is the transient performance disruptions during the transition.

CONCLUSION

Cyber-assurance is warranted for the forthcoming IoT. Unlike traditional IT systems, the IoT network presents a much higher degree of risk and instability and a much higher chance of being attacked. Hence, it is necessary to consider security as an important indicator to take the appropriate measures right at the initial stages of IoT network design, hardware production, and software development. ICDs and IoT network designers and developers should insist on using physical isolation measures in ICD and IoT network design. Embedded key hardware and chips should prevent our enemy from installing components such as defective chips which will lead to serious security issues such as the breakdown of the IoT system, theft of information, and the failure of the chips at critical moments [33].

ICD and IoT developers must persevere in the development of important operating software precluding from the adversary pre-setting hidden attacks, loopholes, and virus programs thus avoiding grave potential APTs to the IoT system.

While the concept of cyber-assurance greatly reduces the overall system complexity through the decomposition of malicious security functions into modular, embedded services, it does call for increased attention to the process of developing, integrating, and testing these services. This is important to monitor the reliability of the implementation of the processes. Since hardware components can degrade and malfunction, and since there can be implementation bugs in the software/firmware running on a device it is important to detect (if not correct) processing errors that occur on the device. When these occur, new and unplanned vulnerabilities may present themselves in a device. As a result, detection of any malfunction in the processing of a device should initiate steps to protect all the information and resources that are being protected by the device. The integration lifecycle can no longer be a sequential waterfall process. Because each individual IoT service or IoT service family may have its own development timeline, waiting to start overall security integration until all services are developed and unit-tested may not be realistic. Rather, the IoT environment will have to incrementally incorporate testing of the services as they become "online", constantly regression-testing the overall IoT system behavior along the way. This will heighten the need for test harnesses, prototypes, and simulators that can act as a surrogate while the true service capabilities are being developed.

REFERENCES

[1] Abad, C., Taylor, J., Sengul, C., Yurcik, W., Zhou, Y., & Rowe, K. (2003). Log correlation for intrusion detection: A proof of concept. In *Proceedings of the 19th Annual Computer Security Applications Conference, 2003* (pp. 255–264). IEEE.

[2] Agosta, G. & Pelosi, G. (2007). A domain specific language for cryptography. In *FDL* (pp. 15–164).

[3] Anderson, E. A., Irvine, C. E., & Schell, R. R. (2004). Subversion as a threat in information warfare. *Journal of Information Warfare*, 3(2), 51–64.

[4] Azar, Y. & Regev, O. (2001). Strongly polynomial algorithms for the unsplittable flow problem. In *International Conference on Integer Programming and Combinatorial Optimization* (pp. 15–29). Springer, Berlin, Heidelberg.

[5] Brooks, T., Kaarst-Brown, M., Caicedo, C., Park, J., & McKnight, L. (2013). A failure to communicate: Security vulnerabilities in the gridstreamx edgeware application. In *2013 8th International Conference for Internet Technology and Secured Transactions (ICITST)* (pp. 516–523). IEEE.

[6] Brooks, T., Kaarst-Brown, M., Caicedo, C., Park, J., & McKnight, L. W. (2014). Secure the edge? Understanding the risk towards wireless grids Edgeware technology. *International Journal of Internet Technology and Secured Transactions 8*, 5(3), 191–222.

[7] Burbridge, T. & Harrison, M. (2009). Security considerations in the design and peering of RFIDdiscovery services. In *2009 IEEE International Conference on RFID* (pp. 249–256). IEEE.

[8] Cai, Z., Liu, F., Xiao, N., Liu, Q., & Wang, Z. (2010). Virtual network embedding for evolving networks. In *2010 IEEE Global Telecommunications Conference* (*GLOBECOM 2010*) (pp. 1–5). IEEE.

[9] Chasaki, D. & Wolf, T. (2010). Design of a secure packet processor. In *2010 ACM/IEEE Symposium on Architectures for Networking and Communications Systems* (*ANCS*) (pp. 1–10). IEEE.

[10] Chakrabarti, A., Chekuri, C., Gupta, A., & Kumar, A. (2002). Approximation algorithms for the unsplittable flow problem. In *International Workshop on Approximation Algorithms for Combinatorial Optimization* (pp. 51–66). Springer, Berlin, Heidelberg.

[11] Cheng, X., Su, S., Zhang, Z., Wang, H., Yang, F., Luo, Y., & Wang, J. (2011). Virtual network embedding through topology-aware node ranking. *ACM SIGCOMM Computer Communication Review*, 41(2), 38–47.

[12] Chowdhury, M., Rahman, M. R., & Boutaba, R. (2012). Vineyard: Virtual network embedding algorithms with coordinated node and link mapping. *IEEE/ACM Transactions on Networking* (*TON*), 20(1), 206–219.

[13] Chowdhury, N. M. K., Rahman, M. R., & Boutaba, R. (2009). Virtual network embedding with coordinated node and link mapping. In *IEEE INFOCOM 2009* (pp. 783–791). IEEE.

[14] Cirani, S., Picone, M., Gonizzi, P., Veltri, L., & Ferrari, G. (2015). Iot-oas: An oauth-based authorization service architecture for secure services in iot scenarios. *Sensors Journal, IEEE*, 15(2), 1224–1234.

[15] Dierks, T. (2008). The transport layer security (TLS) protocol version 1.2.

[16] Dlamini, M., Venter, H., Eloff, J., & Mitha, Y. (2012). Authentication in the Cloud: A risk-based approach. University of Pretoria.

[17] Du, W., Deng, J., Han, Y. S., Varshney, P. K., Katz, J., & Khalili, A. (2005). A pairwise key predistribution scheme for wireless sensor networks. *ACM Transactions on Information and System Security (TISSEC)*, 8(2), 228–258.

[18] Elbe, A., Janssen, N., & Sedlak, H. (2003). *Cryptographic Processor*. U.S Patent Application 10/461,913.

[19] Engebretson, P. (2013). *The Basics of Hacking and Penetration Testing: Ethical Hacking and Penetration Testing Made Easy.* Elsevier, Philadelphia, PA.

[20] Eppstein, D. (1998). Finding the k shortest paths. *SIAM Journal on Computing*, 28(2), 652–673.

[21] Graham, J., Olson, R., & Howard, R. (Eds.) (2010). *Cyber Security Essentials.* CRC Press, Boca Raton, FL.

[22] Hankerson, D., Menezes, A. J., & Vanstone, S. (2006). *Guide to Elliptic Curve Cryptography.* Springer Science & Business Media.

[23] Hershberger, J., Maxel, M., & Suri, S. (2007). Finding the k shortest simple paths: A new algorithm and its implementation. *ACM Transactions on Algorithms (TALG)*, 3(4), 45.

[24] Isa, M. A. M., Hashim, H., Ab Manan, J. L., Adnan, S. F. S., & Mahmod, R. (2014). RF simulator for cryptographic protocol. In *2014, IEEE International Conference on Control System, Computing and Engineering* (*ICCSCE*) (pp. 518–523). IEEE.

[25] Kommareddy, C., Güven, T., Bhattacharjee, B., La, R. J., & Shayman, M. A. (2003). *Overlay Routing for Path Multiplicity* (Vol. 70). Technical Report, UMIACS-TR.

[26] Kovacshazy, T., Wacha, G., Daboczi, T., Erdos, C., & Szarvas, A. (2013). System architecture for Internet of Things with the extensive use of embedded virtualization. In *2013 IEEE 4th International Conference on Cognitive Infocommunications* (*CogInfoCom*) (pp. 549–554). IEEE.

[27] Lee, S., Chung, B., Kim, H., Lee, Y., Park, C., & Yoon, H. (2006). Real-time analysis of intrusion detection alerts via correlation. *Computers & Security*, 25(3), 169–183.

[28] Leventis, P., Chan, M., Chan, M., Lewis, D., Nouban, B., Powell, G., Vest, B., Wong, M., Xia, R., & Costello, J. (2003). Cyclone™: A low-cost, high-performance FPGA. In *Proceedings of the IEEE Custom Integrated Circuits Conference* (pp. 49–52). IEEE.

[29] Li, Z., Taylor, J., Partridge, E., Zhou, Y., Yurcik, W., Abad, C., Barlow, J. J., & Rosendale, J. (2004). Uclog: A unified, correlated logging architecture for intrusion detection. In *The 12th International Conference on Telecommunication Systems-Modeling and Analysis* (*ICTSM*).

[30] Limin, H. (2010). Embedded system for internet of things. *Microcontrollers & Embedded Systems*, 10, 5–8.

[31] Liu, D., Ning, P., & Li, R. (2005). Establishing pairwise keys in distributed sensor networks. *ACM Transactions on Information and System Security (TISSEC)*, 8(1), 41–77.

[32] Luiijf, E. (2012). *Understanding Cyber Threats and Vulnerabilities* (pp. 52–67). Springer, Berlin, Heidelberg.

[33] Ozvural, G. & Kurt, G. K. (2015). Advanced approaches for wireless sensor network applications and cloud analytics. In *2015 IEEE 10th*

International Conference on Intelligent Sensors, Sensor Networks and Information Processing (*ISSNIP*) (pp. 1–5). IEEE.

[34] Parameswaran, S. & Wolf, T. (2008). Embedded systems security — An overview. *Design Automation for Embedded Systems*, 12(3), 173–183.

[35] Park, J. S. & Chandramohan, P. (2004, January). Component recovery approaches for survivable distributed systems. In *37th Hawaii International Conference on Systems Sciences* (*HICSS-37*). Big Island, Hawaii.

[36] Park, J. S., Chandramohan, P., Suresh, A. T., Giordano, J., & Kwiat, K. (2009). Component survivability for mission-critical distributed systems. *Journal of Automatic and Trusted Computing* (*JoATC*), 66, 1390–1417.

[37] Park, J. S., Chandramohan, P., Devarajan, G., & Giordano, J. (2005). Trusted component sharing by runtime test and immunization for survivable distributed systems. In *Security and Privacy in the Age of Ubiquitous Computing* (pp. 127–142). Springer, US.

[38] Porambage, P., Kumar, P., Schmitt, C., Gurtov, A., & Ylianttila, M. (2013). Certificate-based pairwise key establishment protocol for wireless sensor networks. In *2013 IEEE 16th International Conference on Computational Science and Engineering* (*CSE*) (pp. 667–674). IEEE.

[39] Porambage, P., Schmitt, C., Kumar, P., Gurtov, A., & Ylianttila, M. (2014). Two-phase authentication protocol for wireless sensor networks in distributed IoT applications. In *2014 IEEE Wireless Communications and Networking Conference* (*WCNC*) (pp. 2728–2733). IEEE.

[40] Qian, Y., Tipper, D., Krishnamurthy, P., & Joshi, J. (2010). *Information Assurance: Dependability and Security in Networked Systems.* Morgan Kaufmann, Boca Raton, FL.

[41] Rahman, M. R., Aib, I., & Boutaba, R. (2010). Survivable virtual network embedding. In *International Conference on Research in Networking* (pp. 40–52). Springer, Berlin, Heidelberg.

[42] Sabahi, F. & Movaghar, A. (2008, October). Intrusion detection: A survey. In *3rd International Conference on Systems and Networks Communications, 2008* (*ICSNC '08*) (pp. 23–26). IEEE.

[43] Seba, V., Modlic, B., & Sisul, G. (2013). System model with adaptive modulation and frequency hopping in wireless networks. In *Global Information Infrastructure Symposium, 2013* (pp. 1–3).

[44] Tseng, Y. W., Liao, C. Y., & Hung, T. H. (2015). An embedded system with realtime surveillance application. In *2015 International Symposium on Next-Generation Electronics* (*ISNE*) (pp. 1–4). IEEE.

[45] Ukil, A., Sen, J., & Koilakonda, S. (2011). Embedded security for Internet of Things. In *2011 2nd National Conference on Emerging Trends and Applications in Computer Science* (*NCETACS*) (pp. 1–6). IEEE.

[46] Unger, S. & Timmermann, D. (2015). DPWSec: Devices profile for web services security. In *2015 IEEE 10th International Conference on Intelligent*

Sensors, Sensor Networks and Information Processing (*ISSNIP*) (pp. 1–6). IEEE.

[47] Veltri, L., Cirani, S., Ferrari, G., & Busanelli, S. (2013). Batch-based group key management with shared key derivation in the internet of things. In *2013 9th International Wireless Communications and Mobile Computing Conference* (*IWCMC*) (pp. 1688–1693). IEEE.

[48] Wang, L. & Ranjan, R. (2015). Processing distributed internet of things data in clouds. *IEEE Cloud Computing*, (1), 76–80.

[49] Wu, C. H. J. & Irwin, J. D. (2013). *Introduction to Computer Networks and Cybersecurity.* CRC Press, Boca Raton, FL.

[50] Xiang, W., Zexi, Z., Ying, L., & Yi, Z. (2013). A design of security module to protect program execution in embedded system. In *2013 IEEE and Internet of Things (iThings/CPSCom) Green Computing and Communications (GreenCom), IEEE International Conference on and IEEE Cyber, Physical and Social Computing* (pp. 1750–1755). IEEE.

[51] Yan, L., Zhang, Y., Yang, L. T., & Ning, H. (Eds.) (2008). *The Internet of Things: From RFID to the Next-Generation Pervasive Networked Systems.* CRC Press, Boca Raton, FL.

[52] Yang, J. C., Hao, P. A. N. G., & Zhang, X. (2013). Enhanced mutual authentication model of IoT. *The Journal of China Universities of Posts and Telecommunications*, 20, 69–74.

[53] Yang, Y., Zhou, J., Wang, F., & Shi, C. (2014). An LPI design for secure burst communication systems. In *2014 IEEE China Summit & International Conference on Signal and Information Processing* (*ChinaSIP*) (pp. 631–635). IEEE.

[54] Yu, M., Yi, Y., Rexford, J., & Chiang, M. (2008). Rethinking virtual network embedding: Substrate support for path splitting and migration. *ACM SIGCOMM Computer Communication Review*, 38(2), 17–29.

[55] Yuan, Y., Wang, C., Wang, C., Zhang, B., Zhu, S., & Zhu, N. (2015). A novel algorithm for embedding dynamic virtual network request. In *2015 2nd International Conference on Information Science and Control Engineering* (*ICISCE*) (pp. 28–32). IEEE.

[56] Yun, M. & Yuxin, B. (2010). Research on the architecture and key technology of internet of things (IoT) applied on smart grid. In *2010 International Conference on Advances in Energy Engineering* (*ICAEE*) (pp. 69–72). IEEE.

[57] Zhai, X., Appiah, K., Ehsan, S., Howells, G., Hu, H., Gu, D., & McDonald-Maier, K.D. (2015). A method for detecting abnormal program behavior on embedded devices. *IEEE Transactions on Information Forensics and Security*, 10(8), 1692–1704.

[58] Zhou, L. & Chao, H. C. (2011). Multimedia traffic security architecture for the internet of things. *IEEE Network*, 25(3), 35–40, New York, NY.

[59] Zhou, H. (2012). *The Internet of Things in the Cloud: A Middleware Perspective.* CRC press.

Chapter 10

Zero Trust Security in 5G O-RAN Wireless Grid Networks: Designing a System-of-Systems Intrusion Detection System (SoSIDS)

ABSTRACT

The critical need for integrating next-generation 5G networks with zero trust (ZT) principles is imperative. This paper introduces the concept of a zero-trust architecture (ZTA) as a security framework in 5G networks with untrusted components. While software-defined networking (SDN), network function virtualization (NFV), and service-based architectures (SBAs) are key enablers of 5G networks, operating in an untrusted environment has also become a key feature of networks. Further, seamless connectivity to a high volume of devices in multi-radio access technology (RAT) has broadened the attack surface on information infrastructure and for an untrusted environment calls for revolutionary architectures beyond existing static security frameworks. This chapter presents the architectural design of a 5G ZTA upon which modern artificial intelligence (AI)/machine learning (ML) algorithms can be developed to provide information security in untrusted 5G networks. The envisioned architecture adopts a SBA design, similar to the 3GPP specification of 5G networks, by leveraging the open radio access network (O-RAN) architecture with appropriate real-time engines and network interfaces for collecting necessary machine learning data. The chapter also introduces key ZTA principles using a system-of-systems intrusion detection system (SoSIDS) that also incorporates a machine-automated response solution (MARS) which provides intelligent responses to mitigate anomalies in the 5G O-RAN ZTA environment.

OVERVIEW

Wireless communication has become the key enabler of emerging technologies such as autonomous vehicles, vehicle-to-everything (V2X) networks, smart cities, and internet-of-things (IoT). The fifth generation (5G) networks provide a massive volume of heterogeneous devices with seamless connectivity and computational resources for autonomous and intelligent operation. Further, sixth generation (6G) — and beyond — networks incorporate more agile radio environments, including satellite and unmanned aerial vehicle (UAV) communications, to provide a three-dimensional (3D) [1]. However, traditional network security frameworks have obvious weaknesses in providing security assurance in such a complex and dynamic network environment. Traditional network security models assume a network perimeter, as the trust zone, which is protected against unauthorized access. Any subject operating in the trust zone, after appropriate authentication and authorization, is deemed trusted. However, due to the agile radio environment, mobility, and heterogeneity of next-generation tactical networks, identification of the network perimeter is challenging if not impossible [2]. More importantly, such models allow lateral movement of subjects in the trust zone after authentication.

A zero-trust architecture (ZTA) is a solution to address security requirements in a network with untrusted infrastructure (see Figure 1). A ZTA provides network assurance under the assumption that no subject, requesting access to the network resources, can be trusted even after initial authentication and authorization [3]. Every access request is individually authorized and monitored during the access period for compliance with security policy rules. A dynamic trust evaluation for every access request is the key tent of ZT. Authorizing the individual access requests by a subject rather than authorizing the subject requesting access is a key tenet of a ZTA.

Dynamic risk assessments and trust evaluations are key elements of a ZTA. The chapter introduces the architecture of a 5G open radio access network (O-RAN) ZTA which provides a framework to employ artificial intelligence/machine learning (AI/ML) engines for information security in untrusted networks. It also discusses the adoptability of O-RAN for the 5G integration and briefly discusses how the multi-access edge computing

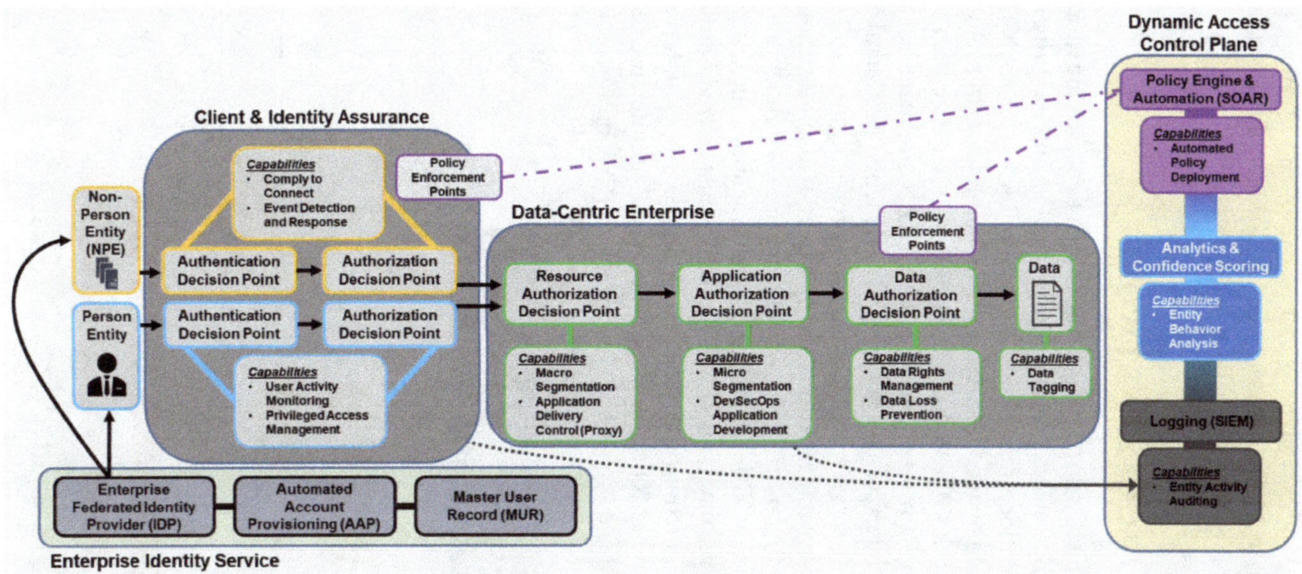

Figure 1. Zero Trust Reference Architecture

Source: https://dodcio.defense.gov/Portals/0/Documents/Library/(U)ZT_RA_v1.1(U)_Mar21.pdf.

(MEC) technology of 5G networks can be exploited to provide resource-constraint devices with the necessary computational resources for realizing the envisioned 5G O-RAN ZTA environment.

OPEN RADIO ACCESS NETWORK

The O-RAN is a totally disaggregated approach to deploying mobile fronthaul and midhaul networks built entirely on cloud-native principles [4]. O-RAN is an evolution of the Next Generation RAN (NG-RAN) architecture, first introduced by the GSMA's 3GPP in their release 15 (5G version 1) technical specification TS 38.401 [5]. The Overall Architecture of O-RAN below provides a high-level view of the O-RAN architecture. It shows that the four key interfaces — namely, A1, O1, Open Fronthaul M-plane, and O2 — connect service management and orchestration (SMO) framework to O-RAN network functions and O-Cloud. It also illustrates that the O-RAN network functions can be virtualized network functions (VNFs), i.e., virtual machines (VMs) or Containers, sitting above the O-Cloud and/or physical network functions (PNFs) utilizing customized hardware. All O-RAN network functions are expected to support the O1 interface when interfacing with the SMO framework. The overall architecture of O-RAN in Figure 2 provides a high-level view of the O-RAN architecture.

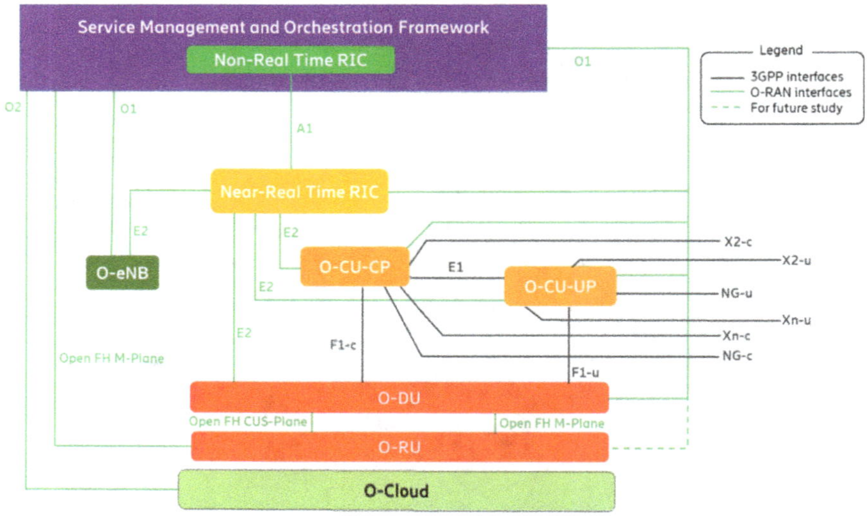

Figure 2. O-RAN Reference Architecture

Source: https://www.o-ran.org.

It shows that the four key interfaces — namely, A1, O1, Open Fronthaul M-plane, and O2 — connect service management and orchestration (SMO) framework to O-RAN network functions and O-Cloud. It also illustrates that the O-RAN network functions can be VNFs, i.e., VMs or containers, sitting above the O-Cloud and/or PNFs utilizing customized hardware. All O-RAN network functions are expected to support the O1 interface when interfacing with the SMO framework.

ZERO TRUST SYSTEM-OF-SYSTEM INTRUSION DETECTION SYSTEM (SoSIDS)

Intrusion Detection Systems (IDS) have been used widely to detect malicious behaviors in network communication and hosts [6]. With the integration of ZT, intrusion detection systems (IDS) management is an important capability for distributed IDS solutions, which makes it possible to integrate and handle different types of sensors or collect and synthesize alerts generated from multiple hosts located in the distributed environment [7]. Facing new application scenarios in ZT and Cloud Computing, the IDS approaches yield several problems since the operator of the IDS should be the user, not the administrator of the Cloud infrastructure [7, 8]. Extensibility, efficient management, and compatibility with virtualization-based context need to be introduced into many existing IDS implementations.

To meet these requirements, this paper proposes to implement a ZT using a system-of-systems intrusion detection system (SoSIDS) architecture, which consists of several sensor planes and a machine-automated response solution (MARS) as shown in Figure 3. The architecture will provide the capability to detect potential adversaries in complicated system-of-systems 5G environments, detect intrusions and adversarial activities in cloud-based environments, and be able to examine the activities of the different subsystems to determine if the adversary is active in the environment.

The realization of ZT principles with 5G O-RAN static policies is overwhelming due to the current technical Cloud environments [9]. Automated real-time monitoring and dynamic security evaluation will be the key features of a ZTA 5G O-RAN architecture. Further, with the growing volume of users, the ZTA components will be dealing more with big data, hence, monitoring, evaluation, and decision-making capabilities (DMC), using AI/ML, are the critical enablers of a ZTA in these next-generation 5G O-RAN networks.

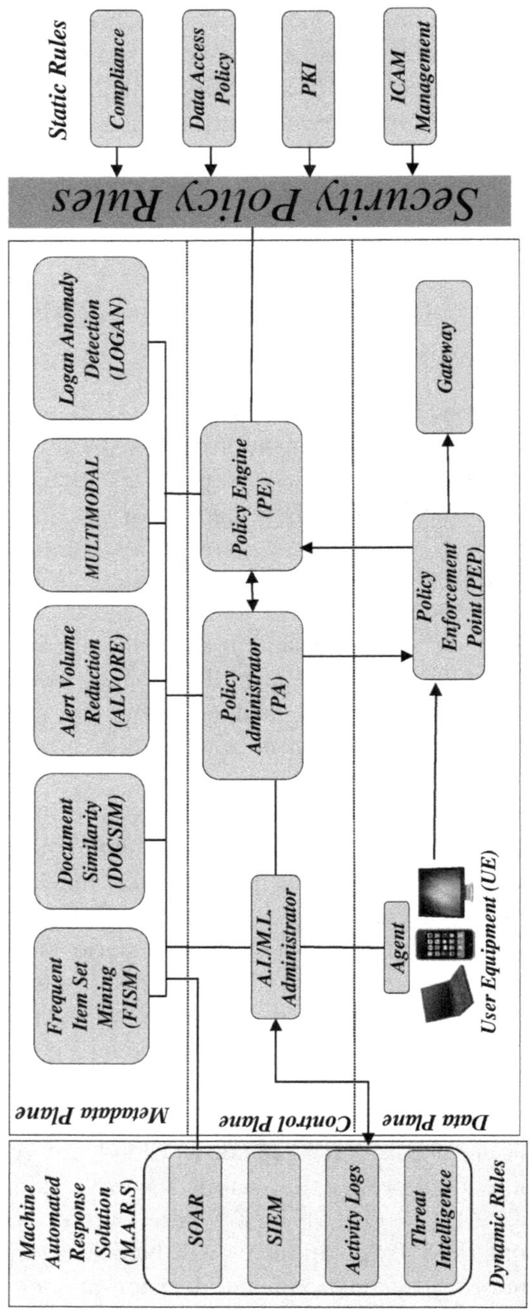

Figure 3. Zero Trust SoSID

The information used by the SoSIDS core to grant and monitor a connection is provided by several DMC peripheral modules as shown in Figure 3. The location of different blocks in this diagram reflects the logical interaction of the components and does not necessarily show their physical locations in the network. In this paper, we use the following terminology when referring to the SoSIDS:

- A *subject* is any user, application, or service requesting access to a network resource.
- The *network assets* refer to all devices, network infrastructure, and functions (including cloud services) involved in the communication.
- The *network resource* contains sensitive information that must be protected against unauthorized access.

The core of the SoSIDS comprises a policy enforcement point (PEP), a policy engine (PE), and a policy administrator (PA). The PEP is the first point of contact for access requests as it establishes the connection between the subject and the requested resource if access is granted. The decision on granting access is made by the PE and it uses all available internal and external information about the security state of the subject and network assets for deciding authorization and authentication. The PE is an automated component that allows administrators to express and enforce usage policies that dictate how users can gain access to the resources and use them.

The PA manages, configures, and monitors the PE and PEP utilizing the AI/ML administrator. The PA also provides quality of service (QoS) resource management based on the overall architecture policy decision scheme for considering management cost and QoS guarantees in the environment. The gateway, residing on the PEP, performs a similar task but is intended for resource-constraint devices, such as IoT and sensor devices. The gateway is directly configured by the PA and also incorporates algorithms from the AI/ML administrator, which work together in a federated learning approach. The other modules in the diagram of Figure 3, are the distinct features of a SoSIDS. These include the AI/ML administrator, the Policy Engine (PE), the metaplane, and the MARS.

AI/ML Administrator

The role of the AI/ML administrator is to provide the network assets, that require access to the resources, with a risk score, and a model for their security posture. The subjects with higher risk values might obtain higher confidence scores in risk assessment by the PE. Through an agent to employ a reinforcement learning (RL) engine that conducts three main tasks: (1) analyzing the traffic of the device in the network which provides an initial risk assessment on the network environment, (2) learning the flow of unnecessary communication in the device that may reduce its confidence level in accessing certain resources, and (3) providing a model for the communication pattern of the device which is passed along with an access request to the PE for overall risk assessment.

The AI/ML administrator is divided into two major components: (1) access request management from resource-constraint devices without computational capability to host agents, and (2) a learning component that supports federated learning of the agents. In addition to the peripherals, the core PEP and PE functions work with the AI/ML administrator engines to realize the entire DMC chain. The AI/ML administrator is the algorithm engine of the PEP which provides devices with situational awareness and the PE makes decisions on granting access based on all information provided by the PEP, PA, AI/ML administrator, and policy rules. Another critical task of the AI/ML administrator is anomaly detection using MARS. The goal of this component is to detect and prevent potential attacks, such as DoS and distributed DoS (DDoS), that target the overall environment. Additionally, MARS protects the network against more subtle DoS attacks. A potential attacker can indirectly make the PE deny access by promoting a hostile network environment, hence increasing the risk of granting access.

Policy Engine

The endpoint of trust evaluation is the PE. Like the AI/ML administrator, the PE incorporates an AI/ML engine to make the final decision on granting requested access based on the agent and network state. The PE employs a neural network with long- and short-term memories to evaluate the risk of granting access to an agent based on all previous activities of the agent and the network. The PE provides a *C*-score as the confidence level of access. The PE policy is optimized through an RL algorithm to minimize the probabilities of false positives and false negatives. After deciding (access grant or denial), the PE monitors the security state of the session (how strictly the agent conforms to the security policy rules). The PE also receives the future state of the agent from the AI/ML administrator to evaluate the reward return corresponding to the decision. The PE uses the collected information to evaluate the risk of the agent for its future transactions.

The Metaplane

The SoSIDS in Figure 3 divides the network into three logical planes: data, control, and metadata. The modules also include data access policy, public key infrastructure (PKI), identity and access management (IDAM), and industry compliance. These modules, collectively, define the security policy rules for secure communication and integrity check rules. The policy rules can be dynamically adjusted by the SoSIDS core. Data communication between the subject and network resources is carried out in the data plane, which also includes the initial access request by the subject. The SoSIDS components (i.e., PEP, PE, and AI/ML administrator) communicate in the control plane for making decisions and configuring connections. These two planes also exist in the current 5G network architectures. The third plane of the SoSIDS is the metadata plane used for communicating all data required by the AI/ML engines. The main components of the SoSIDS metadata plane are as follows:

- **Frequent Item Set Mining (FISM):** It is a critical component in data mining that plays a significant role in network security for the SoSID. It is designed to identify and analyze commonly associated files on a network that are frequently accessed. The underlying principle of the FISM is to establish patterns or associations among sets of items in data repositories. In the context of network security, it provides valuable insights into the behaviors and patterns of network users, particularly with regard to file access. By mapping the frequency and correlation of file accesses, FISM serves as a proxy method for anticipating potential exfiltration trajectories of an adversary. This allows security systems to proactively identify and mitigate potential security risks. By observing the trends in file access and cross-referencing them with known behaviors of security threats, FISM aids in the prediction and prevention of data breaches and unauthorized access, thus fortifying network security.
- **Document Similarity (DOCSIM):** An advanced data analysis technique utilized to identify and compare sets of documents based on their content similarity in the SoSID. Leveraging state-of-the-art ML models, DOCSIM performs complex computations to assess and quantify the

semantic and structural similarity among multiple documents. One of the primary applications of DOCSIM is in policy gap analysis. By identifying sets of similar documents, particularly policy documents within an organization, it can highlight potential inconsistencies, redundancies, or gaps in policy implementation and enforcement. The comparisons drawn by DOCSIM can guide organizations in standardizing and harmonizing their policies, ensuring all critical areas are comprehensively addressed. Moreover, by using machine learning models, DOCSIM can continuously learn and improve its performance, thereby providing increasingly accurate and useful results over time. This method provides a robust tool for organizations seeking to optimize their policy frameworks and strengthen compliance with regulatory standards.

- **MULTIMODAL:** Leverages AI/ML capabilities to build optimized data processing pipelines. These pipelines are designed for the SoSID to manage and process large volumes of real-time data, efficiently filtering, categorizing, and analyzing the incoming information. The strength of MULTIMODAL lies in its adaptability and responsiveness: it enables dynamic protection mechanisms that adjust according to the evolving threat landscape. This is achieved through real-time telemetry, which provides ongoing, precise measurements and tracking of data. This enables MULTIMODAL to identify and respond to cybersecurity threats rapidly and accurately. Furthermore, MULTIMODAL supports adaptive defenses, which can modify their strategies based on detected threats, ensuring that cybersecurity measures are always fit for purpose. This capacity for detecting and remediating cybersecurity threats as they emerge, rather than merely responding after the fact, is a crucial aspect of proactive defense and resilience in modern, data-intensive environments.
- **Logan Anomaly Detection (LOGAN):** Designed specifically for the detection of anomalies within Syslog data. It employs a two-phased approach to enhance the precision and reliability of its results. In the initial phase, LOGAN applies smart log parsing techniques to break down the log data into manageable, identifiable segments. By doing so, it can effectively identify and construct templates for recurring log event types, thereby creating a baseline of “normal” behavior. In the second phase, LOGAN compares incoming log events against this established baseline to identify deviations, or anomalies, that could signal potential cybersecurity threats. Such a methodical approach

ensures that the system not only recognizes potential issues but also understands the context in which they arise. This in-depth understanding aids in reducing false positives and allows for more effective mitigation strategies when genuine anomalies are detected, thereby bolstering the overall integrity of the system it protects.

- **Alert Volume Reduction (ALVORE):** An innovative analytic methodology that aims to streamline and optimize the processing of network alerts. Recognizing the potential overload that an excess of individual alerts can present to an analyst, ALVORE seeks to group together similar alert events originating from the network. This consolidation process results in a reduced, more digestible set of alerts for analyst review. By categorizing and grouping related alerts, ALVORE not only alleviates the burden of sifting through large volumes of alerts but also aids in discerning patterns and commonalities among them. This can enhance an analyst's understanding of the network's security landscape, facilitating more accurate threat identification and more efficient response strategies. In effect, ALVORE transforms a potential information overflow into a streamlined, manageable data set, improving both the efficiency and effectiveness of network security management.

Machine Automated Response Solution

MARS integrates advanced threat intelligence capabilities for pinpointing emerging security vulnerabilities, comprehensive activity logs capturing granular behavioral metadata pertaining to user/assets and network traffic dynamics, a sophisticated security information and event management (SIEM) system for assimilating longitudinal security state data and potential threat vectors, complemented by a security orchestration, automation, and response (SOAR) platform, optimized for streamlined security incident management and the automation of threat countermeasures.

MARS is designed to facilitate automated cybersecurity countermeasures within cloud-centric architectures. Its key functionalities encompass: (1) autonomous response mechanisms operable across the entirety of the OSI stack, encompassing host-level, networking hardware, and protocol-specific interventions, tailored to instantiate direct mitigative effects in the ecosystem, thereby curtailing anomalies and associated repercussions such as DoS events targeting legitimate users; (2) a quantifiable tradeoff space metric, which serves as a comparative index juxtaposing the advantageous impact against the potential deleterious aftermath of a specified counteractive measure; and (3) an intelligent decision algorithm, operational in real-time, purposed for the selection and deployment of the most efficacious countermeasure in response to an anomalous signature, whilst algorithmically assessing the aforementioned tradeoff space. In its overarching methodology, MARS employs a game-theoretic paradigm, leveraging computational mathematical models to decipher and simulate the interplay between adversarial and defensive entities, thereby modeling anomaly-response interactivity.

5G O-RAN ZERO TRUST ARCHITECTURE

In this section, we introduce a 5G O-RAN ZTA framework for information security in untrusted 5G networks. The envisioned ZT SoSIDS opens new research areas in the application domain for information security. The key elements of the ZT SoSIDS include: (1) trust algorithms to authorize access requests based on subject privileges and security state, security policy rules, the network state, and a risk score that reflects the confidence level of the access; specifically, the PE and PEP are envisioned to employ RL to maximize usability with the least privileges (2) the MARS engine to employ anomaly detection to identify potential attacks, (3) the AI/ML administrator to analyze the security posture of the network traffic to the subject and provides it with environmental awareness while keeping a high confidence level of the subject in accessing the network resources.

As shown in Figure 4, the architecture of the SoSIDS is integrated into the 5G O-RAN architecture. The O-RAN further provides appropriate interfaces for near-real-time monitoring of remote devices and services.

The realization of a SoSIDS, with real-time processing of big data, might appear challenging. However, these ZTA next-generation 5G O-RAN network architectures plan to provide appropriate computational resources and interfaces for data collection needed by AI/ML applications. Seamless connectivity in 5G networks implies that multiple RAT technologies are used dynamically in a single session of data communication. Furthermore, heterogeneous devices, with different security specifications, credentials, privileges, and computing resources participate in the communication.

Hence, real-time monitoring and security evaluation of all involved devices is the necessity of an SoSIDS. 5G O-RAN network architectures integrate NVF cloud computing for the realization of real-time functions for intelligent processing engines, with commercial off-the-shelf

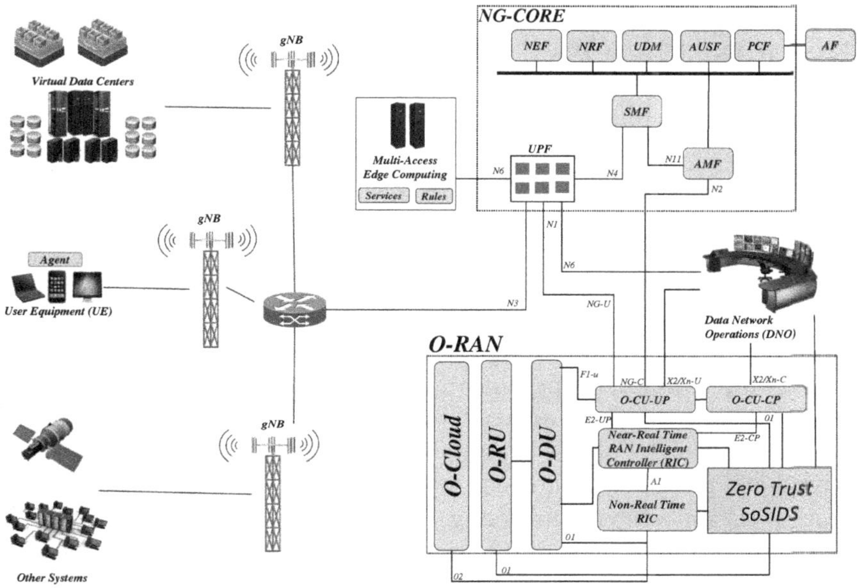

Figure 4. 5G O-RAN Zero Trust Architecture

hardware. A promising example is the O-RAN architecture that provides (near-) real-time (10 ms to 1 s) RAN intelligent controller (RIC), central (CU), distributed (DU), and radio units (RU). While initial use cases of real-time engines in O-RAN focus on connectivity management in multi-RAT and quality of experience (QoE) optimization, integration of SoSIDS functions is an emerging critical application.

Multi-Access Edge Computing Opportunities

Dynamic access in multi-RAT also implies a broadened attack surface for an O-RAN architecture. The multi-RAT network and D2D communications allow attackers to exploit UEs without intrusion into the network. Hence, the envisioned SoSIDS requires all authorized devices to dynamically monitor their network environment for potential risks, as part of the DMC. The major concern, however, is the limited computational resources of UEs, especially IoT node and sensor devices.

For example, multi-access edge computing (MEC) in 5G networks can be leveraged to address this issue [10]. The MEC is a prominent example demonstrating the unique capabilities of 5G networks, which bring the computing resources as close as possible to the network edge [10]. Hence, a high volume of devices, possibly with high mobility, may have access to high-performance computing resources with low-latency connectivity. The MEC adapts a similar service-based architecture (SBA) of 5G networks according to 3GPP specifications. The deployment of MEC can be considered as a mapping onto a network application function (AF) interacting with other network core functions [10].

The MEC hosts are deployed at the edge of 5G RAN to minimize latency and improve user QoE [1]. An interesting feature of this architecture is the exposure of MEC hosts to radio information provided by the CUs and DUs of the RAN [1]. The MEC platform may use radio information, e.g., signal power and quality, to further reduce latency by avoiding unnecessary routing traffic via the core network. While MEC enables the deployment of some DMC components, it is also protected by the SoSIDS. The 5G core incorporates appropriate functions such as NEF and policy control (for traffic steering) and unified data management (for user authentication, authorization, and service continuity) to provide untrusted application functions (AF) with requested services [1]. While these functions provide static security measures, the SoSIDS core provides dynamic security measures to authorize accesses to the MEC and monitor sessions.

Risk Assessments Using a Graph Neural Network Design Analysis Methodology

Risk-based design analysis has become an important systems engineering activity in the design of interconnected, complex, mission-critical computer networks. Another important aspect of trust evaluation is the dynamic risk assessment for every access request in a 5G ZTA. To defend the systems from attack, system engineers and architects must develop a protection strategy based on a subset of the possible cybersecurity protections. Applying the complete set of cybersecurity protections is prohibitively expensive and unnecessary. A suitable protection set must be selected to mitigate risk adequately and realistically. In a 5G network, the mobility of heterogeneous devices in a varying environment calls for a dynamic model of the network state that provides information about the risks of accessing a particular resource by a given subject. This architecture proposes using a graph neural network design analysis methodology (GNNDAM) to model the state of the 5G O-RAN ZTA which is of particular interest in risk assessments by the PE.

The memory of the PE policy is an important feature for risk assessments. An attacker does not deviate from the security policy rules with observable traces; rather, it attempts to exploit multiple network assets by taking incremental steps toward malicious activities or unauthorized access to sensitive information, distributed over space and time [11]. While the spatial security state is modeled by the AI/ML administrator, the PE provides the temporal model. It is important for the PE to incorporate all previous and future states of the subject and the network for risk assessments. All components of the AI/ML administrator work together in a cohesive manner to meet the enhanced security needs of organizations as well as commercial 5G/6G networks in the future. Using this new type of architecture, sensitive applications may benefit from widespread adoptability and low-cost deployment of these networks without compromising information security.

Graph neural networks have been shown to be successful as a scalable approach for resource allocation in Cloud computing and wireless networks [12, 13]. In these applications, the GNN models the channel state between pairs of communicating nodes and the goal is an optimal allocation of spectrum resources to the nodes [12, 13]. The AI/ML administrator employs a GNN to model the communication patterns of a 5G O-RAN network and the goal is to assign risk scores (R-Scores) to the nodes such that the overall metric of security assurance in granting access is maximized. The AI/ML administrator uses the GNN model of the network to detect such activities and potential attacks in conjunction with the M.A.R.S component and employs reinforcement learning to meet the following objectives: (1) compliance with a set of security policy rules, (2) authorizing accesses with the least privileges, and (3) maximizing network usability. The RL algorithm dynamically assigns appropriate scores to all nodes in the network so that an assurance score (as the reward) is maximized, by inspecting how strictly the policy rules are met by the nodes while the network is available to all users.

This GNNDAM is a general, quantitative, risk-based design analysis methodology that efficiently expresses the complete design space. This section describes the GNNDAM's design expression and risk evaluation process. Risk is evaluated in terms of attacks on the system since attack analysis reveals the vulnerabilities that most impact system risk. After the one-time work of developing the attack model for the system is complete, designs are evaluated for risk via an automated calculation. This methodology makes it possible to search the design space, providing a first step toward posing a rigorous risk-based design optimization problem.

The GNNDAM allows the complete design space to be efficiently expressed in terms of the IA protections selected to defend against attacks. An attack model describes the composition of attack-step instances into attacks. Attack-step instances exploit individual vulnerabilities in the system and therefore indicate locations for possible IA protection deployment. For each location, a number of IA protections is possible. By construction, all instances of a given attack step have the same possible protections. A design is a selection of one IA protection for each attack-step instance. The GNNDAM treats each IA protection selection as an independent parameter. The set of all designs, the design space, is therefore complete in the sense that it contains all possible IA protection combinations. The concept of a design space provides a formal means for expressing IA protection strategies.

A design's risk score is a function of the cyber protections selected by the design. The list of attack steps comprising each attack is augmented by the design to create a list of attack-step-protection pairs, the pairing of each attack step with one of its possible IA protections. Each attack-step-protection pair is given quantitative attribute values. The attribute values for the attack step-protection pairs are aggregated to create an attack score, a measure of the risk impact of that attack for the selected design. A design's risk score calculation aggregates all attack scores for that design. The particular selection of attributes and aggregation functions will vary with operational needs and design goals, but, in all cases, the computation of risk scores will be an automated calculation using the attack-step-protection attribute values as inputs.

With the GNNDAM, the design space is expressed completely and the risk calculation is automated. The exploration of the space is therefore possible without iterating the entire process. Figure 5 represents the contrasting workflows of the traditional method and the GNNDAM. Searching the design space is now possible.

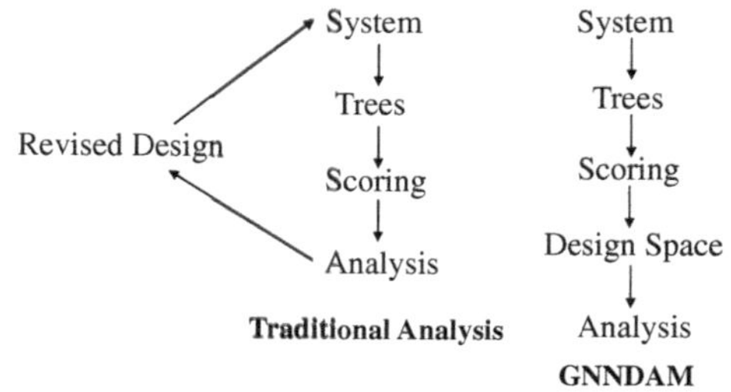

Figure 5. Traditional Analysis Cycle versus the GNNDAM

Attack Steps

This subsection describes how individual attack steps, a_i, and attack-step instances, $a_{i,j}$, are modeled, how they relate to cyber protections, and how attack steps are created to facilitate instantiations. An attack step, a_i, is modeled by the preconditions that must be met by an adversary before attempting the step, the postconditions gained by the adversary after successfully completing the step, and a variable number of cyber protections, $\mathbb{P}(a_i)$, preventing the step's success. An example of an attack step is given in Example 1.

Example 1: An attack step achieving a login shell to a host can be modeled as follows:

Attack Step	
Name	Log On to Host
Preconditions	Electronic access to the host
Postconditions	Login shell to the host
Cyber Protections	1. Static username and password 2. Public key infrastructure (PKI) authentication certificate

Preconditions and postconditions are defined generically so that attack steps can be made independent of the system components they attack. Each attack step is applied to any system component where the preconditions, postconditions, and possible IA protections are the same. Each use of an attack step is an attack-step instance. Attack-step instances can apply to components such as client hosts, legitimate client users, the network on which a client resides, a network device on that network, the client application, the data stored on the client, and the cryptographic implementation (if any) protecting the application data. Similar components could be targeted for other hosts such as data stores, configuration servers, and management servers. Example 2 shows how a single step can be used against multiple system components.

Example 2: An adversary must meet the precondition, *Gain Electronic Access*, before attempting the attack step *Log On to Host* (Example 1). Gaining access depends on the host's network type. Defenses can be both wireless (e.g., Wi-Fi Protected Access, WPA) and wired (e.g., switch port security). A system designer who wishes to compare placing clients and servers on the same network to placing them on different networks can create separate attack-step instances for each. These would be (*Gain Electronic Access*, *Client Network instance*) and (*Gain Electronic Access*, *Server Network instance*).

By distinguishing attack steps and their instances, each component from a set of similar components may be assigned a different protection. This allows the system designer to experiment with, for example, comparing hardened borders to hardened hosts. The expressibility provided by using multiple instances of attack steps is gained for essentially no additional work, making efficient the expression of very granular cyber protection strategies.

Designs

A design, D, is a selection of one cyber protection, $D(a_{i,j}) \in \mathbb{P}(a_{i,j})$, for each attack-step instance, $a_{i,j}$, from the set of all attack-step instances, I. Formally, it is a map from attack-step instances to valid cyber protections,

$$D : I \cup_{\in vI} \mathbb{P}(v)$$

such that, for all v in I,

$$D(v) \in \mathbb{P}(v).$$

The cyber protection selected for each attack-step instance can be independently adjusted, allowing for any combination of protections. Together with the use of multiple instances of a single attack step, this allows for efficient expression of a wide range of designs.

The design space, $\mathbb{D}$, is the set of all possible designs. In a traditional methodology, the amount of design space that can be explored is limited to the number of alternative attack trees developed. In the GNNDAM, the complete design space, $\mathbb{D}$, can be explored, all with a single tree, subject to computational complexity constraints. Designs are a powerful tool for analyzing mitigations to risk. The collection of all possible designs is efficiently expressed by the design space, and, once a design is found, it can easily be translated back into a system description. The entire design space can be explored without modifying the model and without additional input from a subject matter expert (SME). The analysis therefore scales with the work required to calculate risk scores and draw conclusions, rather than with the work required to refine and rescore the trees.

Risk Calculation

Attack modeling is the process of creating a catalog $\mathbb{A}$ of attacks, A_1, A_2, … , A_N, against a system. Attacks are modeled as attack-step-instance sequences, $(a_{1,j1}, a_{2,j2},...,a_{k,jk})$, that must be completed for the attack to succeed.

In practice, we'd used attack trees to model attacks. An attack tree is a tree where leaf nodes are attack-step instances and non-leaf nodes are Boolean operators (AND, OR). The root node of an attack tree represents the adversary's goal; typically, this is to defeat a cyber service of the system, such as confidentiality. A leaf node is satisfied if that attack-step instance is accomplished. A Boolean AND operator is satisfied if each of its child nodes is satisfied. A Boolean OR operator is satisfied if at least one of its child nodes is satisfied. A collection of attack-step instances satisfies the adversary's goal if accomplishing the attack-step instances satisfies the root node of the tree. An attack is an attack step instance set that satisfies the adversary's goal, but for which no proper subset also satisfies the adversary goal (it is also called a minimal cutset[1] in literature).

Attack trees, because they are typically developed in a top-down fashion, are useful in striving for completeness in the model. Also, because of the ability to reuse instances of attacks, entire subtrees can be used as a template in many places. For example, getting superuser access on a host may occur with many attacks against different hosts, but it is likely to be high level for a single step. It is instead represented as a subtree that combines several more granular attack-step instances. After the trees have been developed, the relevant attributes for each attack step are evaluated so that the risk associated with each attack can be computed. Attributes are typically quantitative measures related to the difficulty of the attack steps, such as difficulty, experience or skill required, probability of success, cost, and likelihood of detection.

---

[1] https://www.sciencedirect.com/topics/engineering/minimal-cut-set.

Attack scoring is the process of eliciting SME opinion to assign quantitative attribute values, $s(a_i,p)$, to each attack step, a_i, for each possible cyber protection, $p \in \mathbb{P}(a_i)$. The scoring of individual attack steps requires clear definitions of the possible cyber protections. In reality, the attribute value of an attack can depend on many factors, such as the adversary's talent, the details of the implementations, and luck. The SME must assign a representative value to the attack-step instance's attributes. Example 3 shows how the cost to defeat authentication methods may be scored.

Example 3: Cost to the attacker is a well-understood and accepted risk attribute. The attack step in Example 1 has two cyber protections defined, so it must be scored twice. Guessing a username and password can be done by brute force, which is not technically challenging but does require a considerable time investment. A possible total cost to an attacker for this step could be $1,000. Forging a public key infrastructure (PKI) certificate is significantly more difficult, requiring either an implementation exploit or cryptanalysis. A possible total cost to an attacker for this step could be $50,000.

Attack scoring is typically a time-intensive process requiring specialized expertise. It can comprise a significant portion of the risk assessment effort. Furthermore, scoring provides the quantitative inputs for the risk assessment; misjudgments in inputs can call the outputs into question. Although it may not be possible to entirely eliminate such sources of error, the GNNDAM, by making the attack scoring process more efficient, allows greater care to be taken in the attack scoring phase. The formalization of preconditions and postconditions of an attack step makes the attack-step-protection attributes independent of the attack step's location(s) within the attack tree. Therefore, scoring can be done outside of the attack tree development process, making scoring a more focused effort well-suited for an SME. The GNNDAM allows a single SME to score the attack steps appropriate to his or her expertise. Attack step scoring is organized for all cyber protections by the logical unit of a single attack step.

The gains in efficiency help make it possible to improve the opinion elicitation processes. For example, analysts can now (1) score attack steps outside of tree development, (2) go to the best possible experts with a short list of attack steps tailored to their particular areas of expertise, and (3) have each attack step scored independently by multiple experts and combine the resulting opinions into, say, an average and a measure of confidence. The possibilities afforded by efficiency can help minimize errors in the quantitative inputs.

Given the attack trees, the attack-step-protection pair attribute scores, and the designs, the process of calculating the risk score of a design is an automatable calculation. It proceeds as follows. Each attack receives an *attack score*, $AS_{A,D}$ specified by the design. This is a quantitative measure of the risk associated with the attack, A, on the system with design, D. Boolean operators defined in the attack tree combine attack-step instances, $a_{i,j}$, into the set of all possible attacks $\mathbb{A} = \{A_1, A_2,\ldots, A_N\}$ where $A_i = (a_{1,j1}, a_{2,j2}, \ldots, a_{k,jk})$ is an attack that achieves the attacker's goal. Each attack-step instance, aid, of an attack step, $a_{i,j}$, has a set of possible cyber protections, $\mathbb{P}(a_i)$. A cyber protection, $D(a_{i,j})$, is selected for each attack-step instance, $a_{i,j}$, according to the design, D, to augment the attack to a sequence, $(a_1, D(a_{1,j1}))$, $(a_2, D(a_{2,j2}))$,…, $(a_k, D(_{ak,jk}))$, of attack-step-protection pairs. The attack-step-protection pairs are given scores, $s(a_i, D(a_{i,j}))$. For each attack, A, in the set of all possible attacks, $\mathbb{A}$, a fixed function, AS, aggregates the attributes of a variable number of attack steps to produce an attack score, $AS\,(s(a_1, D(a_{1,j1})), s(a_2, D(a_{2,j2})),\ldots, s(a_k, D(_{ak,jk})))$. The set of all attack scores are then aggregated by another function, R, to produce

Algorithm 1. The Risk Score Computation Algorithm

```
Let AS be the attack score function
Let R be the design risk score function
Let 𝔸 {A_1, A_2,..., A_N} be the set of all attacks given by the attack
    model
Let 𝔻 be the design space
Let D ∈ 𝔻 be a selected design
Let s(a_i, D(a_{i,j})) be the scores associated with the attack-step-protec-
    tion pair (a_i, D(a_{i,j}))
for all attacks A in 𝔸 do
Let a_{1,j1}, a_{2,j2},..., a_{k,jk} be the attack step in-stances in attack A, which
    are instances of the attacks a_1, a_2,..., a_k
Let AS_{A,D} be the attack score for attack A against design D
AS_{A,D} = AS(s(a_1,D(a_{1,j1})), s(a_2,D(a_{2,j2})),..., s(a_k,D(a_{k,jk}))
end for
Let R_D be the design risk score for design D
R_D = R(AS_{A1,D}, AS_{A2,D},..., AS_{AN,D})
```

the risk score, $R(AS(A_1, D), AS(A_2, D), \ldots, AS(A_N, D))$, for design D. In choosing the functions, AS and R, system designers must account for the properties of their system, the elements of the system they are attempting to understand, and the questions they must answer. Algorithm 1 describes the risk computation in detail.

CONCLUSION

Network assurance in the untrusted environment of 5G O-RAN networks demands for dynamic authorization, risk assessment, and monitoring of network assets. Realization of ZT principles, necessary for providing information security in such environments, requires real-time processing of big data. This proposed 5G O-RAN ZTA architecture will help guarantee ZT principles for applications by leveraging distinct technologies of 5G O-RAN networks using a SoSIDS. The 5G O-RAN ZTA core includes the PE and the AI/ML administrator for dynamic authorization of access requests; using RL, with the objective of using federated learning to provide users with a risk score. Dynamic monitoring of the network assets is also realized with M.A.R.S which employs a GNNDAM for network modeling and adversarial learning for risk assessments. It is our sincere hope that the SoSIDS vision discussed in this chapter motivates new research directions in the application of AI/ML for providing information security in untrusted 5G O-RAN ZTA networks.

REFERENCES

[1] Pham, Q. V., Fang, F., Ha, V. N., Piran, M. J., Le, M., Le, L. B., ... & Ding, Z. (2020). A survey of multi-access edge computing in 5G and beyond: Fundamentals, technology integration, and state-of-the-art. *IEEE Access*, 8, 116974–117017.

[2] Zhang, N., Wang, T., & Ji, J. (2021). Analysis of the US military's tactical cloud application based on zero trust. In *ICMLCA 2021; 2nd International Conference on Machine Learning and Computer Application* (pp. 1–5). VDE.

[3] Rose, S., Borchert, O., Mitchell, S., & Connelly, S. (2020). *Zero Trust Architecture* (No. NIST Special Publication (SP) 800-207). National Institute of Standards and Technology.

[4] Singh, S. K., Singh, R., & Kumbhani, B. (2020). The evolution of radio access network towards open-RAN: Challenges and opportunities. In *2020*

IEEE Wireless Communications and Networking Conference Workshops (WCNCW) (pp. 1–6). IEEE.

[5] Sirotkin, S. (Ed.) (2020). *5G Radio Access Network Architecture: The Dark Side of 5G*. John Wiley & Sons, Hoboken, New Jersey.

[6] Hindy, H., Brosset, D., Bayne, E., Seeam, A. K., Tachtatzis, C., Atkinson, R., & Bellekens, X. (2020). A taxonomy of network threats and the effect of current datasets on intrusion detection systems. *IEEE Access*, 8, 104650–104675.

[7] Alevizos, L., Ta, V. T., & Hashem Eiza, M. (2022). Augmenting zero trust architecture to endpoints using blockchain: A state-of-the-art review *Security and Privacy*, 5(1), e191.

[8] Ferretti, L., Magnanini, F., Andreolini, M., & Colajanni, M. (2021) Survivable zero trust for cloud computing environments. *Computers & Security*, 110, 102419.

[9] Nassef, O., Sun, W., Purmehdi, H., Tatipamula, M., & Mahmoodi, T. (2022). A survey: Distributed machine learning for 5G and beyond. *Computer Networks*, 207, 108820.

[10] Taleb, T., Samdanis, K., Mada, B., Flinck, H., Dutta, S., & Sabella, D. (2017). On multi-access edge computing: A survey of the emerging 5G network edge cloud architecture and orchestration. *IEEE Communications Surveys & Tutorials*, 19(3), 1657–1681.

[11] Zheng, L. & Myers, A. C. (2005). End-to-end availability policies and noninterference. In *18th IEEE Computer Security Foundations Workshop (CSFW'05)* (pp. 272–286). IEEE.

[12] Scheinert, D. & Acker, A. (2020). Telesto: A graph neural network model for anomaly classification in cloud services. In *International Conference on Service-Oriented Computing* (pp. 214–227). Springer, Cham.

[13] Wu, Z., Pan, S., Chen, F., Long, G., Zhang, C., & Philip, S. Y. (2020). A comprehensive survey on graph neural networks. *IEEE Transactions on Neural Networks and Learning Systems*, 32(1), 4–24.

Index

X

Y

Z